HELPING THE
Struggling
ADOLESCENT

A companion book will be published by Zondervan in January 1994. *Helping the Struggling Adolescent: A Counseling Guide* will contain further guidance for counselors and others who work with young people, and it will include a collection of more than thirty rapid assessment tools dealing with many of the topics examined in this book.

Helping the Struggling Adolescent: A Counseling Guide is often referred to in this book in the section titled "How To Help" and should also be taken into account for the section "Where To Go for Additional Help."

HELPING THE
Struggling
ADOLESCENT

A Guide to Thirty
Common Problems
for Parents, Counselors
& Youth Workers

Les Parrott III

ZondervanPublishingHouse
Academic andProfessionalBooks
Grand Rapids, Michigan

A Division of HarperCollinsPublishers

Helping the Struggling Adolescent
Copyright © 1993 by Les Parrott III

Requests for information should be addressed to:
Zondervan Publishing House
Academic and Professional Books
Grand Rapids, Michigan 49530

Edited by Robert D. Wood and James E. Ruark
Cover design by P.M. Graphics

Library of Congress Cataloging-in-Publication Data
Parrott, Les.
    Helping the struggling adolescent : a guide to thirty common problems for parents, counselors, and youth workers / Les parrott III
        p. cm.
    Includes bibliographical references
    ISBN 0-310-57821-3
    1. Teenagers—Counseling of—United States. 2. Church work with teenagers—United States. 3. Adolescent psychology—United States. I. Title.
HV1431.P37   1993   92-33998
362.7'0835—dc20   CIP

Printed in the United States of America

93 94 95 96 97 98 /   / 10 9 8 7 6 5 4 3 2 1

*To the two people who provided me
with boundless hope during my adolescent years.
I dedicate this work to my mom and dad,
Les and Lora Lee Parrott,
with love and affection.*

CONTENTS

Acknowledgments   9
How To Use This Book   11

Part One: Effective Helping

1. Adolescence: A Struggle for Identity   15
2. Characteristics of Effective Helping: A Self-Inventory   25
3. The Heart of Helping   30
4. A Parent's Guide to Professional Help   41

Part Two: The Struggles of Adolescents

Abuse   47
Anger   55
Anxiety   65
Body Image   76
Depression   87
Drugs and Alcohol   93
Eating Disorders   105
Forgiveness   119
God's Will   125
Grief   132
Guilt   143
Homosexuality   152
Inferiority   162
Loneliness   173
Masturbation   182
Obsessions and Compulsions   190
Panic Attacks   198
Parents   208
Peer Pressure   218
Phobias   224
Pornography   233
Promiscuity and Premarital Sex   242
Schizophrenia   251

School Work   263
Shyness   272
Siblings   281
Sleep Disturbance   288
Spiritual Doubt   296
Stuttering   303
Suicide   308

Index   316

ACKNOWLEDGMENTS

The first words of this book were written on an airplane as I was returning home to Seattle from Indianapolis, where I had addressed a gathering of parents, ministers, and counselors. They had come from across the country to talk about helping struggling adolescents. Their dedication, compassion, and enthusiasm were self-evident, and a company of people never encouraged a writer more than they did me. *Helping the Struggling Adolescent* was inspired by these people and written for thousands like them.

I am indebted to my colleagues at Seattle Pacific University who understand and encourage my calling to integrate spiritual values with human understanding. I am especially thankful for the prayerful support of my colleagues in the School of Social and Behavioral Sciences and the Department of Psychology.

The pages of this book represent the combined effort and expertise of many professionals who reviewed and critiqued particular chapters. The following specialists deserve not only acknowledgment, but my profound gratitude: Dub Ambrose, Roy Barsness, Alan Basham, Charles Bombardier, John Court, Wendy Fisher, Stan Gaede, Joy Hammersla, Dan Hartman, Donald Joy, James Mallory, David Massey, Steve Moore, Thanne Moore, Carol Parrott, Cliff Penner, Cindy Perrin, Robin Perrin, Kim Lampson-Reif, Michael Roe, Randy Rowland, Denny Rydberg, Suzanne Shelton, JoAnne Smatlan, James Scott Smith, Pat Springle, Les Steele, Scott Willis, Mitch Woltersdorf, Michael Vitiello, and Philip Zimbardo. The discerning questions and thoughtful input of these people have been immensely helpful. Although none of these individuals can be held responsible for weaknesses that remain, they have all made contributions to whatever strengths this book contains.

A debt of thanks is also owed to the people who have helped me improve my craft of writing. Luke Reinsma and Rose Reynoldson generously gave of their time to help me rework the first draft of this manuscript while it still suffered from "the disease of clutter." I am indebted to Jim Ruark, my editor at Zondervan, for his personal touch and heart-felt desire to help those who work with struggling adolescents. I am also grateful for Stan Gundry's vision and confidence in this project. The library work of my research assistants, Sarah Timmons and Steve Scott, was invaluable.

The long, lonely hours in front of my computer were compensated for by the energizing support of friends who put up with my "struggling adolescent obsession." Special thanks go to my pastor, Tharon Daniels, for the cathartic talks while jogging around Green Lake, and to my friend, Steve Moore, for affirming the dream.

To my wife, Leslie, I owe more than gratitude. It is difficult for me to imagine how any human being could give more to another than she has given to me. Her positive spirit helped create an environment that made this book possible. Her patience, vision, and unswerving dedication to our relationship know no bounds. Nor does my love for her.

Finally, I want to thank the adolescents who trusted me with the personal struggles that have defined their pilgrimage. They have taught me much.

HOW TO USE THIS BOOK

Helping the Struggling Adolescent is a practical resource tool for everyone working to understand and help young people. This book is for parents, youth workers, pastors, and other Christians in their day-to-day counseling ministries with adolescents. It is also a guide for educated lay helpers and knowledgeable parents and a suitable text for seminary and college courses on counseling. Here are strategies that beginning lay counselors must learn and that experienced practitioners must continually relearn.

Part One is designed to give a conceptual overview of a Christian perspective on counseling adolescents, and the four introductory issues there may be read consecutively. In Part Two, I deal with thirty specific issues with which adolescents struggle. They are listed alphabetically for ease of access to the reader. Thus the book belongs in a reachable slot on the reference shelf of anyone who routinely works with adolescents. The design of the topical sections will enable you quickly and easily to find vital information for particular problems. Each section, indicated by the symbol ☑, succinctly answers several fundamental questions:

☑ *What* does the specific struggle look like?

☑ *Why* did it happen?

☑ *How* can a counselor help?

☑ *When* should a counselor refer the adolescent to another professional, and *where* can a counselor find additional resources for helping?

The issues of resources and referral are raised in each chapter to avoid the hazard of believing that this handbook can answer every question, and the danger of believing that you can work with *every* struggling adolescent.

PARENTS AS HELPERS

Research indicates that adolescents go first to parents when they are struggling. Mom and dad rank higher than peers, relatives, pastors, teachers, or counselors as resources for advice or help. Research also suggests that when parents are concerned about a serious problem in their adolescent children, they are most likely to turn to their extended family for advice. A trained counselor is consulted only after a number of repeated failures. This book will help parents know how to help more effectively and when to take that next step.

11

A growing body of evidence indicates that parents, with a little guidance from professionals, can successfully help to resolve a number of struggles for their adolescents. For example, with help parents can deal with anger control, critical attitudes, God's will, grief, guilt, loneliness, peer pressure, school work, sibling rivalry, and spiritual doubt. Unfortunately, parents do not receive a great deal of useful information from scientific literature or even from the experiences of other parents. This book attempts to help bridge that gap.

However, parents with even the noblest of intentions must understand that many specific problems must be treated by trained professionals. Adolescents who struggle with abuse, severe depression, suicide, eating disorders, panic attacks, phobias, schizophrenia, and sleep disorders need professional help. While some helping techniques for these problems may be useful for parents to apply, effective treatment requires an objective clinician.

Parents should seek the services of trained mental health professionals in such clear cases or when little or no progress is being made in other problem areas. Chapter 5 provides a checklist to help you decide whether professional help is needed. You will also find help there in selecting a counselor or psychotherapist. In spite of the continuing stigma of psychological treatment and the belief that families should be able to solve their personal problems without outside help—especially in evangelical circles—mental health professionals can be of great value in preparing adolescents to realize in their lives the power of the gospel and the healing comfort of the Holy Spirit.

In this volume I have tried to summarize much of what we know about counseling methods and about the major problems afflicting adolescents today. I have intentionally approached the material as a Christian and as a clinical psychologist. The many helping techniques and practices are based on a thorough review of hundreds of scientific studies, and I carefully chose them to highlight strategies that have proved to be the most therapeutic and consistent with Christian understanding. Each section provides the latest technical knowledge in nontechnical language and demonstrates intervention strategies that a competent counselor should consider before entering into a counseling relationship with a struggling adolescent.

No universal or simple formulas for resolving the complex problems of young people are available. Therefore, I have followed a pragmatic rather than a dogmatic approach to helping the struggling adolescent. When asked how he worked, Einstein once replied, "I grope." I hope that in your work with adolescents, this book will help you grope in the right direction.

All case material is real but disguised, originating from my clinical practice or from that of colleagues.

Part One

Effective Helping

1

A Struggle for Identity

During World War II, Erik H. Erikson coined a phrase that stuck—*identity crisis*. He used it to describe the disorientation of shell-shocked soldiers who could not remember their names. Through the years, this phrase has become a useful tool to describe the struggle of growing up.

Achieving a sense of identity is the major developmental task of teenagers. Like a stunned soldier in a state of confusion, sooner or later, young people are hit with a bomb that is more powerful than dynamite—puberty. Somewhere between childhood and maturity their bodies kick into overdrive and fuel changes at an alarming rate. With this acceleration of physical and emotional growth, they become strangers to themselves. Under attack by an arsenal of fiery hormones, the bewildered young person begins to ask, *"Who am I?"*

While achievement of a meaningful answer to this question is a lifelong pursuit, it is the burning challenge of adolescence. According to Erikson, having an identity—knowing who you are—gives adolescents a sense of control that allows them to navigate through the rest of life.

Without identities, awkward adolescents carry a "how'm-I-doing?" attitude that is always focused on their concern about impressions they are making on others. Without self-identities they will be or do whatever they think others want. They will flounder from one way of acting to another, never able to step outside of a preoccupation with their own performance and genuinely ask others, "How are you doing?" Erikson calls this miserable state "identity diffusion."[1]

The successful formation of self-identity follows a typical pattern. Teens identify with people they admire. Whether in real life or through magazines and TV, they emulate the characteristics of people they want to be like. By the end of adolescence, if all goes as it should, these identifications merge into a single identity that incorporates and alters previous identifications to make a unique and coherent whole.

The quest for identity is scary. Somewhere between twelve and twenty years of age adolescents are forced to choose once and for all what their identity

Four Fundamental Views of the Self

- The *subjective self* is the adolescents' private view of who they see themselves to be. Although this self-view has been heavily influenced by parents and has been hammered out in interactions with peers, it is still one's own assessment.
- The *objective self* is what others see when they view the adolescent. It is the person others think the teen is.
- The *social self* is the adolescents' perception of themselves as they think others see them. It is what they think they look like to others.
- The *ideal self* is the adolescents' concept of who they would like to become, their ultimate goal.[2]

is to be. It is a formidable task. Uncertain which of their mixed emotions are really their true feelings, they are pushed to make up their minds. Their confusion is complicated further when they begin to guess what others, whose opinions they care about, want them to be.

For adolescents who never achieve an integrated identity, "all the world's a stage." In their adult years they will play the part of human beings who change roles to please whoever happens to be watching. Their clothes, their language, their thoughts, and feelings are all a part of the script. Their purpose will be to receive approval from those they hope to impress. Life will become a charade, and players will never enjoy the security of personal identity or experience the strength that comes from a sense of self-worth.

HOW ADOLESCENTS SEARCH FOR IDENTITY

Young people look for identity in uncounted ways. In this section, seven common paths are examined: family relations, status symbols, "grown-up" behavior, rebellion, others' opinions, idols, and cliquish exclusion.

Through Family Relations

Adolescents' families have significant impact on identity formation. To assert individuality and move out of childhood, teenagers will wean themselves from their protecting parents. But individuality may also be found in reaction to the identities of one's brothers and sisters. If the first child, for example, decides to be a serious intellectual, the second may seek individuality in becoming a jokester. Seeing these places already taken, the third child may choose to be an athlete.

In some cases, when young people feel they possess no distinctive talents, they may rebel by separating themselves from the "white sheep." They may become delinquents or prodigals and gain identity by causing trouble.

Through Status Symbols

Adolescents try to establish themselves as individuals through prestige. They seek out behavior or possessions that are readily observable. They purchase sports cars, hairstyles, lettermen's jackets, skateboards, guitars, stereos, and designer clothes in hope of being identified as people who belong. Their status symbols help teens form self-identity because they themselves have what others in their group have: "the jocks," "the brains," "the party types," "the gear-heads," "the rockers." Owning status symbols, however, is not enough to achieve identity. Adolescents quickly recognize a struggling teen who is attempting to carve out an identity by buying the right symbols. In fact, they enjoy detecting these imposters, and reinforcing their own identities by labeling them as "wanna be's" or "posers."

To be authentic, appropriate behavior must accompany the status symbol. A "party girl," for example, must not only wear the right clothes, have the right hairstyle, and buy the right music, she must do the things a party girl does. Soon the behavior will earn the adolescent a reputation—something she must live up to if she is to maintain her identity, and something she must live down if she is to change it.

Through "Grown-Up" Behavior

Adolescents have a strong desire to be like adults. The more mature they appear, the more recognition they receive and the closer they get to feeling that they have achieved identity. Because real maturity is not always visible, young people often resort to behavior that is symbolic of adults. They engage in *tabooed pleasures*—the things parents, preachers, and teachers say they are too young to do.

The most common of these tabooed pleasures are smoking, drinking, drugs, and premarital sex. By the time adolescents reach high school, smoking is a widespread practice. Drinking has become a status symbol for girls as well as for boys, often beginning in the junior high school years. As with drinking, doing drugs usually begins as a group activity. Recent statistics on the number of sexually active adolescents are staggering.[3] Teens engage in these behaviors to gain independence from family restrictions, to increase their social acceptance, or even for adventure or curiosity.[4] Nearly every adolescent will experiment with these "adult" behaviors at some point, but certain adolescents will struggle intensely in these areas. Their problems are addressed more specifically in other sections of this book.

Through Rebellion

Rebellion is a logical consequence of young people's attempts to resolve incongruent ideas and find authentic identity. Rebellion results from a desire to be unique while still maintaining the security of sameness. "But, Dad, I gotta be a nonconformist," the teenager said to his father. "How else can I be like the other kids?"

A rebellious attitude is frequently accompanied by an idealism that prompts adolescents to reject the values of family, school, society, and church. However, their oversimplified and unrealistic ideals are often eventually found to be impractical and rarely held for any significant duration.

Through Others' Opinions

Essential to identity formation is the validation of one's self-image by other people's opinions. Adolescents' perceptions of themselves change, depending on what they believe others think about them. For example, if a young person sees himself as a talented actor but is not offered the lead role in the school play, his identity as an actor may be weakened and he may try to find his identity in academics or sports. If, however, he hears that others believe it was a mistake not to cast him as the lead, his identity may be maintained.

Adolescents do not always fall in line with what others think of them. On the contrary. Because adolescent identity is shaped by their perception of how others see them, they may change in order to contradict their perceptions, even if those perceptions are positive. It may be harmful to tell young people they won't have any problems, that they are the best, or that they will someday be the greatest. Aware of their weaknesses, they feel uncomfortable with an affirmation that leaves no room for error. They will go out of their way to prove parents and counselors wrong and to relieve themselves of the burden of being perfect. For some, relief will come only in identifying with what they are least supposed to be, not in being something that is unattainable.[5]

Through Idols

Especially in their early years, adolescents will often over-identify with famous people to the point of apparent loss of their own individuality. In our star-conscious society literally thousands of rock stars, professional athletes, movie actors and television personalities are available for teenagers to idolize.

Celebrities become "models" because adolescents are looking for a way to experiment with different roles. In their search for identity they latch onto notable personalities in order to explore different aspects of themselves. Idols allow them to test out new behavior and attitudes before incorporating them into their own identity. Idolizing celebrities does not necessarily mean that adolescents endorse idols' lifestyles or values.

Through Cliquish Exclusion

In their search for identity, adolescents may become remarkably intolerant and even cruel as they exclude others on the basis of minor aspects such as dress. They persistently try to define, overdefine, and redefine themselves in relation to others. If they see something in peers that reminds them of what they don't want to be, they will scorn and avoid those people and feel not an ounce of remorse. Teens strengthen their sense of self through ruthless comparisons and persistent exclusions.

Erikson sees the cliquishness of adolescence and its intolerance of

Helping Adolescents in Their Quest for Identity

- At the top of a sheet of paper ask teens to write the question "Who am I?" and then quickly to write twenty answers to the question. Analyze the answers and discuss the process as well as the content. Did the teens self-censor any responses?

- Using old magazines, ask them to create collages, one entitled "Who I Am," and another called "Who I Would Like to Be." When the collages are completed, ask them to write a description of each, indicating the meaning of the pictures they selected. Ask what they learned about themselves.

- To help adolescents discover what is most stable and enduring about their identity, have them draw a set of three concentric circles. In the innermost circle, ask them to list or describe those aspects—qualities, behaviors, values, and goals—that are most important and resistant to change. In the outermost circle, have them identify the least important and least stable aspects of themselves. The middle circle is for those aspects of intermediate importance.

differences as a defense against identity confusion.[6] Usually in late teens adolescents realize that it takes a well-established identity to tolerate radical differences.

WHY ADOLESCENTS STRUGGLE

The establishment of a personal identity is not easy. The danger of identity confusion lurks around every bend. Erikson points out that some confused young people, as in the case of Hamlet, take an excessively long time to reach adulthood.[7] They may regress into a childish state and thus avoid having to make decisions on confusing issues. Other adolescents express their confusion through premature commitments and impulsive actions. They give themselves to poorly thought-out ways of being and end up fighting needless battles.

Adolescence is a period of stress and turmoil for many young people. While the difficulties that occur in adolescence are due in part to lack of experience, at least five common experiences may exacerbate or create significant struggles: physical, sexual, social, religious, and moral changes.

Physical Changes

A fourteen-year-old tried to excuse his poor report card by saying, "My problem is not tests, but testosterone." He had a legitimate argument. The biochemical changes in adolescence may cause more apprehension than studying for an exam. Waking up with pimples, having your voice crack in public, wearing new jeans that are already too short, growing new facial-hair or beginning menstruation and breast development are all traumatic. As hormones set in motion the chain of physiological events that usher in adulthood, nice kids seem to turn into moody, rebellious adolescents. In fact, some parents with well-behaved teenagers worry that their kids aren't developing properly.

Sexual Changes

As the adolescent's body begins to take on the characteristic shape of his or her sex, new behaviors, thoughts, and physiological processes occur. Each reacts to the cultural stereotype of sexual changes. The adolescent boy encounters locker-room comparisons and wonders if his genitals are too small and why he hasn't begun to shave yet. If he gets an erection while dancing with a girl or while reading or merely thinking, he may suffer from a sense that his body has betrayed him. He might resent the lack of control he has over his body and feel he is "doing something wrong."

The adolescent girl also experiences confusion and shame about her sexual maturation. Menstruation is a serious concern, one often compounded by fear and ignorance. It may cause physical discomfort, weight gain, headaches, mood swings, and so on. Because it is commonly referred to as "the curse," a girl's period may encourage her to play the passive role of a martyr. It is not surprising that even the anticipation of this change contributes to other common struggles.

Social Changes

While the biological changes of puberty are dramatic, they are no more significant than the social changes that occur during adolescence. Between the sixth and eighth grades, the structure of school becomes a very different experience. Most young adolescents move from a relatively small neighborhood elementary school to a much larger, more impersonal junior high school. This move has many social ramifications. It disrupts the old peer-group structure, exposes students to different achievement expectations by teachers, and provides new opportunities for different extracurricular activities.

Family relations also shift as boys and girls turn into teenagers. Conflicts in family discussions increase. Male adolescents become more dominant in conversations—especially with their mothers. Feelings of affection toward their parents decline from the sixth to the eighth grades. This does not mean it necessarily becomes negative, but that the change is from very positive to less positive.

Religious Changes

Contrary to popular opinion, adolescents are genuinely interested in religion and feel that it plays an important role in their lives. In *The Search for America's Faith*, George Gallup, Jr., and David Poling report that eighty-eight percent of today's teens say their religious beliefs affect their daily behavior.[8]

However, adolescence is a time when young people question the religious concepts and beliefs of their childhood. They may become skeptical of religious forms, such as prayer, and later begin to doubt the nature of God, but they are on a genuine spiritual quest. This is sometimes mistakenly interpreted as skepticism or doubt. In reality it is sincere questioning. Adolescents investigate their religion to make their faith their own rather than that of their parents. They question, not because they want to become agnostic or atheistic, but because they want to accept religion in a way that is meaningful to them. Still, the quest is often frightening, and the search for faith may lead to involvement in destructive religious cults or other potential problems.

Moral Changes

An important change occurs in adolescents when they realize that their behavior must conform to social expectations without the constant guidance, supervision, and threats of punishment they experienced as children. To become adults, they must replace specific childhood rules with their own moral principles.

Several basic changes occur in the moral thinking of adolescents:

- They become more abstract and less concrete.
- They become more concerned with what is right and less concerned with what is wrong.
- They become more cognitive and less emotional.
- They become more altruistic and less egocentric.
- They become more willing to exert emotional energy on moral issues.[9]

During adolescence, according to Lawrence Kohlberg, teens reach a stage of moral development that is based on respect for others rather than on personal desires.[10] While adolescents are intellectually capable of making this change and creating their own moral code, the task is difficult.[11] Every day adolescents see inconsistencies in moral standards. As they interact with peers of different religious, racial, or socioeconomic backgrounds, they recognize that people have different codes of right and wrong. Some fail to make the shift to adult morality during adolescence and must finish the task in early adulthood. Others not only fail to make the shift but build a moral code on socially unacceptable moral concepts.

Physical, sexual, social, religious, and moral changes all contribute to adolescent struggle for identity and may contribute to potential complications and possible problems.

WHAT ADOLESCENTS DO WITH THEIR STRUGGLES

It is difficult to predict exactly how a specific adolescent will attempt to manage his or her problems. A number of personality traits and environmental factors influence the struggling adolescent's coping style. There are, however, at least three common ways young people contend with their struggles. They either hold them in, act them out, or work them through.[12]

Hold Them In

Many adolescents cope with their difficulties by keeping them to themselves. Like Adam and Eve hiding in the bushes, these adolescents camouflage their struggles, hoping they will eventually disappear. Some adolescents conceal their anxiety by *blocking*—allowing unconscious conflicts to interrupt their flow of thought. Tony, for example, is troubled by having sexual fantasies about a girl he was assigned to work with in his social studies class. At the dinner table he begins to tell his parents about the project. He suddenly gets confused and "forgets" what it is.

Another way adolescents hide their problems is through *sublimation*— transforming unacceptable impulses into behaviors that are more socially acceptable. Angry at his alcoholic father, a young man might disguise his hostility by investing a tremendous amount of energy into basketball.

Adolescents who feel hurt sometimes hide their struggles through *emotional insulation*, keeping potential pain at bay. For example, Carla, a junior in high school, has just been asked to the prom by the boy of her dreams. In order to avoid any possibility of being disappointed, she feels no excitement or joy. She becomes numb for fear that he might drop her at the last minute.

Related to emotional insulation is *intellectualization*—interpreting a situation only at a cognitive level in order to avoid dealing with uncomfortable feelings. When asked how he was doing after being cut from the school drama tryouts, Kevin, who actually hurt very deeply, responds, "I think it is all for the best. God is in charge and he is really teaching me to be a better person through this. It is probably the best thing that could have happened to me."

Perhaps the most common form of hiding one's struggles is through *repression*—pushing thoughts, feelings, impulses, desires, or memories out of awareness. Take Mike, seventeen, who has grown up in the church and is sincerely seeking answers to some of life's difficult questions. He begins to doubt God's existence, but quickly forces this questioning from his awareness because it is "bad." Later this repressed doubt shows up as an inability to be genuine with other feelings. He fails to show normal expressions and becomes legalistic in his spirit.

Act Them Out

Some adolescents cope with struggles by *acting out*—expressing their feelings through impulsive actions to reduce tension. The anxiety they feel about failing a class, for example, is temporarily released through skipping classes, harassment, or vandalism. The tension they feel over not being accepted by their peers may be acted out through sexual promiscuity. Adolescents act out in several different ways.

Young people will sometimes act out their struggle by *displacement*— transferring feelings to a more neutral object. The fifteen-year-old who is angry at his mom might kick over a neighbor's garbage can on his way to school. The payoff is obvious. Telling off one's parents may have costly side effects, but kicking garbage cans vents the hostility for free.

Another way of acting out struggles comes in the form of *regression*—retreating to an earlier developmental period that was less stressful. If Wendy, fourteen, is denied her desire to stay out with her friends past midnight, she may regress to childish behavior and relieve some of her frustration by sulking, crying, or throwing temper tantrums.

Adolescents who are afraid of their own thoughts or impulses may act them out through *projection*—putting them into another person. Neal, a sixteen-year-old "jock," becomes convinced that Craig is a homosexual. To ward off fears of his own sexuality, Neal transfers his sexual confusion onto Craig and acts out his anger by ridiculing him in front of other teammates.

Another common way of warding off uncomfortable emotions is through *denial*—refusing to accept reality. Wayne, seventeen, does this by partying. Regardless of the problem—poor grades, a broken home, depression, anger, and so on—Wayne denies the reality of his pain through two words: "Party, dude!" He avoids having to face up to his struggles by simply pretending they don't exist, "celebrating" by truant behavior, hanging out at the park, and drinking.

Work Them Through

Adolescents who hide their struggles and the ones who act them out have at least one characteristic in common. Both are avoiding *responsibility*—the freedom consciously to choose their actions and attitudes. Both are hung up, at some level, on thinking that says, "Why don't they . . . ?" In other words, both suffer from a tendency to wonder why others do not reduce their own problems. William Glasser sees this lack of responsibility as the central cause of adolescent struggles and even juvenile delinquency.[13] He claims that young people have problems in proportion to the degree they avoid taking responsibility for their actions or attitudes.

By holding their struggles in or acting them out, adolescents avoid having to confront them head-on. It's not that they do not have the capacity to take responsibility. Most psychologists agree with the developmental expert Jean Piaget that by adolescence young people are moving beyond concrete thinking and reaching a stage he calls "formal operations." They are able to look past what seems unchangeable, weed out irrelevant issues, and consider ramifications of choices they were unable to distinguish as children. Adolescents are capable of understanding the present and imagining the future. They can think abstractly and consider the consequences of their actions. Adolescents have the capacity to say, "The trouble with me is me, and I am going to do something about it."

Like most abilities, responsibility is best seen on a continuum. There are extreme cases of psychosis when people are simply unable to recognize that they have a choice. For example the paranoid schizophrenic, who believes someone is out to get him, believes he can do absolutely nothing to change his situation.

At the other extreme, some take on too much responsibility. They are the ones who feel guilty about things for which they have no responsibility—the teenager, for example, who feels guilty about her father's death because she was away at school when he died.

The majority of young people, however, are somewhere between these extremes. Lead them to see that they are sometimes responsible for the things that happen to them and that, even when they aren't, they are free to choose attitudes that will help them transcend debilitating struggles.

This book is designed to help you guide the adolescents with whom you work to a place where they squarely face their struggles and choose to work through them. The techniques outlined in the sections of Part Two are designed to help you allow adolescents to become their own counselors.

When adolescents are able to solve their problems with reasonable success and feel increasingly confident in their abilities to cope, periods of struggle gradually become less frequent and less intense. Only then will fulfillment begin to outweigh struggle.

Notes

1. E. H. Erikson, *Identity: Youth and Crisis* (New York: Norton, 1968).

2. A. Arkoff, *Psychology and Personal Growth*, 2d ed. (Boston: Allyn and Bacon, 1980), 28–32.

3. J. McDowell and D. Day, *Why Wait? What You Need To Know About the Teen Sexuality Crisis* (San Bernardino, Calif.: Here's Life Publishers, 1987).

4. G. M. Smith and C. P. Fogg, "Teenage Drug Use: A Search for Causes and Consequences," *Personality and Social Psychology Bulletin* 1 (1974): 426–29.

5. Erikson, *Identity: Youth and Crisis*.

6. E. H. Erikson, *The Challenge of Youth* (New York: Anchor, 1965).

7. Ibid.

8. G. Gallup and D. Poling, *The Search for America's Faith* (Nashville: Abingdon, 1980).

9. J. Mitchell, "Moral Growth During Adolescence," *Adolescence* 10 (1975): 221–26.

10. L. Kohlberg, *Stages in the Development of Moral Thought and Action* (New York: Holt, 1969). Kohlberg calls this stage "postconventional morality."

11. J. Piaget "The Intellectual Development of the Adolescent," in *Adolescence: Psychosocial Perspectives*, ed. G. Caplan and S. Lebovici (New York: Basic Books, 1969), 22–26. Piaget describes the adolescent as entering a stage of "formal operations."

12. G. K. Olson, *Counseling Teenagers: The Complete Christian Guide to Understanding and Helping Adolescents* (Loveland, Colo.: Group Books, 1984). Olson provides an excellent discussion of defense mechanisms. I have relied upon much of his work in this section.

13. W. Glasser, *The Identity Society* (New York: Harper & Row, 1972).

2

Characteristics of Effective Helping:
A Self-Inventory

The single most important factor in effective counseling is the personhood of the counselor. Regardless of one's education, training, theoretical orientation, or counseling techniques, it is now widely accepted that if certain qualities are not brought to the helping relationship, little chance of successful intervention exists.[1] The following self-inventory will help determine the degree to which these traits are present.

THE EFFECTIVE COUNSELOR

The most important instrument you have to help adolescents is you.[2] Who you are as a person is critical in determining the effectiveness of your counseling. This understanding, however, does not diminish the importance of the Holy Spirit. The point is that your attitude and behavior either help or hinder any healing work the Holy Spirit is prepared to do through you.

Many researchers have attempted to identify the qualities that contribute to successful counseling. They have discovered the importance of sensitivity, hope, compassion, control, awareness, knowledge. The list could fill several pages. However, beginning in 1967 Carl Rogers and his colleagues conducted a four-year study that seemed to cut to the bone.[3] It has been supported by subsequent research and is cited in nearly every text on counseling. The findings are unequivocal. People are more likely to improve when their counselors are (1) warm, (2) genuine, and (3) empathic. Without these traits a person's condition may actually worsen regardless of the technical knowledge of the counselor.

Warmth

Paul Tournier, the renowned Swiss counselor, said, "I have no methods. All I do is accept people." The key to nonpossessive warmth is acceptance. It is an attitude that does not evaluate or require change. It simply accepts the

A Self-Inventory

☞ *Directions:* For each statement indicate the response that best identifies your beliefs and attitudes. Keep in mind that the "right" answer is the one that best expresses your thoughts at this time. Use the following code:

5 = I strongly agree
4 = I agree
3 = I am undecided
2 = I disagree
1 = I strongly disagree

___ 1. Giving advice has little to do with good counseling.

___ 2. I can accept and respect people who disagree with me.

___ 3. I can make a mistake and admit it.

___ 4. I look at everybody's side of a disagreement before I make a decision.

___ 5. I tend to trust my intuition even when I'm unsure of the outcome.

___ 6. I don't need to see immediate and concrete results in order to know progress is occurring.

___ 7. Who you are in counseling is more important than what you do.

___ 8. My presence frees others from the threat of external evaluation.

___ 9. In a tense emotional situation I tend to remain calm.

___10. I know my limits when it comes to helping others.

___ *Total Score*

Total your responses to determine the degree to which you have the qualities necessary to be an effective counselor:

40–50   You are well on your way to being an effective counselor; take special care to maintain the qualities you have.

30–39   You have what it takes to be effective, but you will need to exert special effort to groom the traits described in this chapter.

Below 30   Seek out an occupational counselor who can assess your strengths more accurately.[4]

thoughts, feelings, and actions of the client. This warmth helps a teen develop a base of self-worth: "If my counselor cares about me, maybe I *am* valuable."

Nonpossessive warmth is not necessarily approving of everything a client does. Gary Collins recounts how Jesus showed warmth to the woman at the well: "Her morals may have been low, and he certainly never condoned sinful behavior. But Jesus nevertheless respected the woman and treated her as a person of worth. His warm, caring attitude must have been apparent wherever he went." [5]

Nor is this warmth a kind of smothering sentimentality. It does not skip through the counseling session whistling a happy tune and tossing out platitudes and contrived emotion. Through unconditional warmth we invite struggling adolescents to catch glimpses of God's grace. And grace is the bedrock of growth. When adolescents feel sure they will not be condemned for who they are and that the counselor will make no judgment of them, the power of God's grace begins to turn the wheels of change.

Unconditional warmth frees adolescents from attempting to win their counselor's approval. Young people no longer wonder whether they are loved for who they are or for what they do. Why does this matter? Because teenagers who feel a need to perform to get approval will be troubled by a nagging uncertainty whether their counselors genuinely accept them. In their relationship with God, for example, they will continually chase the carrot of divine approval.

Nonpossessive warmth provides a springboard for struggling adolescents to accept themselves and become strong individuals who do not compulsively conform their personalities to what others wish them to be.

Genuineness

Without honesty there is no way to touch hurting teenagers. Adolescents have built-in radar that spots phoniness even at a distance. They are experts at detecting fabricated feelings and insincere intentions. To every overture of help they apply their own polygraph test. Honest thoughts and authentic feelings may be verbally expressed at appropriate times, but it is just as important for genuineness to come through in all of its subtle forms, in counselors' eyes and posture, for example.

Genuineness cannot be faked. Either you sincerely want to help or you are simply playing the sterile role of a "helper"—hiding behind masks, defenses, or facades. In other words, authenticity is something you *are*, not something you *do*. Genuineness has been described as a lure to the heart. Jesus said, "Blessed are the pure in heart." Or, to put it another way, "Consider the counselor in whom there is no guile." When genuineness is present, a hesitant and skeptical adolescent is likely to stay with you and invest energy in the counseling process.

To maintain the qualities of warmth, genuineness and empathy, routinely ask yourself these questions:

- Do I honestly accept this adolescent without requiring change? Do I value this person in spite of his thoughts, feelings, or behavior?
- Am I more concerned with doing the right things as a counselor than being who I am as a person? Am I aware of my emotions when I am with others?
- How would I act, think, and feel if I were in this adolescent's situation? Do I understand him so accurately that I have no desire to judge him?

Empathy

The best way to avoid stepping on adolescents' toes is to put yourself in their sneakers. I don't know who said that first, but it's surely true. Empathy lets struggling adolescents know you hear their words, understand their thoughts, and sense their feelings. This does not mean you necessarily understand all that is wrong with them. It means you understand what they feel and think. Empathy is void of judgment and says, "If I were you, I would act as you do; I understand why you feel the way you feel."

Two important distinctions about empathy are helpful. First, empathy is not identification. You don't need to wear faded jeans and blare rock and roll on your car radio to enter the adolescent's world. In fact, teenagers want to be seen as unique and complex. They resent blatant attempts by adults to identify with them. To say "I know exactly how you feel" to a struggling adolescent is like telling a Vietnam veteran that his post-traumatic stress is easy and simple to understand.

Second, empathy is deeper and stronger than sympathy. Sympathy is standing on the shore and throwing out a lifeline while empathy is jumping into the water and risking one's safety to help another. And the risk is real. In empathy we risk change. Understanding the aching heart of a struggling adolescent *will* change you in spite of the human tendency to resist change. Yet when we have the courage to enter the pain of a hurting teenager, we begin to build a relationship in which healing can occur.

For struggling adolescents, the best conditions for growth occur when they (1) feel they are accepted unconditionally; (2) feel they are with one who is trustworthy and real; and (3) feel they are deeply understood.

NECESSARY BUT NOT SUFFICIENT

Although these three traits are critical for effective counseling, they do not assure success. They are necessary but not sufficient. Persons who possess these qualities will still vary in their effectiveness as counselors. For instance, crucial to effectual counseling is the practice of active listening, which I describe in the next chapter. A second important factor is a working knowledge of when and how to use practical techniques that have proved helpful in alleviating specific struggles. Part Two provides many of the practical components often overlooked when it comes to helping teenagers with specific problems.

Beware of excessive emphasis on techniques. We counselors are not technicians with boxes of gimmicks and quick fixes. The methods and techniques recommended in this book must be enhanced by counselors' warmth, genuineness, and empathy. The result will be meaningful expressions of love for clients.

Notes

1. D. Brenner, *The Effective Psychotherapist: Conclusions from Practice and Research* (Elmsford, N.Y.: Pergamon, 1982), 2.

2. G. Corey, *Theory and Practice of Counseling and Psychotherapy*, 4th ed. (Wadsworth, Calif.: Brooks-Cole, 1991), 12.

3. C. R. Rogers, G. T. Gendlin, D. V. Kiesler, and C. B. Traus, *The Therapeutic Relationship and Its Impact* (Madison: Univ. of Wisconsin Press, 1967).

4. This self-inventory was designed by the author to provide a quick and rough estimate of a person's helping traits.

5. G. Collins, *Christian Counseling: A Comprehensive Guide, Revised Edition* (Waco, Tex.: Word, 1988), 24–25.

3

The Heart of Helping

John, thirteen, was brought to a counselor's office by his mother because he was having difficulty at school and wouldn't do his homework.

> JOHN: I don't care what they do to me. I'm not going to do another assignment.
>
> COUNSELOR: [With great concern] Do you know you can't graduate if you don't do your homework?
>
> JOHN: I don't care.
>
> COUNSELOR: [In a compassionate tone] I bet you'll care when you start looking for a job.
>
> JOHN: Big deal.
>
> COUNSELOR: [Desperately wanting to help] It is a big deal. It will affect the rest of your life.
>
> JOHN: I don't care.

This endless circle of conversation does not move John one inch closer to doing homework, and it does next to nothing to build a therapeutic relationship. The counselor is rational and is obviously concerned. Why isn't it working?

The missing component is the most important and fundamental skill required for a successful helping relationship—active listening. Adolescents do not readily lay out their thoughts and feelings even for a compassionate counselor. Counselors who build a therapeutic relationship with adolescents do it the old-fashioned way: They "earrrrrrn it." An adolescent's real concerns are often closed off and opened only by continued and careful listening. Like a safecracker, a counselor who listens with skill can spin off the combination that gets through the door of silent pain. "The road to the heart," wrote Voltaire, "is the ear." Look at this brief interaction again with a counselor who is hearing more than just words.

JOHN:	I don't care what they do to me. I'm not going to do another assignment.
COUNSELOR:	Sounds as if you've made up your mind.
JOHN:	Yep. Those teachers are idiots, especially Mr. Wilson.
COUNSELOR:	They're not too smart, huh?
JOHN:	Well, I'm sure they're smart and everything, but they aren't very nice.
COUNSELOR:	They're kind of mean?
JOHN:	Yeah. The last time I handed in my paper, Wilson read it aloud. I didn't write that for the whole world to hear.

Like marriage, counseling is a relationship that may be for better or it may be for worse. Artful listening determines the difference.

LISTENING IS THE HEART OF COUNSELING

Aristotle observed that while an injury to the head can make one unconscious, a wound to the heart is invariably fatal. Active listening—listening with "the third ear" as Theodore Reik called it—is the heart of counseling. It is vital to the life of a helping relationship. Without active listening counseling dies.

Jesus understood the importance of listening. Even as a young boy he was sitting with the teachers in the temple, "listening to them and asking them questions [and] everyone . . . was amazed at his understanding" (Luke 2:46–47). The apostle Paul understood that listening requires diligent work. When he was before Agrippa, he said, "I beg you to listen to me patiently" (Acts 26:3). The book of James tells us to "be quick to listen, slow to speak" (James 1:19). And the book of Proverbs says, "He who answers before listening—that is his folly and his shame" (Prov. 18:13). The word *listen* occurs more than two hundred times in the Bible.

Two major ingredients go into active listening: reflection and clarification.

Active Listening Requires Reflection

Understanding comes through empathic reflection—responding sensitively to the emotional rather than the semantic meaning of a person's expression. Jesus responded on the basis of what he "heard" people *feeling*. After a short exchange, Nathanael declared Jesus to be the Son of God. Jesus reflected Nathanael's meaning and said, "You believe because I told you I saw you under the fig tree" (John 1:50; see vv. 43–51).

Active listening does not mean saying, "I understand." A classic cartoon shows an exasperated teenager telling her mother, "For Pete's sake, will you stop understanding me and just listen?"

Many believe that sincerity assures understanding. But sincerity ignores the fact that we communicate in ways that severely limit our ability to get our real messages across. Between what a person intends to communicate and what others hear stands an unavoidable filter of preconception. "I'm not going to do another assignment" may mean "I was terribly embarrassed by Mr. Wilson for reading my assignment to the whole class." "I won't go" may mean "I don't want to go." Or "Do you really think so?" may mean "I disagree."

Counselors normally target three aspects of a message in their reflections: (1) the content of the message, (2) the thinking behind the message, and (3) the feeling behind the message. Each is equally valid and useful. Here is an example of how a single statement may be reflected at each level.

ADOLESCENT: I couldn't believe he was accusing me for what *he* did.

COUNSELOR: [Reflecting content] He blamed you.

ADOLESCENT: Yeah. He said I was the one responsible because I was there.

COUNSELOR: [Reflecting thinking] You thought he was unfair.

ADOLESCENT: Yeah. I didn't deserve to be blamed.

COUNSELOR: [Reflecting feeling] It must have made you angry.

ADOLESCENT: I was furious. I also felt bad.

By reflecting the content of the message, counselors allow adolescents to elaborate further on what happened. By reflecting the thinking behind the message, counselors allow adolescents to understand their evaluation of what happened. And by reflecting the feeling behind the message, counselors invite adolescents to become aware of emotions resulting from what happened. Here are more examples.

ADOLESCENT: [Sitting down, looking at the floor, hunched over, and silent]

COUNSELOR: [Reflecting content] You've had a bad day.

ADOLESCENT: My dad took away my driving privileges.

COUNSELOR: [Reflecting thinking] I wonder whether you would rather be left alone.

ADOLESCENT: No, I just wish my dad would leave me alone.

COUNSELOR: [Reflecting feeling] Looks as if you don't feel so good.

ADOLESCENT: I guess I feel that I let my dad down, but I'm mad at him.

By reflecting the content, thinking, or feeling of a struggling adolescent, we are not evaluating or advising. We are saying, "I am with you and want to understand you better." Here is another example:

ADOLESCENT: I got accepted to all three schools!

COUNSELOR: [Reflecting content] You got just what you wanted.

ADOLESCENT: Yeah, every one of them sent me a letter.

COUNSELOR: [Reflecting thinking] Your hard work really paid off.

ADOLESCENT: Yeah, I guess I didn't need to worry the way I did.

COUNSELOR: [Reflecting feeling] You got just what you wanted. You must be happy.

ADOLESCENT: I've never been so relieved. I feel great.

However, reflecting comments can be overdone. Eager to build rapport with an adolescent, sometimes beginning counselors reflect everything that rolls across the kid's tongue. Continual "uh-huhs" and constantly nodding or parroting a counselee's comments interfere at best, and may show superficiality and insincerity at worst. Go easy.

Active Listening Requires Clarification

> **Love**
> **isnowhere**

How do you read the two lines above? Some see "Love is no where." Others read "Love is now here." In the same way, we may see an entirely different meaning from the one the counselee intends.

When absurd misunderstandings happened between Abbott and Costello, the famous comedy team, the whole nation chuckled. But in a counseling session, being misunderstood is no laughing matter. Misunderstanding does not result from not hearing the words but from our not clarifying the meaning of the words. The five hundred most commonly used words in the English language carry over fourteen hundred different meanings—an average of nearly three meanings for each word!

In addition, some adolescents have personalized meanings for the words they use. I once heard an adolescent say he was "bailin' for a loc fiesta that's fully amped with no ancients." Translation: he was leaving for an exciting neighborhood party with no adults. Here are some more examples: *dude!* means hello; *dude* means guy; *buds* means friends; *rad* means superlative; *way rad* means extremely cool; *fresh* means cool; *weak* means uncool; *chill* means hang out; *chill* means relax; *fly* means very stylish; *clean* means very attractive; *fundage* means cash; and *bad* means good. No wonder clarification is necessary!

An Exercise in Active Listening

Important feelings are often hidden behind the words of a struggling adolescent. Reflecting an adolescent's feelings is one of the most helpful and difficult listening techniques to implement. Following are some typical adolescent statements. Read each separately, listening for feelings. Make note of the feeling you hear and write a response that reflects the feeling of each statement.

1. I practice all the time, but it doesn't make any difference.
2. Every girl has a date but me.
3. I shouldn't have slammed the door, but she shouldn't have said that.
4. I should be able to stay out past midnight if I want. Jim does.
5. Do you think I did the right thing?
6. I'd like to punch his lights out!
7. I don't want to talk about it anymore.
8. What's the use?
9. What if she laughs at me? I'm not going to ask her.
10. I don't feel anything about it.

Compare your list of reflective statements with those listed on the next page to see how accurately you recognize feelings. Give yourself a 2 on items where your choice matches closely, a 1 on items where your choice only partially matches, and a 0 if you missed altogether.

How you rate on recognizing adolescents' feelings:

16–20	Above average recognition of feelings
11–15	Average recognition of feelings
0–10	Below average recognition of feelings

Clarification serves two basic purposes: (1) to gather additional information; and (2) to help explore an issue more thoroughly—to discover, for example, whether a problem is a greater concern to the adolescent or to you.

One obvious point: Clarification is necessary when you are not sure you heard correctly. Another cartoon says it beautifully: A king in the back seat of his Rolls-Royce is being carried by a group of long-haired guys with no shoes. He leans out the window and says, "I said 'radials,' not 'radicals'!"

WHAT ACTIVE LISTENING DOES

Listening Unearths Hidden Feelings

Active listening allows teenagers' hidden feelings to percolate to the top. Struggling adolescents do not often broadcast their pain. They want someone to sense their hurt without their having to admit it. The cry of fear, for example,

Possible Responses to the Exercise in Active Listening

1. I practice all the time, but it doesn't make any difference.— *Sounds as if you feel discouraged.*

2. Every other girl has a date but me.— *It feels as if you got left out.*

3. I shouldn't have slammed the door, but she shouldn't have said that.— *You feel kind of guilty but, at the same time, justified for what you did.*

4. I should be able to stay out past midnight if I want. Jim does.— *I wonder if you feel that your parents are being overly protective.*

5. Do you think I did the right thing?— *It sounds as if you're not very sure of yourself.*

6. I'd like to punch his lights out!— *You must be really angry.*

7. I don't want to talk about it anymore.— *It sounds as if you're feeling overloaded, as if it is all just too much.*

8. What's the use?— *As you say that, I get a picture of a guy who is discouraged and is crying uncle.*

9. What if she laughs at me? I'm not going to ask her.— *I get the sense that you're a little afraid and that your mind is made up.*

10. I don't feel anything about it.— *I'm wondering whether you have some idea of what you should be feeling and because you do not, you register it as not feeling anything.*

sometimes hides behind a fuming face. Pain is sometimes muted by wordy anger. And depression may lurk behind a stiff smile.

To help adolescents, a counselor needs a sensitive internal seismograph to feel the tremors beneath the external calm. In effect, that is what active listening is—a way to sense the quaking of adolescence. If we have a hunch that Brian, a fourteen-year-old, is not so apathetic as he seems but actually angry because he didn't make the team, we don't blurt out, "You are denying how angry you really are." Instead we may probe gently: "I get the feeling you're angry and you aren't sure that's okay." A statement like this allows Brian to own his buried anger without losing face.

Listening Takes Away the Fear of Feeling

Free from evaluation, active listening creates a safe environment. It provides a place where trembling adolescents may shed defenses and own up to previously feared emotions—and know that their feelings are acceptable. When adolescents are guarded, it is as if they are pressing the accelerator all the way to the floor but keeping the car in neutral and a foot on the brake—using valuable fuel and going nowhere. Counselors' active listening gives struggling adolescents new energy and helps them begin to move in positive directions.

Listening Helps Adolescents Be Their Own Counselors

The counselor's goal is not to be needed. Counseling isn't rescuing. Too often we mistake help with throwing out a line of advice. The problem with solving people's problems is that external solutions foster unhealthful dependence. If you solve a problem for a young person who comes back with a similar problem the next week, you put out the same fire over and over. When we listen to another person, we are saying, "I believe in you." But giving advice says, "I don't trust you to come up with your own solution." Active listening boosts the confidence of struggling adolescents and teaches them to depend on God and themselves for problem solving.

Listening Facilitates True Learning

The only people who really want somebody else to change them are wet babies. The goal of counseling is not to change people. It is to provide a relationship in which persons learn to change themselves—a relationship in which people mature.

True learning, the kind that significantly influences behavior, for the most part is self-discovered. And active listening helps struggling adolescents to discover how they can best cope with their situations. Active listening generates the principle of participation: People are motivated to act or follow through on decisions they have had a part in making. The motivation to act on advice that has been imposed is minimal at best.

TWO COMMON MISTAKES IN ACTIVE LISTENING

In *The Healing Heart*, Norman Cousins reports that medical students usually score higher on measures of empathy when they are entering medical school than they do upon graduation.[1] Somewhere in the process of learning medicine, they shift their focus away from the patient and look solely at the disease. As a result, Cousins believes, many medical students have become superbly trained but poorly educated. Counselors may fall into the same trap. We may become so overly confident of our ability to listen that we lose interest in practicing it. Or we may work so diligently at being sophisticated listeners that we miss what is most evident. To be effective in the art of listening, counselors must not lose their desire or their ear for the obvious.

Desire to Listen

Since most people talk at the rate of 120 words per minute, and since most spoken material can be comprehended equally well at rates up to 250 words per minute, plenty of extra time is available for mental activity during a counseling session.[2] This means that counselors have at least two options: We may use our surplus time for deepening our comprehension of the message, or we may wonder what we are going to have for dinner when we get home. If we are to

Useful Leads for the Active Listener

It sounds as if you're feeling . . .	It seems as if . . .
I get a picture of . . .	What I hear you saying is . . .
Could it be that . . .	It must have been . . .
I wonder if you're thinking . . .	You must feel . . .

remain effective in understanding struggling adolescents, we must maintain a genuine desire to listen. A lack of desire may be a symptom of burnout.

An Ear for the Obvious

While active listening requires an eye for subtleties, it doesn't neglect the obvious—"the last thing a fish will discover is water." In our search for the hidden emotion, we sometimes lose sight of the most visible.

Harold Kushner tells a story that illustrates this point.[3] A factory was having problems with employee theft. Every day, it seemed, somebody stole a valuable item. So the plant hired a security guard to search each employee as he left the building. Most men carried only a lunch pail. But every day one man took out a wheelbarrow filled with trash, which the exasperated security guard had to dig through to determine whether the employee was making off with anything of value. The guard never found anything in the trash, but one day he couldn't stand it any longer. "Look," he howled, "I know you're up to something, but I can never find anything worth stealing in all that trash you carry out. It's driving me crazy. Just tell me what it is and I promise not to report you." The man shrugged and said, "Wheelbarrows. I'm taking wheelbarrows."

WHY ADVICE TURNS SOUR

Too often advice cuts the heart out of counseling. A little advice, like a little garlic, goes a long way. The following reminders may help you keep from overdoing it.

Advice Is Often Self-Centered

When we dole out advice before we have truly actively listened, we may believe we are being skillfully helpful. After all, isn't it the loving thing to relieve adolescents of suffering by helping them see the light? Actually, attempts to change adolescents by giving advice is not only naïve and ineffective but often self-serving. It hurts to see adolescents struggle with psychic pain, so by doing our part—giving advice—we feel better. The driving motivation behind the practice is often a desire to feel good about oneself. Don't be surprised by the chaos that results from self-serving advice.

Advice May Make Counselees Feel Worse

Offering advice may set young people up to feel worse because they cannot or are not ready to follow through on it. This may instill terrible pangs of guilt. The advice that Job's friends gave him in his time of affliction, for example, served only to make poor Job more miserable. The only way a counselor can know when and whether an adolescent is ready for advice is through persistent and sensitive listening.

Advice May Be Threatening

Sometimes giving advice may call counselees' beliefs and attitudes into question. This practice may reflect counselors' insecurity and uncertainty regarding their own beliefs. It is uncomfortable for us to be uncertain of our own values on certain issues. So, we reason, if we convert adolescents to our way of thinking, our discomfort is relieved, and we have reinforced the validity of our convictions. Further, we have once again proved that we are all-knowing counselors. This is much easier than putting ourselves out in an effort to understand adolescent perspectives.

Advice May Be Boring

Being forced to sit through an unrewarding or even irritating monologue causes people to turn off the one-sided "conversation" and put their minds on something else. Bored listeners simply suppress impulses to walk out by taking a mental vacation and sitting it out. Without self-restraint, the bored client feels like the bored youngster in church who said to his mom, "Pay the man and let's go home." Advice given without active listening causes boredom. And as Proverbs 18:13 says, advice is the advice giver's "folly and his shame."

Advice May Be Costly

Advice is effective only when it fulfills the salient needs of the listener. Too often, advice is given without considering how the counselee will feel about it. Those who give advice without listening enjoy the luxury of an opinion without the labor of a thought.

Because a counselor is ready to give advice does not mean a person is ready to receive it. Trigger happy advice is costly. When the price of listening to advice outweighs any gain from it, all of us turn it off. Upon hearing advice that is not given out of active listening, a teenager may say, "I don't want to talk about it anymore!" Therapy is shut down and the counselor is at a deadend. Even good advice isn't worth that price.

The point is obvious. It is difficult to make a mistake with active listening, but advice and recommendations may clog the flow of genuine feelings. Or, to put it another way, active listening will nearly always help a person clear out the clutter.

MAKING ADVICE HELPFUL

Carl Jung said that advice seldom hurts any of us because we so rarely take it seriously. That may be true, but there are ways to help people take good advice to heart. The key is knowing when and how to give it. The Bible states, "Let your conversation be always full of grace, seasoned with salt, so that you may know how to answer everyone" (Col. 4:6).

By now it should be clear that advice will usually backfire if the counselor has not earned—through active listening—the right to give it. Before giving advice, a counselor must understand what the struggling adolescent is really needing. Philosophers have always said it is more important to find someone who knows what the question is than it is to find someone who knows a pat answer to a question. The same holds true in counseling. Listening is not icing on the cake; it *is* the cake.

With the importance of listening in mind, here are some specific ways to minimize the possible negative consequences of giving advice to adolescents, *even when it is appropriate to do so.*

- Advice is heard best by a person who is calm and rational. When a person is drowning, it is not a good time to try to teach him to swim.
- Help adolescents to give the advice themselves. It is sometimes helpful to say, "What would you tell someone in your predicament?"
- Advice will have more impact if it is not given routinely. Like a mailgram from Western Union, infrequent advice will stand out in importance.
- Don't hesitate to be redundant. Restating a suggestion in different ways increases the likelihood that students will get the point.
- Ask what counselees hear you saying. Ask them to state in their own words what you have said.
- Suggest that counselees write down what you have said. Experiments indicate that note taking increases comprehension because it increases attention and personal involvement.[4] Subsequent review of the notes maximize the usefulness of advice.
- Pay attention to the timing of your advice. Information given first and/or last in a session is remembered better than that which is presented in the middle.
- If the counselee does not understand or accept the advice, don't push it. A counselor I know has a plaque in her office that reads, "Lord, fill my mouth with good stuff, and nudge me when I've said enough."

Notes

1. N. Cousins, *The Healing Heart: Antidotes to Panic and Helplessness* (New York: Norton, 1983), 26.

2. E. Foulke, "Listening Comprehension as a Function of Word Rate," *Journal of Communication* 18 (1968): 198.

3. H. Kushner, *When All You've Ever Wanted Isn't Enough: The Search for a Life That Matters* (New York: Summit Books, 1986), 152.

4. D. E. McHenry, *The Effects of Certain Learner, Task and Response Variables on Immediate and Delayed Aural Comprehension of Meaningful Verbal Material* (Denver: Univ. of Denver, 1974).

4

A Parent's Guide to Professional Help

WHEN IS PROFESSIONAL HELP NEEDED?

Nailing down what is normal in adolescence is like trying to nail gelatin to the wall. In general, the shift from "normal" to "abnormal" occurs when teens' behavior begins to interfere with their ability to carry out daily routines or sustain relationships.

The following questions may help you decide whether your teenager is going through a harmless phase or is suffering from a serious problem. If you answer yes to any of these questions, your child needs assessment and professional help as soon as possible.

- Is your teen silent for long periods and often withdrawn socially, having few friends?
- Is your teen considering dropping out or in danger of not completing high school? Failing classes?
- Is your teen obsessed with exercise and diet? Does your teen have an eating disorder?
- Does your teen practice any form of self-mutilation in the form of teeth marks, cuts, or burns? Does he wear homemade tattoos?
- Is your teen involved in any kind of illegal activity? Has he been arrested or in trouble with the law?
- Does your teen show an excessive fear of a particular family member, other relative, or family friend? Could she have been sexually abused and fears to talk about it?
- Does your teen have long periods of feeling worthless, helpless, guilty, or lethargic? Does he suffer from depression?
- Is your home life in chaos because of your teen? Is your well-being or performance at work suffering because of your teen's problems?
- Does your teen show a strong interest in the occult? Does he read about black magic or is he involved in anti-religious activities?
- Does your teen blow up with anger and get into fights a great deal? Has he been involved in vandalism? Is he a threat to someone's physical well-being?

- Are you concerned that your teen may be sexually promiscuous? Is he or she risking venereal disease or pregnancy?
- Does your teen report hearing voices that others do not hear? Does she hallucinate or is she out of touch with reality?
- Is your teen having serious problems with sleep, such as insomnia, repeated wakefulness at night, frequent nightmares, or sleeping too much?
- Does your teen have morbid thoughts, talk about death a lot? Is she suicidal?
- Does your teen run with a peer group that violates the rights of others? Do you have reason to suspect that he is involved in illegal activities or destructive acts?
- Does your teen get drunk? Does he drive while drinking? Is your teen experimenting with drugs that can kill?
- Does your teen experience relatively brief periods of intense anxiety? Does she suffer from panic attacks?

HOW TO SELECT A MENTAL HEALTH OR FAMILY PROFESSIONAL

If you answered yes to any of the above questions, you have no doubt tried many things to help your struggling child. Perhaps you have talked with a trusted friend who has gone through a similar experience with a young person. Maybe you have read a reputable book on the problem or consulted a teacher, guidance counselor, physician, or minister. These are all excellent resources, but when the problem becomes serious it is time to call a professional psychotherapist. That decision can be scary. It's not easy to tell a stranger that all is not well in your home. If you are like most parents, you're not comfortable subjecting your child-rearing skills to professional scrutiny.

The following information is designed to help you become an informed consumer of psychological services. While these suggestions may not reduce all of your fears, they may bolster your confidence and enable you to get the best help possible for your teenager.

The first item of importance in selecting a psychotherapist is to know the different kinds of qualified professionals. An old joke among practitioners asks, "What's the difference between a psychologist and a psychiatrist?" The answer: "About ten dollars an hour." There are a number of different kinds of professionals who provide a wide variety of psychological services today, and the differences go far beyond the fees they charge.

Unfortunately, many states allow almost anyone to put out a shingle and label himself a therapist. This term, however, indicates nothing about the person's education and experience. People seeking therapy should never be shy about asking helping professionals about their credentials. Here are some of the professions genuinely qualified to help:

Clinical psychologists have received Ph.D. or Psy.D. degrees after five or six years of graduate study. They are specialists in diagnosing and treating mental illness. They also do personality and intelligence testing.

Counseling psychologists usually have degrees in education, such as an Ed.D. They frequently work in school settings and specialize in academic, vocational, marriage, and family counseling.

Psychiatrists hold M.D. degrees and have taken postgraduate training in psychiatry. They can prescribe medication for mental, emotional, and behavioral problems.

Marriage and family therapists usually hold M.A. degrees and generally specialize in overcoming relational difficulties.

Psychiatric social workers usually have earned M.S.W. (Master of Social Work) degrees or D.S.W. (Doctor of Social Work). Like counselors, many specialize in marital or family problems of adjustment.

Finding the right mental health professional cannot be done hastily nor can the choice be made at random. And the decision should not be based solely on professional training. Making the right choice also requires careful consideration and cooperation between you and your teen. As much as possible, strive to choose a therapist with your teen, not for your teen.

The first step in choosing a therapist is to have a knowledgeable source of information. One of the best sources is people in the helping professions. Physicians, ministers, nurses, and teachers can often provide excellent referrals. Other informational sources include hospitals, community service societies, referral services, and local professional societies. Their information, however, is usually less candid and thus less helpful. Little can be told about the skills and training from a therapist's phone listing, but the yellow pages of the telephone directory do provide another source of information. If you are especially concerned that the therapist be sympathetic to Christian values and beliefs, several good referral sources can help you. Each of them has a referral base of professional men and women who are committed to Christ-centered psychotherapy:

Christian Association for Psychological Studies 714/337-5117
Focus on the Family 719/531-3400
Minirth-Meier 800/877-4673
New Life Treatment Centers 800/332-8336
Rapha 800/227-2657

Once you have two or three good referrals, the next step is to find out which therapist in your area is the best match for your teen. One way of gathering information concerning a particular professional is to talk with a person who has been in treatment with that therapist. While this is desirable, it is not always possible. I recommend a preliminary phone contact with the therapist followed by an in-person interview before you and your adolescent make a final decision.

Both you and your teenager must feel comfortable before committing to therapy. Ask therapists about several issues before entrusting adolescents to their care. Here are some questions to ask.

- Are they licensed?
- Do they work with adolescents on a regular basis?
- What are their credentials?
- At what university did they earn them?
- What professional associations are they accountable to?
- How will they approach your adolescent's particular problem?
- May clients call them between sessions?
- What do they expect of you regarding their treatment?
- How long do they expect treatment to take?

In the end you will have to follow your instincts by asking yourself whether you and your child like the person. Does he seem understanding and would your teen feel comfortable confiding in him?

Another important concern, of course, is money. How much will therapy cost? Ask the therapist about the fee structure. The average fee for treatment varies depending upon where you live and the credentials of the professional. In major metropolitan cities some psychologists charge as much as $125 an hour. In other areas the same type of therapy may be $40. You should also ask whether the therapist accepts insurance. Your insurance may or may not cover psychological services. Policies vary greatly. Many policies pay nothing at all and others may pay the entire fee. Call your insurance company to find out what your policy covers.

How do you know whether therapy is working? By definition, "successful" therapy helps the person to achieve better adjustment. Thus, a reasonable expectation is improvement, not "cure." For example, if a teen struggles with panic attacks, the long-range goal would, of course, be the elimination of the attacks. Therapy, however, is working if frequency and intensity of attacks are decreasing. Evaluate the effectiveness of your child's therapy based on short-range goals. Therapy should end either when the goals have been completely achieved or when, over time, there has been no progress toward the achievement of goals.

One final word of advice. Growing up often hurts, but sometimes being a good parent can hurt too. Even the best of homes have children with emotional problems, drug dependencies, eating disorders, and other struggles. Do not feel guilty because your teenager needs professional help. Do not blame yourself for your adolescent's struggles, and do not neglect your own needs. Do not punish yourself for perceived inadequacies. Seek help from a professional or join a parents' support group, and your entire family will benefit.

Part Two

The Struggles of Adolescents

ABUSE

☑ WHAT THE STRUGGLE LOOKS LIKE

A horrifying number of adolescents are abused—physically, sexually, or emotionally—by their parents, stepparents, relatives, friends of the family, or others. Each year at least ten percent of young people are reported to have been physically abused by their parents, and another ten percent are reported to be sexually abused. These alarming numbers are considered gross underestimates of the actual situation.[1]

Abuse may come from either parent and may be directed at one or more children, often in a repeated pattern. Physical abuse is typically accompanied by abusive language and humiliating punishment that may not be physical.[2]

Major physical injuries resulting from abuse are most frequently seen in very young children (under three years of age) and early adolescents (twelve to sixteen years old). The number of male and female victims of physical abuse is about equal.[3] Sexual abuse, however, occurs more frequently with female victims.[4]

If the abuse is recent, the signs may be obvious: bruises, scars, burns, or lethargy. Most of the time, however, the damage is not so visible. No single reaction characterizes abused young people. Their reactions can manifest themselves as aggressive behavior, depression, lack of empathy toward others, inability to trust anyone, helplessness, perfectionism, overeagerness to please others, excessive involvement in school or church activities, or a decline in school performance.

Many abused children also struggle with feelings toward their nonabusive parent for failing to protect them from the abuse. Because they may feel that they have somehow "asked for it," abused children are also likely to suffer from guilt, believing they are responsible for the abuse from their parents. As a result it is not unusual for their self-esteem to be damaged well into adulthood. Sexual abuse specifically has been linked to difficulties in healthful sexual functioning, increased sexual awareness, prostitution, drug/alcohol abuse, eating disorders, delinquency, sexual victimization of others, and an artificial acceleration of psychosexual development.[5]

☑ WHY THE STRUGGLE HAPPENS

It would be wonderful if abusiveness could be attributed to a genetic flaw or a wild hormone. It can't. It almost seems that the more we attempt to discover clear causes through research, the cloudier the issue becomes. Patterns of behavior and personality profiles are not consistent. Seemingly reasonable individuals, not just psychopaths or perverts, commit violent abuse. Questions still outweigh answers by a long shot when it comes to the causes of abuse.

The ultimate irony is that abuse may be the biggest cause and effect of abuse. Children who have been abused often become adults who abuse their children, a vicious cycle. Among abusing parents, thirty to sixty percent say they were abused as children. The exact manner in which this cycle is created varies from one case to another, but the child often receives messages that abuse is necessary and productive and that children are powerless possessions of parents.[6] Of course the overarching message is of their worthlessness, else they would not be treated so.

☑ HOW TO HELP

Intervention strategies involving victims of physical or sexual abuse are similar enough to be grouped together. The following techniques should be thought of as working together and always undergirded with personal acceptance and reflective listening. If you do not have specific training and experience in working with victims of abuse, you should refer the young person to a psychologist.

Make Clear Philosophical Assumptions

Abuse by parents or others tests the limits of our ability to be objective in treating hurting adolescents. For this reason, helping strategies designed for teens who are struggling with abuse require a solid undergirding of explicit philosophical assumptions. First, counselors must assume that the problem is treatable and that victims will become survivors. Second, assume that victims are not responsible for the abuse (they are responsible only for their recovery). And third, assume that victims' expression and acceptance of feelings are necessary. These assumptions insure a more effective treatment plan.[7]

Know the Limits of Confidentiality

All fifty states mandate the reporting of all types of abuse. Failure to do so is a misdemeanor if your profession is in mental health, social service, medicine, education, or ministry. Some states do exempt pastors from the reporting requirement. If you are the first to learn about a specific case of abuse, you must report your findings to the appropriate agencies. In most states, the report must be made within a specified period of time, usually somewhere between twenty-four hours and seven days. Reports can be made by phone, in writing, or in person to a local law enforcement agency, the

Case Description

Melody, seventeen, is an only child of divorced parents. She was referred for counseling after being in inpatient psychiatric treatment for a suicide attempt. After about six sessions of outpatient care, Melody began to feel more comfortable with her therapist and to unravel her past. She confessed that her depression and suicidal thoughts were over a fear that she would never have a happy marriage. Upon gentle inquiry from her therapist she began to cry, "I have never told anyone this. . . ."

For the first time Melody confessed her gruesome story. When she was eight years old she was sexually abused several times by the landlord of the apartment complex where she lived. Occasionally, when her mother was going to be working late, she asked the landlord to let Melody into the apartment. The landlord would wait behind the screen door of Melody's apartment when she arrived from school. He would tell her he had a snack for her in the kitchen. It was there he sexually abused her. Until now she had never told a soul. Melody sobbed, "I can still see him standing above me by the kitchen table."

Department of Social and Health Services, or Child Protective Services. Those who report abuse are generally given immunity from liability and can remain anonymous, but normally confidential communication is not protected in court proceedings.

If you suspect abuse and have a reasonable basis for thinking a young person is being abused though the young person does not admit its occurrence, you should report your suspicions. If the victim is over eighteen at the time of the disclosure, reporting abuse may not be mandatory. Still, the counselor may have an ethical obligation to report it if siblings or other children are still at risk.[8] If you are in doubt about the appropriateness of a report, consult informally with Child Protective Services or law enforcement personnel.

Understand Delayed Intervention

Because many children are abused in their preadolescent years and the abuse is not reported, in many situations counselors may be dealing with delayed intervention even though clients are still teenagers. Many of the strategies for delayed intervention are the same as immediate intervention. In delayed cases young people have usually built up arsenals of defenses to cope with the abuse. They may minimize the abuse ("Every dad gets mad now and then") or rationalize ("He couldn't help it; he was drunk"). The counselor must be sensitive to these barriers, which are serving as defenses. One of the most significant difficulties with this kind of defensiveness is reluctance to discover that they are actually victims of abuse.

These adolescents generally come to counseling for problems that seem unrelated to abuse. They may have a presenting problem of sexual misconduct, substance abuse, or peer problems. If you suspect that a teen may have been abused in the past you should ask, "How are things going at home?" This simple inquiry may trigger surprise, anxiety, or secretiveness. If this kind of question does not elicit strong reactions, you may try another avenue by saying, "A lot of young people tell me about painful or unusual things that have happened to them, even if they occurred a long time ago."

If you have good rapport with the young person, it may be best to inquire about abuse directly to indicate that it is okay to discuss this taboo topic. Be careful, however, not to force the counselee to say the "right" thing. Also, be careful not to turn your assessment into an interrogation. Trust and safety are critical. Pressured disclosure can revictimize or retraumatize the young person. If an adolescent does not immediately reveal a history of abuse, you will have planted the seed allowing permission to talk about it later.

Be Alert to Suicidal Risk

It is not unusual for an abused adolescent to say, "I'm the cause of all these problems." The guilt and betrayal most victims experience is so intense that counselors must assume that a high suicide risk exists in every case. Statements such as "they would be better off without me" should be taken seriously. To ease their self-blame, let victims know that their feelings are acceptable and normal. Consult the section on suicide.

Assess the History of Abuse

An information interview is essential for professionals who treat victims of abuse. The goal is to get an accurate picture of counselees' abuse history. Professionals will progress from general questions to a more specific focus in gathering information. They will use open-ended questions and avoid double-edged questions that might imply blame (e.g., "Don't you. . . ?"). They will put potentially embarrassing questions about sex in context (e.g., "I need to ask about . . . because. . . ."). Counselors will document their observations and impressions and include counselees' nonverbal messages, facial expressions, physical appearance, and any physical signs of abuse. Notes provide a baseline on victims' behavior and may be useful if clinicians are subpoenaed for court proceedings.[9]

Give "Permission" To Feel

Abused children normally keep a tight lid on their emotions. Giving them permission to vent their feelings with intensity is critical in the healing process. Repression of feelings is common. For example, they may report an inability to feel angry. When this is the case, an important goal is to increase their affective awareness. Expressing submerged anger in the safety of a counseling relationship can be a powerful and liberating force. Take time to explore feelings that may or may not seem relevant to the abuse. Be aware that abused young people often act out their feelings through aggression or inappropriate sexual behavior. These teenagers need appropriate channels in which to express feelings, and a relationship with a professional counselor often provides this.

Facilitate Grieving

Being abused as a child and trying later to survive as a young adult is to sacrifice growing up. Most adolescents do not easily admit their losses. Grieving the loss of their childhood is a way to honor their pain. Grief work allows them to let go of their secret agony and move into the present with greater self-awareness and control. It allows them to regain some of their stolen vulnerability and prepares them for genuine intimacy with others in the future. See the section on grief for further help in this process.

Keep Your Feelings in Check

A counselor only adds to the young person's confusion if the counselor expresses strong feelings—even if these feelings stem from a desire to be an advocate for the teen. A counselor can be supportive of the child without "offender bashing." Keep your biases of disgust and anger in check. This creates a safer environment for the adolescent and invites the counselee to express intense feelings. It also enables the victim to set the tone and pace of the intervention, further instilling a sense of regaining control.

Facilitate Empowerment

The imbalance of power is a key element for victims of abuse. Young persons are powerless against abusive adults. Teens may exhibit powerlessness by becoming withdrawn, isolated, and helpless. Or to regain control in response to perceived power loss, they may act out sexually or rebel at school. Effective treatment must facilitate healthful empowerment. This goal can be challenging because it requires that assertiveness not turn into aggression. Empowerment is a positive, assertive sense of control and appropriate feelings of control. Empowerment begins with the first report of the abuse.

Being believed and being able to say what really happened is the first step toward regaining control. Young people need reassurance that they did the right thing in reporting the abuse. Affirm them for their courage and acknowledge that they have taken a difficult step toward regaining command of their lives. Don't convey a sense of suspicion or doubt by asking whether the counselee is "absolutely sure" events happened as reported. Young people also need to know that they have the right to say no while maintaining their place in the family.[10] Facilitating empowerment also means teaching them self-protective skills to avoid becoming victims again. Assertiveness-training exercises may empower young people with confidence. Several techniques are outlined in the section on shyness.

Set the Stage for a Survivor Mentality

Victims' distress can be eased by affirming their ability to survive their circumstances. Help them gently to begin looking toward a brighter future. Remind them that having undergone the severe trauma of abuse does not preclude their ability to function normally in the future. Tell them they are instinctively strong to have survived what they have been through. Recognize the success of their coping strategies. Praise their journey toward self-recovery. It may encourage some to know that thousands of abuse victims have become survivors. Suggest that they will feel in greater control of their lives as time goes by. Hope and realistic reassurance will instill a survivor mentality.

Explore Spirituality

A history of abuse can distort young people's concept of God. The last thing those who have been abused by their dads need is another father. They will most likely see God as an abusive parent. At the same time the one thing they need most is the Father. In time they need to see that God is love. If teens are spiritually sensitive, explore their spiritual perceptions and needs. Help them straighten out their crooked concepts and tap into God's love. This is essential to meaningful healing and peace of mind. It may mean, by the way, that they need to express their anger and disappointment toward God. "If God is so loving," they will ask, "how could he let this happen?" Accept their anger and let them know it is all right to express their true feelings to God.

Explore Forgiveness

Forgiveness of abusers cannot be forced on victims. Eventually, however—almost always a long way down the road—youths will need to assess their capacity to give up their need to hurt back. They will need to forgive others as well as themselves. Bitterness and hatred will slowly gnaw at them and cause them to carry the burden of abuse forever. If you focus on forgiveness before victims are ready, it will only stifle a healthful healing process and increase denial. Techniques and strategies that facilitate this process can be found in the section on forgiveness.

Consider Group Work

The use of group therapy may be a dynamic component of the healing process. Groups vary but commonly provide mutual support and information that facilitate survival. Some are oriented toward young victims, others toward parents, and some toward the whole family. Groups are particularly helpful as a strategy in delayed intervention, that is, a year or more after the abuse has occurred. Effective groups reduce feelings of isolation and alienation as well as stigma, which are common in victims. Parents Anonymous for physical abuse and Parents United for sexual abuse provide national networks for support and education and may be helpful resources in locating local groups. The toll-free number of Parents Anonymous is 800/421-0353.

Understand Rape

Physical abuse and sexual abuse are not limited to family members. As adolescents begin dating, their chances of being victimized increase. The incidence of physical violence and rape during a date has become common enough to be labeled *date rape*. According to reports, a growing number of young men and teenage boys, often by using physical force, are forcing their dates to have intercourse or perform other sexual acts against their will. Each year thousands of teenage girls are victims of date rape.[11] Counselors must be aware of and sensitive to this kind of victimization. These victims may not even recognize it as rape and will continue to be in sexual contact with abusers because of confusion.

The crisis-oriented approach to sexual-assault intervention views the counselor's role as an active one. A common obstacle to successful intervention is dealing with victims' ambivalence. Only one in ten victims will use some type of crisis intervention service such as a rape-crisis center or hospital. Once they have agreed to avail themselves of therapy, the emphasis is on assisting the victim to regain a sense of autonomy and control over her life. Treatment focus is on developing crisis-related problem-solving skills to equip girls and women for possible medical and legal procedures. A social support network for victims is also critical.[12] For more information on assisting victims of date rape, consult Robin Warshaw's *I Never Called It Rape.*

☑ WHEN TO REFER

Refer adolescents who struggle with abuse to psychologically astute physicians or to psychiatrists, if physical or sexual abuse is recently inflicted. Refer them to other competent counselors or psychologists when, over time, they become increasingly stuck in a defensive reaction to their dealing with pain or if they experience a growing sense of hopelessness or are increasingly depressed or suicidal. This requires counselors who are willing to recognize their own limitations. Even experienced abuse specialists frequently refer adolescents to achieve the therapeutic goal. If you do not have explicit training and experience in treating abuse victims, referral is imperative.

Where To Go for Additional Help

Allender, D. B. *The Wounded Heart: Hope for Adult Victims of Childhood Sexual Abuse.* Colorado Springs: NavPress, 1990.

Burgess, A. W., L. L. Holmstrom, A. N. Groth, and S. M. Sgroi. *Sexual Assault of Children and Adolescents.* Lexington, Mass.: Lexington Books, 1978.

Feldmeth, J. R., and M. W. Finley. *We Weep for Ourselves and Our Children: A Christian Guide for Survivors of Childhood Sexual Abuse.* San Francisco: HarperCollins, 1990.

Finklehor, D. *Child Sexual Abuse.* New York: Free Press, 1984.

Heitritter, L., and J. Vought. *Helping Victims of Sexual Abuse: A Sensitive Biblical Guide for Counselors, Victims and Families.* Minneapolis: Bethany House, 1989.

Justice, B., and R. Justice. *The Abusing Family.* New York: Human Sciences Press, 1976.

Martin, G. L. *Counseling for Family Violence and Abuse.* Waco, Tex.: Word, 1987.

McGee, R. S., and H. Schaumburg. *Renew: Hope for Victims of Sexual Abuse.* Houston: Rapha, 1990.

Morrison, J. *A Safe Place: Beyond Sexual Abuse for Teenagers*. Wheaton, Ill.: Shaw, 1990.

Russell, D. E. H. *The Secret Trauma: Incest in the Lives of Girls and Women*. New York: Basic Books, 1986.

Sgroi, S. M., ed. *Handbook of Clinical Intervention in Child Sexual Abuse*. Lexington, Mass.: Lexington Books, 1982.

Warshaw, R. *I Never Called It Rape*. New York: Harper & Row, 1988.

Notes

1. R. Emery, "Family Violence," *American Psychologist* 44 (1988): 321–28.

2. B. Justice and R. Justice, *The Abusing Family* (New York: Human Sciences Press, 1976).

3. American Humane Association, *The National Study of Child Neglect and Abuse* (Denver: American Humane Association, 1981).

4. D. Finklehor, *Child Sexual Abuse* (New York: Free Press, 1984).

5. L. Tong, "Personality Development Following Sexual Abuse," *Child Abuse and Neglect* 11 (1987): 371–83.

6. D. Graybill, "Aggression in College Students Who Were Abused As Children," *Journal of College Student Personnel* 26 (1985): 492–95.

7. D. Capuzzi and D. R. Gross, *Youth at Risk* (Alexandria, Va.: American Association for Counseling and Development, 1989).

8. F. Sink, "A Hierarchical Model for Evaluation of Child Sexual Abuse," *American Journal of Othopsychiatry* 58 (1988): 129–35.

9. T. L. Jackson, R. P. Quevillon, and P. A. Petretic-Jackson, "Assessment and Treatment of Sexual Assault Victims," in *Innovations in Clinical Practice: A Source Book*, vol. 4, ed. P. Keller and L. Ritt (Sarasota, Fla.: Professional Resource Exchange, 1985), 51–78.

10. W. G. Wagner, "Child Sexual Abuse: A Multidisciplinary Approach to Case Management," *Journal of Counseling and Development* 65 (1987): 435–39.

11. E. Flax, "Panel Hears Testimony on Causes of Violent Acts by Nation's Teenagers," *Education Week* (24 May 1989): 13.

12. R. Warshaw, *I Never Called It Rape* (New York: Harper & Row, 1988).

ANGER

☑ WHAT THE STRUGGLE LOOKS LIKE

The body of Christ has always had trouble knowing how to express strong emotions appropriately. Especially anger. In some families it is more acceptable to be depressed than angry.[1] But anger is normal and natural. According to David Mace, we are not responsible for being angry, only for how we respond to and use anger once it appears. The apostle Paul understood this when he said, "In your anger do not sin" (Eph. 4:26). Humans were created with a capacity to experience potent emotions, including the passion of anger.[2]

Anger is not easy to define. It occurs in varying degrees of intensity and is expressed in countless ways. In *Counseling for Anger*, Mark Cosgrove sees anger as having three components: emotional (e.g., feeling hurt), cognitive (e.g., "You need to know how much you hurt me"), and behavioral responses (e.g., yelling). These components, he says, are so intertwined that people experience the emotion of anger as one continuous surge. Some young people lose hope when they face this powerful negative emotion because they do not separate feeling and thought from behavior. They lose sight of the thinking and behaving components and focus solely on the surge of emotional arousal.[3]

Physical signs of anger include rapid talking, raised voice, shakiness, trembling, cold hands, rapid breathing, sweating, grinding of teeth, biting lips, a choked feeling, and cracking voice. Paul Eckman, a professor at the University of California and the developer of the Facial Action Coding System, explains that narrowing of the lips is one of the earliest signs of anger. A sensitive observer may detect in a counselee's face a betrayal of the deep emotion before it registers in his or her conscious mind.[4]

Anger is so common during adolescence that many people believe its absence is a maladaptive sign. People expect adolescents to be angry and even slam doors shut now and then. Anger is a part of the important and painful process of individuation. For some quick-tempered adolescents, however, anger becomes more than a developmental phase. It becomes a chronic pattern of self-defeating hostility. In fact, an attitude of anger may become a major component in personality development.

Case Description

Mark was a seventeen-year-old boy of sturdy build. He outweighed his father by twenty pounds and was in outstanding physical condition. Although he had friends at school, they had all learned from experience to let Mark have his way when he got angry. He had a reputation for being hot-headed. He came for counseling because of multiple minor delinquencies and a belligerent attitude toward parental discipline. On several occasions, his parents felt he was forcibly restraining himself from striking them. His mother admitted to extreme fear that he might eventually hurt her. She described him as "a time bomb waiting to explode." While Mark admitted to arguing with his parents, he did not see himself as having a problem with anger.

Adolescents who struggle with anger are more isolated, less successful, and less satisfied than their peers. Many of their relationships are marked by conflict, withdrawal, and loss. At home they fight with siblings and combat their parents. They may express their anger passively by coming home late and offering phony excuses. Or they may be blatantly aggressive and break doors, walls, or furniture. They may be suspended from school or become dropouts because their teachers are hassling them.[5]

Diagnostically, according to the American Psychiatric Association, the intense behavior patterns of destructive anger may be labeled *Conduct Disorder*, *Oppositional Disorder*, *Intermittent Explosive Disorder*, or, if the adolescent is at least eighteen years of age, *Antisocial Personality Disorder*. In any case, the anger of adolescents is like a buoyant basketball forced under water: hard to sit on. When the delicate balance required to hold it down is disturbed, adolescent anger comes rushing to the surface and explodes into the environment. In children we call it a temper tantrum, but the same experience can be seen in many adolescents. When a fit of anger is provoked in adolescents, the reaction may be almost volcanic in intensity. Rage is manifested by a loss of control that erupts in screaming, cursing, breaking objects, and sometimes hitting. While tantrums are expected in young children (ages two to four years), destructive rage is out of bounds for adolescents. Often adolescents who throw tantrums have benefited from them by watching their parents raise the white flag of surrender in the face of angry fits. In this way young people learn to control the environment through outbursts of anger.

From time to time adolescents may come to counseling specifically for anger issues. More likely, however, they will seek help for other problems and in the process the problem of anger will appear. In fact, anger (like guilt) tends to be woven into the fabric of most counseling.

☑ WHY THE STRUGGLE HAPPENS

The list of possible causes of anger seems almost endless: frustration, betrayal, deprivation, injustice, exploitation, manipulation, criticism, violence, disapproval, humiliation, and on and on.[6] The following are just a few of the reasons some adolescents struggle with anger.

Developmental Changes

In adolescence, self-consciousness and concern with identity issues set the stage for frequent demonstrations of anger. Adolescents, more than any other age group, may be angered by an assault on their dignity and self-worth. This may include teasing, bossiness, sarcasm, rejection by others, failure, being lied to, unfairness, or criticism. Adolescents are in the serious business of building a solid personal identity, and even a minor attempt to undermine its construction might provoke retaliation. Also, during this time of continual change, the body's chemistry may interact with emotional processing. Hormone levels, for example, in adolescents have been shown to be related to anger.[7]

Continual Threat

Some adolescents have known nothing but pain and hurt all their lives. They have grown up in homes where they were put down, rejected, unjustly criticized, or even abused. Their learned response to this negative environment is to protect themselves with a heavy armor of anger and aggression. They have been burned. They have learned that relationships are painful and they are not about to let others take advantage of them. Anger then becomes a way of life. It is adolescent insulation from psychic pain.

Social Learning

Adolescents also learn to express their anger from their parents' style of anger. A comprehensive longitudinal study of grade-school children in New York revealed that parents' aggressive behavior at home is associated with aggressiveness in children at school.[8] We hardly need a study to tell us that children model their parents. If children grow up in homes where dads fly off the handle and control their families with physical and verbal abuse, it makes sense to conclude that the children will learn to use anger in the same way.

Unrealistic Expectations

In a desire to build their identities on solid foundations of healthful self-esteem, adolescents may set unrealistic standards for themselves. In fact, they may expect perfection. For example, if they are talented in the classroom and used to receiving grades of *A*, they may burst into fits of anger upon receiving *B-plus*. Young athletes who miss crucial foul shots in basketball games may experience similar surges of anger. Adolescents who expect perfection are condemned to suffer from chronic anger with themselves and others.

☑ HOW TO HELP

It is widely accepted that chronic anger is bad for one's health and destructive of one's relationships. It is also clear that expressing or repressing anger does not get rid of it. In fact, it makes anger worse. However, therapy can help reduce anger.[9] The following techniques are designed to help hostile adolescents manage anger in healthful ways. Therapists and counselees must work together, and counselors must always undergird these relationships with personal acceptance and reflective listening.

Pinpoint the Severity

At the beginning of treatment it is helpful to assess the intensity of the anger. A careful assessment can serve as a point from which to measure therapeutic progress. The State-Trait Anger Scale is a fifteen-item instrument that assesses anger both as an emotional state that varies in intensity and as a relatively stable personality trait. The Novaco Anger Scale is another instrument that can be helpful in pinpointing the severity of one's anger. These measures can be found in my book *Helping the Struggling Adolescent: A Counseling Guide*.

Avoid the Most Common Pitfalls

Daniel G. Bagby, an expert on anger in the church, points to three common misconceptions that govern an inadequate management of anger by religious people. First is the erroneous belief that God does not want us to experience any anger and that all anger is sinful. Second is the belief that angry feelings are best managed by camouflaging or ignoring them. And third, the belief that the painful feelings of anger, if ignored, will vanish and not continue to influence relationships.[10]

Understand Your Own Anger

Many issues people bring into counseling have never been experienced by counselors (for example, alcoholism, anorexia, suicidal behavior, panic attacks). Anger, in contrast, has been experienced by all. To be human is to know anger. Even the best of counselors have lost their tempers and lashed out in frustration. For this reason it is imperative that those who work with angry adolescents understand their anger thoroughly. What is your attitude toward anger? What makes you angry? How do you cope with and redeem your anger? Counselors will facilitate a healthful exploration of anger only if they have examined and understood anger in their own lives.

Help Them Admit Their Anger

Buried anger may be difficult to excavate, but it is imperative for angry young people to confess their struggle. It may be especially threatening if they are directing their anger at family members or God. Helping adolescents talk honestly about their anger requires patience and empathy from caring counselors. Young people are usually more comfortable projecting their bad feelings onto someone else whom they blame for their hot tempers.

If teens resist admitting to their anger, ask them to complete the sentence: "Anger is. . . ." How they define anger may help them (and you) understand their thinking. They may say, "Anger is always justified if you have been hurt"; or "Anger is always wrong, no matter how badly you've been hurt"; or they may say, "Anger is hating my parents." Whatever they say provides clues to their concept of anger and provides them with nonthreatening windows of opportunity to begin to admit their struggle with anger.

Some adolescents may be threatened by their angry thoughts. They need sensitive and supportive recognition of their fears of losing control. They are afraid of the damage they might do and the retribution that might follow. Counselors' focus with these young people should be on recognizing and discussing the fear of loss of control rather than on the anger itself.

Assign a "Hassle Log"

This assignment is used to heighten adolescents' awareness of where, when, why, and how often they get angry. The hassle log is a diary-like means of analyzing provocative events. They keep a record on anger, including places, happenings, persons present, what they did or said, the results, how they felt afterwards, and what they wish they had done differently. They bring their logs to each session. Counselors should review the logs and use situations described in the logs as role-play examples for teaching techniques on dealing with anger.

Discover the True Source of Anger

On the surface, angry adolescents may be mad at their mothers for embarrassing them in front of their friends, at their teachers for unfair grades, at friends for not agreeing with them during lunchroom conversation, at older siblings for failing to pick them up on time. Yet all these things are only symptoms of deeper hurt. At a deeper level, they may be really angry about a close relative's untimely death or parental divorce. By pinpointing the true sources of anger, counselors can begin to deal with the real problems.

Restore Physical Well-Being

Anger increases autonomic activity. Anger creates a surge of energy and physical tension. For the chronically angry, clients may be helped by learning about socially acceptable outlets for excess tension and energy. Jogging, swimming, team sports, even screaming into a pillow and breaking pencils have been found helpful in restoring physical homeostasis within angry people. The key point in suggesting vigorous physical activity is to be sure the conscious intent of the exercise is to reduce tension, not to act out or even fantasize revenge. The aim is to restore physical well-being.[11]

Teach the "Anger Control Chain"

In 1975 Raymond Novaco designed an anger control program that has been supported by extensive research and proved highly effective. Taught incrementally over several sessions, this program centers around "the five links in the anger control chain": triggers, cues, reminders, reducers, and self-evaluation.

Triggers are the external events and internal appraisals (self-statements) that produce anger arousal. A young person's *interpretation* of a situation can become the trigger. Becoming aware of these triggers is the first step to controlling anger. The hassle log mentioned above may be helpful in identifying triggers.

Cues refer to the physiological and kinesthetic experiences that signal anger arousal. The signals include accelerated heartbeat, flushed cheeks, tightening of the muscles, butterflies in the stomach, and rapid shallow breathing. It is analogous to the response a boxer feels to the cue, "and in this corner." Giving attention to cues is important because chronically aggressive adolescents are often impulsive. Becoming aware of their cues helps them slow down the process. It also helps adolescents discriminate among other affective states; it helps them see the difference between fear and anger for example. Once adolescents can identify through these cues when an increase in anger arousal is actually taking place, they are ready for the next link.

Reminders are self-instructional means for lowering the level of anger arousal. Reminders are the opposite of triggers. They are self-statements designed to reduce anger in any situation. Examples include "chill out," "calm down," "cool out," or "I can't win by getting angry."

Reducers continue the effort begun by reminders. They arm young people with an array of means for reducing their anger arousal in provocative, real-life situations. Reducers can be relatively simple: counting backward from ten or a hundred, deep breathing, or imagining a peaceful scene.

Self-evaluation is the final link taught in this anger control chain. Reflecting on their progress enables the young people to appraise how well the links were used, and then to make changes to control anger more effectively.

This is the core of the Anger Control Training program. Contracting, assertiveness training, problem-solving techniques, and relaxation training are also sometimes incorporated into the program. For a thorough description of how to implement this strategy see Raymond Novaco's book *Anger Control: The Development and Evaluation of an Experimental Treatment*.

Teach Rational Alternatives to Enraging Beliefs

Angry adolescents need help to understand that anger is often a symptom of feeling hurt, fearful, or frustrated and that it is the thinking behind these feelings that gives anger the combustion to ignite. Irrational thinking provides the kindling that sparks anger to a full flame. Adolescents may benefit from seeing how this combustion works. Here are three common examples:

Labeling. "You are a total jerk!" "You're a slouch, a loser." Labeling helps young people feel morally superior to those with whom they are angry. Once labeled, people are polarized and represent only the things the angry folks despise. Confront angry adolescents with reality. Ask whether they truly believe that those they are angry with are *total* jerks or just unfair in particular instances. Help them understand how labeling only intensifies their own frustration and results in more intense anger.

Mind Reading. In this distortion counselees invent explanations for actions of other persons. They do not simply hold their personal explanations as hypotheses to be confirmed; they believe them as fact. This generates and intensifies anger by allowing them to get worked up over false premises. Counselees may be helped by asking them to articulate causes of their anger in particular situations, what they believe other persons were feeling, and why they acted the way they did. It may be helpful to reverse the roles as counselors and "mind read" clients' actions and feelings to let them know how inaccurate this distortion can be.

Magnification. In this anger-creating distortion a negative event is blown out of proportion. For example, if teens missed points on an exam because they didn't understand the instructions, they may be momentarily frustrated but realize that it can't make any difference in their final grade. However, they may choose to magnify their frustration out of proportion until they become hot with anger. They may make a catastrophe of the situation by giving one moment more importance than it is worth and therefore erupting with disproportionate anger. Ask teens to recall times when they magnified minor frustrations until they made them boil with anger. Helping them see this process with objectivity will help them reduce its occurrence in the future.[12]

Practice Imagery Exercises

In *Self-Talk, Imagery, and Prayer in Counseling*, H. Norman Wright reports success with imagery exercises to control and reduce anger. He suggests that counselees indicate the five most anger-creating situations they are currently experiencing. Have them close their eyes and use their imaginations to recreate one of these situations. Allow them to hear their self-statements and watch how they usually react with anger. Next, have them relax. Then imagine the same situation but with rational self-statements that slow down the process of anger. This would fulfill the biblical admonition to be slow to anger. Help them visualize themselves responding to the provocation in a calm and relaxed manner. Wright suggests that counselees practice this new version of the experience in their minds many times outside of counseling sessions. With practice, they will change responses the next time they confront real situations.[13]

Be Prepared for Swearing

The issue of bad language is often part of anger in adolescence. It generally falls into three categories: (1) profanity, which is speech involving disrespect for something that is considered sacred or holy, such as the name of God; (2) cursing, which is speech reflecting the wish to harm someone (for example, "damn you"); and (3) obscenity, which is referring to sexual images in a sneering way (for example, "screw you").

Almost all adolescents use bad language sooner or later, and its use in recent years has, not surprisingly, increased.[14] Adolescents will swear to gain attention, to shock, or to rebel and assert their independence.[15] I have found that one of the best ways of dealing with it in a counseling setting is to ignore it. If counselees see that their language is not startling or upsetting to you, they will not have reason to continue using it. However, it is also important to be empathic. When they curse as a response to their frustration, try to recognize the distress and let them know you understand. At the same time, it may also be appropriate to express disapproval and set down limits for their behavior. If they continue to use profanity, for example, you may express your understanding of their feelings, but tell them that it is also upsetting for you to hear them dishonor God and that you would appreciate it if they would not use profanity while they are in your office. This also helps them see a constructive way of making requests without verbal emotional aggression.

Explore Anger Toward God

The angry counselees need to know that it is okay to shout at God. God has seen anger before; he has even experienced anger. If counselees are blaming God for something, allow them to say so. Allow them to talk freely about these feelings. Sometimes it is helpful to have them write an honest letter to God telling him how they feel about him and their circumstances. Once they have expressed their feelings, suggest that they also listen to God.[16]

Teach Forgiveness

Angry clients who are filled with bitterness and hatred ultimately need the healing of forgiveness. They need to learn how to forgive others as well as themselves. Forgiveness holds more promise for aiding an effective resolution to the problem of chronic anger than any other therapeutic intervention. Anger exists only in the present. Contrary to what many claim, anger does not accumulate or build up in an inner reservoir. We don't have anger left over from yesterday like an athlete with a sore muscle. We may have painful memories of yesterday that cause us to re-create feelings of anger, but anger itself is in the present. The *memories* of the hurtful events are what keep anger alive. The solution, in these cases, lies not in forgetting or even in anger-management techniques, but in breaking the power of clients' memories to re-create the feelings of hurt. The solution is forgiveness.[17] For techniques and strategies that facilitate this process, see the section on forgiveness.

☑ WHEN TO REFER

Refer angry adolescents to psychologically astute physicians or to psychiatrists when physical symptoms are present. Possible physical consequences of chronic anger include skin rashes, ulcers, muscle-tension aches, high blood pressure, grinding teeth, and clenched jaws.[18]

Refer youthful clients struggling with anger to other competent counselors or psychologists when, over time, they are feeling more out of control and angry. Refer them when you recognize your own unresolved anger issues are interfering with treatment (for example, if their situations or personalities are generating strong negative feelings in you).

Where To Go for Additional Help

Augsburger, D. *Caring Enough to Confront*. Ventura, Calif.: Regal, 1981.
Bry, A. *How To Get Angry Without Feeling Guilty*. New York: New American Library, 1976.
Carter, L. *Good 'N' Angry*. Grand Rapids: Baker, 1985.
Feindler, E. L., and R. B. Ecton. *Adolescent Anger Control: Cognitive-Behavioral Techniques*. New York: Pergamon, 1986.
Goldstein, A. P., and H. Keller. *Aggressive Behavior: Assessment and Intervention*. New York: Pergamon, 1987.
Hart, A. *Unlocking the Mystery of Your Emotions*. Waco, Tex.: Word, 1989.
Novaco, R. *Anger Control: The Development and Evaluation of an Experimental Treatment*. Lexington, Mass.: Lexington, 1975.
Olson, G. K. *Counseling Teenagers: The Complete Christian Guide to Understanding and Helping Adolescents*, chap. 10. Loveland, Colo.: Group Books, 1984.
Rubin, T. I. *The Angry Book*. New York: Collier, 1970.
Tavris, C. *Anger, The Misunderstood Emotion*. New York: Simon & Schuster, 1982.
Walters, R. P. *Anger: Yours and Mine and What To Do About It*. Grand Rapids: Zondervan, 1981.
Warren, N. C. *Make Anger Your Ally: Harnessing Our Most Baffling Emotion*. Garden City, N.Y.: Doubleday, 1983.

Notes

1. D. G. Bagby, "Anger," in *Dictionary of Pastoral Care and Counseling*, ed. R. J. Hunter (Nashville: Abingdon, 1990).

2. For a discussion of the issue of when anger becomes sinful, see Frank B. Minirth and Paul D. Meier's book *Happiness Is a Choice*, chap. 13 (Grand Rapids: Baker, 1978).

3. M. P. Cosgrove, *Counseling for Anger* (Waco, Tex.: Word, 1988).

4. D. Mace, *Love and Anger in Marriage* (Grand Rapids: Zondervan, 1982).

5. P. York et al., *Toughlove* (Garden City, N.Y.: Doubleday, 1982).

6. For a more thorough discussion of the etiology of chronic anger, see Cosgrove's *Counseling for Anger*.

7. E. J. Susman et al., "Hormones, Emotional Dispositions, and Aggressive Attributes in Young Adolescents," *Child Development* 58, (1987): 1114–34.

8. L. R. Huesmann et al., "Stability of Aggression Over Time and Generations," *Developmental Psychology* 20 (1984): 1120–34.

9. J. L. Deffenbacher et al., "Cognitive and Cognitive Relaxation Treatments of Anger," *Cognitive Therapy and Research* 12 (1988): 167–84.

10. Bagby, "Anger."

11. C. F. Alschuler and A. S. Alschuler, "Developing Healthy Responses to Anger: The Counselor's Role," *Journal of Counseling and Development* 63 (1984): 26–29.

12. H. N. Wright, *Self-Talk, Imagery, and Prayer in Counseling* (Waco, Tex.: Word, 1986).

13. Ibid.

14. R. B. Bloom, "Therapeutic Management of Children's Profanity," *Behavioral Disorders* 2 (1977): 205–77.

15. A. Montague, *The Anatomy of Swearing* (New York: Macmillan, 1967).

16. Scriptures that address anger include Ephesians 4:26, Psalm 4, Colossians 3:8, and James 1:19.

17. A. Hart, *Unlocking the Mystery of Your Emotions* (Waco, Tex.,: Word, 1989).

18. F. Stearns, *Anger* (Springfield, Ill.: Charles C. Thomas, 1972).

ANXIETY

☑ WHAT THE STRUGGLE LOOKS LIKE

The twentieth century has been termed the Age of Anxiety and the Century of Stress. Many see anxiety as the most pervasive psychological phenomenon of our time.[1] In defining this common struggle, it is helpful to differentiate the shades of meaning in the cluster of words we often use interchangeably to describe this prevailing emotion.

Worry. This is perhaps our most common form of human suffering. It is a chain of negative and relatively uncontrollable thoughts and images. Worrying is like a rocking chair; it will give you something to do but it won't get you anywhere. Perhaps the definition that captures its essence best is that "worry is interest paid in advance on a debt you may never owe." About fifteen percent of the population of the United States are chronic worriers.[2]

Fear. Even the bravest people among us have experienced fear in some form at some time, such as a sudden scare at the sight of a harmless snake, a dry mouth before beginning a speech, or sweaty palms on a flight through bumpy air. Fears are different from phobias. The critical distinction between a common fear and a phobia is the degree to which it interferes with everyday life. This difference is explained further in the section on phobia.

Stress. This is the alarm reaction that activates the body to prepare for "the fight or flight response." It mobilizes us to cope with an emergency. In stress our heart rate, breathing, and perspiration increase. Our pupils dilate and our adrenaline kicks into overdrive.[3]

Concern. This refers to mental activity that focuses on a problem with a view toward taking action to resolve the problem. Concern springs naturally from caring and is directed toward a constructive end.

While worry, fear, phobia, stress, and concern are all related to the struggle that is the focus in this section, they are different from anxiety. Anxiety is all of these emotional factors rolled up together and gone too far.

The *Diagnostic and Statistical Manual of Mental Disorders* (3d ed. rev.) of the American Psychiatric Association (DSM-III-R) discusses generalized anxiety as a disorder characterized by chronic diffuse anxiety and apprehensiveness. ("Chronic" is defined by APA as anxiety of at least one month's duration.) The most prominent emotional component is an unpleasant sense of apprehensiveness and impending calamity. Because this type of anxiety may not seem to stem from any particular threat, it is said to be free-floating.

Clinical anxiety is almost always accompanied by several physical symptoms. The list of symptoms is long, but a quick review is helpful as we highlight some of the most important ones. The person with generalized anxiety experiences varying combinations of these physical symptoms:

- Rapid, pounding heart rate
- Diarrhea
- Fainting
- Profuse sweating
- Frequent urination
- Shortness of breath
- Loss of appetite
- Dizziness
- Sleeplessness
- Tremors and shaking

Adolescents who struggle with anxiety experience some of these symptoms on a day-to-day basis. They are more or less in a constant state of tension, worry, and diffuse uneasiness. Those suffering from anxiety can be overly sensitive to interpersonal relationships and be socially uneasy most of the time. They usually have difficulty concentrating and making decisions for fear of making a mistake. They may exhibit strained and tense posture and movements. They often complain of muscular tension, sleep disturbances, and cold hands.[4] Anxious adolescents feel as though they have no control over what is happening to them. They feel terrified. If you ask them what they are frightened of, they will say, "I don't know." They feel an impending sense of doom, but they don't know why.

To be clinically diagnosed with an anxiety disorder, adolescents must exhibit excessive or unrealistic anxiety for a period of six months or longer, as indicated by the frequent occurrence of at least four of the following:

- Excessive or unrealistic worry about future events
- Excessive or unrealistic concern about the appropriateness of past behavior
- Excessive or unrealistic concern about competence in one or more skills, e.g., athletic, academic, social
- Somatic complaints, such as headaches or stomachaches, for which no physical basis can be established
- Marked self-consciousness
- Excessive need for reassurance about a variety of concerns
- Marked feelings of tension or inability to relax[5]

One further clarification is in order. A panic attack is an intense burst of anxiety accompanied by physiological uproar and many strange changes in bodily feelings. The attack lasts from a few minutes to a few hours, and each attack will leave the victim feeling shaken and exhausted. The treatment

Case Description

Teresa is seventeen. She is popular at school, conscientious, and attractive. She also suffers from an almost unbearable amount of anxiety and stress. She worries about driving on the freeway, about saying something "stupid" in front of her peers, about embarrassing her parents, about failing in the classroom, and just about anything else that pops into her head. This is nothing new for Teresa. She has struggled with anxiety for at least a year and it seems to be getting worse. She sometimes gets stomachaches as a result of the worry, and of course that makes her worry all the more. She simply can't relax.

strategy with panic attacks requires a different approach from a general struggle with anxiety. For further help, refer to the section on panic attack.

Adolescence is a crucial period for learning how to deal with anxiety and stress. The coping style developed then will influence the rest of life.

☑ WHY THE STRUGGLE HAPPENS

Among the adolescent population anxiety is a widespread condition with numerous causes. Here are some of the major reasons for its occurrence.

Negative Self-Talk

Teenagers' self-talk, that is, their evaluation of an event, can produce anxiety. When a young person is faced with a stressful situation, he or she interprets it in terms of pairs of declarative sentences. For example, a male adolescent who fears rejection and humiliation might react to meeting an attractive young woman with the following two sentences: "She may not like me enough to go out on a date. That would mean that I am hopeless and no good." Albert Ellis, the founder of Rational Emotive Therapy, suggests that youths struggling with anxiety create their own anxiety through negative self-talk as seen in the second sentence in the example.[6]

Insecurity

The major cause of anxiety for most young people is a lack of inner security. A pattern of chronic worry is set up when adolescents feel unsafe and are awash in self-doubts. Feelings of rejection may come in greater force because they are sensitized for signs of rejection. When they look for rejection they usually find it, which in turn reinforces their insecurity. The cycle starts all over again. Insecurity breeds anxiety.

Inconsistency

Adolescents who have little stability in their lives will probably suffer from anxiety. Parents and teachers who are inconsistent in their relations with adolescents promote anxiety. Typically, one parent expects one thing and the other expects the opposite. Adolescents are caught in the middle. A teacher can add still another element of unpredictability. If students are affirmed one day for creativity on an assignment and marked down the next on a similar project for not following directions, the inconsistency creates anxiety over not knowing what is desired.

Legalistic Criticism

A steady diet of intense legalism and criticism from adults or even peers can lead to anxiety. Adolescents are already swimming in a pool of self-criticism. To be continually evaluated, judged, and exposed unjustly to additional criticism will bring about intense worry. Legalism and a bombardment of criticism make adolescents feel as if they are constantly being tested. They receive enough examination in the classroom.

Permissiveness

Some adolescents may feel anxious when there are no clearly defined boundaries. Without guidelines of behavior that will please others, teens must rely on themselves to discover the real limits. Some teenagers are almost seeking to be punished just to know that some things are off-limits.

Perfectionism

Adults' expectations of perfection directly lead to anxious reaction in a significant number of adolescents. Very high achieving, uncaring, or easygoing adolescents escape the anxiety of not fulfilling adults' expectations. But others develop tension and worry about not doing well enough. The standards are too high and the teachers, pastors, or parents never seem satisfied.

Neurology

Some anxiety is caused by disturbances in the brain's chemistry. Neurochemicals, the normal tranquilizers of the brain, can be dislodged, causing anxious thoughts and states of mind. Ignorance of this component can produce a great deal of misunderstanding about some anxiety.[7]

Physical Disorders

Anxiety symptoms can be caused by physical disorders that mimic anxiety reactions. Here are some examples: cocaine abuse, alcohol withdrawal, diabetes, hypoglycemia, psychomotor epilepsy, and hyperthyroidism. There are numerous others. For this reason, a complete medical examination by a physician is necessary when treating an anxiety disorder.

Meaninglessness

Existentialist Viktor Frankl holds that our main motivation is to find meaning in our existence. Without this meaning we suffer from an "existential vacuum" and anxiety. According to Frankl, each of us needs to find his or her own meaning, and we do this through working for the benefit of others, experiencing and appreciating the things of life, and taking an uplifting attitude toward life. Existentialists believe that if we have a *why* to live for we can bear almost any *how*.[8]

☑ HOW TO HELP

Counseling anxious adolescents is not easy. The challenge for counselors and other helping professionals who work with youth is to help young people learn to balance the stress in their lives to ensure maximum physical, psychological, and social well-being. The following suggestions are geared to provide a holistic approach to anxiety and stress management.

Pinpoint the Severity

At the beginning of treatment it is helpful to assess the intensity of the adolescent's anxiety. A careful assessment can serve as a point from which to measure therapeutic progress. The Clinical Anxiety Scale is made up of twenty-five items and is designed to quickly measure the amount, degree, or severity of generalized anxiety. The Self-Rating Anxiety Scale is a twenty-item test consisting of the most commonly found characteristics of an anxiety disorder. It can be used to help quantify anxiety symptoms. The Stressors Rating Scale can also be useful in assessing the severity of a young person's struggle with anxiety. All these measures can be found in my book *Helping the Struggling Adolescent: A Counseling Guide*.

Require a Physical Examination

A careful history and a physical examination with particular attention to anxiety symptoms is essential. Prior to embarking on a psychological treatment approach, organic disorders must be adequately ruled out.

Help Adolescents Face Their Anxiety

Young people, like most people, will do almost anything to avoid a direct confrontation with their anxiety. Like a person terrified of going to the dentist, the anxious teenager will ignore the problem while it festers and causes further psychic decay. Our society is ashamed to admit anxiety. We want to be heroes who bravely withstand the unexpected jolts and worries of daily life just as Rambo singlehandedly defeats an entire army. A young person told me he was being tempted by his friends to drag race on a busy highway. He said he played the macho game for a minute and then confessed he was chicken. He said he could immediately feel the anxiety roll away. However, adolescents who acknowledge their anxiety turn out to be stronger than those who equate anxiety with cowardice. In fact, true courage seems to begin with the admission of anxiety. Paul Tillich spoke of the basic need for "courage to be." This courage includes the willingness to accept and face personal anxiety.

Avoid Pat Answers

It is both callous and misleading to say to a young person struggling with anxiety, "Your problem is normal. All you have to do is pray and trust God more and everything will be all right." In teaching great numbers of students in counseling courses, I have heard responses like the above over and over again in practice role plays. Anxiety is assumed, unfortunately, to be a sign of spiritual and psychological weakness, which is far from the truth. Pat answers to anxiety problems isolate troubled adolescents and push them down into deeper pain.

Recognize the Strengths of Anxiety

Franklin Roosevelt became famous for telling a frightened nation that our greatest fear is of fear itself. Well spoken! To become free of anxiety it is necessary, first, to stop fearing it and to recognize that anxiety can even work in a person's favor. Anxiety, for example, is the emotional force behind much learning activity. An anxious student under the pressure of a final exam in algebra may be motivated to pick up the book, burn the midnight oil, and cram. A more carefree classmate, not anxious enough to study, may flunk. Anxiety can also be a sign that a moral code has been violated. Furthermore, it can help prepare a young person for a future stressful situation. The adolescent who is to give an oral presentation, for example, may be goaded by anxiety to rehearse the speech until the anxiety lessens in intensity. Anxiety that motivates a young person to take corrective action is healthful. All anxiety is not bad.

Recognize Anxiety as an Agent of Growth

Some developmental periods are almost always accompanied by anxiety. A young person who leaves home for an extended time expects to experience anxiety. I talked with a young woman who was recently graduated from high school. She was obviously tense and very anxious. She said that her coming to college was the first time she had ever been away from her family. She was determined to become independent, but she would have to do it in the face of anxiety. She described how she had always been overprotected by her mother and three older brothers; leaving home was the hardest thing she had ever done. She could have stayed near home in Illinois and gone to college there, but she decided it would be better for her to travel to a distant city, Seattle, and learn to develop into an independent and mentally healthy young woman. I have seen other students, who could not face the anxiety of separation, decide to remain home, tied to mom and dad, and never achieve individuation and full maturity. Anxiety can be a means of personal growth.

Neutralize Some of the Anxiety

Sometimes therapy cannot proceed until some anxiety is dissipated. Various methods can be used to aid relaxation. First, speak in a soft voice, slowing down your own verbal pace. This helps set the tempo and create a climate that allows teens to move unconsciously at a slower pace. Second, universalize clients' experiences. Tell them about the thousands who experience similar feelings. Reassure them that there are successful techniques for dealing with the problem. Generally, in this setting, young people take courage and grasp hope and become perceptively more relaxed. Once the anxiety is more manageable, counseling can proceed.

Focus on Thought Patterns

One of the best ways to alleviate chronic anxiety is to exercise mental willpower. A recent study at Oxford University found cognitive therapy superior to other forms of treatment in helping patients identify the exaggerated thoughts that made them anxious and helping them develop more realistic ways of thinking that would generate positive influences on their feelings and behavior. Six months after treatment ended, patients who had been taught to use their minds to help control their emotional state continued to show signs of marked relief from anxiety. Their ability to identify and assess anxiety-provoking thoughts improved.[9] Adolescents who can learn to control their thought patterns can change the way they feel. A great deal of undue anxiety in adolescents is related to school performance. Academic anxiety is often caused, at least partially, by unrealistic thought patterns. See the section on school for a discussion of ways to cope with this specific kind of anxiety.

Practice Positive Self-Talk

Self-talk strategies may be used alone or with other relaxation strategies. Many adolescents have not learned to stop saying negative or anxiety-producing comments to themselves. The first step is to stop self-statements such as "I'll never fall asleep"; "I know something terrible is going to happen"; "No one would ever want to go with me." The next step is to suggest positive self-talk. Ask adolescents to practice positive statements aloud in your office. "I'm upset now but things will get better soon. When I start to worry, I am going to relax. Nobody is perfect. Worry doesn't help; action does." The goal is to help them say things to themselves that enhance relaxation. When they are confronted by problems at school, for example, they will be able to say to themselves, "Calm down and relax."

Teach Deep Muscle Relaxation

Anxious adolescents need to gain mastery over their overwhelming emotions and uncontrolled physiological state. Deep muscle relaxation techniques can help them do this. Explain how a person cannot be in a state of anxiety and relaxation at the same time. The body and the mind will not allow contradictory actions simultaneously. Progressive muscular relaxation teaches us to be aware of varying degrees of muscle tension throughout the body.

A deep state of relaxation can be produced through a series of exercises alternately tensing and relaxing various muscle groups. Particular emphasis must be placed on perceiving and feeling the transition from the state of the muscular tension to the state of relaxation. The process may be repeated with successive muscle groups throughout the body until deep muscular relaxation is achieved. Here is a sample script for a portion of the exercise:

> Turn your attention to your head, wrinkle your forehead as tight as you can. Now relax and smooth it out. Let yourself imagine your entire forehead and scalp becoming smooth and at rest. Now frown and notice the strain spreading throughout your forehead. Let go. Allow your brow to become smooth again. Close your eyes now, squint them tighter. Look for the tension. Relax your eyes. Let them remain closed gently and comfortably. Now clench your jaw, bite hard, notice the tension throughout your jaw. Relax your jaw. Let yourself appreciate the contrast between tension and relaxation.[10]

This relaxation technique does not require mental imagery or special equipment, and the rationale for its use is understood by most adolescents. The following case illustrates the use of the progressive muscular relaxation technique with an adolescent:

> A fifteen-year-old girl undergoing chemotherapy for a lymphoma began to experience extreme anxiety each time intravenous therapy was instituted. She described many kinesthetic sensations during these episodes that included coldness of the extremities, abdominal discomfort, goosebumps, and tachycardia. Although she was unable to use mental imagery techniques successfully, she was receptive to the progressive muscular relaxation technique. With sequential tensing and relaxing of various muscle groups and attention to the consequent sensations over a fifteen-minute period, she was able to attain a state of deep relaxation and decreased anxiety. She was able to tolerate subsequent intravenous procedures without undue anxiety while listening to a tape recording of the technique.[11]

Practice Biofeedback

Biofeedback techniques traditionally require equipment and specialized training. However, the principles of biofeedback can be applied with minimal investment (described further below). Biofeedback provides electronic signals of physiological variables such as muscle tension, skin temperature, and skin moisture. These signals are amplified and displayed to the adolescent usually as auditory or visual information. Through this feedback the client can learn to alter any physiological activity.

Skin temperature biofeedback is commonly used to train people to warm their hands. Since blood flow to the skin of the hand is predominantly a function of the sympathetic nervous system, vigorous efforts to influence the skin temperature are usually unsuccessful. It is only when one achieves a relaxed passive state that the desired warming occurs. While specificity of biofeedback training is debatable,[12] it can be used to augment other relaxation training. The procedure has also been shown to be attractive to adolescents who may be less receptive to simple relaxation or imagery techniques.[13] In addition, the feeling of mastery and control frequently is reinforced with successful biofeedback training.

The counselor or therapist who does not have access to expensive biofeedback equipment can reap its benefits through temperature dots. I have used these with children as well as adolescents with positive results.[14]

I am indebted to Archibald Hart in regard to these strategies. In his book *Adrenaline and Stress*, he provides an excellent strategy for managing stress and anxiety through the use of temperature dots. It is based on the now well-established principle that the temperature of the skin fluctuates in response to stress and arousal (in technical jargon, this is called "peripheral vasoconstriction").

In recent years, round plastic dots have been developed with liquid crystal imbedded in them. These little dots change color in response to the change in skin temperature. The backs of the dots are coated with adhesive, and by placing one of these dots on the hand in a nonintrusive position one can have a simple yet effective form of biofeedback. If one remains in a stable room temperature the dot will provide a convenient and accurate estimate of skin temperature.

A supply of temperature dots can be ordered from Mindbody, Inc., which developed them. They offer audio cassettes that combine taped relaxation exercises with biofeedback tools. For a brochure and price list, write or call

Mindbody, Inc.
50 Maple Place
Manhasset, NY 11030
407/495-4700

Place a temperature dot on the top of an adolescent's hand between the thumb and index finger. After a brief moment, note the color of the dot before you begin. Instruct the adolescent to lie on his or her back, hands at the side, legs uncrossed. After the counselee's eyes are closed lead the client through a relaxing exercise. Be sure to speak softly and slowly.

"Relax. Let your jaw muscles relax. Take a deep breath and count to five: 1 . . . 2 . . . 3 . . . 4 . . . 5. Breathe in slowly and then exhale. Feel the tension leave your body. Now concentrate on your hands. Picture yourself lying in the warm sun. Imagine that you are on a beach and feel the sun beating down on your hands. Hold this image. Feel your hands getting warmer. Feel the blood vessels of your hand becoming larger. Imagine more and more blood filling your hands as they become warmer and warmer. Say to yourself, 'My hands are becoming warmer. I can feel them getting heavier.' Repeat this over and over. [Remain quiet for a moment or two.] Now, when you are ready, slowly open your eyes, feeling relaxed and calm."

Now note the color of the temperature dot. If it shows a "warmer" color, this kind of exercise will probably be helpful for the client to practice alone. You may suggest that the youth follow the procedure once or twice daily (the exercise can be done sitting up as well). The client's hands, with practice, will become noticeably warmer and will provide a concrete example of how the young person can control anxiety.

Explore Spiritual Issues

If adolescents are receptive to Christian values, try to incorporate a biblical approach. Gary Collins, in his book *Christian Counseling*, outlines the Bible's formula for overcoming anxiety. It involves five actions: (1) *Rejoice*. With the knowledge of God's promises we can celebrate the security of his peace and not let our minds be wracked with anxiety; (2) *Forbear*. A negative condemning outlook on life supports anxiety, while a gracious forbearing attitude reduces it; (3) *Pray*. Philippians 4 gives several instructions about prayer in times of anxiety. Such prayer should be specific, include thanksgiving, and be accompanied by the expectation that supernatural peace will be forthcoming;[15] (4) *Think*. Philippians 4 also instructs us to let our minds dwell on positive things; (5) *Act*. The Christian's task is to do what the Bible teaches and not simply sit listening.[16]

☑ WHEN TO REFER

Refer adolescents suffering from intense anxiety to psychologically astute physicians or psychiatrists when physical symptoms are present or when the anxiety is severe enough to warrant medication for temporary relief.

Refer anxious adolescents to other competent counselors or psychologists when, over time, they feel more out of control and increasingly stressed and anxious. You will want to refer if they have been unable to establish some awareness of the feelings that threaten to overwhelm them, or if their anxiety initially subsided, only to return and continue at a higher level of intensity.

☑ WHERE TO GO FOR ADDITIONAL HELP

Agras, S. *Panic: Facing Fears, Phobias, and Anxiety.* New York: W. H. Freeman, 1985.

Benson, H. *The Relaxation Response.* New York: Morrow, 1975.

Charlesworth, E. A., and R. G. Nathan. *Stress Management: A Comprehensive Guide to Wellness.* New York: Ballantine, 1984.

Colten, M. E., and S. Gore. *Adolescent Stress: Causes and Consequences.* Hawthorne, N.Y.: Aldine de Gruyter, 1991.

Davis, M., M. McKay, and E. R. Eshelman. *The Relaxation and Stress Reduction Workbook.* Richmond, Calif.: New Harbinger, 1980.

Hart, A. D. *Adrenaline and Stress.* Waco, Tex.: Word, 1986.

———. *Overcoming Anxiety.* Waco, Tex.: Word, 1989.

Osborn, C. *Release From Fear and Anxiety.* Waco, Tex.: Word, 1978.

Walker, E. *Learn to Relax.* Englewood Cliffs, N.J.: Prentice-Hall, 1975.

Notes

1. E. A. Charlesworth and R. G. Nathan, *Stress Management: A Comprehensive Guide to Wellness* (New York: Ballantine, 1984).

2. A. D. Hart, *Overcoming Anxiety* (Waco, Tex.: Word, 1989).

3. H. Selye, *Stress Without Distress* (New York: Signet, 1974).

4. *Diagnostic and Statistical Manual III-R* (Washington, D.C.: American Psychiatric Association, 1987).

5. Ibid.

6. A. Ellis, *A Guide to Rational Living* (North Hollywood, Calif.: Wilshire Books, 1961).

7. A. Hart, *Adrenalin and Stress* (Waco, Tex.: Word, 1986).

8. V. Frankl, *Man's Search for Meaning: An Introduction to Logotherapy* (New York: Simon & Schuster, 1962).

9. L. Emanuel, "Thinking Away Anxiety," *Health* (June 1991): 59.

10. M. Davis, M. McKay, and E. R. Eshelman, *The Relaxation and Stress Reduction Workbook* (Oakland, Calif.: New Harbinger, 1980), 25.

11. M. S. Smith and W. M. Womack, "Stress Management Techniques in Childhood and Adolescence," *Clinical Pediatrics* 26 (1987): 581–85.

12. B. V. Silver and E. B. Blanchard, "Biofeedback and Relaxation Training, the Treatment of Psychophysiological Disorders: Or Are the Machines Really Necessary?" *Journal of Behavioral Medicine* 1 (1978): 217–39.

13. Smith and Womack, "Stress Management Techniques," 581–85.

14. L. Parrott, "Helping Children Manage Stress," *Child and Family Behavior Therapy* 12, no. 1 (1990): 69–73.

15. Archibald Hart, however, makes a helpful observation concerning prayer and the person suffering from anxiety: One may use prayer as a way of worrying without feeling guilty.

16. G. Collins, *Christian Counseling: A Comprehensive Guide* (Waco, Tex.: Word, 1980).

BODY IMAGE

☑ WHAT THE STRUGGLE LOOKS LIKE

The fastest-growing medical specialty today is plastic surgery. In the 1980s, the number of people undergoing cosmetic surgery increased nearly ten percent each year. And a growing number of those opting for aesthetic surgery are girls still in puberty.[1]

Adolescents are obsessed with that question, "How do I look?" They may be wondering about their new haircut, whether their clothes are wrinkled, or whether food is caught between their teeth. But what they really want to know is whether others see them as physically attractive.

Christian musician Randy Stonehill graphically describes in a song this generation's obsession with looks: "Cosmetic fixation, we pursue it with dedication; / Cosmetic fixation, it's overtaking the nation. / Are her legs real long? Is her hair real blonde? / Does she look real foxy on the party lawn?"

The overwhelming majority of adolescent girls aren't satisfied with what they see in the mirror. The Gallup Poll found that eighty percent of all women report disliking or being totally repulsed by some part of their bodies, and sixty-two percent of them would like to lose eleven to twenty pounds. It is no wonder that high school girls are twice as likely as boys to suffer from depression.

Interestingly, women who are unhappy with their bodies don't necessarily suffer from low self-esteem. This may be because they're in good company. It helps a young woman who wants to lose ten pounds to know that most of her friends feel the same about themselves.

There is one group of male and female young people, however, that suffers a disproportionate amount of pain and humiliation because of their body image—obese adolescents. These are the teens who are most likely to show up in a counseling office because of body-image struggles. Adolescents who are not obese and struggling with body image are more likely to be suffering from an eating disorder (refer to the section on eating disorders).

Ten to fifteen percent of all adolescents are truly obese, girls more than boys.[2] Obesity among adolescents is a serious health problem. Longitudinal

76

Case Description

Peter is an extremely overweight fourteen-year-old boy. He has above-average intelligence and does reasonably well in school when he wants to. His eating is out of control. More than once he has eaten a half-gallon of ice cream at one sitting. He stands in front of the mirror each morning and tries various combinations of shirts and pants somehow to "reduce" his size. Some mornings he has even ditched school because he is ashamed of his weight. When he is at school, his general mode is to withdraw and avoid much social contact. Peter's heaviness haunts him every minute, but he has never forced himself to throw up nor exhibited other signs of having an eating disorder. Peter has been called every "fat" name in the book, and his self-esteem is just about shot. Peter would give anything to look "normal."

studies show higher levels of risk factors for cardiovascular disease, joint disease, and gynecological disorders in obese adolescents. The National Institutes of Health recommends that weight reduction be considered for anyone with one of the following medical conditions: family history of diabetes, high blood pressure, coronary disease, or history of obesity in childhood.[3]

Being overweight, however, not only represents a health hazard, it also affects adolescent social relationships, self-esteem, ego-identity development, and emotional adjustment. Furthermore, if an obese teenager has a history of weight problems and does not reduce as an adolescent, the odds are twenty-eight to one that she or he will become and remain an obese adult.[4] People who hope that an obese adolescent will grow out of it are awaiting an unlikely event.

Some may indeed grow out of it, but the pain and suffering that heavy adolescents endure should not be minimized. This quote depicts the hurt: "My name is Marcy Lewis. I'm thirteen years old and in the ninth grade. All my life I've thought I looked like a baby blimp with wire-frame glasses and mousy brown hair. Everyone said that I'd grow out of it, but I was convinced that I'd become an adolescent blimp with wire-frame glasses, mousy brown hair, and acne."[5]

Many factors determining obesity status are simply arbitrary judgments of variable criteria, for example, the "large size of skinfolds" measured by skin calipers (most often applied to the triceps). However, the best criterion, generally, is measured against a weight index (normed for age, sex, and height). Most experts consider anything above the ninetieth percentile to be an adequate indicator to diagnose obesity.[6] Experts, however, also classify the degree of the adolescent's obesity. *Mild* obesity, ranges from fifteen percent overweight to an upper limit of about thirty-five percent. *Moderate* obesity ranges from thirty-five to a hundred percent overweight. *Severe* obesity is defined as being more than a hundred percent overweight. This severe degree may carry a dangerous risk to life, and a surgical approach to treatment (gastroplasty) should be considered if behavioral treatments have failed.[7]

☑ WHY THE STRUGGLE HAPPENS

Why does obesity develop in the first place? What makes obesity aggravatingly resistant to change? The causes of obesity are not simple. Most experts agree that it is a multidetermined problem. Genetic, biological, behavioral, familial, cultural and even economic factors interact in complex ways to affect the development and maintenance of this struggle. Here is what some of today's researchers are telling us about its etiology.

Genes

It seems that some adolescents are born to be overweight. Selective breeding experiments and twin studies have shown a strong genetic contribution to obesity. In one investigation, researchers analyzed weight and height records. Their study of identical and fraternal pairs of twins found that siblings reach and maintain similar body weights whether or not they are reared in different families (and that they are much more likely to grow up looking like their natural parents than their adoptive ones). Their conclusion? If both biologic parents are overweight, an eighty percent chance exists that their kids are going to be overweight.[8]

Biology

Biological barriers have also been shown to work to maintain or increase weight in the obese. Studies of adipose cells and of metabolic adaptations to weight reduction make it clear that biology plays a major role in obesity. Positive biological energy must exist for obesity to occur. That is, for obesity to develop, the amount of energy consumed must be greater than the amount of energy expanded. Further support of the biological view is attributed by some to studies that show adolescents of parents who are obese are much more likely to be obese than adolescents whose parents are lean.[9]

External Causes

Considerable evidence shows that less biologically oriented factors contribute to the problem. For example, significant correlations are found between the weights of spouses and measures of obesity as well as the weights of obese foster parents and their children.[10] Studies have even correlated the weights of pet owners with their dogs to show the influence of less biologically oriented factors.[11]

Eating Style and Behavior Patterns

Obese adolescents typically show a "high density" eating style. This eating style includes excessive eating, with more gulping and less chewing than in their leaner peers.[12] An obese adolescent I once worked with would buy a box of Twinkies and eat one after the other—whole! Some evidence, not surprisingly, also shows obese adolescents to be less active than their leaner counterparts.[13] And if activity level is low, of course, fat accumulates because metabolism declines. Some, out of ignorance, are quick to label the inactivity as lazy. More often, it is probably avoided out of embarrassment. David Elkind, in his book *All Grown Up and No Place to Go*, quotes the following passage from Paula Danzinger's *The Cat Ate My Gymsuit*. It poignantly illustrates the embarrassment felt by every obese adolescent. It is a picture of a sensitive overweight girl avoiding gym.

> I just sat there. Trying to change into a gymsuit while hiding my mini bra and fat body would have been a gymnastic feat in itself. Once the class started, I walked up to the gym teacher, Schmidt. "All right, Lewis, what is it this time?" "The cat ate my gymsuit." She shook her head, frowned, and wrote another zero in her marking book. I sat down to watch my eighty millionth volleyball game.[14]

Food Preference

Obese adolescents do not necessarily eat more food overall, but they almost always prefer foods that are calorically dense and highly flavored. Furthermore, their physiological responses tend to encourage this consumption and do not become inhibited after the food is consumed. After eating foods high in carbohydrates or sugars, their insulin levels are elevated, which increases hunger and food consumption. In fact, just the sight and smell of foods can elevate the insulin level in obese people.[15]

Family Factors

The beginnings of obesity may be found in the early relationships between parents and their children. Childhood for many obese adolescents was characterized by intense parental involvement, overprotectiveness, and rigidity. The parents may have an unusually high concern for their children's welfare. For example, in an interview with the family, parents frequently speak for their obese children or correct them when they attempt to speak for themselves. In extreme cases, they may not want their obese children to be put on a diet because they don't want to deprive them of anything.[16]

Psychological Factors

Eating is often a greater positive reinforcement for obese people because they find it to be a more pleasurable activity than do people of normal weight. On the flip side, eating can also be used as a means of self-punishment. With a poor self-image, weight gain becomes a way of reinforcing negative self-conceptions and proving their self-perceptions. Adolescents who are obese, already feeling ineffective, may become more inactive and withdrawn and turn to eating as a form of comfort and security.[17]

☑ HOW TO HELP

Counseling and psychotherapy have been successful in treating obesity.[18] The following techniques should be undergirded with personal acceptance and reflective listening. They are designed to create alternatives for the adolescent to replace dysfunctional behavior and attitudes.

Assess the Conditions

Several measures are available to assess the severity of the adolescent struggling with body image and obesity. One preliminary measure that is often helpful assesses adolescents' belief in their ability to control weight loss. The Internal Versus External Control of Weight Scale is made up of five items and will give the counselor some idea of whether the adolescent is optimistic about change. The Compulsive Eating Scale can be used to measure the adolescent's tendency to eat uncontrollably (especially during times when they are not necessarily hungry). It is one of the few assessments on eating that was developed specifically for adolescents. It is a simple eight-item instrument. Both scales may be found in *Helping the Struggling Adolescent: A Counseling Guide*.

Require a Physical Exam by a Physician

The most successful approaches to treating obesity recognize that it is a multicausal problem encompassing genetic, metabolic, environmental, familial, and emotional factors. Counselors cannot effectively treat this problem without incorporating the expert assistance of medical consultation to provide them with a complete picture of the struggle. Physical complications may be present, which a physician, not a therapist or counselor, should be treating. If an unusually low-calorie diet is prescribed, it is especially essential that medical assessment and follow-up be built into the treatment program.

Plan for the Long Run

Adolescents vary a great deal in their response to treatments for obesity. One thing is certain, however. There are no quick cures for obesity. Counselors should plan on long-term treatment. If all other factors are equal, it is desirable to meet with obese adolescents at least once a week for eight to twelve months, longer if needed. Research has shown that sustained, weekly therapist contact can facilitate maintenance of key strategies and improve weight loss. Even after goal-weights are achieved, weekly contact should be sustained for several months to promote generalization of behavior changes.[19]

Assess the Goals

At the beginning of treatment, it is important to assess the appropriateness of young people's goals for weight loss. Although improvement in physical appearance is usually a major motivation for most obese adolescents beginning counseling, such motivation may be problematic because the weight loss achievable by many may not alter physical appearance dramatically. The goals teens have in mind may be unrealistic, and the time to tackle this situation is at the beginning of treatment. Help them shift their therapeutic goals away from entirely cosmetic considerations.

Boost Confidence

Obese adolescents are rejected by their peers more than any other minority-type person.[20] The damage to their self-esteem can be horrendous. Many believe obese people are simply lazy, stupid, and weak. This stereotype leads to overweight people being treated as second-class citizens, especially among adolescents. It is not at all uncommon for obese adolescents to grow up hearing names like "Crisco" or "fatso." Overweight adolescents need to hear that the problem is with their bodies, not themselves. As persons they are not defective; they simply have the special challenge of managing their bodies. Without self-confidence and a sense that they can learn to control their bodies better, treatment is useless. They need to believe that change is possible and achievable. For additional help in this foundational treatment step, see the section on inferiority.

Confidence, by the way, is especially important to instill after a setback. Backsliding is inevitable in a weight-control program. The adolescent may eat too much pizza on a Friday night, for example, or not follow through on an exercise goal because the weather was bad. Catastrophic thinking by the young people in these circumstances is not unusual. Without acceptance and encouragement they may give up altogether.

Begin a Weight Graph and Eating Diary

Assist adolescents to construct personalized charts for a record of weight changes. The Y-axis should include incremental amounts of weight. The X-axis should be labeled "dates." They should enter their weight about once a week and record the date. This does not have to be highly regimented, but it can serve as a helpful reinforcer to keep them accountable. Besides, the chart gives them visual access to their progress.

Adolescents should also keep an eating diary, recording when, where, what, and with whom they eat. This exercise allows them to observe their eating habits with more objectivity. It helps answer questions like the following: Do I eat mostly when I am alone? Do I often eat between meals? Does a certain feeling precede my eating?

A sample eating diary is shown on page 82.

Modify Eating Style

As noted under the causes of obesity, heavy adolescents exhibit a high-density eating style. They eat rapidly, with big spoonfuls, gulping food by chewing relatively little for the amount of food consumed. This eating style can increase the body's propensity to store excess nutrients as fat. Effective treatment must emphasize the change in eating styles through a sustained self-monitoring of their eating behavior. Give an assignment to adolescents to help them modify these habits. Help them to take time to appreciate their food—its color, aroma, texture, and so on. Require them to take a two-minute time-out during each meal. If they cannot remember to do this, suggest they set an alarm

EATING DIARY

Date	Time	Food Eaten Quantity	Food Eaten Type	Social State Alone	Social State With Whom	Where	Event Before	Mood
1/4	7 a.m.	2	Bagels	✓		Kitchen	Woke up	Tired
	9:15 a.m.	1	Milky Way		Jim	Locker	Math	Bored

to go off in the middle of each meal. Or teach them to divide their meal and rest before eating the second half. To slow down eating further, they should pause briefly after each bite and put down their utensils before taking another bite. This allows them to become more aware of stomach fullness and eventually change their high-density eating style.[21]

Implement an Exercise Routine

It is becoming clearer that weight-control interventions must focus on increasing physical exercise in addition to the traditional goal of changing eating patterns. Evidence suggests that exercise can even decrease appetite. One study found that including a ten-minute exercise period before lunch reduced the caloric intake of obese adolescents just as effectively as nutritional education.[22] The problem with trying to increase the exercise activity of sedentary adolescents is that they often don't follow through on the plan. A variety of interventions must be considered to make this effort successful. For example, we know that people tend to maintain exercise regimens better if (1) they enjoy their exercise, (2) if the exercise is convenient to do, and (3) if the exercise includes other people (e.g., a team sport). These points must be considered when setting up an exercise routine. In sum, research says that the best advice for counselors in this area is to encourage the use of specific weekly (not daily) planning to increase exercise in obese adolescents' lives.[23]

Use Behavioral Contracts

A behavioral contract is an explicit agreement specifying expectations and plans for the changing of behavior. The contract should be written rather than verbal and include specific target behavior and consequences. It is often desirable to have clients write out their own contracts with the counselor each week and include the week's goals, which, by the way, should be challenging yet achievable. For example, the adolescent might include in his or her contract "to record calorie intake; to play soccer three times, to enter my weight on my weight-loss graph once; to avoid ice cream or other dessert foods." The reward for achieving contracted goals can be anything that may further motivate them. Have youths deposit the modest sum of five dollars, which will be returned to them at the end of the week if they have kept the terms of the contract. Research has shown that the amount of reward does not usually influence the outcome.[24] Other rewards may include positive social events or special privileges at home.

A sample behavioral contract is shown on page 84.

Activate Parental Involvement

Since eating plays a central role in family life, it is helpful to include parents in the treatment strategy. If adolescents agree with the idea, it may be helpful to meet with their parents. Encourage parents to be sensitive to buying or making calorie-dense foods, serving meals that are excessively high in fat, and keeping the refrigerator stocked with foods that are high in calories. If

---

Contract for the Week of _____

This week I will—

1. Self-monitor my food at least six out of seven days
2. Jog at least twice for at least thirty minutes
3. Eat only in the kitchen for at least four days
4. Read a chapter of my book on nutrition
5. Walk home from school on three days
6. Enter my weight on my weight graph

If I meet these goals successfully, I will be refunded my deposit of five dollars.

_____

Signature, Date

---

parents ask about cookbooks with recipes that are in line with this treatment, the following may be useful: *American Heart Association Cookbook* (New York: Ballantine Books) and *The Living Heart Diet* by Michael DeBakey, Antonio M. Gotto, Lynne W. Scott, and John P. Foreyt, (New York: Raven Press). Also urge parents to model routine physical exercise.

If frequent conflict occurs in the home, consider training the parents in child-management skills to reduce the turmoil. Studies have shown that families who experience patterns of relational chaos have less adequate dietary habits than other families.[25]

Consider Intensive Treatment Centers

One method that has been devised for overweight adolescents is to send them to a residential weight-management camp. One group of researchers studying the success of these camps chose a Tacoma, Washington, camp that emphasizes three aspects: (1) nutrition education, (2) behavior modeling, and (3) physical activity. Participants attend for only five days, but follow-up studies six months after camp revealed permanent weight loss, leading researchers to conclude that this is a useful approach to adolescent weight-management therapy.[26] Similar intensive treatments include hospital settings. The Oaks Treatment Center in Austin, Texas, has a twelve-week program for teenagers that consists of nutrition classes, exercise classes, monitored diets, and so on. Before recommending a specific camp, counselors must be fully informed of its validity and effectiveness.

Examine Your Expectations

These strategies are some of the best available for treatment of this painful problem. There is, of course, much more to treating obesity effectively. This chapter is simply a springboard into other excellent resources that describe in greater detail therapeutic interventions for obese adolescents. Some of them are noted at the end of this chapter. Counselors of obese adolescents must also be aware of the difficulty of this assignment. Examine your expectations for treatment. Are they unrealistic? Remember that small weight loss or simply stopping the inevitable rise in weight with increasing age can enhance health.

☑ WHEN TO REFER

Refer obese adolescents to psychologically astute physicians or psychiatrists for a complete physical examination at the beginning of counseling treatment. The purpose is to address the presence or absence of physical problems that are beyond the scope of counseling or that might interfere with treatment.

If counselors do not feel qualified to deal with problems of obesity, they should refer clients to their colleagues. Several studies have shown that behavior therapists are superior to nonbehavior therapists in treating obese adolescents.[27] If your orientation to counseling does not lend itself to incorporation of the strategies of this modality, you should probably refer.

If it becomes clear that adolescents' struggles with obesity signal the generalized problems and conflicts within the family, focused training in child management or more intense family therapy is in order. Consult a competent marriage and family therapist if this is not your area of training and expertise.

Where To Go for Additional Help

Brody, J. *Jane Brody's Nutrition Book*. New York: Bantam, 1981.
Collipp, P. J. *Childhood Obesity*. New York: Warner Books, 1986.
Kirschenbaum, D. S., W. G. Johnson, and P. M. Stalonas. *Treating Childhood and Adolescent Obesity*. New York: Pergamon, 1987.
LeBow, M. D. *Child Obesity: A New Frontier of Behavior Therapy*. New York: Springer, 1984.
Lipe, D., and J. Wolff. *Help for the Overweight Child: A Parent's Guide to Helping Children Lose Weight*. New York: Scarbrough, 1978.
Powers, P. S. *Obesity: The Regulation of Weight*. Baltimore: Williams and Wilkins, 1980.
Wolman, B. B. *Psychological Aspects of Obesity: A Handbook*. New York: Van Nostrand Reinhold, 1982.

Notes

1. B. Hey, "Portrait of an Obsession," *Health* (June 1991): 68–70.
2. United States Department of Commerce, Bureau of the Census. *Statistical Abstract of the United States*. Washington, D.C.: U.S. Government Printing Office, 1987.
3. National Institutes of Health Consensus Development Conference Statement, "Health Implications of Obesity," *Annals of Internal Medicine* 103 (1985): 1073–77.
4. K. D. Brownell, "Obesity: Understanding and Treating a Serious, Prevalent, and Refractory Disorder," *Journal of Consulting and Clinical Psychology* 50 (1982): 820–40.
5. P. Danziger, *The Cat Ate My Gymsuit* (New York: Dell, 1973), 7.
6. D. S. Kirschenbaum, W. G. Johnson, and P. M. Stalonas, *Treating Childhood and Adolescent Obesity* (New York: Pergamon, 1987).

7. W. S. Agras, *Eating Disorders: Management of Obesity, Bulimia, and Anorexia Nervosa* (New York: Pergamon, 1988).

8. *Time* (4 June 1990), 80.

9. S. M. Garn and D. C. Clark, "Trends in Fatness and the Origins of Obesity," *Pediatrics* 57 (1976): 443–56.

10. Ibid.

11. E. Mason, "Obesity in Pet Dogs," *Veterinary Record* 86 (1970): 612–16.

12. D. S. Kirshenbaum and A. J. Tomarken, "On Facing the Generalization Problem. The Study of Self-Regulatory Failure," in *Advances in Cognitive–Behavioral Research and Therapy*, ed. P. C. Kendall (New York: Academic, 1982), 1:121–200.

13. K. D. Browness and A. J. Stunkard, "Behavioral Treatment for Obese Children and Adolescents," in *Obesity*, ed. A. J. Stunkard (Philadelphia: W. B. Saunders, 1980).

14. D. Elkind, *All Grown Up and No Place To Go* (New York: Addison Wesley, 1984), 34.

15. J. Rodin, "Obesity: Why the Losing Battle?" in *Psychological Aspects of Obesity: A Handbook*, ed. B. B. Wolman (New York: Van Nostrand Reinhold, 1982), 30–87.

16. R. J. Brone and C. B. Fischer, "Determinants of Adolescent Obesity: A Comparison with Anorexia Nervosa," *Adolescence* 23 (1988): 155–69.

17. J. Sobal, "Group Dieting, the Stigma of Obesity and Overweight Adolescents," *Marriage and Family Review* 7 (1984): 9–20.

18. J. Meer, "Psychotherapy for Obesity," *Psychology Today* 18 (March 1984): 10.

19. Kirschenbaum et al., *Treating Childhood and Adolescent Obesity.*

20. M. D. Lebow, *Child Obesity: A New Frontier of Behavior Therapy* (New York: Springer, 1984).

21. Kirschenbaum et al., *Treating Childhood and Adolescent Obesity.*

22. L. H. Epstein, B. J. Masek, and W. R. Marshall, "A Nutritionally Based School Program for Control of Eating in Obese Children," *Behavior Therapy* 9 (1978): 766–78.

23. Kirschenbaum et al., *Treating Childhood and Adolescent Obesity.*

24. Ibid.

25. A. C. Israel, L. Stolmaker, and C. A. G. Andrian, "The Effects of Training Parents in General Child Management Skills on a Behavioral Weight Loss Program for Children," *Behavior Therapy* 16 (1985): 169–80.

26. G. Brandt, T. Maschhoff, and N. S. Chandler, "A Residential Camp Experience As an Approach to Adolescent Weight Management," *Adolescence* 15 (1980): 807–22.

27. J. P. Wollersheim, "The Effectiveness of Group Therapy Based Upon Learning Principles in the Treatment of Overweight Women," *Journal of Abnormal Psychology* 76 (1970): 462–74.

DEPRESSION

☑ WHAT THE STRUGGLE LOOKS LIKE

Depression, the "common cold of psychopathology," touches everyone's life. Whether it be as a temporary mood or as a suicidal psychosis, no one is exempt—especially adolescents.

As young people travel the rugged road that leads to adulthood, it should come as no surprise that symptoms of depression often hover overhead like a black cloud. When adolescents leave the less demanding life of childhood and struggle for identity, many experience a sad sense of loss. Saying good-bye to the security of having their decisions made for them, they slowly accept responsibility, dragging their heels and echoing the words of Peter Pan: "I don't want to grow up." And understandably so. Failing to make the junior high basketball team, sitting alone in a crowded cafeteria, not having the right answer when a teacher calls on them in class, or not having a date on the weekend can strike a powerful blow to the wobbly underpinnings that guard against adolescent depression.

Some depression in adolescence is normal, and is probably better thought of as feeling down or blue. However, a point comes at which feelings of discouragement take on the debilitating characteristics of depression. The early signs include a sad facial expression, a loss of interest in school, church, or leisure-time activities, being easily agitated and irritated, feelings of inferiority, worthlessness, helplessness, or guilt. As depression worsens, the loss of energy is accompanied by insomnia or hypersomnia, loss of appetite or excessive eating, social withdrawal, pessimism, difficulties in concentration, and an inability to enjoy pleasurable events. The most important symptoms to watch for occur together: a sad mood and a loss of interest in one's environment.[1]

Depressions come in various types. Archibald Hart, in *Depression: Coping and Caring*, outlines the three major categories of depression. *Endogenous* depression comes from a biochemical disturbance in the hormonal system, the nervous system, or even from an infection in the body. It seems to rise spontaneously, is usually found in the elderly or in psychotic disorders, and requires medical intervention.

Case Description

Cindy is a seventeen-year-old in high school. She is overweight, her facial expression is sad and pained, and her eyes are lifeless. Her hair is limp and oily. She came for counseling because her life had lost the joy and energy it once had. As a child she loved school and church and looked forward to the days when she could go out with boys as her older sisters did.

Cindy's depression seemed to be the consequence of her inability to deal with herself and her external circumstances. She views the world in negative terms and blames her former boyfriend for her negative internal state. If she had a date every weekend, however, she would find another reason to be unhappy. In other words, the source of her depression is her attitude. Listening to Cindy, I felt that if only someone would ask her out she would no longer be depressed. The truth is she needs to restructure her outlook and take responsibility for her feelings. For some reason she has made her feelings solely dependent upon other people's responses to her.

Reactive (or exogenous) depression occurs as a result of a real, imagined, or threatened loss and usually lasts no longer than a few months. This is the typical depression found in adolescence, and counseling is the usual treatment. *Neurotic* depression is a lifestyle response to stress and anxiety. It is used to escape from other emotions and develops over a long period of time. Another type of depression noted by some professionals is *masked* depression. This depression is hidden by other symptoms. For example, teenagers who have lost parents may cover their depression by acting out sexually or by drug abuse.

Adolescent depression is a complicated condition, difficult to describe with accuracy, but it is certain to be seen repeatedly by every Christian counselor.

☑ WHY THE STRUGGLE HAPPENS

Researchers have isolated several possible causes for depression during the teen years. Although it is difficult to label a specific source when working with a counselee, it is safe to say that depression is probably a combination of several causes.

Biochemical Causes

Although it is not believed that people inherit depression, some evidence suggests that people can inherit a predisposition to depression.[2] Some researchers also believe that in certain cases changes in hormone levels contribute to depressed feelings.[3] While physical causes can be complicated (e.g., glandular disorders, brain tumors, etc.), they can also be as simple as medication side effects, improper diet, and lack of sleep.

Life Experience

Although life experiences do not have to lead to depression, they do increase the probability of its occurrence. When adolescents, for example, have grown up with parents who set their expectations and standards beyond the ability of their children, failure becomes inevitable and teens will eventually become depressed. Even a short life of perceived failure or rejection can increase the likelihood of depression.

Social Rewards

Some assert that people become and remain depressed because of the rewards they obtain, usually in special attention, when they appear sad in front of others.[4] The sympathy and concern they receive reinforces their depression. Well-meaning people who comfort a depressed adolescent girl, for example, can potentially be sustaining her symptoms. She may not want to risk loss of their attention by getting well.

Learned Helplessness

People can also become depressed when they think they have no control.[5] If teens believe that there is nothing they can do to cause change—to help parents understand them, for example—or that their actions are futile no matter how hard they try, they will eventually give up and be depressed.

Faulty Logic

Negative thinking can result in depression. High school students who think they are total failures because they didn't say the right thing at the lunch table is an example. They selectively concentrate on a single mistake to convince themselves they are worthless. When teens feel inadequate or view life as a burden or see their future as going nowhere, they are likely to trigger a downward spiral of depression that reinforces their negative expectations.

To assume that depression is the result of only one cause, biochemical for instance, is too simplistic. Several factors contribute to depression, including the physiological, sociological, and psychological. In other words, the causes of depression are not mutually exclusive.

☑ HOW TO HELP

The following techniques should be thought of as working together and should be undergirded with genuine acceptance and reflective listening. They are designed to create alternatives to dysfunctional behavior and attitudes.

Pinpoint the Severity

At the beginning of treatment it is helpful to assess the intensity of the depression. A careful assessment can serve as a point from which to measure therapeutic progress. The Self-Rating Depression Scale is made up of twenty items and can be used to assess depression as a clinical disorder and quantify the symptoms of depression. The Generalized Contentment Scale is a twenty-five item test designed to measure the degree, severity, or magnitude of depression. Since depression is often the result of irrational and pessimistic thinking, it can be helpful to assess the young person's general attitude. The Dysfunctional Attitude Scale is a forty-item instrument designed to identify cognitive distortions, particularly the distortions that may underlie or cause depression. Using these measures, counselors can easily chart the counseling. Each of these measures can be found in my book, *Helping the Struggling Adolescent: A Counseling Guide.*

Challenge Irrational Thinking

Many depressed adolescents define their life situations in global terms like "*everything* is hopeless," "*nothing* is going right," "I'm a *total* jerk." As long as they continue to see themselves or the world in bleak, generalized terms, they will remain depressed. When challenged they will often answer affirmatively to questions like the following: "Is *everything* hopeless or basically only the chances of you and Dan getting back together?" "Is *nothing* going right or only the way things are going on the basketball court?" "Are you really a *total* jerk or did you act like a jerk only during lunch?" As you help them to chip away slowly at their irrational thinking, they can decrease their overwhelming feeling of depression and begin to see themselves and the world more realistically.

Evaluate the Secondary Gains

Through reflective listening, clarification, and sensitive questioning, seek out any potential social rewards. For example, if you suspect that the sixteen-year-old girl in your office is depressed in part because she receives extraneous attention from her boyfriend, gently probe. "I wonder," you might say, "whether there are any benefits, any good things, to feeling down." Though none may be acknowledged, it will at least begin the internal process of self-questioning and eventual heightened awareness.

Provide Community

Adolescents struggling with depression often feel that they are the only ones who have ever suffered as they have. It is a feeling of being alone. Effective counselors not only attempt to provide a sense of empathic community within the counseling session, but when possible, outside of it as well. A concerned group in their church or other social institution (peers or adults) can do much to melt the ice of loneliness and instill hope. In fact, when people without support and other resources experience a loss, they are more likely to see their situations as hopeless.[6] Adolescents who are not alone are better equipped to conquer depression. A note of caution, however, is in order. Teenagers in this lonely and depressed state often reject what they want and need. And they will certainly bristle at overly expressive warmth or support. Tread softly.

Encourage Physical Activity

While little can sometimes be done to change depression-producing circumstances, it is possible for depressed adolescents to change their actions; and actions influence feelings. Depression seems to put people into slow motion. In fact, depressed teenagers find it easy to stay in bed, passively pondering their misery. Gently pushing depressed people into activity and exercise can have effective results. Aerobic exercise and long-distance running have been found to increase a sense of control and to elevate the body's chemicals, which are depleted by depression.[7] A moderate but specific exercise (one at which counselees are likely to succeed) can be assigned to adolescents.

Evaluate the Risk for Suicide

Since depressed people often contemplate suicide, counselors must be alert to its signals: self-injurious talk, feelings of hopelessness, sudden and unexplainable shifts to a cheerful mood, knowledge about the most effective suicide methods, a history of prior suicide attempts, etc. The issue of suicide should be addressed directly with any adolescent who is depressed. Do not hesitate to ask, "Do you ever have thoughts of harming yourself? Have you ever attempted suicide?" Direct questioning forces counselee to confront the issue in a rational setting. If the answer is unclear, ask, "Do you think about killing yourself?" If the answer is affirmative ask, "Do you have a plan?" A more thorough discussion of helping suicidal adolescents is found in the section on suicide.

☑ WHEN TO REFER

Refer depressed adolescents to psychologically astute physicians or psychiatrists when physical symptoms are present or when the depression is severe enough to warrant medication for temporary relief.

Refer depressed adolescents to other competent counselors or psychologists when, over time, counselees feel more out of control and increasingly depressed, hopeless, or suicidal. Refer them also if you recognize that you are encouraging dependence in an already depressed and dependent adolescent (so that you yourself can feel needed and powerful).

Where To Go for Additional Help

Beck, A. T. *Depression: Causes and Treatment.* Philadelphia: Univ. of Pennsylvania Press, 1967.

Hart, A. D. *Depression: Coping and Caring.* Arcadia, Calif.: Cope Publications, 1981.

————. *Coping With Depression in the Ministry and Other Helping Professions.* Waco, Tex.: Word, 1984.

Lloyd-Jones, D. M. *Spiritual Depression: Its Causes and Cure.* Grand Rapids: Eerdmans, 1965.

Notes

1. A. D. Hart, *Depression: Coping and Caring* (Arcadia, Calif.: Cope Publications, 1981).

2. J. D. Barchas et al., "Neuropharmacological Aspects of Affective Disorders," in *Depression: Clinical Biological and Psychological Perspectives*, ed. G. Usdin (New York: Brunner/Mazel, 1977).

3. M. M. Weissman and G. L. Klerman, "Sex Differences and the Epidemiology of Depression," *Archives of General Psychiatry* 34 (1977): 98–111.

4. R. P. Liberman and D. E. Raskin, "Depression: A Behavioral Formulation," *Archives of General Psychiatry* 24, no. 6 (1971): 515–23.

5. M. E. Seligman, *Helplessness: On Depression, Development, and Death* (San Francisco: W. H. Freeman, 1975).

6. G. W. Brown, T. Harris, and J. R. Copeland, "Depression and Loss," *British Journal of Psychiatry* 130 (1977): 1–18.

7. K. E. Callen, "Mental and Emotional Aspects of Long-distance Running," *Psychosomatics* 24 (1983): 133–51.

DRUGS and ALCOHOL

☑ WHAT THE STRUGGLE LOOKS LIKE

One of the most challenging problems facing society today is the use and abuse of chemical substances by teenagers. The numbers of seniors in high school who report using drugs "at some time in their lives" are startling:

Alcohol—93%	Inhalants—14%
Stimulants—27%	Tranquilizers—13%
Cocaine—16%	Opiates—10%
Hallucinogens—15%	LSD—9%
Sedatives or barbiturates—14%[1]	

The number-one drug problem, without a doubt, is alcoholism. About three hundred thousand Americans are addicted to heroin, but about nine million are addicted to alcohol. When alcohol abusers are added to the number of hard-core alcoholics, the number is estimated to be over fifteen million. Each day Americans consume 15.7 million gallons of beer and 1.2 million gallons of hard liquor. Another statistic paints a graphic picture of the problem: every twenty-seven minutes a person dies in an alcohol-related automobile crash.[2]

Alcohol is clearly the substance with which adolescents have the most experience. Statistics vary but the best estimates indicate that there could be more than four million American alcoholics under the age of eighteen. And the age of experimentation is getting younger. Today's junior highers are facing decisions about drugs that were once reserved only for older youth. Trying alcohol today is already more common among current fifth graders than it was among current eighth graders when they were in the fifth grade. The percentage of youth who drank alcohol "ten or more times in the last twelve months" doubles between the eighth and ninth grades. Substance use among adolescents is a problem the size of Goliath. Each weekend thirty to forty percent of the youth in America use alcohol and drugs.[3]

Even the best of adolescents become addicts and their parents often have no idea. Stephen Arterburn and Jim Burns, in their insightful book *Drug-Proof Your Kids*, quote a sixteen-year-old who is an active church youth group member: "I don't think it even entered my parents' minds that I was a teenage alcoholic. . . . They didn't suspect that almost every day for the past two years, I was getting high." Parents today do not have the luxury of not worrying about their families being threatened by drugs. Almost every young person experiments with drugs or alcohol, and the statistics for heavy drug use for churched and unchurched kids are almost identical.[4]

The warning signs of teenage alcohol and drug abuse include social withdrawal, deterioration in school performance, resistance to authority, behavior problems, high-risk behavior such as stealing, extreme mood swings (which include signs of depression), sexual promiscuity, physical complaints, changes in relationships, changes in eating habits, plus the more observable signs such as alcohol on the breath, slurred speech, staggering, appearing "spaced out," dilated pupils, and the presence of drug paraphernalia (pipes, pill boxes, straws, spoons), and clothing depicting drug themes.

The *Diagnostic and Statistical Manual* (3d ed. rev. [DSM-III-R]) makes a helpful distinction in understanding pathological use of substances. It defines two categories: psychoactive substance abuse and psychoactive substance dependence. Together they constitute Psychoactive Substance Use Disorders. Substance dependence can be thought of as an addiction. It is the abuse of a drug accompanied by impairment in social and occupational functioning and by psychological dependence upon it. Substance abuse is a less severe version of dependence. It is diagnosed when the use of a substance is maladaptive but not severe enough to meet the criteria for dependence.

The DSM-III-R defines psychoactive substance *dependence* as the presence of at least three of the following symptoms for at least one month.

1. The person uses more of the substance or uses it for a longer time than intended.
2. The person recognizes excessive use of the substance and may have tried to reduce it but has been unable to do so.
3. Much of the person's time is spent in efforts to obtain the substance or recover from its effects.
4. The person is intoxicated or suffering from withdrawal symptoms at times when responsibilities need to be fulfilled, as school or work.
5. Many activities are given up or reduced in frequency because of the use of the substance.
6. Problems in health, social relationships, and psychological functioning occur.
7. Tolerance develops, requiring larger doses (at least a fifty-percent increase) of the substance to produce the desired effect.
8. Withdrawal symptoms develop when the person stops ingesting substances or reduces the amount.
9. The person uses the substance to relieve withdrawal symptoms. For example, one may drink alcohol early in the morning because one feels withdrawal symptoms coming on.[5]

The DSM-III-R defines psychoactive substance *abuse* as the presence of at least one of the following:

1. Continued use despite knowledge of having a persistent or recurrent social, occupational, psychological, or physical problem that is caused or exacerbated by use of the psychoactive substance.
2. Recurrent use in situation in which use is physically hazardous. For example, driving while intoxicated.[6]

The counselor's task is to distinguish the adolescents who use drugs primarily for sociocultural reasons from those youngsters who use drugs in a desperate effort to hide or correct a perceived personal deficiency. Drug and alcohol use varies considerably from one adolescent to another. Rich Van Pelt, in his helpful book *Intensive Care*, lists five stages in adolescents' progression toward alcohol addiction. He credits Larry Silver of the National Institute of Mental Health for their development.

Stage 0. Curiosity in a world where alcohol is readily available.

Stage 1. Learning the mood swing. Adolescents learn how easy it is to feel good with few if any consequences, except perhaps mild guilt.

Stage 2. Seeking the mood swing. Rather than using alcohol as an accompaniment to social events, the youngster decides to get drunk as a goal and arranges to have his or her own supply.

Stage 3. Preoccupation with the mood swing. Being drunk is the main goal of life. Students who drink daily may plan their days around trips to euphoria.

Stage 4. Drinking to feel okay (addiction). The euphoria becomes harder to achieve; larger amounts are needed.[7]

I also find it helpful to distinguish four possible and common types of adolescent drug users.

1. *The Experimenter.* This adolescent experiments with drug use up to four or five times in order to gain acceptance and be "in the know." Their use is short-term and low in frequency.
2. *The Recreationist.* This young person uses drugs to share pleasurable experiences with friends, not to achieve a mood or mental effect from the substance.
3. *The Seeker.* This adolescent seeks an altered state and uses drugs and/or alcohol regularly to achieve a sedative or intoxicant effect.
4. *The Drug Head.* This is a "sick" adolescent who has moved to regular use of hard drugs like cocaine or heroin. He or she is addicted.

John E. Meeks, in his book *The Fragile Alliance: An Orientation to the Outpatient Psychotherapy of the Adolescent*, says the "Drug Head" or "sick" users may often be identified by observing more than a high frequency of drug use. They show serious deficiencies in interpersonal relationships. They

Case Description

Matt is sixteen. He was brought into counseling by his mom who was tired of dealing with his drug-abuse problems. Matt's school was also threatening him with expulsion unless he secured immediate treatment. He was caught drinking alcohol in the morning on school property two months ago and more recently school officials discovered marijuana in his locker. He denied having a problem with drinking or drugs ("It's as if I committed murder or something"), but did report smoking marijuana "now and then." As a young boy Matt was pleasant and never seemed to cause much trouble.

In junior high, however, he began to hang out with young people his mom and dad did not like. "He started listening to loud music," his mom reported, "and he begged and begged to go to a Pink Floyd concert with his friends until I just had to let him go." Four years ago Matt's parents were divorced, but they live in the same town and still see each other. In the first session Matt's father joined his former wife in the intervention. He described discovering that Matt and his friends use an old rusted-out van that is up on blocks in a neighbor's back yard as their "drug club." As he described how it was sealed up to keep the smoke contained and thus increase its effect, Matt began to roll his eyes.

compensate for these deficiencies through group membership in a drug subculture, where the only thing members have in common is their drug experience. They simply prefer drug intoxication over pleasures derived from relationships.[8]

Before discussing the causes of this struggle, it is helpful to review the kinds of drugs that are often abused. It is perhaps most useful to define them by how they affect the body. When classified this way, four major types of drugs evolve.

1. *Depressants.* These slow down the activity of the nervous system. They include alcohol, inhalants (including glue, nail polish remover, cleaning fluid, lighter fluid, antifreeze, and gasoline), minor tranquilizers (including valium), and sedatives (including barbiturates, Quaaludes, and PCP). All depressants except PCP can be obtained legally.
2. *Stimulants.* These stimulate activity, suppress the appetite, and ameliorate emotional depression. They include the legal drugs caffeine and nicotine as well as the legal and illegal amphetamines and the illegal methadrine and cocaine.
3. *Hallucinogens.* These are mind-distorters. They have no medical use and create altered perceptions. They include marijuana, LSD, and mescaline. All hallucinogens are illegal.
4. *Narcotics.* These have an analgesic effect. They relieve physical pain and make surgery possible, but they are highly addictive. They include morphine, codeine, and heroin.

☑ WHY THE STRUGGLE HAPPENS

Drugs are readily available in our society, and most teens will experiment with some of them—usually alcohol, tobacco, and marijuana. Experimenters should not be considered in the same category as those who regularly use or abuse drugs. The following is a list of some of the reasons for regularly using drugs. As is often the case, research is not consistently clear on causes, but most experts agree that drug use entails a variety of risk factors.

Media Influence

Movies, television, and advertisements often glamorize drinking. There is an average of ten to eleven "drinking acts" (defined as ingestion of alcohol or preparation to drink) per hour of prime-time television. For many TV viewers this means witnessing about twenty drinking scenes almost every evening. Of course, marketing alcohol is serious business. By the time the average teen is eighteen years old, he or she has seen 100,000 TV beer commercials. The goal of advertisers is to increase the percentage of those who drink and increase the number of times people drink.

In *It's Killing Our Kids*, Jerry Johnston points out that Michelob Beer's ad campaign began a decade ago with the catchy slogan "Weekends are made for Michelob." Soon the ad evolved into "Put a little weekend in your week." Then the sales pitch became "The night belongs to Michelob." In about one decade, Michelob moved from advocating drinking as a way to unwind on the weekend to promoting drinking as a habitual nightly activity.[9]

Despite the legal drinking age of twenty-one in most states, adolescents are becoming a major target group for advertising campaigns featuring alcohol. These companies know that winning the brand loyalty of a young person may result in loyalty for several years. The alcohol industry also knows that the largest portion of beer drinkers is between eighteen and twenty-four, with college students spending two billion dollars annually on beer.[10]

Peer Pressure

Half of all seventh graders have been pressured to try marijuana, and by the twelfth grade, more than half of them have given in.[11] "It's cool to get drunk," according to many teens. Peer pressure in social environments of heavy party drinking is inescapable for virtually all students. Drinking at a party can even become a sign of prestige and respect. You might hear adolescents praise a classmate by saying, "What a man! Bill is still on his feet after a whole fifth. Bill can really hold his liquor." During a typical two-week period, forty percent of high school seniors participate in binge drinking of five or more drinks in a row.

Family Factors

The literature is replete with studies citing the parent-child relationship as the primary factor in adolescent drug use. Parents who themselves use alcohol, tobacco, and prescription drugs (especially amphetamines, barbiturates, and tranquilizers) are more likely to have children who use drugs.[12] The Children of Alcoholics Foundation states that children of alcoholics are at greater risk by four times of developing alcoholism than children of nonalcoholics. There are 28.6 million children of alcoholics in the United States today; 6.6 million of them are under the age of eighteen.[13] As you may guess, parental warmth and positive control are correlated with absence of drug abuse.

Inheritance

Inherited addictive predispositions might be a factor in abuse. The research is not even close to conclusive in this area, but by studying adopted children whose biological parents were alcoholics, researchers have found them to be more likely to be alcoholics themselves, regardless of whether their adoptive parents abuse alcohol. Still, it must be noted that over one-third of all alcoholics have no family history of alcoholism.[14]

Personality Factors

Research has shown that a "certain kind" of adolescent is more vulnerable to drug use. This young person typically struggles with low self-esteem, has low expectations for personal achievement, lacks impulse control, is highly adventuresome and independent, and is seeking inclusion in a social group. Basically, the adolescent who is low on inner resources is most vulnerable. Drugs, for this young person, sometimes make unbearable feelings bearable.[15]

☑ HOW TO HELP

Once it is determined that intervention is needed, the counselor must explore treatment options. Research has shown that intervention strategies for the adolescent struggling with substance use and abuse are most likely to be successful if the following guidelines are practiced:

- Parents are involved in the intervention process.
- Information about drugs is provided truthfully and as the young person demonstrates interest.
- Opportunities are offered for drug-related behavior to be replaced with health-promoting behavior.
- Health-promotive alternatives for use of free time are explored and developed.
- Students are given opportunities to explore capabilities and ways to contribute in meaningful ways to school and their families. This helps them form their identity.
- The adolescent respects the counselor and can use him or her as a model for socially acceptable behavior.
- Opportunities are given for continued support as the young person begins to make changes toward a more healthful lifestyle.[16]

In addition to these general guidelines, the following techniques have been helpful in treating adolescent drug and alcohol abuse.

Pinpoint the Severity

Adolescents who admit to use of alcohol or other drugs might find it helpful to conduct a self-assessment to determine the seriousness of their use. One helpful self-assessment is the Teen Alert Questionnaire. It consists of twenty-seven items and is designed primarily to heighten awareness. The Michigan Alcoholism Screening Test is an instrument of twenty-five items designed to detect alcoholism. Both of these assessments appear in *Helping the Struggling Adolescent: A Counseling Guide.*

Consider Confidentiality and Safety Issues

Assure adolescents that your counseling is a private matter held in the strictest confidence. Let them also know the limits of that confidentiality. Adolescents should be told that confidentiality will be broken if counselors feel the drugs are dangerous to health or if the sale of drugs is potentially dangerous to other youngsters. Counselors must clearly explain that they will do whatever is possible to interrupt these destructive activities. A reasonable therapeutic alliance cannot exist when counselors permit behavior that is clearly self-destructive. This does not mean the adolescents' parents are automatically and quickly apprised of details of their adolescents' behavior. One must assess the ability of the parents to deal constructively with situations and be willing to explore other alternatives for control of the behavior with their adolescents.

Know the Language

It can be very difficult for counselors to communicate with adolescents who are deeply into the world of drugs if terminology is not clarified. Here are some of the more common drug-related terms that have a specialized meaning:

Trip refers to the feelings, thoughts, and perceptions one experiences while under the influence of a hallucinogenic. A "bad trip" results in panic and terror.

Pot, reefer, spliff, weed, nickel, joint, roach, dime, bone, bong, hit, hooch, doobie, grass, shake, and *smoke* are used to refer to marijuana.

Burnout is the disorientation, confusion, and possible memory loss resulting from long-term and heavy use of hallucinogens or amphetamines.

Skin popping refers to injecting drugs under the skin. *Mainlining* is injecting drugs directly into the vein. *Slamming* is injecting speed, cocaine, or heroin.

Crash or *crashing* refers to coming down from a speed or cocaine high.

Bag or *baggie* refers to an amount of marijuana in a plastic bag. A *dime bag* is a ten-dollar bag of marijuana.

Blitzed, lit, ripped, wasted, freaked, blasted, buzzed, and *cooked* are used to refer to getting or being high.

These are just a few of a number of terms that adolescents who are into drugs frequently use. Beth Polson and Miller Newton in *Not My Kid* provide a more extensive slang glossary of drug terms. Counselors, however, need not learn a new language. They should be honest and ask for clarification of any terminology used by young people that is confusing. Most adolescents enjoy educating their counselors in this way.

Consider Inpatient Treatment

Teenage drug abuse and addiction is a serious problem that may require intensive treatment by a professionally trained staff in a hospital setting. Hospital-based programs generally last six to eight weeks with several months of follow-up. You are performing a great service when you connect adolescents and their families to an agency that can help them overcome their struggle.

Hospitalization should be considered in these cases:

1. Adolescents have unsuccessfully tried to quit or stop abusing drugs several times on their own.
2. They have been unsuccessful in outpatient treatment programs.
3. There has been an overdose, or the potential for one is strong. For example, they are mixing street drugs and alcohol.
4. Medical attention is necessary to control severe withdrawal symptoms.
5. Suicidal thoughts, bad trips, and flashbacks are occurring.
6. Adolescents' behavior is out of control. They are truant, failing school, stealing to obtain drugs, or in denial when confronted with evidence of drug abuse.
7. Family members are emotionally drained from the roller coaster ride of mood swings, social problems, and arguments that accompany drug abuse.[17]

Your local telephone directory or directory assistance is an immediate means of accessing an inpatient service. To find agencies in your area, look up the following listings in your directory: adolescent clinics, county department of health, mental health clinics, general hospitals, or psychiatric hospitals.

Century HealthCare Corporation offers a variety of programs to help young people fighting addictions. It has programs in more than seventeen cities that provide preventative education services, evaluation, outpatient services, crisis intervention, and residential treatment. You can obtain more information about HealthCare at 800/782-8336.

When psychiatric treatment within an explicitly Christian context is desired, several programs are worth investigating: New Life Treatment Centers, Minirth-Meier Hospitals, Rapha Hospitals, and Lifegate (a division of HealthCare). Each offers professional treatment in hospitals staffed by men and women who are committed to Christ-centered treatment. The programs have several locations across the United States where treatment is immediately available. For information about New Life Treatment Centers, call 800/332-8336. For information about Rapha, call 800/227-2657 (in Texas call 800/445-

2657. For information about Minirth-Meier services, call 800/877-4673. For information about Lifegate services, call 602/256-0310.

Use Psychoeducational Programs

A psychoeducational approach is designed to clarify values; improve communication, coping, and problem-solving skills; establish goals and a sense of direction; increase awareness of cues that trigger drug use; build support systems; and explore nonchemical highs. In these programs young people have opportunity to commit themselves publicly to nondrug use and to hear testimony from others struggling to resist peer pressure and personal desires. Their successes are also strengthened and reinforced. Many of these programs incorporate the twelve steps made popular through Alcoholics Anonymous, the largest and most widely known self help group in the world. It currently has thirty thousand chapters and a membership of more than a million.

The twelve steps, which are the guiding principles of AA's "one-day-at-a-time" philosophy, have been adapted for young people by the authors of the helpful little book *Young Winners' Way: A Twelve Step Guide for Teenagers*:[18]

1. We admitted we were powerless over alcohol—that our lives had become unmanageable.
2. We came to believe that a Power greater than ourselves could restore us to sanity.
3. We made a decision to turn our wills and our lives over to the care of God, as we understood Him.
4. We made a searching and fearless moral inventory of ourselves.
5. We admitted to God, to ourselves, and to another human being the exact nature of our wrongs.
6. We were entirely ready to have God remove all these defects of character.
7. We humbly asked Him to remove our shortcomings.
8. We made a list of all persons we had harmed and became willing to make amends to them all.
9. We made direct amends to such people wherever possible, except when to do so would injure them or others.
10. We continued to take personal inventory and when we were wrong, promptly admitted it.
11. We sought through prayer and meditation to improve our conscious contact with God, as we understood Him, praying only for knowledge of His will for us and the power to carry that out.
12. Having had a spiritual awakening as the result of these steps, we tried to carry this message to alcoholics and to practice these principles in all our affairs.

Explore Cognitive Distortions

Adolescents' distorted self-talk surrounding drug use is usually so automatic and subtle that they are not aware of its effect. Once this self-talk is mirrored back to the struggling young person and clarified, he or she will move toward reality. Old beliefs about the necessity of using drugs to create excitement and adventure, to feel good, and to suppress unpleasant feelings can be replaced with new self-statements and beliefs that eliminate the necessity for drugs as part of the lifestyle. Here are three commonly used distortions by young drug users:

1. *Selective Abstraction.* This tunnel vision is revealed in self-statements like "The only way I can have fun is to get high."
2. *Overgeneralization.* Examples include "I stopped drinking for two days once, so I know I can stop anytime" or "I didn't have a single friend before I began to drink."
3. *Superstitious Thinking.* This is often an excuse to avoid anxiety. For example they may do drugs just before exams because "When I take this stuff I have powers I never dreamed of" and "I do my most creative work with a few drags from a joint."[19]

Teach Stress Management

Many adolescents turn to drugs as a way of escaping stress. Therapy can show better ways of coping with the pressures of life. Stress in general can be discussed, but actual stress reduction techniques can be taught and practiced. Refer to the sections on anxiety and panic attack for descriptions of a variety of stress-management techniques.

Prepare for Follow-up Care

The likelihood of a relapse must be addressed. Progress and change do not always go as planned. For the adolescent recovering from drug abuse, each day is filled with land mines of setbacks and relapses. To insure their safety and to avoid these dangers, it is necessary to plan ahead. Joseph White recommends three things:[20]

1. The plan should first of all incorporate maintenance of a solid support system. Adolescents need to be around encouraging peers who reinforce drug-free living. AA organizations, youth centers, teen hot lines, and drug-abuse programs can usually connect teens to long-term support groups. Overcomers Outreach is a Christian twelve-step support group for teens with hundreds of programs in forty-two states. For more information contact Overcomers Outreach, Inc., 2290 W. Whittier Blvd., Suite A, La Habra, CA 90631; 213/697-3994.
2. The plan should also recognize relapse warning signs. These include being dishonest with one's self, justifying or rationalizing how one can resume using drugs without abuse, drifting back to old drug-abusing peers, expecting life to be perfect and becoming depressed or angry

when it isn't, and denying that one has to worry about drug abuse anymore.

3. Finally, the plan should incorporate a relationship with a primary resource person. This is typically the counselor or therapist they have been meeting with. There should be an open invitation to youths to meet periodically to discuss the concerns of growing up. This should not be a flip invitation. It must be backed up with specific dates and a promise to be accessible if an emergency arises.

☑ WHEN TO REFER

Refer adolescents struggling with substance dependence and abuse to physicians for medical examination if they have long histories of alcohol and/or drug use. Require a comprehensive medical examination early on in treatment. Young people who are high-frequency and high-intensity drug users may be suffering physical side effects and nutritional deficits caused by poor eating habits and lack of physical exercise.

In extreme cases, young people may need an alcohol and drug-free environment and an external structure, such as hospitalization, for detoxification. This should be done immediately if they are a danger to themselves (through physical problems or accidents) or to others (through accidents).

Referral to Alcoholics Anonymous or similar group meetings is also a necessary step in helping teens with addiction. These groups provide needed support and constructive options for dealing with dysfunctional patterns.

If, during the treatment process, substance abuse is being rationalized and the adolescent is increasingly out of control, referral to a substance-use specialist or another therapist is necessary.

Where To Go for Additional Help

Armor, D. J., M. J. Polich, and H. Stambul. *Alcoholism and Treatment*. New York: Wiley, 1978.

Arterburn, D. *Drug-Proofing Your Kids*. Pomona, Calif.: Focus on the Family Publishing, 1989.

Johnston, J. *It's Killing Our Kids: The Growing Epidemic of Teenage Alcohol Abuse and Addiction*. Waco, Tex.: Word, 1991.

McGee, R. S., P. Springle, and S. Joiner. *Overcoming Chemical Dependency*. Dallas: Word, 1991.

The National Association of Parents for Drug-Free Youth has established a toll free line, 800/554-KIDS, that can assist you in treatment strategies.

Nelson, D. D., and J. T. Nolan. *Young Winners' Way: A Twelve Step Guide for Teenagers*. Minneapolis: Comp Care Publications, 1983.

Polson, B., and N. Miller. *Not My Kid: A Parent's Guide to Kids and Drugs*. New York: Avon, 1983.

Strack, J. *Drugs and Drinking: What Every Teenager and Parent Should Know*. Nashville: Nelson, 1985.

The Will Rogers Institute has a series of booklets on the effects, composition, motives, treatment, and consequences of psychoactive drugs. These free booklets are available from the Will Rogers Institute, 785 Mamaroneck Avenue, White Plains, NY 10605. The telephone number is 914/761-5550.

These organizations can also be helpful in providing information to the counselor working with adolescents struggling with substance use:

Alcoholics Anonymous
P.O. Box 459
Grand Central Station
New York, NY 10163

Alateen
P.O. Box 182
Madison Square Garden
New York, NY 10159-0182
212/254-7230

National Institute of Drug Abuse
5600 Fishers Lane
Rockville, MD 20857

Notes

1. G. Beschner, "Understanding Teenage Drug Use," in *Teen Drug Use*, ed. G. Beschner and S. Friedman (Lexington, Mass.: Health, 1986).

2. J. Johnston, *It's Killing Our Kids: The Growing Epidemic of Teenage Alcohol Abuse and Addiction* (Waco, Tex.: Word, 1991).

3. P. Benson, D. Williams, and A. Johnson, *The Quicksilver Years: The Hopes and Fears of Early Adolescence* (New York: Harper & Row, 1987).

4. D. Arterburn, *Drug-Proofing Your Kids* (Pomona, Calif.: Focus On the Family Publishing, 1989), 1.

5. American Psychiatric Association, *Diagnostic and Statistical Manual of Mental Disorders*, 3d rev. ed. (Washington, D.C.: American Psychiatric Association, 1987).

6. Ibid.

7. R. Van Pelt, *Intensive Care: Helping Teenagers in Crisis* (Grand Rapids: Zondervan, 1988).

8. J. E. Meeks, *The Fragile Alliance: An Orientation to the Outpatient Psychotherapy of the Adolescent* (Baltimore: Williams and Wilkins, 1971).

9. Johnston, *It's Killing Our Kids*.

10. Ibid.

11. L. Johnston, P. O'Malley, and J. Bauchman, *Highlights from Drugs and American High School Students, 1975–1983* (Rockville, Md.: U.S. Institute on Drug Abuse, 1984).

12. M. A. Sheppard, "Peer or Parents: Who Has the Most Influence on Cannabis Use?" *Journal of Drug Education* 17 (1987): 123–28.

13. Johnston, *It's Killing Our Kids*.

14. D. W. Goodwin, "Alcoholism and Heredity: A Review and Hypothesis," *Archives of General Psychiatry* 36 (1979): 57–61.

15. D. Capuzzi, and L. L. Lecoq, "Social and Personal Determinants of Adolescent Use and Abuse of Alcohol and Marijuana," *Personnel and Guidance Journal* 62 (1983): 199–205.

16. B. J. Wagner, "Intervening with the Adolescent Involved in Substance Abuse," *Journal of the National Association of Social Workers* 54 (1984): 244–46.

17. J. L. White, *The Troubled Adolescent* (New York: Pergamon, 1989).

18. D. D. Nelson and J. T. Nolan, *Young Winners' Way: A Twelve Step Guide for Teenagers* (Minneapolis: Comp Care Publications, 1983).

19. G. W. Rowatt, *Pastoral Care with Adolescents in Crisis* (Lousville: Westminster/John Knox, 1989).

20. White, *The Troubled Adolescent*.

EATING DISORDERS

☑ **WHAT THE STRUGGLE LOOKS LIKE**

"Thin is in!" Our nation is obsessed with slimness. Exercise programs, diet centers, weight-loss groups, and figure salons cannot meet the demand. Dieting is one of the fastest growing businesses in the United States. Some estimate that over twenty million Americans are seriously dieting and that we spend more than ten billion dollars yearly to do so. The media do their part to preach the slim and thin message. Slinky models smile at us from the covers of magazines, billboards, and the television. Their message is clear: "If you want to be happy and succeed, you cannot be too thin."

Most people are not overly convicted by the "thin is in" idea. They may see it as desirable to lose weight, but that's about as far as it goes. However, this message deeply disturbs two groups of people. Their passion for thinness is overwhelming and out of control. It is pathological. Thinness takes priority over everything else and becomes a dangerous obstruction to well-being. The two groups are anorexics (those who starve themselves) and bulimics (those who binge-eat and purge).

Anorexia nervosa literally means "nervous loss of appetite." In actuality the anorexic generally suffers extreme hunger pains but refrains from eating in order to achieve thinness. The American Anorexia Nervosa Association defines anorexia as a "serious illness of deliberate self-starvation with profound psychiatric and physical components."[1] Anorexia is a life-threatening, self-induced starvation syndrome characterized by the relentless pursuit of thinness and a morbid, near-phobic fear of being fat. It can impair biochemical functions such as hormonal balance, pulse and heart rate, body temperature, and the menstrual cycle.[2] Expressions of concern from others cannot penetrate the distorted image the young person has of her body. Even when weight has been reduced by more than twenty-five percent of the original body weight, an anorexic adolescent cannot see her emaciated state.

As many as four percent of the adolescent population suffer from anorexia nervosa, with more than ninety percent of its victims being female, predominantly from middle- to upper-middle-class white families.[3] It is most frequently seen in early adolescence, and it usually peaks between the ages of fourteen and eighteen. The natural course of anorexia usually extends over a period of three to four years, but it can last much longer. Pop singer Karen Carpenter died in 1983 of unexplained heart failure at the age of thirty-two. After her death, her family revealed that she had been suffering from anorexia *for twelve years.* Cherry Boone O'Neill, Pat Boone's oldest daughter, described her ten-year struggle with anorexia in *Starving for Attention.* Anorexia is not a problem that will simply go away. Without serious intervention, it can be fatal. Some studies report a death rate from anorexia nervosa as high as twenty-two percent.[4]

The primary characteristics of anorexia include the following:

1. Intense fear of becoming obese, which does not diminish as weight loss progresses.
2. Disturbance of body image. For example, victims may claim to "feel fat" even when emaciated, or believe that one area of the body is "too fat" even when they are obviously underweight.
3. Refusal to maintain body weight over a minimal normal weight for age and height, and failure to make expected weight gain during a period of growth.
4. In females, the absence of at least three consecutive menstrual cycles when they are otherwise expected to occur.
5. No known physical cause of weight loss.[5]

Bulimia nervosa literally means "ox hunger" or "insatiable hunger." It is characterized by repeated cycles of binge eating and compensation for food intake by self-induced vomiting, laxative abuse, diuretic abuse, and/or fasting and excessive exercise. Bulimic individuals are usually within the normal weight range, with frequent weight fluctuations due to their binge-purge episodes. During the binge phase, most people consume enormous amounts of high calorie, energy-rich, fattening foods like ice cream, candy, and junk foods. The binge phase, usually about two hours or less, is terminated by physical exhaustion, exhaustion of food supply, self-induced vomiting, sleep, abdominal pain, exercise, laxative use, or interruptions by visitors. To restore a sense of control, relieve painful fullness, and reduce anxieties about weight gain, the bulimic engages in self-induced vomiting, laxatives, diuretics, fasting, exercise, or severe diets. Between these binge phases, the adolescent is likely to maintain a strict diet and avoid energy-rich foods.

In bulimia, the weight loss is not so extreme or so life-threatening as in anorexia. The major consequences of repeated cycles of binge-eating, purging, and fasting are potassium depletion, deterioration of tooth enamel (from the gastric acid vomiting creates), abdominal pains, kidney problems, dehydration, and electrolyte imbalances (which can cause heart irregularities).[6] Also, in bulimia, unlike anorexia, the adolescent is aware that her eating pattern is abnormal, and she is likely to suffer depression and self-criticism about her eating behavior.

Binge eating typically begins around age eighteen. It occurs primarily in

Case Description

Jennifer is fourteen years old, in the eighth grade, and on the honor roll. Her dad is a banker and her mom is an administrator for a successful retail chain. A school counselor referred Jennifer to a psychologist. She is five feet, four inches tall and has lost about thirty pounds in the past year. She originally weighed 110 pounds, but now weighs 80 pounds and wants to lose more. Jennifer is "grossed out" by fat women. She wants to be "athletic looking without flabby curves." She originally started dieting because some of her friends were losing weight. For lunch Jennifer usually eats plain yogurt with fruit. For breakfast she has a stick of sugarless gum. If she eats dinner at all, it is usually carrot sticks or a salad. Despite her skin-and-bones appearance, Jennifer exercises almost two hours daily and denies that she has or might have any physical symptoms. She says her only problem is arguments with her mom about her diet. She says her mom is "jealous because she would like to lose weight too."

middle-class late adolescence and in young adult white females of average weight who are beginning college. Research indicates that ninety percent of bulimic young people are females.[7] There are levels of severity in bulimic behavior. One-half to two-thirds of college-age females report regular binge eating. The incidence of actual bulimia nervosa reported on college campuses is one to fourteen percent. The average duration of bulimia is about five years.[8]

The most frequently mentioned precipitating factors for a bulimic episode are stress, loneliness, interpersonal conflict, depression, boredom, developmental transitions, and tensions built up from continual attempts at strict dieting. Most bulimics prefer to binge at home, alone, or in secret. However, in recent years, the binge-purge cycle has become more of a shared experience. Most young women now know someone who binges and purges. Adolescents teach others how to binge and purge in mutual enforcing interactions.[9]

Primary characteristics of bulimia nervosa include the following:

1. Recurrent episodes of binge eating in which large amounts of food are consumed rapidly in a discrete period of time.
2. A feeling of lack of control over eating behavior during the eating binges.
3. Regular self-induced vomiting, use of laxatives or diuretics, strict dieting or fasting, or vigorous exercise to prevent weight gain.
4. A minimum average of two binge-eating episodes a week for at least three months.
5. A persistent overconcern with body shape and weight.

It is critical that counselors and parents distinguish between these two groups of struggling adolescents, the anorexic and the bulimic. In the book *Walking a Thin Line: Anorexia and Bulimia*, P. Vredevelt and J. Whitman make

Anorexia	Bulimia
Voluntary starvation often leading to emaciation and sometimes death.	Secretive binge eating. Can occur regularly and may follow a pattern. Caloric intake per binge can range from 1,000 to 20,000 calories.
Occasional binges, followed by fasting, laxative abuse, or self-induced starvation.	Binges are followed by fasting, laxative abuse, self-induced vomiting, or other forms of purging. Person may chew food but spit it out before swallowing.
Menstrual period ceases. May not begin if anorexia occurs before puberty.	Menstrual period may be regular, irregular, or absent.
Excessive exercise. Hands, feet, and other parts of the body are always cold.	Swollen glands in neck beneath jaw.
Dry skin. Head hair may thin, but downy fuzz may appear on other parts of the body.	Dental cavities and loss of tooth enamel.
Depression, irritability, deceitfulness, guilt and self-loathing.	Broken blood vessels in face. Bags under eyes.
Attitude: "I'm much too fat," even when emaciated.	Fainting spells. Rapid or irregular heartbeat.
Obsessive interest in food, recipes, and cooking.	Miscellaneous stomach and intestinal discomforts and problems.
Rituals involving food, exercise, and other aspects of life.	Weight fluctuation due to alternating periods of binges and fasts.
Perfectionism.	Desire for relationships and approval of others.
Introverted and withdrawn. Avoids people.	Loses control and fears she cannot stop once she begins eating.

helpful distinctions in the symptoms of each problem, as shown on the chart on page 108.[10]

Eating disorders are a staggering problem among adolescents today. Counselors working with young people must be equipped for the increasing numbers who need help. Reports indicate that anorexia and bulimia affect as many as twenty-five percent of today's adolescent population.[11]

☑ WHY THE STRUGGLE HAPPENS

Eating disorders are the result of a complex web of factors that include at least the following matters.

Stressful Situations

Stressful life situations for which adolescents do not possess adequate coping skills often play a role in the development of eating disorders. Such a situation may be a rejection or perceived rejection, a sexual encounter, or any number of other events. The peak age of onset for anorexia coincides with the transition from junior high to high school; bulimia most often occurs during the transition from high school to college. The rigid and perfectionistic attitude that characterizes anorexics is exacerbated in even the smallest changes or transitions. The one thing, however, they believe they can control is their quest to lose weight.[12]

Developmental Change

Adolescence is a period of great vulnerability to all kinds of struggles. For this reason, eating disorders are often seen as reactions to the stresses of puberty. The hallmark of puberty for females is physical changes in shape and the onset of menstruation. Some therapists theorize that anorexia is a rejection of female sexuality and an attempt to remain a "little girl." Intimacy issues and responsibility may also be avoided to some degree through maintenance of an eating disorder. Anorexics are characterized by extraordinary skill at following clear-cut rules. They are the model children who have mastered good behavior. Pre-anorexics are almost too good to be true. The familiar territory of rules governing their success, however, changes and becomes enigmatic as they mature into women. Societal expectations and women's roles have changed dramatically in recent years. Being overly compliant may cause difficulty in their becoming autonomous and forming personal identity.[13]

Biology

Studies have clearly established that disturbances in hypothalamic function exist in eating disorders. However, it is unclear whether an eating disorder produces the physiological changes or vice versa. Some researchers suggest that women may be biologically susceptible to eating disorders since they are far more likely than males to experience appetite fluctuation in response to stress.[14]

Case Description

Carla is an eighteen-year-old college freshman. She broke up with her high school boyfriend about six months ago. At that time she found herself overeating as a way of coping with feelings of loss and loneliness. At the same time she was trying to diet. Her former boyfriend is now dating a girl who is "prettier and a lot skinnier." Carla thought that by losing weight she could keep her next boyfriend. She was about five pounds above the average for her age and height. A friend of Carla told her that she wouldn't have to worry about weight gain if she would binge and purge. At the time Carla came into counseling, she had been binge-eating and purging by self-induced vomiting about twice a week for the previous four months. A typical binge would start with a large bowl of peanut M & Ms, eight or nine candy bars, a dozen cookies, a large bowl of popcorn, and a huge serving of ice cream. She would eat until she was exhausted or until she ran out of food. Her binge-purge episodes were followed by renewed efforts to diet, but that would last only three or four days before she would start again. Carla is ashamed and concerned that others will learn of her struggle.

Society

Two potent societal influences affect the increasing incidence of eating disorders. The first is the heightened consciousness of nutrition and physical fitness. In the last two or three decades, health and fitness have become major concerns. Health food and vitamin sales are soaring. Many people religiously read nutritional labels and steer away from additives and preservatives. The second factor is our national obsession with slimness. In fact we are willing to compromise the first factor, health, to achieve slimness. When the federal Food and Drug Administration banned cyclamates and artificial sweeteners because the agency thought them to be carcinogenic, a public outcry ensued. People didn't want to give up low-calorie Coke, even if it did supposedly cause cancer. A thin body is more important than a healthy one.

Family Issues

Many agree that the family plays a leading role in the etiology of eating disorders—especially anorexia. First, anorexic adolescents tend to come from families concerned about food. Perhaps the concern results from special dietary needs of a family member, or simply from an emphasis on nutrition. Food may be used as a sign of love and caring or as the center for family gatherings. Mothers of adolescents who struggle with eating disorders are often dominant and intrusive and frequently have episodes of depression. Fathers are described as aloof or passive, yet with high expectations. However, no single set of parental personality traits has definitely been shown to exist universally.

Salvadore Minuchin, a recognized expert on family systems, has described the internal politics of a typical anorexic family. The features include enmeshment (entangled personal boundaries), rigidity, overprotectiveness, and lack of conflict resolution. Awareness of the kinds of family dynamics that may promote anorexia or bulimia will be decidedly helpful in treatment. Read more about these dynamics in Minuchin's book, *Psychosomatic Families: Anorexia Nervosa in Context.*

Peer Relationships

Most people have between six and ten close friends and another thirty acquaintances with whom they interact regularly.[15] During adolescence, peer groups are vital in easing the transition from childhood to adulthood. An absence of close friends is considered to be one feature in the onset of an eating disorder. Anorexics have a pattern of developing only one relationship at a time, and those relationships are repeatedly short-lived. Often, anorexics are overly involved with and dependent upon family to the exclusion of outside relationships. They cheat themselves out of the aid of peers to help them through the process of individuation.

☑ HOW TO HELP

The following techniques are not exhaustive. They are a place to begin. Eating disorders are difficult to treat because they have developed over a lifetime and are therefore deeply ingrained. Don't expect a quick cure and don't rely solely on this section for resources. However, treatment can be effective when it addresses the contributing factors mentioned above and incorporates the following techniques.

Pinpoint the Severity

At the beginning of treatment, assess the intensity of counselees' eating disorders. A number of helpful instruments to measure this intensity are available. The Are You Dying To Be Thin Scale indicates tendencies toward anorexia nervosa or bulimia nervosa. The Bulimia Test assesses the symptoms of bulimia as defined by the *Diagnostic and Statistical Manual* (3d ed. rcv. [DSM-III-R]). The test is a thirty-two-item instrument arranged in a multiple choice format. This test may also be helpful in ruling out anorexia nervosa. The Concern Over Weight and Dieting Scale is a fourteen-item instrument that measures dieting behavior. The Eating Attitudes Test is a forty-item test that measures a broad range of behaviors and attitudes characteristic of anorexia nervosa. The Goldfarb Fear of Fat Scale contains ten items and measures the fear of gaining weight. The Restraint Scale is a ten-item instrument measuring the ability of a person to refrain from eating in order to maintain a particular weight. These assessment tools may be found in *Helping the Struggling Adolescent: A Counseling Guide.*

Require a Medical Examination

Medical assessments of adolescents' status are essential because of the severe medical problems related to starvation and malnutrition. Adolescents' vital signs are often lowered, including blood pressure, heart rate, body temperature, and respiration rate. A physical evaluation is necessary to confirm that no other illness has caused the weight loss and to assess the severity of malnutrition. This is true for both anorexia and bulimia. The most predominant danger in bulimia is electrolyte imbalance due to purging by vomiting or abusing laxatives and diuretics. Because electrolyte imbalances may be fatal, it is imperative that medical doctors assess adolescents prior to counseling.

Focus on Nutrition

Nutritional rehabilitation is the first step in any treatment program. Although the restoration of body weight may seem intrusive to adolescents, it is necessary for the preservation of thinking and to increase abstract thought. Starvation greatly affects cognitive and affective functioning. Only after an appropriate weight is reestablished and a full range of food is restored will bulimic and anorexic adolescents be able to focus on psychological reasons for their problem.

Of course the method of weight restoration used depends on the severity of the illness. If the illness is in its early stages and hospitalization is not needed, consultation with a dietitian is helpful. Often the initial goal is weight maintenance; then after a week a weight gain of one or two pounds per week is advised.[16] The young person should be invited to participate in all decisions regarding her treatment. This obviously requires enormous delicacy on the part of the therapist, who essentially has the awkward role of "enforcer" even while advocating choice. The process of relearning how to eat in a normal way is time-consuming but important to overcoming the fear of food. The young person must be reassured that she will not get fat and that weight gain will not be excessive or rapid. Tell her that you do not want to see her get fat and that great care will be taken not to produce excessive weight gain. Stress a gradual return to a target weight.

Consider Inpatient Treatment

If on the initial visit the adolescent is already emaciated, decide at once whether she should initially be treated on an outpatient basis or immediately hospitalized. If the client's weight is twenty-five percent below what it should be, hospitalization is imperative. In the marginal ranges, therapists must use their clinical judgment in consultation with physicians. Patricia Neuman and Patricia Halvorson, in their book *Anorexia Nervosa and Bulimia*, suggest several key factors to consider when deciding whether to hospitalize:

1. Consider the rapidity of the weight loss. The more rapid the weight loss the more dangerous.

2. Consider the presence or absence of obesity prior to the weight loss. An obese person can tolerate a greater weight loss.
3. Consider the physical status of the individual. This includes the physician's testing for potassium deficiency, dehydration, cardiac irregularities, and so on.
4. Consider the presence or absence of starvation symptoms. These include decreased concentration and indecisiveness, irritability, anxiety, depression, sexual disinterest, social withdrawal, fatigue, and loss of menstruation.

Hospitalization provides, at the very least, separation from the family and from anxiety-producing stressors in the patient's life. It also insures adequate nutritional intake. Outpatient treatment is almost always necessary upon discharge. Hospitals differ in their treatment programs. Therapists should familiarize themselves with the approaches taken by hospitals nearest them. For hospitalization that incorporates a Christ-centered approach to therapy, consider Rapha. Rapha has several locations across the United States where treatment is immediately available; for additional information call tollfree 800/227-2657 (in Texas, 800/445-2657). Another chain of inpatient settings with a Christian focus is the Minirth-Meier Clinics; reach them tollfree at 800/877-4673. A Christian treatment center that specializes in eating disorders among women is Remuda Ranch in Wickenburg, Arizona; the tollfree number is 800/445-1900. Consider also New Life Treatment Centers, based in Laguna Beach, California (800/227-LIFE).

Establish Trust

Once you begin individual treatment with the adolescent, the most pivotal element in achieving success is the establishment of a relationship of trust. While this may seem obvious because it is a basic ingredient to all effective therapy, it is exceptionally challenging to achieve trust with anorexic or bulimic clients. They are noted for their resistance to therapy and their ability to sabotage the process. Unlike other struggling adolescents, a young person with an eating disorder does not want to give up her symptoms, and she will regard the counselor as one with whom to do battle, as another one of the many who are trying to "fatten her up." A therapeutic alliance is crucial. For this reason it is imperative that counselors sharpen their empathic skills to build solid platforms of relational trust.

Gather a Detailed History

Effective work is based on accurate and detailed information. One of the best ways to gather historical information about the young person's food intake, weight changes, exercise patterns, and so on is through a questionnaire. Use the information you gather to begin an empathic discussion of her experience. Two excellent eating disorder questionnaires are (1) the Stanford Eating Disorder Questionnaire, which can be found in Stewart Agras' book, *Eating*

Disorders, and (2) the Eating Disorder History Form, which can be found in Patricia Neuman and Patricia Halvorson's book, *Anorexia Nervosa and Bulimia*.

Assign a Diary

It is often helpful to ask the adolescent to keep a daily diary of the type and amount of food she eats, the time and place it is eaten, and the feelings and thoughts she has before, during, and after eating. The purpose of this exercise is fourfold. First, it heightens the adolescent's awareness of her feelings. Second, it helps identify the kinds of thoughts that lead to trouble so that appropriate refuting statements may be developed. Third, it provides a relatively objective record of changes that do or do not occur. And it is helpful in discovering behavioral patterns.[17]

Explore the Meaning of the Weight Loss

After some degree of trust has been built and information has been gathered, a discussion of the meaning of weight loss becomes possible. You may want to ask what her original target weight was when she first began to diet. Ask how she thought she would feel upon reaching that weight. Ask what she actually felt upon reaching it. Does she realize that the weight loss will never be good enough because that is the nature of the illness? The dieting that began as a lift and a thrill with an accompanying sense of accomplishment becomes a terrifying burden because losing weight becomes harder and harder to do. Does the client see that the promises of losing weight are not being realized? Exploring these issues may help her realize that the very thing that was supposed to liberate her has entrapped her and made her increasingly unhappy. This simple realization may be an important step in allowing the adolescent to join with you in fighting the problem. Once a collaborative effort is established, you are on your way to making a difference.

Explore Cognitive Distortions

Correcting faulty thinking and beliefs is a major task in treating the eating-disorder patient. The anorexic and the bulimic adolescent must learn to think differently. This requires gentle challenges. On the one hand, affirm the young person's experience as real. On the other hand, present alternative ways of seeing the world and herself. This takes patience. A major distortion, of course, involves misperceptions about the physical body. But at the root of much of her faulty thinking is perfectionism.

Anorexics see total failure as their future unless *everything* is done perfectly. Yet the harder they try for perfection, the worse the ensuing disappointment. The young person with an eating disorder must be challenged on this style of black-and-white thinking. She must realize that if she fails a test, it does not mean she is an idiot, and that if she gains weight, it does not mean she is fat. Ask her to identify the thoughts that lead to a binge or a period of starving. Simply writing out these thoughts or saying them aloud often lessens their intensity. Once she is conscious of her irrational thoughts, she can begin to refute them by replacing them with more constructive ones. You may find the section on guilt helpful in exploring how to refute these kinds of cognitive distortions.

Explore Feelings

Another primary therapeutic goal in treating eating disorders is the genuine and appropriate expression of feelings. Anxiety and anger are two emotions that are likely to be particularly troublesome.[18] Help counselees explore these frightening feelings and allow them to discover what is going on within them. They need to know that these feelings are normal and acceptable. Your office may be the only place they regard as safe. Once these feelings are identified and acknowledged, adolescents can learn healthful options and responsible choices to help them cope more effectively with their once-unconscious emotions. Ultimately, this self-awareness leads to greater self-confidence and self-esteem. You may find the section on inferiority helpful in exploring feelings.

Consider Family Issues

Developing autonomy is hard enough for a healthy adolescent. The task is magnified for the eating-disordered adolescent who is trying to separate from her family. In many cases, the counselor's work with the family is helpful. In fact, several researchers believe that family therapy is a necessary part of all treatment of eating disorders unless the family is extremely hostile or intrusive.[19] The goals of family counseling are to help each member deal with concerns about the eating-disorder problem, become more autonomous, resolve conflict, and encourage appropriate coalitions among family subsystems. Specific goals in therapy may depend on the stage of the family-life cycle, but experts suggest the following general principles in working with families of eating-disordered victims:[20]

1. Approach families in a nonblaming way.
2. Assume that families have done their best.
3. Recognize that families are tired from stress.
4. Assume that families want to help.

Obviously, family therapy is a complex intervention strategy. Such therapy should not be approached without formal training and/or co-therapy with a trained professional. Some resources for learning more about family therapy include *Families and Family Therapy* by Minuchin, and *Family Therapy: Theory and Practice*, edited by Philip J. Guerin, Jr.

Consider Group Treatment

Group therapy can be an important adjunct to individual and family therapy for anorexic individuals. It provides an opportunity to work on peer relationships, to explore feelings about family, and to increase self-awareness and self-expression. Reestablishment of close peer relationships is especially important in the treatment of anorexia. Groups are also helpful in correcting perceptual and cognitive distortions. Group treatment, however, is not for everyone. If adolescents are still in denial of the illness and need medical management because of starvation symptoms, they are not good candidates for group work.[21]

Help Parents Cope

Parents who have an adolescent struggling with an eating disorder are often grateful for guidance from a therapist. The American Anorexia Nervosa Aid Society recommends several dos and don'ts for parents:[22]

DON'T

1. Do not urge your child to eat, and do not watch her eat. Do not even discuss food intake or weight with her. Leave the room if necessary. Your involvement with her eating is her tool for manipulating you. Take this tool out of her hands by letting her alone.

2. Do not allow yourself to feel guilty. Most parents ask, "What have I done wrong?" Perfect parents do not exist. Once you have checked out her physical condition with a physician and made it possible for her to begin counseling, getting well is her responsibility. It is her problem, not yours.

3. Do not neglect your marriage partner or other children. Focusing on the sick child can perpetuate her illness and destroy the family. She needs to know that she is important to you, but no more important than any other member of the family.

4. Do not be afraid to remove the child from the home if it becomes obvious that her continued presence is undermining the emotional health of the family.

5. Do not put the child down by comparing her to her more "successful" siblings or friends. Her self-esteem is a reflection of your esteem for her. Do not ask, "How are you feeling?" or "How is your social life?" These questions only aggravate her feelings of inadequacy.

DO

1. Love your child. Love makes anyone feel worthwhile.

2. Trust your child to find her own values, ideals, and standards rather than insisting on yours.

3. Do everything to encourage her initiative, independence, and autonomy. Be aware though, that anorexics tend to be perfectionistic. Thus, they are never satisfied with themselves.

4. Be aware of the long-term nature of the illness. Anorexics do get better; many get completely well; very few die. Be prepared for months and sometimes years of treatment and anxiety. A support group such as a parents' self-help group may make a significant difference to your family's survival.

☑ WHEN TO REFER

Refer adolescents struggling with eating disorders to specialists in eating disorders, if you are not thoroughly trained to work with anorexia or bulimia.

Refer to psychologically astute physicians or psychiatrists when unusual physical symptoms are present or when eating disorders are severe enough to warrant medication and/or hospitalization. Refer adolescents to other competent counselors or psychologists when, over time, they are not making noticeable progress in weight rehabilitation. Refer young people to family therapists if family work is called for and you are not trained in this method.

Where To Go for Additional Help

Agras, W. S. *Eating Disorders*. New York: Pergamon, 1987.
Anderson, A. E. *Practical Comprehensive Treatment of Anorexia Nervosa and Bulimia*. Baltimore: Johns Hopkins Univ. Press, 1985.
Brownell, K. D., and J. P. Foreyt, eds. *Handbook of Eating Disorders: Physiology, Psychology, and Treatment of Eating Disorders*. New York: Basic Books, 1986.
Brunch, H. *Eating Disorders*. New York: Basic Books, 1973.
Crisp, A. H. *Anorexia Nervosa: Let Me Be*. New York: Grune and Stratton, 1980.
Guerin, P., ed. *Family Therapy: Theory and Practice*. New York: Gardner Press, 1976.
Minuchin, S. *Families and Family Therapy*. Cambridge, Mass.: Harvard Univ. Press, 1974.
Minuchin, S., B. L. Rosman, and L. Baker. *Psychosomatic Families: Anorexia Nervosa in Context*. Cambridge, Mass.: Harvard Univ. Press., 1978.
Neuman, P. A., and P. A. Halvorson. *Anorexia Nervosa and Bulimia: A Handbook for Counselors and Therapists*. New York: Van Nostrand Reinhold, 1983.
Palazzoli, M. *Self Starvation*. New York: Jason Aronson, 1978.
Reif, D., and K. Lampson-Reif. *Eating Disorders: Nutrition Therapy in the Recovery Process*. Gaithersburg, Md.: Aspen Publishers, 1992.
Vredevelt, P., and J. Whitman. *Walking a Thin Line: Anorexia and Bulimia*. Portland, Oreg.: Multnomah, 1985.
The following organizations are also excellent resources. Although they were developed primarily for victims and those close to them, they may have value for the professional helper as well.

American Anorexia Nervosa Association
133 Cedar Lane
Teaneck, NJ 07666
201/836-1800

Anorexia Nervosa and Related Eating Disorders, Inc.
P.O. Box 5102
Eugene, OR 97405
503/344-1144

The Center for the Study of Anorexia and Bulimia
Institute for Contemporary Psychotherapy
1 West 91st Street

New York, NY 10024
212/595-3449

Notes

1. P. A. Neuman and P. A. Halvorson, *Anorexia Nervosa and Bulimia: A Handbook for Counselors and Therapists* (New York: Van Nostrand Reinhold, 1983), 2.

2. D. M. Garner and P. E. Garfinkel, eds., *Handbook of Psychotherapy for Anorexia Nervosa and Bulimia* (New York: Guilford Press, 1985).

3. C. L. Grant and I. G. Fodor, "Adolescent Attitudes Toward Body Image and Anorexic Behavior," *Adolescence* 21 (1986): 269–82.

4. M. J. Maloney and W. M. Klykylo, "An Overview of Anorexia Nervosa, Bulimia, and Obesity in Children and Adolescents," *Journal of the American Academy of Child Psychiatry* 22 (1983): 99–107.

5. Adapted from American Psychiatric Association, *Diagnostic and Statistical Manual of Mental Disorders*, 3d rev. ed. (Washington, D.C., 1987).

6. J. E. Mitchell, "Bulimia: Medical and Physiological Aspects," in *Handbook of Eating Disorders: Physiology, Psychology, and Treatment of Eating Disorders*, ed. K. D. Brownell and J. P. Foreyt (New York: Basic Books, 1986).

7. A. E. Bayer, "Eating Out of Control," *Children Today* (December 1984): 7–11.

8. C. Johnson and R. Larson, "Bulimia: An Analysis of Moods and Behavior," *Psychosomatic Medicine* 44 (1982): 341–51.

9. R. H. Striegel-Moore, L. R. Silberstein, and J. Rodin, "Toward an Understanding of Risk Factors for Bulimia," *American Psychologist* 41 (1986): 246–63.

10. P. Vredevelt and J. Whitman, *Walking a Thin Line, Anorexia and Bulimia* (Portland, Oreg.: Multnomah, 1985), 29–31.

11. Maloney and Klykylo, "An Overview of Anorexia Nervosa, Bulimia, and Obesity in Children and Adolescents."

12. Neuman and Halvorson, *Anorexia Nervosa and Bulimia: A Handbook for Counselors and Therapists.*

13. W. S. Agras, *Eating Disorders: Management of Obesity, Bulimia, and Anorexia Nervosa* (New York: Pergamon, 1987).

14. D. Jones, "Structural Discontinuity and the Development of Anorexia Nervosa," *Sociological Focus* 14 (1981): 233–45.

15. Ibid.

16. M. Strober and J. Yager, "A Developmental Perspective on the Treatment of Anorexia Nervosa in Adolescents," in *Handbook of Psychotherapy for Anorexia and Bulimia*, ed. D. M. Garner and P. E. Garfinkel (New York: Guilford Press, 1985).

17. Neuman and Halvorson, *Anorexia Nervosa and Bulimia: A Handbook for Counselors and Therapists.*

18. Ibid.

19. A. E. Anderson, *Practical Comprehensive Treatment of Anorexia Nervosa and Bulimia* (Baltimore: Johns Hopkins Univ. Press, 1985).

20. J. E. Hedblom, F. A. Hubbard, and A. A. Andersen, "Anorexia Nervosa: A Multidisciplinary Treatment Program for Patient and Family," *Social Work in Health Care* 7 (1981): 67–86.

21. A. Hall, "Group Psychotherapy for Anorexia Nervosa," in *Handbook of Psychotherapy for Anorexia Nervosa and Bulimia*, ed. Garner and Garfinkel.

22. American Anorexia Nervosa Aid Society, *AANAS Newsletter* (January–February 1981).

FORGIVENESS

☑ WHAT THE STRUGGLE LOOKS LIKE

While forgiveness has been a continuing struggle for millions of people throughout history, modern psychology is relatively quiet on the topic.[1] In spite of the silence, forgiveness is important as a therapeutic issue.

A struggle with forgiveness occurs when a person experiences a violation that causes emotional or physical pain. The wronged person experiences both frustration and loss. The loss may be concrete (such as physical possessions), or abstract (such as a dream or a sense of dignity). Almost instantaneously hurt people feel angry toward violators and want revenge. In the heat of the moment they may even vow to "get even, if it is the last thing they do." This typically leads to vindictiveness and unfocused hostility. In general, the younger the person, the more insidious and pervasive are the effects of failing to forgive.[2]

Adolescents who struggle to forgive those who have harmed them nurture their anger in order to pay back the offenders with even greater pain than they received. In a more general sense they become rigid in other relationships and their trust in others decreases. They develop a pattern of not giving until they are sure they will receive something in return. In short, they become bitter and resentful. That is, unless they experience forgiveness.

Archibald Hart says it straight out: *Forgiveness is surrendering our need to hurt back.* The apostle Paul laid down the essence of forgiveness: "Do not repay anyone evil for evil. . . . If it is possible, as far as it depends on you, live at peace with everyone. Do not take revenge, my friends, but leave room for God's wrath" (Rom. 12:17–19).

In the Sermon on the Mount, Jesus sums up the principle of forgiveness by saying, "Turn the other cheek." The old law had called for "eye for eye and tooth for tooth" (Matt. 5:38). But the problem with the old law is that we can't stop at just one eye or one tooth. We feel that we only even the score when our offender has suffered more than we have. So Jesus says to give up your need to hurt back. Forgive. Ironically, forgiveness does not give our offender the advantage; it protects us from further offense, from outdoing our offender's harm again and again. Forgiveness is for our own protection.[3]

119

Case Description

April, seventeen, came to counseling because, as she put it, she was being "sabotaged by her best friend." About four months ago her friend Julie started dating one of April's former boyfriends. April was madly in love with this boy at the time of their breakup. They had dated for almost a year. April never understood why he broke up with her—until two months ago. The pieces fell into place when her former boyfriend started dating Julie. As it turned out, April learned that Julie had instigated the breakup by giving the boy the false information that April wanted to dump him. The boy, in an attempt to save face, decided to break up with her before she called it off. That's when Julie began flirting with him. April was understandably furious. She could not stand even to see Julie at school. She spent most of her time thinking about how to hurt and embarrass Julie. It became an obsession. Julie's dating relationship with the boy was short-lived, but April still cannot bring herself to forgive Julie for the wrong she did her.

Helping adolescents learn the principles of forgiveness is a significant gift and may be very rewarding. For the rest of their days they will bump up against even well-meaning people who hurt them. Knowing the power of forgiveness will empower them to heal untold numbers of relationships.

☑ WHY THE STRUGGLE HAPPENS

In short, the reason people struggle with forgiveness is that they can't or won't give up their right to hurt back. The following characteristics increase the power of this struggle.

Legalism

Some sincere teenagers have a legalistic mentality that results in a continuing need to seek revenge against anyone who hurts them. In Jesus' day, the Pharisees were religious purists who emphasized rules over relationships. Such views are still with us and keep some from experiencing the joy and freedom of surrendering their legalistic belief of "an eye for an eye."

Pride

An attitude of swollen pride keeps forgiveness at bay. Proud people get satisfaction from contemplating their superior position; thus, they are unable to empathize with others. The self-focus of pride makes troubled adolescents determined to retaliate. They have a driving need to even the score by somehow harming offenders.

Bitterness

Anger over offenses naturally fuels the fires of resentment and the desire to retaliate. If forgiveness does not do its healing work at that point, the blaze will become the white heat of bitterness. When this occurs, all of life turns sour. Offended people project their anger on everything and everybody. They become experts in fault-finding. In a word, they become bitter. This entrenched disposition makes the struggle to forgive doubly difficult.

Modeling

Parents who struggle with forgiveness are often emulated by their children. They may come to believe that refusal to forgive offenses is proper. They hear their parents scheme about how to repay injustices done against them, so teenagers believe they are to do the same. In addition, children may be the brunt of parental lack of forgiveness. This, of course, makes it all the more difficult for young people to forgive others.

False Forgiveness

Some people struggle with genuine forgiveness because they "forgive" too much. They forgive even the mildest of mistakes at the drop of a hat. Because forgiveness has been trivialized, it loses its power and meaning. Young people who forgive too easily will struggle with genuine forgiveness because they are avoiding their real pain by repressing traumatic offenses.

Faulty Theology

Some adolescents struggle with forgiving others because they believe God can never forgive them. They may even believe that God wants them to be punished. While their beliefs may be sincere, they are obviously wrong. God does forgive them: "Whoever believes in him is not condemned" (John 3:18). The quality of young people's relationships with God has a major bearing on their capacity to forgive.

☑ HOW TO HELP

The following techniques should be thought of as working with and undergirded by personal acceptance and reflective listening.

Move Slowly

No one can be forced to forgive. Counselors cannot wheedle teenagers into forgiving their enemies. Coerced "forgiveness" facilitates a kind of trigger-happy forgiver who fires off forgiveness at the least offense.[4] Counselors must be alert to sensitive adolescents who may be especially quick to forgive. These youngsters are probably forgiving out of a sense of duty. This, of course, is not forgiveness at all. It comes closer to excusing than forgiving. Counselors must not be hasty in concluding that such cases are cured when working with problems of forgiveness. They must be long on patience.

Clarify the Goal

Forgiveness is not the same as reconciliation. One may forgive the violations of another person yet not continue a relationship with the offender. This may be the case, for example, when the offense is physical or sexual abuse. While forgiveness is an indispensable prelude to reconciliation, it does not require a continuing relationship with the violator. Even if young people are able to give up their anger and its distilled bitterness, they may judge the probability of the violator's change in a positive direction to be so slight that they decide to avoid reconciliation. In this case, the goal of therapy is to achieve an emotional position in which the offended are willing not to seek retribution from offenders.

Help Them Own the Need

If we didn't want anything from people, they could not hurt us, we would not get angry, and there would be no need for forgiveness. Help adolescents reexamine the hurt caused by violators. Help them see violators' unmet needs, those wounds to the spirit inflicted by other offenders. Violators' deep need may be to be trusted, loved, or respected. Labeling offenders' needs is the first step toward stirring up the personal resources that will help those who have been offended eventually to forgive. When they own their need, they are not so quick to lay all the blame on offenders, no matter how despicable the offense.[5] Owning the need requires a humbling of self, and the process often takes time. Move slowly and gently in uncovering this sensitive area.

Help Them Move Beyond the Need

Once adolescents have identified what they want from their offenders, they need to move beyond seeing the persons only in terms of their own needs. To achieve forgiveness they must come to an understanding of the others' needs and motives for acting the way they did. Perhaps the best example is Jesus' endurance of the pain of the cross: "Father, forgive them, for they do not know what they are doing" (Luke 23:34). The goal is to empathize with offenders and understand, in even a small way, that the violators were trying to protect or enhance their own interests, albeit in a misguided way.[6]

If adolescents struggle to forgive their parents for not letting them use the car, they must enter the world of their parents as much as possible to see that they are trying to be the best parents they can. Adolescents don't have to agree with parental actions, just view them from their parents' perspective. Again, this perspective requires putting aside angry defensiveness. Don't expect adolescents quickly to become vulnerable to this degree. The journey may be so gradual that they will pass over the line of empathy without realizing it.

Recognize a Common Misconception

Many adolescents believe that to forgive others is to condone their actions. This may cause them to hold onto their anger and keep them from experiencing the freedom of forgiveness. Clarify this point to insure that it does not slow down the process. Help them realize that their forgiveness of offenders must not depend upon any change in offenders' behavior. Nor should those who have been hurt anticipate any guarantee that offenders will not hurt them again. Forgiveness is for forgivers' own protection, not offenders'.[7]

Explore the Disguises of Forgiveness

It is not uncommon for people to believe that as long as they don't think about the pain caused by others' offenses, they have achieved forgiveness. They equate forgiveness with a denial of their pain. Suppression is not forgiveness. Forgetting is not even a test of genuine forgiveness. The test lies in the healing of the lingering pain of the past. It is also a mistake to confuse forgiveness with excusing. Excusing is letting a person off the hook. Forgiveness keeps people accountable for their behavior. Nor is forgiveness tolerance. We do not have to tolerate what people do just because we have forgiven them for doing it.[8]

Consider Inner Healing

Intervention may have positive results for religious persons who struggle to forgive others of specific and traumatic offenses. Sometimes people cannot forgive because the memories are too painful. They may be afraid of falling apart if they forgive. Inner healing is a prayerful process whereby the counselor symbolically introduces the presence of Jesus into painful memories. As hurting people, with the aid of the counselor, relive painful memories, they are encouraged to see Jesus with them, perhaps holding them and protecting them. This procedure may not bring about instant results, but it may begin a process of healing that will empower young people to forgive. Approach inner healing cautiously, and never force the experience upon clients. The decision to use this technique should be mutually agreed upon.[9]

One of the most helpful approaches to healing memories and damaged emotions is espoused by David Seamands. He suggests several general biblical principles to facilitate this process:[10]

1. *Face the problem squarely.* With ruthless honesty, the hidden memory must be confronted.
2. *Accept responsibility in the matter.* The blame must be taken off others and ownership for the situation must be embraced.
3. *Ask yourself whether you really want to be healed.* Healing the memory means it will no longer be there as a crutch to help gather sympathy from others.
4. *Practice forgiveness.* Healing cannot begin until genuine forgiveness has been accomplished.
5. *Forgive yourself.* A lack of self-acceptance and forgiveness can short-circuit healing.
6. *Ask the Holy Spirit to show you how to pray.* God can help point to the real need.

For a more thorough description of this healing process, see David Seamands's books *Healing for Damaged Emotions* and *Healing of Memories*.

Rely on God's Forgiveness

Leslie Weatherhead said, "The forgiveness of God is the most powerful therapeutic idea in the world. If a person can believe that God has forgiven him, he can be saved from neuroticism." All human forgiveness is predicated on the grace and forgiveness of God. It is central to the Gospel and our salvation. Ideally, counselors should help young people who are in the process of forgiving others to participate in God's forgiveness for themselves. What people cannot accomplish through psychological techniques and principles can still be achieved with the help of the Holy Spirit. Obviously, counselors must be sensitive to adolescents' expressed spiritual beliefs and values.

☑ WHEN TO REFER

Refer adolescents who struggle with forgiveness to other competent counselors or psychologists when, over time, they are feeling increasingly resentful, frustrated, depressed, hopeless, or suicidal. Refer them if you recognize that you have personal unfinished business involving forgiveness. Don't allow your personal issues to contaminate your counseling.

Where To Go for Additional Help

Augsburger, D. *Caring Enough to Forgive*. Ventura, Calif.: Regal, 1982.
Seamands, D. *Healing for Damaged Emotions*. Wheaton, Ill.: Victor, 1982.
_____. *Healing of Memories*. Wheaton, Ill.: Victor, 1985.
Smedes, L. B. *Forgive and Forget: Healing the Hurts We Don't Deserve*. San Francisco: Harper & Row, 1984.

Notes

1. F. C. Shontz and C. Rosenak, "Psychological Theories and the Need for Forgiveness: Assessment and Critique," *Journal of Psychology and Christianity* 7 (1988): 23–31.

2. J. M. Brandsma, "Forgiveness," in *Baker Encyclopedia of Psychology*, ed. D. G. Benner (Grand Rapids: Baker, 1985).

3. A. D. Hart, *Feeling Free: Effective Ways To Make Your Emotions Work for You* (Old Tappan, N.J.: Revell, 1979).

4. L. B. Smedes, *Forgive and Forget: Healing the Hurts We Don't Deserve* (San Francisco: Harper & Row, 1984).

5. D. Seamands, *Healing for Damaged Emotions* (Wheaton, Ill.: Victor, 1982).

6. D. Augsburger, *Caring Enough To Forgive* (Ventura, Calif.: Regal, 1982).

7. Hart, *Feeling Free: Effective Ways to Make Your Emotions Work for You*.

8. Smedes, *Forgive and Forget*.

9. J. M. Alsdurf and H. N. Malony, "A Critique of Ruth Carter Stapleton's Ministry of 'Inner Healing,'" *Journal of Psychology and Theology* 8 (1980): 173–84.

10. Seamands, *Healing for Damaged Emotions*.

GOD'S WILL

☑ WHAT THE STRUGGLE LOOKS LIKE

Invariably, the spiritually sensitive adolescent will ask, "How can I know God's will for my life?"—or some variation of that theme.

While young people of previous generations usually found major choices in life to be culturally or parentally determined, typical Christian teenagers today are faced with an incredible diversity of opportunity and choice. Their decisions are complex and often lead to confusion about the matter of knowing God's will for them.

The concern is generally not over God's sovereign or moral will, but more often over his individual will—his ideal life plan, uniquely designed for each believer. Henri Nouwen defines God's individual will as the unique way in which God's love becomes manifest in one's life: "It is an active claiming of an intimate relationship with God," says Nouwen, "in the context of which we discover our deepest vocation and the desire to live that vocation to the fullest."[1] The will of God, according to Lloyd Ogilvie, is a relationship with God in which he discloses his purpose, power, and plan for our lives.[2]

Of course, God's ultimate will is that we know him, love him, and glorify him. Difficulties arise in trying to decide, in specific terms, how best to do that. Occupational choice, for instance, can be miserable for some sincere young people seeking to serve God. Adolescents feel under pressure to choose a vocation. Most of their lives they have been asked, "What do you want to be when you grow up?" Some teens become frustrated in the decision process by their perception of God's aloofness. Some become frozen in fear that they will miss out on God's will if they make the wrong decision. And still others believe that God will want them to do something they will hate. So they stall.

☑ WHY THE STRUGGLE HAPPENS

Several factors contribute to adolescent frustration regarding assurance of God's will. The following are just a few of the reasons some teens get hung up.

Case Description

Walt is eighteen and anxious about his future. He is a model student and deeply sincere about his faith. Walt is also a gifted adolescent and considering a career in graphic design. His SAT scores are above average, and his chances of getting into a very prestigious art school look promising. His teachers and others whom he respects have encouraged him, but he still feels uneasy about making the decision to apply. Walt is afraid God may not want him to go into this field. He struggles with the thought that he may miss out on what God has planned for him if he goes to art school. Walt has a strong compassion for the homeless, and sometimes feels that God is calling him to devote his life to meeting their needs. While parts of this social work attract Walt, other parts repel him. He is tormented by trying to know what God really wants.

The Myth of a Standard Formula

Different decisions require different approaches to God's will. Sometimes teenagers do not understand the variance in the import and meaning of decisions. They seek to know God's will in very specific terms on every decision they make. They believe they must approach simple decisions in the same way they would approach complex ones. Searching for a standard formula for finding God's will in everything, they deliberate over questions that are straightforward or simply a matter of preference.

Confusion Over What "God's Will" Means

Many adolescents seek the will of God before intelligently understanding what the concept means. Some equate God's will with a detailed map for their lives. God does have a "wonderful plan" for each of us that is worthy of emphasis, as the famous Campus Crusade evangelistic tract, "The Four Spiritual Laws," tells us. But God does not outline a personalized plan that settles every future decision. That would be determinism, a philosophy that contradicts free will. In fact, the Bible nowhere teaches that knowledge of the future is necessary or even helpful for effective decision making.

Overconcern with the Future

Some young people get hung up on the matter of God's will for them because they are focused more on the future than the present. Though a tentative outline of what God is planning for our lives is not to be avoided, an obsession with knowing everything about one's future years can deter a person from discovering God's will for today.

Unrealistic Expectations of the Bible

Some sincere young people are frustrated by their failure to discern God's will because they expect to find specific answers to every conceivable question delineated in God's Word. They may feel compelled inadvertently to distort passages of Scripture that are irrelevant to their decisions. They may become superstitious about the Bible and attempt to treat it like a crystal ball. An example is the absurd story of the man who married a woman named Grace because he read the verse that says, "My grace is sufficient for thee." Some teens struggle with God's will because of the futility of this approach.

☑ HOW TO HELP

Helping adolescents who struggle with discerning God's will requires patience and sensitivity on the part of counselors. The following techniques should be undergirded with personal acceptance and reflective listening. They are designed to clear up foggy thinking, bring about a spiritually open attitude, and energize intelligent action.

Reframe the Attitude

Many adolescents struggle with confusion over God's will because they approach it as if it were a perplexing puzzle to to be arduously and mysteriously solved. These young people need to see that God's guidance is ultimately up to him. They can rest assured that God will make his desires known to them. Psalm 32:8 states, "I will instruct you and teach you in the way you should go." God wants to reveal his will even more than we may want to receive it. Help teens achieve a sense of security in believing that in his own good time God will reveal his will to those who are open to his direction. Some teens are afraid they will miss it if they are not obsessed with ascertaining God's will. They superstitiously look for signals that will reveal his will. This sort of anxiety is not necessary. God has promised to guide his followers, just as a shepherd guides his sheep. While this does not mean that people are to shirk all responsibility in the guidance process, it does mean they are to give God more credit for making his desires known. Gary Friesen proposes that a person should not even ask, "How do I find the will of God?" Instead, a better question to pursue is, "How do I make good decisions?"[3] This shift in attitude can do much to help the struggling young person.

Clarify the Assignment

While adolescents can rest in the assurance that God will initiate his guidance for them, they can also be helped by understanding their assignment to hear his direction clearly. Blaine Smith, in his helpful book *Knowing God's Will*, outlines four basic aspects of the quest to embrace God's will:[4]

1. Adolescents must be willing to hear God's will. Are they determined to understand that God will enable them to be effective in his kingdom? If openness and willingness are not present, it is doubtful that a genuine understanding of God's will can occur.
2. Christians need to ask God for guidance as they pray. In the New Testament the most explicit command to pray for knowledge of God's will is

given in James 1:5–6: "If any of you lacks wisdom, he should ask God, who gives generously to all without finding fault, and it will be given to him. But when he asks, he must believe and not doubt." Through prayer young people may begin to glimpse God's perspective on their lives, and ask for the strength to do his will.

3. Young people need to study Scripture, not to find final answers to specific complex decisions, but to understand God and his principles for fulfilled living. This comes through regular and frequent study of the Bible.

4. Teens must use their God-given reason to make intelligent choices. Paul is a biblical example of a person who used his rational faculties to make decisions. For him, discerning God's will was primarily a matter of making logical judgments based upon that which would bring the greatest glory to God. Eventually, a person must trust that God, in his providence, will give all the information needed to follow his will.

Clarify the Types of Decisions

Some sincere teens are overwhelmed with finding God's specific will for almost every decision regardless of its importance. They wonder about whether they are to wear the blue or red sweater, for example. For these young people it is helpful to explain the degree of importance among decisions. Blaine Smith notes several types of decisions that can be delineated. *Moral decisions* are straightforward. They include such matters as stealing or premarital sex. For Christians there is a clear moral principle that simply needs to be understood and applied.

Nonmoral decisions are also straightforward. They deal with choices about actions that have no moral implications. They are simple decisions, such as whether to eat an apple or an orange. *Complex decisions* concern important personal decisions like what college to attend, whether or not to marry, how to spend money, and so on. These decisions require more than simply applying straightforward moral principles. On this level of decision making, one finds a great deal of flexibility and choice. But these are the decisions that commonly cause adolescents to wrestle with knowing God's specific will. Help young people realize that every decision does not call for an equal amount of time and thoughtfulness.

Distinguish God's Plan for the Future from God's Desire for Now

God's plans for people's future are different from his wishes for their present circumstances. Predicting their specific future is not the concern of Christians. God normally reveals his specific plans for people in portions.[5] Undue anxiety is caused by thinking that one needs to know the future to understand God's will for the present. Struggling young people should be encouraged to focus more on God's desires for them right now and not jump to conclusions about tomorrow. Their future cannot be indisputably determined. For example, a young person may feel led to go on a date with a certain person, but that does not necessarily mean that God intends them to become engaged.

Help the young person avoid the need to "know" what God plans for them years from now.

The highest will of God is revealed when people are doing, right now, what pleases God most.[6] They may feel led, for example, to study for the pastoral ministry, but that does not mean they will ever become pastors. At the same time, of course, young people should never be deterred from an enthusiastic vision of their future and from moving toward specific goals. Making a distinction between God's plan for the future and God's wish for the present helps youth whose anxiety renders them unable to make any decisions.[7]

Explore the Use of Intuition

Feelings are like a compass for most adolescents. An emotional surge is more powerful for most than a rational deliberation. Sometimes hunches (intuition) or feelings are regarded as inward signs of God's leading. Some view intuition as the direct voice of the Holy Spirit. While God may certainly influence our feelings in order to tell us something, we must be cautious about putting too great an emphasis on intuition.

Nowhere does the Bible tell us that we should attempt to discern God's will merely through inner feelings. Intuition is helpful in providing insight into one's unconscious. It reveals some of our deepest desires and may tell us something about what God desires for us. However, we cannot conclude that every desire is directly from God. Desires are influenced by further information and experiences. Feelings are important in discovering God's will, but they are not the infallible voice of God.[8]

Facilitate Sound Decision Making

A struggle with knowing God's will almost always results from knowing how to make competent decisions. Blaine Smith presents a helpful fourfold process that should be considered by young people making complex decisions.[9]

1. Consider one's personal desires. Many sincere adolescents believe that a Spirit-led decision will always lead to suffering. They may, for example, believe they should marry out of sympathy or a sense of duty. I know one young man who thought that, in order to be sure he was doing God's will, he should go into an occupation he would not enjoy. This twisted logic ignores the biblical evidence that God creates desires within the sanctified heart that draw us into his plan. Self-denial and sacrifice may be part of the decision, but they are a subset of the overarching enthusiasm for reaching one's goals. Personal desires must be affirmed to recognize and energize God's will. Sometimes it is helpful to ask teens how they would advise others who are faced with their situation. Their answers may give insight into their deepest feelings. One final note on personal desires: Desires should be given, as Smith says, time to "season." It is important, especially during adolescence, to put desires to a time test, to check whether they are worthy of a commitment.

2. Assess competence and abilities for handling the responsibilities of a

particular decision. Young people must examine their skills or potentials before choosing vocations. While this seems obvious, a surprising number of young people do not consider this matter or they may regard it as irrelevant. They are walking "in faith" without considering whether they are suited to such a "call." Encourage them to experiment with it. If, for example, they want to be missionary doctors, they should enroll in some of the hard sciences to see whether they are cut out for that difficult program. Help adolescents take into account everything they can about their personalities and abilities. For some this may mean consulting career counselors or psychologists who can administer a personality assessment.

3. Young people should examine their circumstances to see what opportunities are available to them. What things prevent them from taking certain actions? What options are simply out of the question because the door has been closed? What alternatives are wide open? Circumstances should not play a predominant role in discerning God's will, but they often suggest new avenues to explore and sometimes confirm leanings.

4. There is the matter of counsel. When adolescents desire to move in directions for which they are equipped and for which they have opportunity, they should seek counsel from people they respect. Determining God's will is not the place to exercise rugged individualism. Encourage young people to share their decision process openly with a select group of knowledgeable people who are concerned about their best interests. They should avoid advisers who have their own agenda for the adolescents. The book of Proverbs is packed with wisdom on this theme; for instance, "Plans fail for lack of counsel, but with many advisers they succeed" (15:22). Encourage teenagers who wrestle with important decisions to find several sources of wise guidance.

For a more detailed description of this decision process see *Knowing God's Will* by Blaine Smith. You may also wish to consult *Living God's Will* by Dwight Carlson. Employing a ten-step procedure for knowing God's will, Carlson discusses the four actions noted above:

1. Be obedient to God's already-revealed will.
2. Be open to any means or results.
3. Examine God's Word for principles of guidance.
4. Utilize prayer.
5. Acknowledge the work of the Holy Spirit.
6. Utilize the counsel of others.
7. Consider providential circumstances.
8. Evaluate yourself and your environment.
9. Make the decision.
10. Ask whether you have God's peace about the decision.

Carlson also provides an organized checklist of "things to consider before making any major decision in your life." This may be helpful to use with some adolescents who need more structure to contain their anxiety about uncovering God's will. The checklist is found in *Helping the Struggling Adolescent: A Counseling Guide*.

☑ WHEN TO REFER

Refer adolescents who struggle with determining God's will to other competent counselors or pastors when, over time, they feel more confused and uncertain. Referral may be necessary for career counseling or personality assessment that can inform their decisions. Refer them to competent psychologists if they begin to show signs of depression or hopelessness. Refer them if for any reason you are uncomfortable with assisting them in spiritual counsel.

Where To Go for Additional Help

Carlson, D. L. *Living God's Will*. Old Tappan, N.J.: Revell, 1976.
Friesen, G. *Decision Making and the Will of God*. Portland, Oreg.: Multnomah, 1980.
Johnson, B. C. *Discerning God's Will*. Louisville: Westminster/John Knox, 1990.
Ogilvie, L. J. *God's Will in Your Life*. Eugene, Oreg.: Harvest House, 1982.
Smith, M. B. *Knowing God's Will: Biblical Principles of Guidance*. Downers Grove, Ill.:
    InterVarsity Press, 1979.

Notes

1. H. J. M. Nouwen and J. Imbach, "God's Will," in *Dictionary of Pastoral Care and Counseling*, ed. R. J. Hunter (Nashville: Abingdon, 1990), 466.

2. L. J. Ogilvie, *God's Will in Your Life* (Eugene, Oreg.: Harvest House, 1982).

3. G. Friesen, *Decision Making and the Will of God: A Biblical Alternative to the Traditional View* (Portland, Oreg.: Multnomah, 1980).

4. M. B. Smith, *Knowing God's Will: Biblical Principles of Guidance* (Downers Grove, Ill.: InterVarsity Press, 1979).

5. D. L. Carlson, *Living God's Will* (Old Tappan, N.J.: Revell, 1976).

6. Ibid.

7. Smith, *Knowing God's Will*.

8. B. C. Johnson, *Discerning God's Will* (Louisville: Westminster/John Knox, 1990).

9. Smith, *Knowing God's Will*.

GRIEF

☑ **WHAT THE STRUGGLE LOOKS LIKE**

Grief is a natural and normal response to the loss of something or someone cherished or loved. Doug Manning, in his book *Don't Take My Grief Away*, writes, "Grieving is as natural as crying when you are hurt, sleeping when you are tired, eating when you are hungry, or sneezing when your nose itches. It is nature's way of healing a broken heart."[1]

Grief is succinctly defined by Elisabeth Kübler-Ross in *On Death and Dying* as the "process of separation."[2] Grief is not limited to death. The process of adolescence is separation from childhood and movement toward becoming an adult. Adolescence is fraught with grieving. Grief is a natural response to the breaking of attachments through the loss of a person, thing, activity, status, romantic relationship, or anything that has become significant. Grief has the power to disrupt and disorganize one's total life. It is preoccupying and depleting. Generally, grief is a process, not a state. Bereaved people move through various stages of grief that allow them to reorganize life in positive ways.

According to Kübler-Ross, grief is a gift. "When it is unfiltered, it is right and good and healthy," she writes. "It needs no work or change or therapy. It heals itself. But when we begin to filter our grief through sieves of guilt, anger, resentment, bitterness or self-pity, then we need more help."[3]

Clinically, the signs and symptoms of grief have been noted for decades: somatic distress, preoccupation with the image of the deceased, guilt, regret, fear, hostile reactions resulting from unresolved anger, and loss of conduct patterns previously influenced by the deceased.[4] The *Diagnostic and Statistical Manual* (3d ed. rev. [DSM-III-R]) describes a category of uncomplicated bereavement. In this, a depressive syndrome is frequently normal. After a death, guilt, if present, is largely about things done or not done by the survivor at the time of the death. Thoughts of death, according to *DSM-III-R*, are usually limited to one's thinking that one would be better off dead, or that one should have died with the deceased. The reaction to the loss may not be immediate but rarely occurs after the first two or three months.[5]

Teenagers who suffer significant loss experience more stress than other teens. Research has shown, however, that they often emerge as healthier people when their grieving process continues to a resolution and acceptance. For example, they are more reflective, have better relationships with parents and peers, improve school work (after temporary difficulties), have a sense of increased maturity relative to other adolescents, and moral values are heightened.[6]

Adolescents grapple with death better than do some adults. The American poet William Cullen Bryant, best known for his poem "Thanatopsis," expresses Erik Erikson's goal of ego integrity and trust. Bryant wrote:

> So live, that when thy summons comes . . .
>   Thou go not, like the quarry-slave at night,
> Scourged to his dungeon, but, sustained and soothed
>   By an unfaltering trust. . . .

Bryant wrote this poem when he was eighteen—an adolescent!

From her work with terminally ill patients, Kübler-Ross found common responses to news of impending death. She identified five stages of dying: denial, anger, bargaining, depression, and acceptance. While these stages are similar to the stages of grief, there are differences. Her theory is directed specifically to the dying patient. To force her stages of dying on a person who is struggling with grief, according to David Switzer, is distorting and misleading.[7]

Pastoral theologian, Wayne Oates, has proposed a helpful theory of grief that outlines a progression of stages: the shocking blow of the loss in itself, the numbing effect of the shock, the struggle between fantasy and reality, the breakthrough in a flood of grief, selected memory and stabbing pain, the acceptance of the loss and the affirmation of life itself.[8]

John Bowlby suggests three basic stages of grief teens go through: protest and denial, despair and disorganization, and finally reorganization.[9] A more complete picture of the process is provided by Y. Spiegel.[10] In this model the bereaved person moves through four stages:

1. *The Shock Stage.* Adolescents in this stage will be characterized by disbelief, emotional numbness, occasional outbreaks of pain and tears, a frequent lack of awareness of external events and conversations, and difficulty in thinking clearly.
2. *The Control Stage.* This is characterized by a stoic self-control on the part of grieving adolescents (as well as a control on the demands by other persons around them). Here young people may be passive, having difficulty in carrying out decisions, experiencing distance between themselves and the external world, a sense of the unreality of it all, depersonalization, feeling empty or dead inside, and trying to act as if the loss had not occurred.
3. *The Regression Stage.* Here adolescents can no longer be sustained under the impact of the reality of the loss. Earlier forms of feeling and

reacting begin to dominate and are often independent of the realities of their present environment. Once again grieving teenagers experience pain, uncertainty, fragmentation, heightened emotion of all kinds, weeping, anger, complaining, often becoming exhausted and withdrawing, having a seeming apathy, self-centeredness, preoccupation with and often idealization of the deceased, a grasping at overly simplistic explanations, a pervasive sense of helplessness, and a variety of defense mechanisms directed against the pain and the fear of loss of control.

4. *The Adaptation Stage.* In this final stage, a step-by-step giving up of regressive behaviors occurs. In their place more adaptive responses arise as the loss is recognized to its full and final extent. This makes necessary the very painful giving up of expectations of life being again as it was, accompanied by a restoration of the deceased within one's own individual personality. In so doing, reconnecting with the present external world takes place.

Since grief is a process with stages, it is essential for adolescents to go through each one of the stages completely in order to reach a positive resolution of the whole grief reaction. To repress and suppress the feelings involved in grief, to go about as if nothing had been lost, to attempt to skip stages of the grieving process, indicate that the process of resolution and reorganization has been thwarted. Pathological or unresolved grief occurs when the usual movement through recognized stages of grief is blocked, although it is not uncommon to go through the stages a bit out of order or to be in more than one stage at the same time.

Signs of pathological grief in adolescents include starting to use alcohol or drugs to "ease the pain," intense feelings of guilt, hurting others because they have been hurt, dropping activities or relationships that once were important and meaningful, experimenting with sex to get close to someone, not talking to people they are close to about what troubles them, causing trouble, behaving recklessly or trying to hurt themselves (although suicidal thoughts are often a natural part of grieving), and playing the role of the "scapegoat" or "bad guy" so as to appear tough.

Everyone's grief, like a physical wound, is on a unique timetable. Some wounds are uncomplicated and heal easily and quickly. But other wounds are more complicated and require professional intervention. So it is with grief. Some losses are grieved over and resolved quietly and alone. Others are complicated and need more help. If, after six to eight months, an adolescent has not made significant progress in the grief process, it is a good indicator that professional intervention may be necessary.

Facilitating the grieving process for bereaved adolescents involves helping them to express feelings, remember, accept the reality of physical death, experience their own value as persons, and discover meaning in their lives in

Case Description

Dorothy, a sixteen-year-old, came to counseling two months after losing her father in an automobile accident. He died upon impact. Dorothy had not expressed any feelings of grief about her father's death, but she could talk at length about it in a factual manner. Her mother reported that Dorothy had not been sleeping well and seemed rarely to be hungry since the accident. But Dorothy said she was fine. She had not confessed her pain to anyone, even her closest friend or older sister. In the second session of counseling Dorothy began to express her sorrow. It started in the latter half of the session when she said she was angry at her father for leaving. He had promised her a trip for her upcoming birthday, and she was angry that it would never happen. More powerful than her anger, however, was her guilt about feeling angry. For twenty minutes, tears streamed down her cheeks as she buried her face in her hands and sobbed.

the midst of the events. Grief work can be a rewarding challenge and provide adolescents with some of life's most meaningful experiences.

☑ WHY THE STRUGGLE HAPPENS

The cause of grief, in one sense, is simply loss. A struggle with pathological grief, however, is more complicated. The question is how to identify those young people who are most at risk. In brief, those most at risk include young people with parents who have themselves been depressed, with a history of serious illnesses requiring hospitalization, and with a genetic inheritance pattern for affective disorders.[11] Gary Collins, in his book, *Christian Counseling*, outlines several additional influences of pathological grief.

The Griever's Beliefs

Most young people are taught from their earliest years how to acquire things, not how to lose them. Even when a youngster loses a pet to an accident, it is often replaced on the next Saturday. Most children are not taught how to think about long-term loss, and there are some who are also taught to bury any sorrow that surrounds loss. They come to believe that showing any signs of grief or seeking comfort and help in dealing with their loss is a personal weakness. They believe they should not be affected even by the loss of a loved one through death. Also, teens who have no religious support or belief in hope for the future and who cannot find comfort in supernatural peace in times of mourning have a greater potential for suffering pathological grief.

Personal History

Grieving is always difficult, but for some adolescents it seems to hit harder than for others. This is especially true if they have had difficulty in other personal separations and losses. Adolescents with personal histories of previously unmastered losses—for example, parents' divorce or a romantic breakup—are more likely to suffer from complicated and dysfunctional grief. In other words, if adolescents have learned to deny earlier losses rather than work them through, they may not be prepared to respond to severe losses. They have no experience on which to draw.

Social Environment

Adolescents who grow up in social environments that try to deny the reality of death are provided little warmth or in-depth social support. They have no intimate or continual relationships to facilitate the grieving process. Because of their environment they learn to bury their feelings and grieve alone, if at all. These adolescents are likely to get stuck in the grieving process and suffer from pathological grief.

Circumstances Surrounding the Loss

A sudden and tragic loss is generally the most difficult for young people to assimilate in healthful ways. If a loss was anticipated, such as an elderly or sick grandparent, the grief is less likely to be pathological. When a sibling dies, there is often a strong sense of guilt ("It should have been me"), especially if one had ambivalent feelings toward a brother or sister, and a stronger feeling of personal mortality ("There but for the grace of God go I").[12] Essentially, the greater the loss, the greater the intensity of the grief.

☑ HOW TO HELP

Several strategies have been tried and proved effective in treating grieving adolescents. The following techniques should be undergirded by personal acceptance and reflective listening. They are designed to create alternatives for adolescents to replace dysfunctional behaviors and attitudes with ones that will lead to successful resolution of the loss.

Pinpoint the Severity

At the beginning of treatment it is helpful to assess the intensity of the grief. While few if any measures are designed specifically to measure this process, the Beck Depression Inventory may be helpful. In addition, the Novaco Anger Scale may be used to assess grieving adolescents' anger reaction to their losses. The latter is found in *Helping the Struggling Adolescent: A Counseling Guide*.

Understand Their True Needs

It is imperative for counselors who work with the bereaved to understand accurately what the grieving need. David K. Switzer has described eight needs that must be fulfilled for effective resolution of the grieving process, especially when it is the result of death:[13]

1. To accept the reality and finality of physical death (or loss).
2. To become aware of and express all the feelings they have about the loss or toward the deceased. Sometimes this concerns the way the deceased died (e.g., suicide, accident, etc.).
3. To break the emotional ties with the deceased. In other words, they need to refrain from investing emotionally in the deceased and behaving toward the deceased as if he or she were still physically present.
4. To break habitual patterns of speech and other behaviors that assume the deceased person is physically present.
5. To affirm that they themselves are worthwhile apart from interaction and connection with the deceased.
6. To reaffirm and therefore allow to come back to life those characteristics and behaviors that contribute to the ongoing and growing life of the grieving adolescent.
7. To cultivate both old and new relationships.
8. To rediscover meaning in one's own life.

Know What To Avoid

Even the most experienced counselors sometimes need to be reminded of the importance of reflective listening while working through grief issues. It is particularly painful to watch young people suffer heartbreaking grief. We may be tempted to solve problems for them as a means to our own comfort. Effective counselors must avoid rushing the grieving process simply to help adolescents avoid more pain. Comforting grieving youth is more like comforting a teething baby than like keeping a child away from a hot stove. The core of the work is listening to their pain and suffering, not keeping them from it. Bereaved adolescents do not need advice, and they certainly do not need to be told how or what to feel. They don't need to hear statements such as "I know what you're going through," or "God is going to teach you something wonderful through this," or "It just takes time to grieve," or "Don't be so down; things could be a lot worse." Avoid all pat answers.

Examine Your Own Unresolved Grief

Unlike many problems that clients bring to therapy, grief is often a reminder to counselors of their own grief issues involving death and loss. Furthermore counselors confront their own mortality in grief counseling. Awareness of death is always tempered by a degree of denial, which helps us to function effectively. As Duc François de La Rochefoucauld said, "Neither the sun nor death can be looked at steadily." Counselors working with grieving adolescents, however, do need to review and examine their attitudes toward loss, experiences with death and grieving, and their degree of comfort with emotions that surround these issues. Failure to do so can block a healthful grieving process for adolescents and lead to undesirable consequences. Counselors cannot substitute knowledge about grief for personal processing of their own grief issues. Those who have learned what it means to experience the complete grieving process are tremendous help to others who are just learning how to grieve.

Help Them Admit Their Grief

Some adolescents will come for counseling to work on their grief, but will act "recovered." They will say that they're okay and force themselves to smile. They seem put together and may even say they want to help the family deal more effectively with grief. John James and Frank Cherry call this "Academy Award Recovery."[14] These young people want the approval of others in their time of sorrow. They want to be praised for the way they have overcome the loss. Effective counselors will help this kind of young person gently discover their unresolved mourning. It is helpful to ask how they have changed since the loss. Has their sleeping or eating changed? Do they have difficulties concentrating? Do they express emotions differently? Do they talk with their friends just as they always have? It may even be helpful to have them write letters to the deceased to express what they never had a chance to say. These kinds of questions and exercises help clients to see and eventually admit that they are suffering from unresolved grief. Sometimes all they need is permission and time to grieve.

Consider Including the Family

When death has occurred in an adolescent's family, it often helps to work with all of the family members (sometimes in addition to individual therapy with the adolescent). Mary Elizabeth Taylor Warmbrod, professor of psychology at the University of Manitoba, has devised a three-stage process of working with bereaved young people and their families. In each of the three stages, the focus is on a different aspect of the family's life. The first stage is the focus on the death and the funeral of the loved one; next, the consideration of what the dead person was like, what the family did together and so on; finally, a focus on the present with reference to adjustments and sources of comfort.[15]

1. *The Beginning: The Death and Funeral.* This stage of counseling begins with asking the family strictly factual questions: When did the person die? Of what? How were you each told that he or she was dead? What was it like going to the hospital? Where was everyone at the time of death? Questions about the funeral or memorial naturally follow: Who came to the funeral? Where was it held? What did you think of the funeral or memorial service? Where is the person buried? Have you been to the grave? In this stage it is important for the counselor fully to appreciate what each family member went through. This stage may take more than one or two sessions.

2. *The Middle: The Past and Memories.* Having reviewed the death and funeral, the next stage takes the family back to the time before the person died. It is important to hear what each one's memories are. Begin with questions about appearance: What did the person look like? Do you have any pictures to

show me? What did you enjoy doing together? What did the person do that you did not like? This last question often brings the answer, "Nothing!" A simple, quiet reply that no one is perfect may be appropriate here. It may set the stage for a time when family members can admit that there were things about the deceased that they did not like. It is important in this stage to let the family remember that the deceased was a fallible human being.

3. *The End: The Present and Future.* The final stage involves attention to the present and plans for the future. The kinds of questions to be discussed are: When do you miss him or her the most, in the morning or evening? To whom do you talk when you think of him or her? Where do you cry? What do you do when you see someone else cry? What would you like from others when you start to cry? How is it at school? Do people at school know? Questions like these give family members opportunity to tell one another how they are grieving together. Interwoven with the focus on support is a concern about plans for the future. Counselors should check with parents about financial conditions while adolescents are present.

Teens worry about finances, and it is better for them to know the facts rather than create terrifying fantasies. Over the course of these sessions, pain may subside. What ideally results is a satisfaction with having known the deceased, a willingness to think about him or her at special times, and confidence that the future offers hope and that the memory of the deceased will continue to influence the family in positive ways. Before concluding therapy, wise counselors will point out how the family has matured through the process and how family members can help one another through difficult times in the future and may seek help from further counseling as needed.

Consider Social Support

Social support has been shown to affect adaptation of adolescents to the deaths of family members. In one study, teenagers who scored higher on a measure of social support were significantly less depressed than were those who scored lower on the same measure. Adolescents who do not find support from the surviving parent are helped the most by social support. Bereaved teenagers report that the most helpful persons are peers. Teenagers in social support groups also report great emotional support from their counselors.

Typically, in the first group session, participants tell the group the details of who has died and how. The leader encourages all members to take their turn but does not pressure them. After the first meeting, the content of group discussion is generally determined by participants. Topics typically include feelings of guilt and anger, difficulties with surviving family members, memories about the deceased, school problems, and problems with fears of others dying. These groups typically range from eight to twelve weeks, and the ideal group size is from five to nine.[16]

Prepare for Anniversary Dates

Even after grief work has been resolved, times will come that will sadden adolescents. These times are predictable. Any date that had significant meaning for survivors and the deceased is considered an anniversary date. Survivors need to prepare for these by having a safe place to talk about their feelings. During the first year of grieving, they should make a list of the upcoming dates that have potential to bring sadness—the birthday of the deceased, the date of death, holidays, and so on. It makes no difference what the day or occasion is; the grieving should have a place to express their pain and sorrow. This may be with counselors or trusted friends. The same considerations should be given to places or events that have the potential for sadness. Again, they should not experience these alone.

Incorporate Meaningful Activity

Grieving adolescents who have difficulty expressing their feelings may benefit from activities that express their grief. For example, they may plant a tree or a rose bush in memory of the deceased. Its growth will be enjoyed as a symbol of life and hope for the future. Providing fresh flowers on special days in the church may be cathartic. Wearing a special piece of jewelry in memory of the deceased may be a symbol of their love. Donating books or clothes of the deceased may be therapeutic. Making and enjoying memories may sooth adolescents who struggle with grief.

Utilize the Power of Prayer

If your clients are open to prayer, incorporate it into your sessions. Having an example to model in spiritual strength is helpful to adolescents battling grief. Suggest that they also pray on their own. Suggest they ask God to comfort them. Encourage them to tell God all of their feelings, to see the deceased with Jesus, and, when they are ready, to thank God for his care. For those who need to say good-bye or express something to the deceased, this quiet moment of prayer provides a wonderful healing moment. Psalm 23 continues to be one of adolescents' favorite Bible passages. This may be a helpful resource for them in helping them to pray during their grief.

☑ WHEN TO REFER

Refer bereaved adolescents to other competent counselors or psychologists when, over several weeks of time, they are stuck in the grieving process or suffering more grief and becoming increasingly depressed, hopeless, or suicidal. Refer if you recognize that your own grief issues are interfering with and complicating the treatment strategy or if you find that you are becoming impatient with their pain and want to "fix" them. Refer if you discover that you are encouraging an unhealthful sense of dependence on you to mend their heartbreak—if you are becoming a replacement for the deceased.

Where To Go for Additional Help

Dershimer, R. A. *Counseling the Bereaved*. New York: Pergamon Press, 1990.

James, J. W., and F. Cherry. *The Grief Recovery Handbook: A Step-by-Step Program for Moving Beyond Loss*. New York: Harper & Row, 1988.

Kennedy, A. *Losing a Parent*. San Francisco: Harper & Row, 1991.

Kolf, J. C. *Teenagers Talk About Grief*. Grand Rapids: Baker, 1990.

Kuenning, D. *Helping People Through Grief*. Minneapolis: Bethany, 1987.

Switzer, D. K. *The Dynamics of Grief*. Nashville: Abingdon, 1970.

Tatelbaum, J. *The Courage To Grieve: Creative Living, Recovery, and Growth Through Grief*. San Francisco: Harper & Row, 1984.

Yancey, P. *Where Is God When It Hurts?* Grand Rapids: Zondervan, 1977.

_____. *Disappointment with God*. Grand Rapids: Zondervan, 1988.

Compassionate Friends is a nationwide support group for bereaved parents and siblings who mourn the death of a child, brother, or sister. Newsletters, brochures, and other information are available by writing them.

The Compassionate Friends, Inc.
P. O. Box 3696
Oak Brook, IL 60522-3696

Compassion Book Service provides more than 200 titles available on death, grief, comfort, and hope. A free catalog is available upon request.

Compassion Book Service
216 Via Monte
Walnut Creek, CA 94598
415/933-0830

Notes

1. D. Manning, *Don't Take My Grief Away* (New York: Harper & Row, 1979).

2. E. Kübler-Ross, *On Death and Dying* (New York: Macmillan, 1974).

3. Ibid.

4. E. Lindman, "Symptomatology and Management of Acute Grief," *American Journal of Psychiatry 101* (1944): 141–48.

5. American Psychiatric Association. *Diagnostic and Statistical Manual of Mental Disorders*, 3d ed., rev. (Washington, D.C.: American Psychiatric Association, 1987).

6. D. Balk, "Effects of Sibling Death on Teenagers," *Journal of School Health* (January 1983): 14–18.

7. D. K. Switzer, "Grief and Loss," in *Dictionary of Pastoral Care and Counseling*, ed. R. J. Hunter (Nashville: Abingdon, 1990).

8. W. Oates, "Anxiety in Christian Experience Bereavement," *Psychiatry* 33 (1970): 444–67.

9. J. Bowlby, *Attachment and Loss*, vol. 3 of *Loss, Sadness and Depression* (Markham, Ont.: Penguin, 1980).

10. Y. Spiegel, *The Grief Process: Analysis and Counseling* (Nashville: Abingdon, 1977).

11. B. J. McConvill, "Assessment, Crisis Intervention, and Time Limited Cognitive Therapy with Children and Adolescents Grieving the Loss of a Loved One," *Crisis Intervention Handbook*, ed. A. R. Roberts (Belmont, Calif.: Wadsworth, 1990).

12. R. A. Kalish, *Death, Grief, and Caring Relationships*, 2d ed. (Monterey, Calif.: Brooks-Cole, 1985).

13. Switzer, "Grief and Loss."

14. J. W. James and F. Cherry, *The Grief Recovery Handbook: A Step-by-Step Program for Moving Beyond Loss* (New York: Harper & Row, 1988).

15. M. E. T. Warmbrod, "Counseling Bereaved Children: Stages in the Process," *Social Casework: The Journal of Contemporary Social Work* (June 1986): 351–58.

16. R. E. Gray, "The Role of School Counselors with Bereaved Teenagers: With and Without Peer Support Groups," *School Counselor* (January 1988): 185–93.

GUILT

☑ WHAT THE STRUGGLE LOOKS LIKE

Almost no one is exempt from guilt. It strikes in unaccountable ways among all ages in all circumstances. Some believe guilt is potentially the most dangerous and destructive of all emotions.[1] I have heard scores of guilt stories in my work as a psychologist. Working mothers, sincere pastors, competent counselors, dedicated teachers, successful business executives—nearly everyone experiences guilt now and then. But I know of no group more prone to suffer the ravages of guilt than adolescents.

Everyone who works with adolescents works with guilt. Talk with young people who struggle with depression, loneliness, inferiority, alcoholism, drugs, critical attitudes, premarital sex, eating disorders, anxiety, spiritual doubt, God's will, masturbation, grief, or almost any other problem and you will find adolescents who struggle with guilt as well.

Guilt is the thud-in-the-gut feeling that occurs when a great gulf separates who we are and who we think we ought to be. According to Bruce Narramore, this emotion is experienced in three typical forms:

1. Self-punishment—"I deserve a good swift kick."
2. Self-rejection—"Nobody could love me, especially God."
3. Self-shame—"I feel worthless."

Adolescents will vary greatly in their experience of guilt, but generally they will experience one of these three forms or a combination of them.[2]

Guilt is so prevalent that several types have been identified. Social scientists and other scholars talk about *objective* or *legal* guilt where a violation of the laws of society has occurred, regardless of whether the person feels any remorse; *social* guilt when a person breaks unwritten but socially expected rules; *personal* guilt when a person breaks personal standards or resists the urgings of conscience; and *theological* guilt, which involves a violation of the laws of God.

The most troubling form of guilt, however, is *irrational* or *false* guilt. Paradoxically, guilt often hits hardest those who have very little or no real

143

Case Description

Jenny is seventeen, attractive, energetic, a cheerleader at her high school, and a top student. Jenny is also wracked with guilt feelings. Not a minute goes by that she doesn't blame herself for something. If she's not thinking about how she is doing something wrong in the present, she will dredge up something from her past. It is not that a specific event seems to fuel her guilty conscience; Jenny just has a general compulsion to hit herself over the head with a sense of guilt. She feels guilty about not being a better daughter, the B she got in French, the negative thoughts she has about one of the other girls on the cheer squad, the ice cream she ate at lunch, and on and on. Jenny believes she is never good enough at home, school, church, or anywhere else. She almost always feels guilty.

reason to be affected by it. I remember one teen who came to see me because of her struggle with guilt. In the third grade she had lost five dollars she was to turn in from selling school raffle tickets. She reported the circumstances and no questions were asked. That night she cried herself to sleep. She wrestled with false accusations from her conscience, which demanded that she be perfect. She finally made a promise to herself: She would put all of her allowance into the church collection plate the next Sunday as a form of restitution for her negligence. Only the coldest of hearts would say that this little girl needed to feel guilty. Yet she carried the residue of guilt feelings from this incident into her teen years. As an adolescent she was still suffering from nightmares about it. Was she guilty? Obviously not. The feelings were irrational.

Irrational guilt is particularly dangerous in adolescence because it can become a personality trait, a predisposition or a prevailing mood. When this happens young people live in a maze of condemnation and a prison of "oughts" and "shoulds." Carrying guilt feelings may become a way of life that must be challenged if adolescents are to reach their potential.

☑ WHY THE STRUGGLE HAPPENS

While causes of guilt feelings are as numerous as the adolescents who experience them, there are several clusters of reasons that explain why young people generally suffer from these feelings.

Unrealistic Expectations

Perfectionism is a major cause of obsessional guilt. Perfectionists measure their self-worth in terms of unachievable goals or accomplishments and productivity. Any deviation from the perfectionistic goal is likely to be accompanied by self-criticism and feelings of guilt.[3] Perfectionists have only a thin thread of fulfillment, which snaps quickly with the heavy weight of unrealistic expectations. Some examples of these expectations include: "I should always be at the top of my class"; "I should never disappoint anyone";

"I should always succeed at whatever I attempt to do"; "I should like everyone and everyone should always like me." Unrealistic expectations like these increase the stranglehold of obsessional guilt around the necks of adolescents prone to hold unrealistic expectations of themselves.

Legalism

I once heard of a woman who chastised her neighbor for cutting his grass on a Sunday afternoon. "Don't you know this is the Sabbath day of rest?" she hollered. "You shouldn't be cutting your lawn." The man replied, "God made the Sabbath for man, not man for the Sabbath." To which she said, "Two wrongs don't make a right!"

Legalism is another cause of irrational guilt. Though it is only a substitute for responsible human behavior and understanding, it pulls many young people into its corner. It finds rules for everything and thus mathematically increases the likelihood of fault and error. Legalism takes policies to an extreme and seeks absolute consistency. It reduces the spirit of law to specific, rigid rules. Legalism obscures and distorts guidelines and is blind to options and possibilities. The absoluteness of legalism is a strong temptation for many struggling adolescents. They can be attracted to its simplicity.

Social Pressure

The sense of feeling on-stage is common in adolescence. They feel exposed, as though others can see inside them, see their faults and defects, know their fears and imaginings. Every day adolescents are immersed in an ocean of social evaluation. They are soaked in mutual criticism. And every day that pressure may move them closer to falling into the clutches of irrational guilt. Every day adolescents are bombarded with statements like "You should have asked her to go out while you had the chance"; "I can't believe you missed that shot"; "Can't you ever get it right?"; "You are so conceited"; "We could have won if it weren't for you"; "You promised you would always stand up for me"; "You were such a jerk at the lunch table today." For a conscience already tender, statements like these will most certainly strengthen the grip of guilt feelings in youthful lives.

A Faulty Conscience

I often ask people, "Who said, 'Let your conscience be your guide?'" Some want to credit the apostle Paul. It was actually Jiminy Cricket in Walt Disney's story of *Pinocchio*. If you let your conscience be your guide, you may get into trouble. This popular maxim fails to recognize that consciences differ greatly from person to person. One's conscience is home grown. It does not come pre-packaged with the Ten Commandments, the Sermon on the Mount, the special rules of your church, or the laws passed by Congress. We were not born with internal emotional thermostats to determine the heat and cold of right from wrong.

Parents are the primary molders of conscience. To avoid punishment, gain rewards, or simply maintain love, children accept their parents' standards of behavior. As children, we were conditioned by "stop that," "no, no," or "naughty, naughty." The more we heard these words, the meaning of right and wrong came into focus. We felt good when we did the right thing and guilty when we did wrong. Developmental psychologist Jean Piaget has shown that the moral judgments of young children are attributed to a kind of magical divine authority given to adults. In other words, children are influenced by the consciences of their parents. Our consciences are cultivated through teaching, and sometimes that teaching is faulty.

In the New Testament Paul makes a distinction between a strong and a weak conscience (see 1 Cor. 8). For Paul a weak conscience is focused rigidly on the letter of the law. The weak conscience, for example, insists upon refraining from meat dedicated to idols, even though idols have no divine reality. The strong conscience, on the other hand, is not bound by the falseness of idolatry. It can bend like a palm tree and adjust to an awareness of circumstances and to the environment. It lives in consideration of principles and in a commitment to ideals. The strong conscience is discerning. It brings all of the elements to bear in a process of moral evaluation. The strong conscience balances a concern for rules with a concern for relationships.

In and of itself, the conscience, contrary to popular opinion, is not ordained of God. While the capacity for a conscience is a divine endowment built into the fabric of personality, it is often informed by distortions that should in no way be regarded as reliable moral guides. The conscience is unreliable unless transformed by Christ.

Evil

Before the Fall, Adam and Eve had no need for conscience. They had no knowledge of good or evil and thus no sense of guilt (see Gen. 2 and 3). However, after their disobedience they realized their wrongdoing and tried to hide from God. At that point, according to Gary Collins, "objective theological guilt and subjective guilt feelings entered God's creation."[4] We fool ourselves if we believe that we are without sin (see 1 John 1:8). Awareness of our guilt comes from the Holy Spirit (see John 16:8–11), and Jesus offers us forgiveness.

Our struggle with guilt, however, comes in realizing that Satan can create guilt feelings. The Bible states that Satan accuses God's followers day and night (see Rev. 12:10). We see him accusing God's people both in Job and Zechariah (see Job 1:6–11 and Zech. 3:1–2). The false experience of guilt is one of the ways he causes us to stumble. Ephesians 6:11 says, "Take your stand against the devil's schemes." Satan certainly causes sincere believers to feel guilty and unforgiven, even when they have done nothing wrong.

☑ HOW TO HELP

The following techniques should be thought of as working with and undergirded by personal acceptance and reflective listening. They are designed to create alternatives for adolescents to replace dysfunctional behaviors and attitudes.

Pinpoint the Severity

At the beginning of treatment it is helpful to assess the intensity of counselees' guilt feelings. Measures of guilt, however, are difficult to come by. The Mosher True–False Guilt Inventory is one of the only guilt measures I know of. However, it is quite long, and portions of it may be inappropriate for young people. I have designed a simple Guilt Scale made up of twenty-five items. While it is not empirically validated, it can serve as a spring board to exploring the intensity of a young person's guilt feelings. The measure can be found in *Helping the Struggling Adolescent: A Counseling Guide*.

Differentiate Between True and False Guilt

Most adolescents who suffer guilt, suffer in silence. When they do talk about it, counselors' first step is to discover whether the sense of guilt is rational or irrational. True guilt is the result of wrong or sinful behavior. In other words, adolescents with true guilt feel guilty because they are guilty. Where there is true guilt, the course of action is clear. Confession, forgiveness, and, in some cases, restitution are needed. Remind youth who struggle with true guilt that God is ready and willing to forgive them. Earl Wilson, Christian psychologist, suggests several questions to ask to determine whether clients are dealing with true or false guilt:[5]

- Is what you feel guilty about a result of real sin?
- If you had to ask forgiveness for some thought or action, what would it be?
- If you had to ask forgiveness of a person, who would it be?

If clients cannot clearly answer these questions, Wilson suggests that the struggle is probably with false guilt. The following questions may unearth adolescents' false guilt:

- What expectation that you are not meeting do you have of yourself?
- Do you feel that you have let down your parents or other people?
- Are you putting demands upon yourself that you cannot meet?
- What action might you take now to move closer to where you would like to be?

These questions will help reveal the impossibilities of adolescent perfectionistic thinking and help young people turn off the false alarm. Wilson sometimes asks, "Could Jesus have satisfied your parents?" A smile of recognition could be the first step toward resolving a struggle with false guilt.

Examine Unrealistic Expectations

The false guilt alarm is often set off by unrealistic expectations. I know a high school student who was nearly destroyed by her self-imposed, false guilt.

She grew up in a family that had great expectations of high academic performance. This girl always seemed to be at the top of her class. When she entered college, she found herself in competition with students who were also at the top of their classes. For the first time she was not the best. She believed she had let her parents down. She punished herself by getting depressed, not sleeping much, and studying all weekend without taking a single break for fun. I helped this young woman see that not being at the top was not a sin. She learned that no reason existed for her to punish herself as she had been doing. She saw that her expectations were irrational.

Adolescents who battle false guilt confuse realistic with unrealistic expectations. The distortion probably stems from a long list of unspoken "shoulds," ironclad rules that are not to be transgressed. These teens feel compelled to be or do something, but they never bother to ask objectively whether particular achievement goals are worth the pressures upon them that the goals create. Karen Horney called this syndrome the "tyranny of the shoulds."

Here is a list of some of the most common and unreasonable "shoulds" that struggling adolescents hold dear:

- I should be the epitome of generosity, courage, and unselfishness.
- I should never feel hurt.
- I should be the perfect friend, sibling, son/daughter, and so on.
- I should be able to find a quick solution to every problem.
- I should be able to endure any hardship and difficulty without complaining.
- I should always feel loved and accepted by everyone all the time.
- I should understand and know everything.
- I should never feel emotions like anger or jealousy.
- I should never make mistakes.
- I should never get sick or even be tired.

Ask adolescents to write their own lists of unreasonable shoulds to heighten their awareness of unrealistic expectations about academic abilities, spiritual dedication, relational devotion, athletic skill, and so on.

Explore the Misuse of Confession

I spent a Friday evening in an unmarked car with a detective friend to observe his work firsthand. A tour of the homicide unit confirmed something I had suspected. Every notorious murder provokes many innocent people to "confess" to the crime. I lived in Los Angeles during the reign of the "Night Stalker." Before the true criminal was caught, at least five people confessed to being that murderer. People with a great amount of guilt are looking for any way they can to assuage their consciences, even confessing to crimes they don't commit in order to receive punishment they are convinced they deserve.

Some people find freedom from guilt through confession while others are propelled further into the guilt trap by this same act. The endless "guilt-confession cycle" looks like this:

> **Guilt Feelings** . . . which lead to . . . **Confession in order to Feel Better** . . . which leads to . . . **Temporary Relief** . . . which leads to . . . **Falling into the Same Behavior or Attitude** . . . which leads to . . . **More Guilt Feelings** . . . which lead to . . . **Confession in order to Feel Better** . . . and on and on.

Confession may be an attempt to manipulate God and avoid the consequence of sin. That is, confession may serve as a temporary way of getting God off our backs, rather than a means to true change of behavior and attitude.

Sincere confession that makes a lasting difference involves a deep repentance, admission of one's inability to meet God's holy standards without his help, and recognition of the futility of trying to earn God's acceptance. Only this level of repentance and change can break up the self-glorifying function of confession.

Genuine confession is painful and frightening. It may also be humiliating. But sincere confession has its rewards. Once a truth is spoken aloud, it is much harder to hide from that truth again. Confession brings a sense of responsibility for behavior and attitudes. It may steer adolescents away from self-blame and from blaming others for difficulties. Confession may help young people avoid what I call the "chain of blame." We rarely enjoy accepting responsibility for something bad, and everyone is an expert at shifting responsibility and blame to somebody or something else. Adam blamed Eve, Eve blamed the serpent, and away we went. However, heartfelt confession may break that chain.

There is another risk to confession that is worth mentioning. Confession may be used as a further means of self-punishment. When one's problem is fear of punishment or self-inflicted punishment, confession tends to lessen the need for punishment and thus releases a sense of guilt. But if the problem is more of a feeling of inadequacy and low self-esteem, confession may actually magnify one's sense of inferiority.[6] This is why some Christians find that confession reinforces their feelings of inadequacy and failure rather than providing reassurance of forgiveness.

Explore Secondary Gains

Counselors who do guilt work quickly become aware of the vigorous desire many have to hold on to their guilt feelings. Clients have made restitution, they have been forgiven by those whom they wronged, they are assured of God's forgiveness, and relationships are restored. But the guilty continue to hold onto their guilt. Usually this is a sign of powerful payoffs or secondary gains. The person is receiving something that makes the suffering of guilt bearable. If the guilt were gone, they would lose the payoff.

One common secondary gain for guilty adolescents is control. They can turn guilt feelings on and off as needed to manipulate those around them. If they don't want to do something, they have a guilt attack. Sometimes they can immobilize their parents by donning their sense of guilt. Sometimes guilt helps them become the center of attention. Ask adolescents what good things they would lose or be forced to give up if they were released from their guilt feelings. For the healing of guilt fixation, explore and expose the secondary benefits that guilt-ridden people cherish.

Examine the Attitude of Perfectionism

Certain jobs require near perfection, such as those of an airline pilot, a surgeon, an architect, or an accountant. But when this trait overflows into relationships and everyday life, it leads directly to guilt feelings. Perfection is the ultimate illusion. It simply does not exist. Everything can be improved, from the space shuttle to peanut butter. In a hit song by Huey Lewis, the chorus says, "There ain't no livin' in a perfect world."

Ask adolescents struggling with a sense of guilt whether they have ever done anything perfectly. Ask whether the benefits of trying to be perfect outweigh the downside. Assign projects to them in which they will be in the wrong yet have the goal of not feeling guilty. Give them permission to make mistakes! This may seem humorous, but it will probably lead them to feel as if a giant weight has been lifted from their shoulders.

Encourage Assertiveness

Ask adolescents what they would do in a circumstance like this: "You have saved money to deposit in CDs, and a friend asks for a loan to help buy new Nike shoes. Can you say no and not feel guilty?" Some young people believe that passive agreeableness is the same thing as virtue, decency, and honor. It is not. This has more in common with wimpishness than civility or good manners. Affirm the natural desire to help others, but let clients know that it is okay to disagree and it is also okay to say no if they want to. Let them know that they can take care of themselves without feeling guilty.

Focus on "Being" Rather Than "Doing"

Trying to look good will make the strongest adolescents weary. It is much less exhausting to focus on trying to be good. Help adolescents turn their spotlight away from doing the right thing and help them work instead on being the right persons. It will help spiritually sensitive teens to know that God does not want them to perform so that he will accept them; he has accepted them, so now they can perform. Ask them to think about being with close friends who accept them in spite of their mistakes. They know they don't have to perform perfectly to receive love and acceptance from this kind of friend. On the other hand, the company of friends who withhold their acceptance until your clients measure up to group expectations will be deflating. When the focus is on *doing* rather than *being*, adolescents are more likely to lose control and slide down the slippery slope of guilt.

☑ WHEN TO REFER

Refer adolescents who struggle with guilt to psychologically astute physicians or psychiatrists when physical symptoms (e.g., rashes) are present. Refer "guilty" adolescents to other competent counselors or psychologists when, over time, counselees feel more guilty and increasingly depressed, hopeless, or suicidal. This may be due to counselors' temptation to preach or teach "down" to clients struggling with guilt feelings. Another pitfall counselors may encounter is the effort to relieve young people with injunctions such as "all you have to do is trust God." Be careful not to create another layer of guilt by implying that solutions are so apparent that clients should already know of them. If you find yourself displaying this kind of attitude, consider referrals.

Where To Go for Additional Help

Carlson, D. *From Guilt to Grace*. Eugene, Oreg.: Harvest House, 1983.
Counts, W., and B. Narramore. *Freedom from Guilt*. Santa Ana, Calif.: Harvest House, 1974.
Justice, W. G. *Guilt and Forgiveness*. Grand Rapids: Baker, 1980.
Narramore, S. B. *No Condemnation: Rethinking Guilt Motivation in Counseling, Preaching, and Parenting*. Waco, Tex.: Word, 1984.
Oden, T. C. *Guilt Free*. Nashville: Abingdon, 1980.
Tournier, P. *Guilt and Grace*. New York: Harper & Row, 1962.
Wilson, E. D. *Counseling and Guilt*. Waco, Tex.: Word, 1987.

Notes

1. G. W. Kisker, *The Disorganized Personality* (New York: McGraw-Hill, 1964).
2. B. Narramore, *No Condemnation* (Grand Rapids: Zondervan, 1984).
3. B. Sorotzkin, "The Quest for Perfection: Avoiding Guilt or Avoiding Shame?" *Psychotherapy* 22, no. 3 (1985): 564–71.
4. G. Collins, *Christian Counseling* (Waco, Tex.: Word, 1980), 122.
5. E. D. Wilson, *Counseling and Guilt* (Waco, Tex.: Word, 1987).
6. Narramore, *No Condemnation*. Narramore provides a thorough discussion of the use and misuse of confession in this excellent book.

HOMOSEXUALITY

☑ WHAT THE STRUGGLE LOOKS LIKE

Few topics trigger more emotional reaction and controversy today than homosexuality. The issue ignites heated debates in virtually every aspect of society: schools, local elections, the military, the courts, sports, science, professional societies, the entertainment world, business and industry, the media, and especially the church. All are caught in the crossfire. On one end of the continuum are gay bashers who are bent on condemning and harassing homosexuals. At the other extreme are the gay liberationists who are intent on making homosexuality an approved way of life, nothing more than an alternative lifestyle.[1] Most of those between these extremes make up an uneasy spectrum of individuals who grapple with the issues and try to make sense of the still-evolving realities and our understanding of causes of homosexuality. Some lean more toward tolerance, others toward condemnation. But they want to do it with thorough understanding rather than bumper-sticker philosophies.

I do not aim in this section to convert you to any one theory or to generate debate. While it is impossible to write on this topic without offending some people, my goal here is to equip you with practical helping techniques that are grounded in compassion rather than condemnation. Debating the issue has its place, but the concern here is to help struggling adolescents.

It is impossible to know how many young people, including Christians, struggle with homosexual urges. Most are understandably afraid to admit their thoughts and feelings (sometimes even to themselves) because of potential rejection or misunderstanding. Somewhere between five and ten percent of the population are homosexual, while some estimate that a larger percentage engage in bisexual activity.[2]

Part of the confusion over homosexuality arises because it is not easily defined. The emphasis should be on behavior rather than on disposition. Christian psychiatrist John White endorses this emphasis in *Eros Defiled*. He writes, "A homosexual act is one designed to produce sexual orgasm between members of the same sex. A homosexual is a man or woman who engages in homosexual acts."[3] Others, who may be motivated by a desire to broaden the base of the homosexual community by including greater numbers, define it as erotic attraction toward persons of the same gender.[4]

Difficulty arises with this definition when one recognizes that gender orientation is not straightforward. It varies in degree. The 1948 Kinsey report suggested a scale with seven points in which zero represents a person who is exclusively heterosexual, three is midpoint, and six represents a person with exclusively homosexual tendencies and actions. Kinsey researchers concluded that few people are at the zero and six points on the scale. However, the plainest definition of homosexuality emphasizes the practice of homosexual acts. This is the sin evangelical Bible scholars identify in Genesis 19.

Homosexuality is not merely one stereotyped behavior pattern. There are many variants of homosexual arousal. Mansell Pattison outlines several types of homosexuality.[5] Anyone of the following may show up in a counseling office where Christian professionals must find ways to be redemptive within the context of moral purity and Christian theology:

Experimental homosexuality usually refers to adolescent experimentation with degrees of sexual interaction with both genders. At a minimal level some adolescents engage in "homoerotic" activity such as arousal as the result of comparing sexual organs. At the extreme end is adolescent experimentation in sexual intercourse with both sexes. Usually this experimentation leads to an exclusive heterosexuality.

Homosexual panic is a phenomenon seen often in young people. An adolescent may encounter nude persons in a shower room after a gym class and suddenly experience sexual arousal. Usually this does not represent homosexual urges, but merely generic sexual arousal from seeing nude bodies.

Situational homosexuality involves homosexual behavior when heterosexual relations are not available. Prisons are the most common example. Sexual release is the primary motivation with affection or intimacy being absent.

Reactive homosexuality involves fear of heterosexual encounters. Although heterosexuality is preferred, homosexual behavior is chosen as less threatening and dangerous.

Social-role homosexuality represents the adoption of homosexual behavior as part of a required social role. Pattison cites as one of the clearest examples a New Guinea tribe in which all males from eight to sixteen are required to play a passive homosexual role and from sixteen to twenty-two an active homosexual role. They are required to marry and remain heterosexual thereafter. More than ninety-five percent of tribal males successfully follow these socially prescribed sexual role behaviors.

Obligatory homosexuality refers to the sense of sexual orientation that some people experience as an internal necessity. They feel no heterosexual arousal but instead sense a homosexual response. Often they find little pleasure in typical adolescent dating, although they may have excellent social relationships

Case Description

Todd, seventeen, managed to convince his parents to arrange for him to go to counseling by telling them that he was worried about possible academic failure. He soon told the counselor that his real concern was related to homosexual fears. Todd remembers trying to "do it" with his younger sister, but he was really too young to know what "it" was. Nevertheless, his father caught them in an undressed state and told Todd how bad he was for what he was doing. Todd attributes his fear of sex with women to that incident. He has never acted out his fear that he is gay, but he is convinced that his early years have "caused" him to be homosexual.

with the opposite gender. They simply feel no attraction. When they begin to experience homosexual arousal, usually in later adolescence, they are surprised, as if against their will. They feel obliged by their own feelings to respond to the same gender. Pattison suggests that this pattern describes the majority of homosexual persons.

Preferential homosexuality occurs in those with bisexual arousal. Many homosexual persons experience heterosexual impulses and perform heterosexual acts with satisfaction. They may simply choose homosexual experiences over heterosexual ones.

Experimental homosexuality and homosexual panic are probably the most common types of adolescent homosexual struggles. Many adolescents who are troubled with their homosexuality enter counseling for other problems. These may include anxiety, depression, compulsive masturbation, grief over a dissolved relationship, or family conflict regarding sexuality. On occasion young people will come to counseling specifically with the presenting issue of clarifying or changing their sexual orientation.[6]

☑ WHY THE STRUGGLE HAPPENS

Space does not permit a full discussion of the etiology of homosexuality. A debate on the diversity of its causes will be left to others. Suffice it to say at this point that no one can accurately pinpoint why a person has such an orientation. The following are some of the most frequently espoused reasons. None of these reasons can be declared as causal, but they are often viewed as factors that increase the likelihood of homosexual predisposition.

Psychological Influence

Adolescence is the period during which emerging sexual identity is tested. Homosexuality, according to many, is due to a profound disturbance in parent-child relationships. A boy, for example, may have a father who is distant, detached, and hostile and a mother who is overly warm, possessive, and controlling. As a result of the rejection of the father, the boy's desire to identify with the father is frustrated, and the seeds of fear and a longing for closeness to a male are planted. The mother's smothering ways further decrease the likelihood of the boy's establishing a complete male identity.[7] Research on this theory has not proved it to be causal, but it is still a commonly espoused view.[8]

Social Influence

Social interaction provides some information on the acceptability of sexual self-expression. Learning principles such as association, reinforcement, and avoidance conditioning are often used to explain a great variety of heterosexual as well as homosexual practices and preferences. According to some, young people, in part, *learn* their sexual behavior through social influence. Aversive conditioning of the sexual response toward the opposite sex and positive conditioning toward the same sex, for example, will tend to produce an inclination toward a gay orientation.[9] One researcher concludes after years of study that while homosexuality may develop without operative genetic or hormonal factors, it generally does not develop without the influence of learning and socialization.[10]

Early Seduction

Some experts theorize that homosexual seduction may play a significant role in creating homosexual desires, especially at an early age. During the early years when sexual choice is still relatively undifferentiated, seduction may have a profound impact. A child is not old enough to understand what is happening, and the homosexual experience may become a reinforcer of sexual expression. In these cases, homosexual patterns may develop before heterosexual habits have an opportunity to be explored. Homosexual seduction certainly does not always result in a gay lifestyle, but in some cases it may be a causal factor.[11]

☑ HOW TO HELP

The role of counselors as a source of positive intervention with adolescents who question their sexual feelings and experiences can be significant. Although some people argue "once a homosexual, always a homosexual," the following strategies side with those who say change is possible but difficult—even with counseling.

Avoid Shock and Express Acceptance

When an adolescent announces, "I think I'm gay," what is your reaction? First of all, do not register any visible shock. Effective help can be offered only if you express an unflappable sense of genuine care. Stay calm. Expressing shock at the sexual proclivities young people reveal in counseling will greatly hamper healthful exploration that may lead to healing. This is especially true when a teen confesses a struggle with homosexuality. Create an atmosphere of warm acceptance. Check your attitude as objectively as possible, and if you cannot achieve a genuine sense of acceptance for the young person, you should refer the client to another competent counselor who can.

Obtain an Accurate History

While I know of no valid and reliable measure that can be used to assess the intensity of homosexuality accurately, a good assessment interview will take a great deal of guessing out of the therapeutic process. A thorough interview usually takes a couple of hours. It is best to prepare clients by saying, "I need to understand as much as possible about your circumstances. This means that I must ask you a lot of questions. I'll try not to be obnoxious, but I am going to want details. If you can't come up with verbal answers, you may want to write them down and give them to me later."

Earl Wilson, in *Counseling and Homosexuality*, provides a number of broad areas that need to be explored as you assess young people.[12] A thorough assessment interview that follows these guidelines is probably not necessary with youth who are experiencing sudden homosexual panic. These questions are most helpful with adolescents who are practicing homosexual behavior.

1. *Family of origin.* Assess home life. Is it supportive? How do people relate to one another?
2. *History of the relationship with same-sex parent and opposite-sex parent.* Learn about clients' feelings and beliefs as well as their experiences related to their parents. How close are they? How do they express affection? How do clients regard their own masculinity or femininity? What are the predominant messages they send? Have they ever been abused by their parents?
3. *Relationships with brothers and sisters.* Sexual behavior is sometimes learned by imitation. What kind of behavior have they learned from their siblings?
4. *Impressions of parents' affectional life together.* What did they learn about relationships from observing their parents?
5. *History of his or her sexual confusion.* When did it start? What incidents were especially puzzling?
6. *Specific history of opposite-sex relationships and encounters.* What is their feeling about the opposite sex? Have they had crushes on people of the opposite sex? Have they kissed people of the opposite sex?
7. *Specific history of same-sex relationships and encounters.* Do they have fantasies about same-sex relationships? What kinds of things have they actually experienced?
8. *Detailed account of current sex practices.* What is the content of their current thought life surrounding sex practices? Are they acting out their fantasies? What about masturbation?
9. *Current views of homosexuality.* How do they view their struggles with same-sex preference? How do they view their future sex life?

Of course, this is only an abbreviated version of the questions to ask in an interview. A more thorough discussion may be found in Wilson's book.

Address Client Fears Directly

Counselors do not cause adolescents to become homosexual by allowing them to explore their anxieties in an open and accepting way. You do not need to walk around the edges of adolescents' true concerns. If young people are simply questioning the possibility that they may become gay, it is probably not the best time to "process" the concern in a lengthy manner. Calm their anxieties as much as possible. Reassure them that their fears are not uncommon in this culture and that they are not homosexual. Most "homosexual" feelings during the teen years actually resemble pseudo-homosexuality. State flatly and with conviction that the clients are worried heterosexuals and are simply in process of constructing their sexual identity.

Clarify and Assess the Therapeutic Goal

An obvious concern of treatment is the outcome. While some secularists argue that homosexual orientation should be affirmed in therapy, many Christians believe that homosexuality should be eradicated through counsel and the power of God. Clients will ultimately determine the goal they desire. The Christian's therapeutic responsibility is to provide the environment and information that will most likely aid clients both to choose and to be able to follow the most healthful course of action, one that is also consistent with God's will. This would include refraining from homosexual behavior.

Ask adolescents what they expect. Make a distinction between *ego dystonic* homosexuality, in which people experience inner conflict over their sexual desires and what they want them to be, and *ego syntonic* homosexuality, where they are satisfied with their gay orientation and behavior. If they sincerely want to enrich their gay lifestyle through therapeutic intervention and this desire conflicts with counselors' values, little will be achieved through debating the proper goal of therapy. Counselors can offer only as much help as clients will receive. An old joke asks, "How many psychologists does it take to change a light bulb?" The answer: "Only one. But the light bulb has to want to change." It is impossible to work with adolescents who are genuinely satisfied with their homosexual lifestyle regardless of how upset their families and others may be. As long as people have come to terms with any particular sin and are nonrepentant, little chance of change exists.

Encourage adolescents who come to counseling with the hope of changing their sexual orientation. But also warn them that it is not always an easy journey. It may be a wrenching and long process. Do not instill false hope. Sometimes clients may not change to a heterosexual orientation, but they can be helped to live a victorious, meaningful life, free of homosexual behavior. Their desire to change is one of the best predictors of whether they will become heterosexual. Research has also found other predictors of positive change: clients with fewer traits of the opposite gender, under age thirty-five, the first homosexual experience occurring after age sixteen, and evidence of some heterosexual arousal.[13] The presence of sexual ideals and values along with moral attitudes toward homosexuality also increases the likelihood of change.[14]

Earl Wilson notes several specific precautions counselors should heed in therapy that focuses on homosexuality.[15]

1. Goals must be specific and tied to behavior whenever possible.
2. Goals must be addressed one at a time.
3. Goals should be related whenever possible so that they build on each other.
4. Goals must be specified by the counselee and agreed to by the counselor.
5. Goals must be significant to counselees but not so extensive that they are unreachable.

Correct Misinformation

Much confusion surrounds the topic of homosexuality. Young people may, for example, labor under the misinformation that homosexuality is a mental disorder or that the condition is always irreversible. Perhaps they believe they have committed the unpardonable sin and will never be acceptable to God. Maybe they blame their parents for "making" them this way. Correcting misunderstandings is appropriate. An enlightened attitude can change attitudes and therefore empower teens to overcome their difficulties.

According to James Mallory, chairman of Rapha's Medical and Clinical Advisory Board, homosexuality is best understood by utilizing an addiction model. Addictive behaviors share in common a predispositional vulnerability. Variables such as relationships with parents; learned attitudes of masculinity and femininity; biological, psychological and social ability to manifest masculine/feminine traits; early sex abuse; quality of relationships with both genders during developmental phases—all may contribute to vulnerability to homosexual behavior, but none is causal. At some point, however, individuals decide to engage in the behavior that is destined to become addictive. Temporarily, according to Mallory, people receive reinforcement and possibly relief from emotional pain and thus conclude, "This must simply be the way I am." They feel trapped or fatalistic about their situation. Counselors have the opportunity and responsibility to correct erroneous conclusions that adolescents may have drawn about their sexual orientation.[16]

Teach Effective Social Skills

Heterosexuality, for many young people, is buried under a mountain of fear. Therapy must include active encouragement of appropriate heterosexual behaviors. A lack of success in dating perpetuates the vicious cycle of heterosexual failures. Learning basic dating and conversational skills may boost confidence. The boy who is wracked with fear about being gay may find it difficult to approach girls with the necessary degree of self-assertion, masculine pride, and self-confidence to attract them. In the process he may also need to learn that men can be self-respecting, assertive, and competent without being cruel, overbearing, or domineering. The section on shyness provides several strategies for teaching social skills.

It should also be noted that girls place a higher priority on personal relationships than on group activities, whereas boys' social priorities are just the opposite.[17] This difference in priorities also tends to distinguish homosexual from heterosexual males. Many adolescent males who have homosexual leanings experience difficulty in developing friendships with heterosexual males. While gay males may want to "share feelings," straight males are more likely to want to relate through shared activities like sports.

Some adolescent males who struggle with this can be helped by focusing on skills and interests that will help them develop friendships with other males who are not gay. Joseph Nicolosi, in *Reparative Therapy of Male Homosexuality*, recommends that some male clients can be encouraged to become athletic to help them discover their masculine strength. He reports that typically the prehomosexual boy misses out on physical play. Masculinity is inherently connected with the body, and when an adolescent boy has little or no physical activity, his sense of masculinity diminishes.[18]

Reinforce Change

Verbal reinforcers may be effective with young people caught in the trap of feeling bound by same-sex attractions. If counselees tell you about talking with opposite-sex students during lunch hours, say, "That's terrific." If they recount their feelings of being attracted to someone of the opposite sex, say, "Good for you." These seemingly small comments may be a real boost to insecure teenagers.

Teach Thought Control

Many adolescents who fear that they are homosexual or are practicing a gay lifestyle are preoccupied with sexual thoughts. They may have difficulty thinking about anything else. Words or images repeatedly invade their mind. Help them prepare a list of alternative thoughts they can focus upon. Quoting Scripture or imagining a relaxing walk through a meadow are possibilities. Certain verses of great hymns or inspirational songs may be memorized and used as needed. The key is to substitute another thought for the obsession. Relaxation training is also effective in helping people stop their obsessions. Several relaxation exercises may be found in the sections on panic attack and anxiety. If young people practice these strategies, they will find that before long the obsessions are dead.

Allow Emotional Release

Repressed fears, hostilities, and painful memories are common in youth struggling with homosexuality. They have sensed the risk inherent in sharing their true feelings with anyone. While such a revelation is too unbearable to examine consciously without support, once teens establish safe relationships with counselors, they must freely release these feelings to resolve internal conflicts and ease tensions. Allow them to delve into their unconscious feelings. Take plenty of time for emotional release.

Insure Social Support

Young people fighting a same-sex preference should be involved in an active social support group. Through social support, a number of Christian ministry groups help homosexuals change. Many are represented by Exodus International and Homosexuals Anonymous. These groups offer a variety of approaches, but generally agree that change is a difficult and painful process of renouncing their practices and attitudes and relying on God for help. You may receive literature and counseling referrals for local social support by contacting

> Exodus International
> P. O. Box 2121
> San Rafael, CA 94912
> 415/454-1017

Consider Co-Counseling

G. Keith Olson suggests that a male-female counseling team may be especially effective in working with teens who struggle with homosexuality. At initial sessions, the same-sex counselor, alone with the counselee, gathers information. Only after this is done and the two have established a therapeutic alliance does the teen begin meeting with the male-female counseling team. This approach enables adolescents to interact with both male and female role models. The method facilitates a quicker resolution of pain and anger toward both sexes. It also helps teens learn to interact with both men and women. The team approach may be a powerful strategy with adolescents.[19]

Expect Fatigue

Counseling youth who struggle with homosexuality is an emotionally draining task. One reason is that counselors will experience a plethora of feelings directed toward them from clients. Counselors may sense suspicion, anger, fear, admiration, ambivalence, love, mistrust, or a yearning for friendship. To make matters more intense, many of these contradictory feelings will be experienced during the same hour.[20] One way that counselors may fight this fatigue is to expect it. Prepare for intense emotions when working with young people who are attracted to the same sex.

☑ WHEN TO REFER

Refer adolescents who struggle with homosexuality to other competent counselors or psychologists if you are not genuinely compassionate and comfortable with their issues or if you are not fully aware of and comfortable with your own sexuality. Also refer if their therapeutic goals conflict with your values. Seek help from other qualified experts if, over time, counselees feel more disillusioned and frustrated.

Where To Go for Additional Help

Atkinson, D. *Homosexuals in the Christian Fellowship*. Grand Rapids: Eerdmans, 1979.

Comeskey, A. *Pursuing Sexual Wholeness: How Jesus Heals the Homosexual*. Altamonte Springs, Fla.: Creation House, 1989.

Jones, S. L., and D. E. Workman. "Homosexuality: The Behavioral Sciences and the Church." *Journal of Psychology and Theology* 17 (1989): 213–25.

Nicolosi, J. *Reparative Therapy of Male Homosexuality: A New Clinical Approach*. Northvale, N.J.: Aronson, 1991.

Payne, L. *The Broken Image: Restoring Personal Wholeness Through Healing Prayer*. Westchester, Ill.: Crossway Books, 1981.

Van den Aardweg, G. *Homosexuality and Hope*. Ann Arbor: Servant Books, 1985.

Wilson, E. D. *Counseling and Homosexuality*. Waco, Tex.: Word, 1988.

Notes

1. *Homosexual* describes only one aspect of a person. In this section I am using the word only as shorthand for "a homosexual person" whose homosexuality is but one aspect of a diverse life. In the same vein, *gay* is used merely for convenience.

2. C. Tripp, *The Homosexual Matrix* (New York: Meridian, 1987).

3. J. White, *Eros Defiled* (Downers Grove, Ill.: InterVarsity Press, 1977).

4. E. M. Pattison, "Homosexuality: Classification, Etiology, and Treatment," in *Baker Encyclopedia of Psychology*, ed. D. G. Benner (Grand Rapids: Baker, 1985).

5. Ibid.

6. E. Coleman and G. Remafedi, "Gay, Lesbian, and Bisexual Adolescents: A Critical Challenge to Counselors," *Journal of Counseling and Development* 68 (1989): 36–40.

7. I. Bieber, "A Discussion of Homosexuality: The Ethical Challenge," *Journal of Consulting and Clinical Psychology* 44 (1976): 163–66.

8. S. L. Jones and D. E. Workman, "Homosexuality: The Behavioral Sciences and the Church," *Journal of Psychology and Theology* 17 (1989): 213–25.

9. Ibid.

10. J. Money, *Gay, Straight and In-Between* (New York: Oxford Univ. Press, 1988).

11. G. K. Olson, *Counseling Teenagers: The Complete Christian Guide to Understanding and Helping Adolescents* (Loveland, Colo.: Group Books, 1984).

12. E. D. Wilson, *Counseling and Homosexuality* (Waco, Tex.: Word, 1988).

13. J. Bancroft, *Deviant Sexual Behavior: Modification and Assessment* (Oxford, Eng.: Clarendon, 1974).

14. E. M. Pattison and M. L. Pattison, " 'Ex-Gays:' Religiously Mediated Change in Homosexuals," *American Journal of Psychiatry* 137 (1980): 1553–62.

15. Wilson, *Counseling and Homosexuality*.

16. Personal conversation with James Mallory (Northwest Medical Center, Atlanta, Ga.).

17. J. Sanford and G. Lough, *What Men Are Like* (Mahwah, N.Y.: Paulist, 1988).

18. J. Nicolosi, *Reparative Therapy of Male Homosexuality: A New Clinical Approach* (Northvale, N.J.: Aronson, 1991).

19. Olson, *Counseling Teenagers*.

20. Wilson, *Counseling and Homosexuality*.

INFERIORITY

☑ WHAT THE STRUGGLE LOOKS LIKE

Maxwell Maltz estimated that ninety-five percent of all people in our society feel inferior.[1] I believe the percentage is even higher among adolescents. Millions of young people suffer from a strong sense of inadequacy.

Inferiority and self-esteem receive more attention than any other topics in adolescent psychology—and with good reason. Healthful self-esteem is like a vaccine against other common teenage problems. Feelings of inferiority have been found to be a factor in anxiety disorders, poor social adjustment, compulsive overeating, poor academic performance, expulsion from school, vocational aspirations, cheating, depression, delinquency, drug abuse, and unwed pregnancy, to name a few.[2] In addition, youth who struggle with a sense of inferiority upon entering adolescence are very likely to enter adulthood with the same negative feelings, if they do not receive help.[3]

Teenage years are particularly critical for cultivating positive self-esteem. With a new capacity to become self-conscious and introspective (i.e., from a formal operations stage of cognitive development), adolescents gather evidence to help them evaluate themselves: Am I intelligent? Am I competent? Am I attractive? They compare themselves with their own ideals and those of others, an experience that is often painful. The ideal self is built on aspirations that are either realistic, too low, or, for the adolescent struggling with inferiority, too high. Ideal selves that are realistic lead to self-acceptance. Those that are too low impede accomplishment. Those aspirations which are too high lead to frustration, self-depreciation, and inferiority.

Self-esteem is the subjective evaluation of one's worth. It expresses approval or disapproval. It has been referred to as the single most significant key to behavior and the mainspring that launches every child for success or failure in living. Another helpful way of defining self-esteem is SE = RS − IS. *Self-Esteem equals Real Self minus Ideal Self.* All adolescents have images of the persons they would like to be. Not a frivolous wish (I'd like to be a rock star), but a sincere desire to possess certain "ideal" attributes. When the real and ideal selves are fairly close together, young people's self-esteem will be positive. When they are quite different, inferiority emerges.

There are several indicators of low self-esteem or inferiority in adolescence. One is *locus of control*. This refers to whether adolescents believe their success or failure is due to their own actions and internal ability or to external influences such as luck or chance. Adolescents struggling with inferiority will invariably ascribe their failures to internal causes and all successes to external causes.[4] If they flunk a test, it's because they are stupid. If they pass a test, it's because it wasn't as difficult as usual.

Another indicator of inferiority is a lack of confidence, or more accurately, *self-efficacy*. This refers to the conviction one has about successfully executing behavior required to produce a desired outcome. It refers to whether adolescents believe they can make a difference in their situation. Those who believe they can make a difference exhibit more endurance and purpose. Those who don't will withdraw and drop out. Adolescents struggling with inferiority are more likely to exhibit feelings of helplessness or powerlessness. They are more likely to suffer from a lack of self-efficacy.[5]

Defensiveness is another common indicator of inferiority. Adolescents with low self-esteem feel hurt. To protect themselves from further pain they erect barriers. They may exhibit a disproportionate amount of hostility, criticism, bragging, suspiciousness, or denial. It is too risky for these struggling adolescents to be exposed to additional hurt, so they wear psychic armor. Perhaps the most common defense for these young people is apathy. It is as if they have been injected with emotional novocaine that leaves them with a lethargic I-don't-care kind of attitude.

Adolescents with low self-esteem may be distractible, shy, withdrawn, inhibited, or anxious. They are more likely to daydream and want to be in situations with minimal competition. They have few, if any, expectations of success. They often lack a sense of belongingness and fear new experiences. They usually have a poor physical appearance and a low energy level.[6]

It is easy to become confused when thinking about self-esteem. The vocabulary becomes unclear and is often used interchangeably. Here are some important related terms:

Self-concept. The constellation of things we use to describe ourselves.

Self-esteem. The evaluation of the information contained in our self-concept.

Self-love. The affection and care we express to ourselves.

Self-efficacy. The confidence to make a difference in a situation.

Self-confidence. The trust, security, and belief we have in ourselves.

Self-acceptance. The respect, dignity, and approval of our personhood.

Self-ideal. The image of the person we would like to be.

Case Description

Ron is fifteen years old. He is withdrawn, and not doing well in school. He grew up in a home where mom and dad held extremely high expectations for him. His father rarely gave compliments—even when Ron used to bring home sterling report cards. Today, Ron cannot remember a single time his dad affirmed him for an accomplishment. He readily admits that he "gave up" school, but he claims that his dad had nothing to do with it. Ron believes he just does not have what it takes to succeed. He feels guilty, not because he sees his behavior as bad; he believes that he, himself, is bad, defective. Ron is also highly sensitive to criticism. Any attempt to correct, encourage, or suggest is heard as a put-down. When asked about his future, he expresses a lack of concern and aloofness. He came to counseling because he thought he was depressed. However, Ron showed few serious signs of depression. He felt frustrated and accepted his situation as fate, believing he could not change. His struggle was with feeling inferior.

One other issue deserves attention before we explore etiology and treatment issues. A great deal of confusion reigns over the biblical view of self-esteem.[7] Charles Ridley has pointed out that true humility, not pride, is the biblical counterpart of positive self-esteem. *Humility* is based upon self-love, not self-negation, and owes its affirmation to God's unconditional regard for humankind. *Pride* is connected with achievement and attempts to take glory due to God for one's self. *False humility*, the counterpart of negative self-esteem, is a reverse form of pride in one's badness.[8]

☑ WHY THE STRUGGLE HAPPENS

Many factors contribute to feelings of inferiority. Many of them relate to parental influences. These "causes" may persist through life to keep self-esteem low unless someone intervenes.

Perfectionistic Expectations

Some parents fall into the trap of having overly high expectations for their children. While no one has ever achieved a state of perfection, these parents believe their children somehow have a chance and they tell them so in no uncertain terms. They permit no error or weakness. They are constantly frustrated, critical, and impatient with their children. These adolescents try harder and harder to be what they are not and eventually learn they will never satisfy mom or dad. They will always be inadequate. This heavy burden alone almost guarantees feelings of inferiority.

Overprotectiveness

Children who are smothered with protection never have a chance to learn to cope for themselves. They never have opportunities to trust their own judgment. They grow up to become timid and afraid of making mistakes. As they struggle to achieve independence they feel vulnerable and become easily hurt and incapable of fending for themselves. They have no track record to construct a sense of confidence, efficacy, and an internal locus of control.

Inconsistency

To establish a sense of well-being, adolescents need consistency from their parents. They need to know what to expect from their mom and dad. Consistency and known limits provide security and structure. If something is permissible one day and the next day they are punished for the same thing, they obviously experience confusion that instills inferiority. When predictability in relationships is missing, the result is insecurity and low self-esteem.

Modeling

Parents who, themselves, suffer from inferiority are often emulated by their children. In addition, they may treat their children with the same lack of respect they feel for themselves. Their children come to believe that not thinking much of themselves is natural. They hear their parents' comments on the way others are always more successful than themselves, so the children believe that they are not meant to succeed.

Physical Influences

Inherited physical characteristics such as physique, appearance, and handicaps also influence developing self-concepts and inferiority. These physical attributes may influence others' perceptions and behavior toward young people. Others may, for example, respond negatively to struggling adolescents' handicapping conditions or physical appearance and thus affect the adolescents' self-esteem. Adolescents who mature later than others are also more likely to be treated like children while most of their peers are progressing more quickly into the adult world. This can invoke low self-esteem as well.

Faulty Thinking

Sometimes adolescents make up self-statements that have little or no basis in reality. With little evidence they conclude, "We're not good-looking enough," "We're not smart enough," "We're not outgoing enough." They live these lies as if they are truth and suffer from inferiority as a result. Unrealistic expectations also develop low self-esteem. Bruce Narramore points to three common expectations that are enemies of self-acceptance: (1) I must meet other people's expectations if I am to be accepted and loved; (2) whenever I fail to reach my goals I need to be punished; and (3) I must master my world.[9] Each of these beliefs is irrational and undermines self-esteem.

Faulty Theology

Some adolescents struggle with low self-esteem because they assume God does not see them as significant. Other sincere Christian young people believe

God wants them to feel inferior. They believe that humility is the same as self-condemnation and that self-love is sinful. While their beliefs may be heartfelt, they are wrong. God does not want us to feel inferior. The Bible continually affirms that human beings are valuable to God and urges us to love ourselves as God loves us.

☑ HOW TO HELP

The following techniques should be thought of as working with and undergirded by personal acceptance and reflective listening. They are designed to create alternatives for adolescents who struggle with feelings of inferiority and allow them to replace dysfunctional behaviors and attitudes with healthful alternatives.

Pinpoint the Severity

At the beginning of treatment it is helpful to assess the intensity of adolescents' feelings of inferiority. The Hare Self-Esteem Scale is a thirty-item instrument that measures self-esteem in young people. Another assessment is the Index of Self-Esteem. This is a twenty-five-item scale designed to measure the degree, severity, or magnitude of adolescent self-esteem. In addition to these measures, it is helpful to assess adolescents' self-efficacy. The Self-Efficacy Scale contains twenty-three items and measures general levels of belief in one's own competence. Each of these instruments may be found in *Helping the Struggling Adolescent: A Counseling Guide*.

Focus on Being Genuine

Adolescents who struggle with inferiority have an internal and highly sensitive radar system for detecting phoniness. Research has shown that these young people respond negatively to expressions of affirmation that are not genuine.[10] Counselors should be cautious about dispensing praise and affirmation that is not warranted and real. According to Gary Collins, it is more helpful to give acceptance, continuing support, gentle encouragement, and mild but sincere approval for achievements that can be clearly evaluated as good.[11] False platitudes not only do nothing to strengthen adolescent self-esteem; they undermine its development.

Explore Their Understanding of Self-Esteem

Many adolescents are confused about how they should feel toward themselves. David Carlson, in his book *Counseling and Self-Esteem*, suggests that counselors ask several questions to identify the situation, people, and circumstances in which this kind of confusion occurs.[12] These questions may be given for homework but are probably more helpful if discussed and clarified during a counseling session.

- How much do I confuse humiliation with humility?

- How much do I confuse putting myself down with putting down my sinful self?
- How much do I confuse self-degradation with self-denial?
- How much do I confuse worthless with unworthy?
- How much do I confuse selfishness with self-love?
- How much do I confuse self-conceit with self-affirmation?
- How much do I confuse self-worship with self-worth?
- How much do I confuse self-absorption with self-awareness?

It is important to keep these questions from making the adolescent feel worse. Their purpose is to help them clarify their understanding of self-esteem.

Localize Inferiority Feelings

It is often useful to look at adolescents' feelings of inferiority in localized areas of their lives. Here is a list of questions to ask yourself as you attempt to discover whether teenagers struggle with pervasive low self-esteem or only primarily in certain areas.

- *Social:* How do they feel about themselves as friends of others? Do they possess social skills that are needed to achieve relationships? Are they satisfied with the quantity and quality of their peer relationships?
- *Academic:* Do they feel good enough? Are they satisfied with their academic performance? Do they set reasonable standards for their performance so that they regularly experience success?
- *Body Image:* Are they satisfied with their appearance? Do peers accept their physical appearance and abilities?
- *Pervasive:* Do they approach new situations with confidence? Do they generally avoid self-critical statements?

Low self-esteem arises from a discrepancy between the perceived self and the real self in each of these areas. It obviously saves time to zero in on a particular area if it is the one causing most of the frustration.

Help Set Reachable Personal Goals

Adolescents need to decide for themselves how they want to be different. I ask nearly all of my clients, young and old, "If you could press a magic button, how would your life be different?" This can help them to think about their goals and what they are doing to achieve them. For the young person struggling with feelings of inferiority, an exercise may be used to help them set into operation some of the behavior and attitudes they would like to change. Ask them to make a list under the heading, "Things I get down on myself about." Once they have the list, ask them to identify their level of willingness to change each behavior according to a five-point scale:

1. "I am not ready to change this yet."
2. "I am confused about what I want to do about this."
3. "I want to work on this in the future."

4. "I am working on this one step at a time."
5. "I am working hard to change this."

Next, ask them to lift out those behavior patterns they want to change most and discuss strategies for implementing ways to improve. Help them begin to take incremental steps toward reaching their goals. For example, a teenager who has an academic C average might say, "One thing I get down on myself about is thinking I'm not smart enough." The youth may want to set a goal of getting all A's next term. Of course, this is probably going to lead to disappointment, frustration, and a deeper sense of inferiority. The teen needs incremental subgoals that are achievable to carry one toward one's larger objectives.

A beginning goal for this student might be to separate the academic record from one's value as a person—or even one's intelligence. Another might be to complete homework before watching TV. The point is to allow clients to think creatively about ways they can become the persons they want to be. Working out their goals with counselors helps them be realistic and keeps them accountable to reaching their objectives.[13]

Teach Problem Solving

For adolescents who have grown up in homes where they have been smothered with overprotection, problem solving is an essential intervention. While it may seem ridiculously basic, this process should not be made light of. These are fundamental skills that overly protected adolescents have never learned. The process is broken down into several steps in the following sequence. I will illustrate the process with Jackie, a fifteen-year-old.

1. *Recognize a problem exists.* Jackie feels uncomfortable in a group of her friends. This is her cue that she has a problem to solve.
2. *Stop and think.* Jackie should take no further action until she identifies the problem and decides what to do. After thinking about it, she realizes that she feels she is being made fun of.
3. *Decide on a goal.* Jackie decides she wants her friends to stop teasing her.
4. *Generate possible solutions.* She now considers a number of possibilities without evaluating them. She allows herself to be farfetched and creative. She could tell them to stop. She could leave. She could tease them. She could tell them how it makes her feel. She could laugh it off.
5. *Consider consequences.* Jackie then thinks about the consequences of each of these actions. If she tells them to stop they will probably do it all the more, and so on.
6. *Choose a solution.* She decides that the best choice is a combination of two solutions. She decides to laugh it off and then tell them in private how it makes her feel. She considers this alternative to have the best consequences for her present situation and her future relationships with them.

7. *Implement the solution.* Jackie deflects her discomfort by not taking the teasing seriously and shrugs her shoulders. She decides to meet one of her friends after school to tell her how the teasing makes her feel, and she will talk with the other one on the phone that night. She won't try to punish them (that would have negative consequences), only to let them know how she feels.

It is helpful to practice these seven steps of problem solving in a counseling session. Counselors provide guidance as necessary but allow the clients to do most of the work. Young people who learn systematic problem-solving strategies tend to cope more effectively with stress and frustration. Their competence is heightened and their increasing autonomy becomes a source of healthful self-efficacy and positive self-esteen.[14]

Develop Positive Self-Statements

It is important to determine whether young people use private speech to construct negative self-images. One way of doing this is to ask teenagers to describe in an open-ended way what they are like. Note the kinds of descriptors used. Then ask what they are like in school, in sports, and with other kids. If you determine that adolescents are undermining their self-esteem through negative self-statements, the following exercise will prove helpful.

First explain the concept of self-talk (how we all carry a mental tape player that goes on automatically). Give some examples ("I'm stupid," "I could never ask a girl out"). Second, help them identify their self-statements. One of the easiest ways to do this is to read the following phrases to them and note how they complete the sentences. Encourage them to answer spontaneously with the first thing that pops into their head.

- When I make a mistake I think to myself . . .
- When I look in the mirror I think . . .
- When my parents yell at me I say to myself . . .
- Everybody should . . .
- When I don't succeed at something I am trying I think . . .
- When I get a bad grade I think . . .

Record their answers as they respond. Go back over their responses with them and ask whether they find themselves sending these messages. Try to establish which ones are most automatic and habitual. Next, work on arguing away negative self-statements with positive alternatives. It is important to let adolescents come up with alternatives for themselves. Talk about situations that are likely to elicit self-statements and how they can substitute their new ones. Have them imagine being in specific situations and experiencing their old self-statements and arguing them away. You may suggest that for a week they keep a log of their self-statements. This process may be slow, but it may also be very powerful and rewarding.

Modify Unrealistic Standards

When adolescents experience success or failure, they are measuring their performance against inner standards. Sometimes these standards are explicit and conscious, while some are less clear-cut and do not even enter awareness. When this happens, the potential for dissatisfaction and self-condemnation increases. Help your clients become aware of their standards by asking about times they have been successful and times they have failed. Ask to what extent they feel they can modify their goals and standards so that they are more or less strict than they are. Use concrete examples provided by the clients, and discuss whether their standards are reasonable or unrealistic. Now present the steps involved in modifying standards.[15]

1. Make concrete, explicit statements about what equals a success and what equals a failure in a particular experience. Is there a middle ground?
2. How often does your performance fall into each of these categories?
3. Decide whether you are feeling as though you fail more than you need to. In other words, are you feeling bad about yourself too often?
4. If you are feeling bad too often, think about ways you could modify your standards. Could you lower your standard for success? Could you lower your standard for failure? Could you do both and make your middle ground larger?
5. Examine your self-statement after performances that fall into success, middle ground, or failure categories. Your thoughts should be helping you feel good about success, neutral about middle ground, and disappointed but not destroyed about failure.

Use these steps to work through several standards in major areas of adolescents' lives. The point is to help them establish standards at a level that brings them fulfillment.

Confront Destructive Tendencies

Maurice Wagner, in his helpful book *The Sensation of Being Somebody*, notes that the person with an inadequate self-concept usually has destructive tendencies that serve only to advance and nurture low self-esteem. These include the tendency to treat people as objects, to give up when proved wrong, to become angry if not in control of situations, to be unwilling to act when afraid, to dread problems instead of accepting them as challenges.[16] When young people exhibit destructive tendences like these, counselors should hold a figurative mirror up to help them objectively see the destruction they create. Counselors may begin by asking teenagers what benefits they receive from these tendencies.

Explore Their Theology

Young people who struggle with low self-esteem and are sensitive to biblical values may have distorted theological views. Little work can be done if teenagers believe that inferiority is the same as humility and that self-esteem is equivalent to sinful pride. They must be helped—gently—to see the biblical teachings about human worth and self-esteem. They must be reminded that they are made in the image of God and that self-condemnation is both destructive and wrong in the sight of God. While this information may take a while to sink in, they must shed their faulty theology before true work can be accomplished in developing a healthful self-esteem. You may find the section on guilt helpful in working with young people who see self-condemnation as a mark of true spirituality.

☑ WHEN TO REFER

Counselors should remember that self-esteem often takes time to grow. Still, refer adolescents who struggle with feelings of inferiority to other competent counselors or psychologists when, over time, they feel more inadequate or if they begin to appear depressed, hopeless, or suicidal. Refer them if you recognize that you are encouraging dependence in already insecure and dependent adolescents.

Where To Go for Additional Help

Bednar, R. L., M. G. Wells, and S. R. Peterson. *Self-Esteem: Paradoxes and Innovations in Clinical Theory and Practice.* Washington, D.C.: American Psychological Association, 1989.

Carlson, D. E. *Counseling and Self-Esteem.* Vol. 13, *Resources for Christian Counseling.* Waco, Tex.: Word, 1988.

Clarke, J. I. *Self-Esteem: A Family Affair.* Minneapolis: Winston, 1978.

McAllister, D., and R. S. McGee. *The Search for Significance: Youth Edition.* Dallas: Word, 1990.

McKay, M., and P. Fanning. *Self-Esteem.* New York: St. Martin's Press, 1987.

Narramore, S. B. *You're Someone Special.* Grand Rapids: Zondervan, 1978.

Osborne, C. G. *The Art of Learning To Love Yourself.* Grand Rapids, Zondervan, 1976.

————. *Self-Esteem: Overcoming Inferiority Feelings.* Nashville: Abingdon, 1986.

Pope, A. W., S. M. McHale, and W. E. Craignead. *Self-Esteem Enhancement with Children and Adolescents.* New York: Pergamon, 1988.

Wagner, M. E. *The Sensation of Being Somebody: Building an Adequate Self-Concept.* Grand Rapids: Zondervan, 1975.

The Alliance for Invitational Education (Room 216, Curry Building, University of North Carolina, Greensboro, NC 27412) publishes a comprehensive newsletter on self-esteem and sponsors one national conference and several regional conferences yearly.

The Center for Self-Esteem (P.O. Box 1532, Santa Cruz, CA 95060; 408/426-6850) sponsors an annual conference, publishes a free newsletter, and distributes curricula, books, and tapes.

Notes

1. Maltz, M. *Psychocybernetics* (New York: Essandes, 1968).

2. D. L. Yanish and J. Battle, "Relationship Between Self-Esteem, Depression and Alcohol Consumption Among Adolescents," *Psychological Reports* 57 (1985): 331–34.

3. F. P. Rice, *The Adolescent: Development, Relationships and Culture*, 6th ed. (Boston: Allyn and Bacon, 1990).

4. L. Y. Abramson, M. E. P. Seligman, and J. D. Teasdale, "Learned Helplessness in Humans: Critique and Reformulation," *Journal of Abnormal Psychology* 87 (1978): 49–74.

5. S. H. Shelton, "Developing the Construct of General Self-Efficacy," *Psychological Reports* 66 (1990): 987–94.

6. G. Domino, and E. Blumberg, "An Application of Gough's Conceptual Model to a Measure of Adolescent Self-Esteem," *Journal of Youth and Adolescence* 16 (1987): 87–90.

7. Several passages of Scripture are helpful in delineating the biblical principles involved in self-esteem: Mark 12:31; Romans 12:3; Ephesians 5:1–2.

8. C. Ridley, "Self-Esteem," in *Dictionary of Pastoral Care and Counseling*, ed. R. J. Hunter (Nashville: Abingdon, 1990).

9. S. B. Narramore, *You're Someone Special* (Grand Rapids: Zondervan, 1978).

10. R. M. Baron, "Social Reinforcement Effects as a Function of Social Reinforcement History," *Psychological Review* 6 (1966): 529–39.

11. G. Collins, *Christian Counseling: A Comprehensive Guide* (Waco, Tex.: Word, 1980).

12. D. E. Carlson, *Counseling and Self-Esteem*. Vol. 13, *Resources for Christian Counseling* (Waco, Tex.: Word, 1988).

13. A helpful resource for parents wanting to instill the principle of goal setting in their children is a book by Lanson Ross, *A Kid's Goal-Setting Guide* (Wheaton: Tyndale, 1985).

14. A. W. Pope, S. M. McHale, and W. E. Craignead, *Self-Esteem Enhancement with Children and Adolescents* (New York: Pergamon, 1988).

15. Ibid.

16. M. E. Wagner, *The Sensation of Being Somebody: Building an Adequate Self-Concept* (Grand Rapids: Zondervan, 1975).

LONELINESS

☑ WHAT THE STRUGGLE LOOKS LIKE

Feeling alone and neglected is becoming an emotional epidemic in America. Loneliness—the painful awareness that we are not meaningfully connected with others—floods the lives of millions. It is one of "the most universal sources of human suffering."[1] It knows no boundary of class, race, or age. One hit song of the Beatles asked this question: "All the lonely people, where do they all come from?" Many of them come from adolescence! Loneliness strikes everyone from time to time, but especially adolescents.

While experts consider loneliness a serious personal problem for at least ten percent of the general adult population,[2] large-scale studies have found that fifteen to twenty percent of all adolescents experience painful levels of loneliness.[3] A study that explores the severity of loneliness in all age groups shows that the loneliest people proved to be low-income, single, adolescent mothers. Alcoholics were next, followed by freshman college students and rural high school seniors.[4]

It should be no surprise that a large proportion of teenagers feel lonely. Their attempts at social connectedness are riddled with fear of rejection. Tony Campolo paints a vivid scene of the adolescent in a new group:

> At first he simply observes, attempting not to reveal any of his own thoughts or feelings. He plays it cool, trying to communicate an air of detachment. Because he is careful not to respond with either enthusiasm or contempt to what the other members of the group are doing, his face may appear almost emotionless. He plays it cool to allow himself time to figure out what the members of the group expect him to be. Once he has the feel of the group he will gradually begin to behave in ways which he believes will earn him approval and acceptance.[5]

If an adolescent doesn't earn approval and acceptance, the trap of loneliness is sprung. Without the tools described in this section adolescents are almost certain to be snared by loneliness—in and out of the church. According to Campolo, a strong probability exists that lonely young people will never return to a church gathering if they do not gain quick acceptance. On the other

Case Description

Peter is fourteen, has red hair, and is a bit overweight. He was an only child until four years ago when his sister was born. His dad is a stock broker and his mom works in sales. They moved to a new city a few months ago, and Peter has never felt lonelier. In a counseling session he says, "I've been alone most of my life, so this is nothing new. I come home from school and stay all alone until around six o'clock when mom or dad come home from work. I watch TV but it gets pretty boring. Maybe I'll be friends with my sister when she's older." His mother encourages him to meet friends, but Peter believes friendships "should just happen." He spends a lot of time sitting around listening to music with a Walkman.

hand, rejection by the "in" group at school can result in the wounded teen being tremendously dedicated to the church that offers acceptance. "The church has always attracted society's losers," says Campolo, "because they can feel like winners within its fellowship."[6]

When young people come to a gathering and sit back detached and emotionless, you can be sure they are not feeling secure. That kind of adolescent is what some call a "jellyfish in armor." They come because they want to be accepted by the group and to gain popularity in their eyes. But the needed warmth is not yet available.

It is difficult to overestimate the impact of having no one to sit with on the school-sponsored bus trip, or eating alone in the cafeteria, or staying at home on another dateless Friday evening. Loneliness is painful. Remember the haunting words of the popular song "At Seventeen"? For the struggling adolescent, loneliness is waiting for what appears will never come.

The feeling of being alone and neglected, however, need not isolate struggling adolescents in a shadowy corner. They may be helped to move beyond its desolate darkness.

Before exploring the causes and cures of loneliness, let's make sure we understand its dimensions. One research team has identified five "Cs" to define the different parts of loneliness. They are seen when the lonely adolescent is feeling a lack of (1) *congruence*—feeling out of touch with parts of the self, (2) *companionship*—the perception of self as separate from another, (3) *community*—the feeling of being ostracized by others, (4) *custom*—the feeling of separation from others because of cultural change, and (5) *communion*—the feeling of separation or alienation from God.[7] Others have identified these same dimensions in different terms: psychological, interpersonal, social, cultural, and cosmic.[8]

☑ WHY THE STRUGGLE HAPPENS

Growing up has never been easy. The road to maturity is treacherous. Maybe kids today are no more lonely than kids of a hundred years ago, but the reasons for adolescent loneliness have certainly changed.

The Spirit of Our Age

Shortly after World War II Paul Tournier wrote, "Loneliness results from the spirit of our age."[9] Today's experts agree. The push toward efficiency and convenience in our high-tech age has driven many to feel smaller and less needed. Today's adolescents do not have so much rootedness. The widespread mobility of our society tears up friendships and separates families. Even the possibility of moving may keep some adolescents from forming close friendships. Urbanization has led to a fear of strangers. Portable music headphones, hand-held video games, and, of course, television may separate us from others. It seems that many adolescents interact more with screens than people. The list could continue. The point is that our society has lost many of the traditional sources of relationships that helped adolescents of earlier generations avoid the pain of loneliness.

Developmental Separation from Parents

During adolescence the relationship to parents is realigned. Young people are trying to grow out of childish ways of relating. A lapse into teens' previous mode of dependency may surprise parents who are adjusting to the new independence. Since parents often do not perceive their faltering teenagers as "dependent children," the latter may experience psychological isolation.[10] They are forced to mourn the loss of their identity as children and give up certain childhood beliefs and attachments. The role of parents in this turbulent separation is critical. Parental responses vary from the most helpful—supportive understanding to the most destructive—premature withdrawal from the children or attempts to undermine the separation by prolonging preadolescent attachments.[11] Inevitably the progressive change in this important attachment/detachment process will be heavily invested with loneliness.

Emotional Maturation

"I want to feel the heat with somebody." Those are the words of a pop hit song by Whitney Houston, and they express the white-hot need for relatedness of the maturing adolescent. The capacity and desire for intense intimacy develops rapidly during the teen years. Such changes bring about strong needs for new emotional connectedness. Couple this with high expectations for dating activity and social popularity, and young people are bound to face deficits in desired levels of tender attachments.

Desire for Autonomy

Adolescents strive for independence in every area of life. They want autonomy in their behavior, their morals, their religion, and their ideas. To achieve this, of course, means they must depend on their own reserves. Each one must become his or her primary decision-maker. This kind of responsibility is frightening and risky. "Every time we grow more autonomous, create our own thoughts, assert our own identity," writes one expert, "we risk moving away from others and therefore risk loneliness."[12] For this reason some degree of loneliness in adolescence must be expected.

Social Comparison

Adolescents have an internal yardstick to measure how well they stack up against everyone else. Their comparisons are bound to magnify feelings of failure and rejection. They will perceive others as more popular, more successful, and less lonely. Some adolescents may even compare their experience with the imagined glamour of young musicians, media stars, and sports figures. Such unrealistic comparisons can easily drive struggling adolescents to overestimate their feelings of aloneness and neglect.

Poor Relations with Parents

Lonely adolescents often report negative relationships with parents. They don't feel supported. Mom and dad seem to instill no vision or purpose in their future. Parents may label their teenagers as failures or simply show no interest or provide no nurture. Parents may also pressure their adolescents into membership in peer groups that do not offer them acceptance. In this case they not only do not fit in with a particular peer group, but alienation in the home also results due to failure in living up to the parents' goals.[13]

Striving for Significance

Adolescents experience a "quiet joy" when they use their newly emerging abilities for the first time.[14] Whether in the classroom, on the ball field, or on an auditorium stage, adolescents are yearning for a place to show their importance and significance. According to Rollo May, adolescents who do not find a way to demonstrate significance typically fall into boredom, aimlessness, meaningless-ness, and eventually loneliness. Without the freedom to participate in activities that allow for a demonstration of significance, adolescents will stumble into the dark pit of social isolation and loneliness.

☑ HOW TO HELP

Only in the last decade or so has loneliness been described as a unique clinical problem. Traditionally it has been viewed as a small component of a more encompassing struggle like depression or anxiety.[15] Perhaps this is why until recently no approaches to treat loneliness in adolescents had been published. While loneliness in adolescents was studied in the 1980s, it is a struggle that requires further therapeutic attention in the 1990s.[16] The following techniques are the strongest ammunition we have to combat this problem and help young people who feel painfully alone.

Pinpoint the Severity

Adolescents experience different degrees of loneliness. Identifying whether the feeling is transient or chronic will guide your treatment strategy. This can be done by administering an assessment to a client on two or three different occasions. One of the most helpful and widely used measures of loneliness is the Revised UCLA Loneliness Scale (RULS). It is a twenty-item scale designed to measure loneliness in adolescents and other populations. The measure is located in *Helping the Struggling Adolescent: A Counseling Guide*.

Affirm Their Courage and Explore the Causes

When adolescents admit to feeling lonely, you can be pretty sure they are serious about wanting help. In our society confessing loneliness is tantamount to admitting to being a misfit. Affirm them for the courage it takes to talk about this problem and comfort them by letting them know they have a lot of company—almost everyone feels lonely from time to time. Knowing they are not "freaks" can alleviate much discomfort. Also help them consider the variety of reasons they are suffering from loneliness. This allows you to work on the sources, not just the symptoms of the struggle. You may choose to refer to the causes of loneliness outlined earlier in this section.

Loneliness is one of the few struggles discussed here that begins to be alleviated simply by talking about it. Once you affirm adolescents' courage, they will feel empowered by the realization that they are doing something to overcome loneliness.

Accept the Process

Young people who struggle with loneliness often feel that it is a permanent condition—as unending as an Arctic winter. But unlike depression and other struggles, recovery from loneliness is not always long and tedious. Loneliness may melt away quickly, almost instantly, when a new relationship emerges. However, for long-lasting results that build a strong hedge against feelings of loneliness in the future, a process must begin that leads to a celebration of solitude. The journey, as we shall see next, begins with helping adolescents see activity and intimacy as premature solutions.

Avoid the Myth of Activity as a Premature Solution

Almost a half-century ago David Reisman wrote a groundbreaking book, *The Lonely Crowd*, to tell us how isolated people feel even though constantly surrounded by others.[17] Since then popular magazines and best-selling books have been filled with writings lamenting our inability to be with others. They have suggested dozens of active remedies: join a club, be positive, become assertive, win friends, travel, listen to music, watch television, take up a hobby, volunteer, and so forth.

The perception of activity is misleading, however, if the heart of loneliness is not understood. Adolescents are not lonely because they lack activity and distractions. Most of them lead hectic lives in crowded schools. Adolescents are lonely, not because they are isolated from others, but because *they are alienated from themselves*. They need to make friends with solitude and embrace their sense of self. Only then will the counsel to become active prove to be genuinely helpful.

Avoid the Myth of Intimacy as a Premature Solution

Some years ago a song of Barbra Streisand's soared to the top of the charts. Its words, "People who need people are the luckiest people in the world," seemed to touch a nerve. The song made us feel good because *all* of us need people. Actually, the most fortunate people are those who need people for healthy reasons—to love and be loved in return. Some adolescents need people, however, to avoid being alone and to avoid facing themselves. Becky, a student who came for counseling, was like that. She saw the quest for intimacy as an antidote to her loneliness. She believed she could escape isolation if she could just find the right guy. She sought romance to avoid intimacy with herself.

Thomas Merton says that the person "who fears to be alone will never be anything but lonely."[18] A counselor can help lonely adolescents study their drive for intimacy, which is not an escape from loneliness. Nor is intimacy a prize package that young people can hope to find or work hard enough to deserve. Intimacy is an attitude and a way of being that comes only from embracing the anxiety of being alone and working on the most basic of relationships—the one on which all others build—the one an adolescent has with his or her self.

Encourage Healthful Solitude

I learned to celebrate solitude as a junior in college. The lesson, however, didn't come from a textbook. I enrolled in a wilderness course in the Cascade Mountains of Canada. The trip was designed to help me to go beyond myself physically, mentally, and spiritually. Toward the end of the course each of us was given the challenge to go solo. Isolated on a mountainside I did not see another face or hear another voice for more than twenty-four hours. My task was to meditate, evaluate, reflect, delight in my existence, and write in my diary. The lesson behind this solo venture was to teach me I could grow from such solitude. And I did.

Adolescents don't need to be in the wilderness to learn the pleasure of solitude. It may be found in an empty football stadium or a corner of the library. Solitude presents adolescents with opportunities to take stock, pray, and simply feel the calm of quietness soak in. These are the times that help us get in tune with our deepest and most important feelings. Encourage teens in these circumstances to keep journals to process their experience. Lonely adolescents at home on a Friday evening may be empowered by understanding that being alone and feeling alone are two very different experiences. Being alone is marked by introspection and renewal. Feeling alone is marked by self-pity and feelings of abandonment. The difference is not found in circumstances but in attitude.

Dispute Irrational Thinking

Irrational beliefs and faulty perceptions may ignite like high-octane fuel in the otherwise quiet engine of loneliness. Struggling adolescents need to clean out their unrealistic self-talk. Fortunately, most adolescents catch on quickly with disputation—it requires the same skills they have mastered while arguing with others. A good disputation is built on four legs: (1) evidence, (2) alternatives, (3) implication, and (4) usefulness.

If a lonely adolescent says, for example, "I eat by myself in the cafeteria because nobody is interested in me," the first question to ask is "What *evidence* do you have for this belief? Show me the evidence that *nobody* is interested." This usually helps the young person see the absurdity of the overreaction. Next, examine the *alternatives*. Ask, "Can you think of any less destructive way to look at eating alone in the cafeteria?" This helps adolescents avoid latching onto the most dire possible belief and to generate alternative explanations (e.g., "I never invite others to sit with me"). What if the negative beliefs adolescents hold are true? Even if the beliefs are correct some relief may be found in unearthing the *implications*. Does the predicament imply that these teens are any less intelligent than others? Does it imply that the situation can't be changed?

The final leg that will support a platform of more rational thinking is found in questioning the *usefulness* of the belief. Perhaps believing that others should naturally eat with you without being invited is not serving a good purpose. It is like a technician doing bomb demolition and thinking, "This could go off and I might be killed." The belief itself serves no purpose. It causes his hands to shake and so on. Through roleplaying and in-session practice lonely adolescents may learn to use these strategies on their own to dispute their irrational thinking and unfounded self-accusations. Help them examine the evidence, alternatives, and usefulness of their irrational thoughts.[19]

Encourage Social Risks

We are designed for community with God and others. Relationships are the foundation of any solutions leading to an escape from loneliness. If adolescents can avoid the compulsion to seek activity and intimacy as hasty solutions, and if they recognize that embracing solitude is the first step toward escaping the dark days of loneliness, and if they are equipped with the tools of disputation, then they are ready to consciously seek healthful activity and genuine intimacy by learning to take social risks.

Reaching out to others is essential if they are to overcome the feeling of being alone and neglected. Research has shown that about forty percent of people suffering from loneliness never talk about it.[20] With patience and encouragement, however, the tight lid of hesitation can be loosened and a lonely adolescent may learn to muster up the courage to take social risks and venture into new relationships. If appropriate to instill optimism, you may briefly disclose an uplifting example from your own experience. Ask them to think of those to whom they can reach out and in what ways. A sense of accountability to counselors may motivate them to smile and say "Hi" to interesting-looking people. It may give them the impetus to compliment the appearance of someone they find attractive. Assign them to ask acquaintances to go to McDonald's. Genuine relationships often begin over a bite to eat. Companions originally were people who shared bread together.

Do not hesitate to encourage lonely adolescents to take social risks and then affirm them for their effort. Suggesting social risks is commonsense counsel found in maxims like "I went out to find a friend but could not find one there. I went out to *be* a friend, and friends were everywhere!" Proverbs 18:24 (KJV) says, "A man that hath friends must show himself friendly." The phone company puts it this way: "Reach out and touch someone." Regardless of the phrasing the point is that loneliness does not have to paralyze a teenager.

Consider Faith Issues

If it can be done with sensitivity, exploring the adolescents' spiritual well-being is helpful in fighting loneliness. For adolescents with sincere faith, a reminder that God is very real and present instills strength and comfort. Loneliness is rarely discussed in Scripture, but it is seen repeatedly in the lives of numerous Bible characters. David, Moses, Job, Elijah, Paul, and Jesus all struggled with moments of loneliness.

Consider Shyness and Inferiority

If you suspect that self-consciousness, poor social skills, and shyness are at the root of counselees' loneliness, you will want to study the section in this book on shyness and the chapter on inferiority and incorporate their tools into your treatment strategy.

☑ WHEN TO REFER

Refer lonely adolescents to psychologically astute counselors when, over time, counselees feel more lonely. If they are showing signs of hopelessness, I recommend serious consultation and consideration of referral because hopelessness may indicate thoughts of suicide. With compassion confront adolescents (and possibly refer them) when you recognize that they are using your counseling sessions as their main relationship. In other words, if you suspect that lonely adolescents are not progressing rapidly because they do not want to terminate their counseling sessions for reasons of personal attraction to you, delicately confront the issue and consider referral. Of course the reverse may be true. If you find yourself facilitating adolescents' experience to find solace from loneliness only in you, you must refer.

Where To Go for Additional Help

Durham, C. *When You're Feeling Lonely: Finding a Way Out*. Downers Grove, Ill.: InterVarsity Press, 1984.

Ellison, C. W. *Loneliness: The Search for Intimacy*. Chappaqua, N.Y.: Christian Herald
    Books, 1980.
Gaev, D. M. *The Psychology of Loneliness*. Chicago: Adams Press, 1976.
Gordon, S. *Lonely in America: A Portrait of America—Young, Old, Married, Single, in
    Groups and Alone*. New York: Simon & Schuster, 1976.
Parrott, L. *CareNote: Feeling Alone*. Saint Meinrad, Ind.: Abbey Press, 1993.
Peplau, L. A., and D. Perlman. *Loneliness: A Sourcebook of Current Theory, Research and
    Therapy*. New York: Wiley, 1982.
Tournier, P. *Escape from Loneliness*. Philadelphia: Westminster, 1962.

Notes

1. H. Nouwen, *Reaching Out* (Garden City, N.Y.: Doubleday, 1975).
2. M. E. Bragg, "A Comparative Study of Loneliness and Depression" (Ph.D. diss.,
UCLA, 1979), *Dissertation Abstracts International* 39 (1979): 79/13710.
3. E. Ostrov and D. Offer, "Loneliness and the Adolescent," in *Adolescent Psychology*, ed.
S. Feinstein (Chicago: Univ. of Chicago Press, 1978).
4. N. Medora and J. C. Woodward, "Loneliness Among Adolescent College Students at a
Midwestern University," *Adolescence* 21, no. 82 (1986): 391–402.
5. T. Campolo, *The Success Fantasy* (Wheaton, Ill.: Victor, 1980).
6. Ibid.
7. L. J. Richmond and E. D. Picken, "A Model for Working with Lonely Clients: Sadler
Revisited," in *Loneliness: A Sourcebook of Current Theory, Research and Therapy*, ed. S. M. Natale
(New York: Wiley, 1986), 351–78.
8. W. A. Sadler, Jr., "Dimensions in the Problem of Loneliness: A Phenomenological
Approach," *Journal of Phenomenological Psychology* 9 (1978): 1–2.
9. P. Tournier, *Escape from Loneliness* (Philadelphia: Westminster, 1962).
10. R. S. Weiss, *Loneliness: The Experience of Emotional and Social Isolation* (Cambridge,
Mass.: MIT Press, 1973).
11. H. Stierlin, *Separating Parents and Adolescents* (New York: Norton, 1973).
12. Ostrov and Offer, "Loneliness and the Adolescent," 34.
13. S. M. Natale, *Loneliness and Spiritual Growth* (Birmingham, Ala.: Religious Education
Press, 1986).
14. R. May, *Man's Search for Himself* (New York: Delta Books, 1953).
15. D. Russell, L. A. Peplau, and L. H. Gerstein, "The Revised UCLA Loneliness Scale:
Concurrent and Discriminant Validity Evidence," *Journal of Personality and Social Psychology* 39,
no. 3 (1980): 472–80.
16. B. T. McWhirter, "Loneliness: A Review of Current Literature, with Implications for
Counseling and Research," *Journal of Counseling and Development* 68 (1990): 417–22.
17. D. Reisman, *The Lonely Crowd* (New Haven: Yale Univ. Press, 1961).
18. T. Merton, *Thoughts in Solitude* (New York: Doubleday, 1968).
19. D. Meichenbaum, *Cognitive Behavior Modification: An Integrative Approach* (New York:
Plenum, 1977). This book will give you a detailed strategy for using disputation and other cognitive
interventions.
20. C. A. Anderson, L. J. Horowitz, and R. French, "Attributional Style of Lonely and
Depressed People," *Journal of Personality and Social Psychology* 45, no. 1 (1983): 127–36.

MASTURBATION

☑ WHAT THE STRUGGLE LOOKS LIKE

"[Masturbation] is one of the most frequently discussed, most roughly condemned and most universally practiced forms of sexual behavior."[1] From ancient times to the present, no sexual practice seems to have been more controversial than masturbation—"the sexual self-pleasuring that involves some form of direct physical stimulation."[2]

In the 1800s abstinence from this kind of "self-abuse" was lauded as crucial to health. The Rev. Sylvester Graham, the promoter of Graham Crackers, wrote *Lecture to Young Men* in which he beseeched them to abstain from masturbation to avoid a reduction in health-reserving "vital fluids" and to avoid moral and physical degeneracy. John Harvey Kellogg, M.D., carried Graham's work further and developed the corn flake as an antimasturbation food and extinguisher of sexual desire.[3]

In a 1918 *Encyclopedia of Health and Home*, one could find diagnostic criteria for the adolescent "addicted to the habit":

> He is timid and bashful, the face is apt to be pale, while the eyes look dull and languid, a general slowness of growth, nervousness and unsteadiness of the hands, loss of memory, an inability to study or stupidity, he cannot look anyone steadily in the face, but will drop the eyes as if guilty of something mean. Few ever know how many of the unfortunate inmates of our lunatic asylums have been sent there by this dreadful vice.[4]

Contemporary views reflect conflicting beliefs about masturbation, even within the church. The most frequently cited arguments against masturbation, according to *Baker Encyclopedia of Psychology*, are these:

1. Only the immature person masturbates.
2. It is condemned in Scripture.[5]
3. Masturbation is unsocial or antisocial.
4. It violates the divinely intended purpose of sex.
5. It causes fatigue and physical debilitation.
6. It is a manifestation of low self-control.

Case Description

Tim came to counseling because he was troubled by his "thoughts." It wasn't until the third session that he confessed his real struggle, which was with masturbation. Tim was a junior in high school. He dated occasionally but had no steady girl friend. He was not exactly the studious or the athletic type. He enjoyed carpentry. Tim, however, was finding that he could not even concentrate on his work because he was bombarded with thoughts about sex. Once a sexual image came into his mind he could not function until he found relief through masturbation. Tim masturbated as much as two or three times a day. He felt tremendous guilt and was convinced he was terribly abnormal.

7. The fantasies associated with masturbation are emotionally unhealthy.
8. It is sexually frustrating and not as satisfying as sex relations with a marital partner.
9. It is an indication of selfishness.
10. It leads to undesirable feelings like guilt and anxiety.

Many experts see these arguments as being oversimplified and even false.[6] Still, the debate of whether masturbation is right or wrong is not settled. Ethical judgments about masturbation run all the way from viewing it as a sin more serious than fornication, adultery, or rape to placing it in the same category as head scratching.[7] Regardless of one's position on the subject,[8] it cannot be argued that masturbation among adolescents is rare.

More than ninety percent of males and fifty percent of females have masturbated to orgasm at some point in their lives. The average age for beginning to masturbate is thirteen for boys and fourteen for girls. However, some research reports that women tend to learn about masturbation over the entire life cycle. In contrast, the onset of masturbation for men appears to be an adolescent phenomenon, with eighty percent of males masturbating by about age fifteen.[9]

Not only do more young men masturbate earlier, they masturbate more frequently. A study done on college youth reports that the frequency of masturbation for men is about once per week and about once per month for women.[10]

Anyone who writes or speaks about masturbation is open to criticism. In the absence of clear biblical guidance on this issue, we are left with a variety of conflicting opinions. Most agree, however, that effective counseling may be extremely useful for adolescents struggling with masturbation.

☑ WHY THE STRUGGLE HAPPENS

While they may not be conscious of many of their motivations, adolescents masturbate for a variety of reasons. Here are some of the most widely cited.

Arousal and Orgasm

This is perhaps the most obvious reason. Adolescents enjoy masturbation. In one study, college women reported that experiencing pleasurable sensations and physical release of sexual tension were their primary motives for masturbation.[11]

Physically Ready

In adolescence, hormones increase the erogenous sensitivity of the maturing sex organs in preparation for procreation. Near the end of puberty the young are reproductively mature, with all the drives toward sexuality and sexual behavior of adults. They are physically ready to enjoy arousal and orgasm. To expect them not to have these experiences would be like expecting a family in a house with new plumbing not to open up the faucets for a few years.

Environmental Stimulation

Adolescents today live in a sex-saturated society that emphasizes immediate sexual gratification. Films, magazines, television programs, and advertisements are blatantly designed to arouse sexual urges and desires. The environment is sexually supercharged, and masturbation is a means to cope with this environmental stimulation.

Self-Exploration

Secular sex educator Eleanor Hamilton recommends masturbation to adolescents as a way of becoming "pleasantly at home with their own sexual organs."[12] Teenagers learn about their personal sexual responses through masturbation. The practice teaches them about their capacity to control their sexual urges; however, masturbation may also be misused and result in lower control of sexual desires. Adolescent boys are almost instantly at the peak level of arousal, a stimulation akin to driving a turbo-charged five-speed Porsche for the first time. Masturbation has the potential to teach an adolescent how to control unbridled sexual desires.

Escape

Masturbation may sometimes be a way to escape boredom, relieve tension, or temporarily avoid pressures of life. At least one-fourth of those people who masturbate do so when suffering from loneliness or rejection. Some adolescents, however, may use masturbation to their detriment, as a means of escape into fantasy and avoidance of meaningful interpersonal relationships.

☑ HOW TO HELP

The following techniques should be undergirded by personal acceptance and reflective listening.

Pinpoint the Severity

A common concern about masturbation is "doing it too much." Even in writings where masturbation is said to be "normal," masturbation "to excess" is often presented as a problem. The question that naturally follows is what "excessive" means. Once a year, twice a week, after every meal? If adolescents masturbate so much that it interferes with certain aspects of their lives, there would be cause for concern. However, in that case masturbation would be a manifestation of the problem rather than the problem itself. For example, adolescents who experience intense emotional anxiety because of conflicts with parents may masturbate as an attempt to escape and release the anxiety. Assess the intensity of the adolescents' struggle with masturbation by asking them directly how often they masturbate.

Listen with Sensitivity

This, of course, should underlie all intervention strategies, but it is sometimes forgotten when counseling adolescents on sexual issues. This means undergirding your sessions with the skills discussed in Part One of this book, but it also means avoiding particular pitfalls. Avoid expressing embarrassment, shock, or excessive curiosity. Monitor your discomfort with the issue to insure calm acceptance. Don't give pat answers. This may alleviate your discomfort with the subject, but it will also alienate adolescents who had the courage to talk to you about the struggle in the first place.

Alleviate Fears and Anxiety

An almost inevitable belief for young people troubled by masturbation is that their behavior is abnormal. Unaware that the practice is so prevalent, many adolescents struggle with numerous fears about their masturbatory behavior. Several sex experts, however, have written of the normalcy of masturbation, and fearful adolescents may be assured of their "okayness" with this information. It has been jokingly said that "ninety-nine percent of teenage boys admit they masturbate, and the other one percent are liars."[13] Masturbation is normal, and there is no medical evidence to indicate that the practice is harmful to the body or that it interferes physically with subsequent sexual intercourse.

Counselors should also alleviate any fears surrounding myths that the adolescent is carrying. Some of the most common of these myths say that masturbation causes pimples or insanity, that it indicates a dirty mind, that it may be controlled by cold showers, and so on. The teenagers who struggle with these and other myths need reassurance that these notions are false. Research, by the way, indicates that masturbation decreases when any anxiety connected with it is alleviated.[14]

For a few adolescents masturbation may be secondary to their fear of being exposed. Sometimes teens may be discovered masturbating. For example, a camp counselor, a parent, or a sibling walks in on them. An older brother may even use this discovery as a form of blackmail to manipulate his sibling. The focus in counseling, obviously, should then become the resulting fear and humiliation.

Work Through Guilt

An adolescent once told me, "Every time after I masturbate I pray and promise God that I will never do it again." Guilt over sexual matters abounds. Adolescents often worry about their particular idiosyncrasies and personal preferences. During the writing of this section an adolescent confessed to me in a counseling session that he sometimes masturbates before going to church and feels extremely guilty for doing this on Sunday. Guilt over masturbation may be one of Satan's major ways of attacking sincere Christian youth.

Mary Ann Mayo in her book, *A Christian Guide to Sexual Counseling*, says, "I have seen people invest forty-eight hours of self-wallowing condemnation and guilt as a result of four minutes of self-indulgent pleasure!"[15] On the other hand, the young person's guilt may be genuine. The apostle Paul wrote, "If anyone regards something as unclean, then for him it is unclean" (Rom. 14:14). Allowing adolescents to investigate their guilt and shame is healing. You may wish to consult the section on guilt for further suggestions on how to work through guilt issues effectively.

Understand Its Developmental Context

According to Christian ethicist Lewis Smedes, moral concern about masturbation ought to focus on young people's total development toward a more wholesome heterosexual life.[16] For wholesome growth it is important for children to learn to understand their own bodies and to accept the ways in which they respond to stimulation. Adolescents are absorbed in establishing their psychosexual identity and are curious about erogenous areas, sensitive swellings, and seminal emissions. If they are encouraged to appreciate these things, many lasting difficulties may be avoided. Masturbation provides a laboratory situation in which adolescents' bodily functions and pleasures may be experienced under controlled circumstances. This experience may aid them as they grow toward mature intimacy in marriage.

Think Through Your Personal Theology

Masturbation may be a major source of spiritual problems for adolescents. The question they are asking is whether or not it is a sin. Scripture, of course, does not address the issue directly. Because of this, Christians have come to different conclusions concerning it. Where are you as a counselor on the continuum? Do you see masturbation in general as a sin or not very serious? Masturbation is one of those areas where we must be careful not to judge others but to remain faithful to our own understanding of biblical principles. Counselors working with this issue in the therapeutic setting must know where they stand in their personal theology.

Facilitate Personal Exploration

Help adolescents understand masturbation in more neutral terms. Advice or ideas that suggest the practice should be resisted at all costs will likely promote the cycle of defeat and guilt. However, suggesting that masturbation may be the way to deal with sexual pressures may also add to the frustration. Lustful fantasies beget lustful fantasies, and Jesus clearly condemns this (Matt. 5:27–30). One of the most constructive approaches for counselors is simply to listen without embarrassment or the need to judge. David Seamands says, "When there is open communication on masturbation it will no longer be a problem."[17] An accepting response to teens' explorations can help them "rebuild their self-esteem and propel them into more meaningful and satisfying interpersonal relationships."[18] Effective counselors model the assurance of God's grace, underlining his total and unconditional acceptance.

Examine Obsessions and Compulsions

Sometimes adolescents are consumed by sexual thoughts and fantasies. Their masturbatory habits may become highly ritualized. This is a deeper problem than simply enjoying self-stimulation. In a life stage that is typically fraught with insecurity, anxiety, and turmoil, the search for the pleasures of masturbation may become compulsive. When this occurs, compulsiveness, not masturbation, is the problem that needs to be addressed. Adolescents need not be obsessed with or mastered by masturbation.

Explore the Use of Pornography

Pornography is accessible to today's teens, and many boys and some girls at least occasionally make use of pornographic materials during masturbation. In one study only about thirty percent of the boys said they never looked at pornography while masturbating.[19] If this is a problem for teens you are counseling, you will find further suggestions in the section on pornography.

Assist Avoidance

For adolescents who conclude that masturbation is wrong for them and are trying to control the practice, Stephen Grunlan offers these suggestions: Avoid the time and places where masturbation has been practiced; avoid sexual stimuli in movies, television, music, or magazines; do not fight thoughts about masturbation but work at replacing them with other thoughts; take it one day at a time; commit the matter to God in prayer.[20] Remember that masturbation is rarely helped by a direct determination to quit. This seems only to magnify the issue, increase anxiety, and make failure more incriminating.

Do Not Neglect Potential Danger

Before concluding this section on how to help adolescents who struggle with masturbation, I must add a word of caution about a rare but very dangerous experiment with masturbation. It is called autoerotic asphyxia or "scarfing." It happens when a teenager (almost always a male) masturbates while constricting his throat or chest to create an altered state of consciousness by reducing the brain's oxygen supply. Some experts say this deprivation may physiologically create intensified sensations of sexual pleasure in the brain. Others say it is simply the power of the suggestion that heightens the pleasure. In either case, it is a deadly endeavor. Fatal cases are usually found hanging naked in a closet or bathroom.

The FBI reports that as many as one thousand young people die from autoerotic asphyxia each year. That means an adolescent dies every eight hours from this practice. The warning signs of autoerotic asphyxia include repeated appearance of bloodshot eyes; a fascination with ropes, chains, and leather belts; and neck abrasions or bruises.[21] If you suspect this activity, do not hesitate to ask directly: "Have you ever done anything unusual or dangerous to enhance your masturbation experience?" The inquiry could save a life.

☑ WHEN TO REFER

If you are embarrassed, ill-at-ease, overly curious, or uncertain how to proceed with adolescents struggling with masturbation, referral to other counselors is necessary. It is important to let adolescents know that the referral is not a rejection of them but a way of getting them the best help possible. If you suspect autoerotic asphyxia, you should immediately initiate a professional consult with an expert.

Where To Go for Additional Help

Carnes, P. *Out of the Shadows*. Minneapolis: CompCare, 1983.

Johnson, J. "Toward a Biblical Approach to Masturbation." *Journal of Psychology and Theology* 10, no. 2 (1982): 137–46.

Johnson, W. "Masturbation." In *The Adolescent Experience: A Counseling Guide to Social and Sexual Behavior*, ed. J. Semmens and K. Krantz. London: Macmillan, 1972.

Mayo, M. A. *A Christian Guide to Sexual Counseling*. Grand Rapids: Zondervan, 1987.

Penner, C. "A Reaction to Johnson's Biblical Approach to Masturbation." *Journal of Psychology and Theology* 10, no. 2 (1982): 147–49.

Penner, J. J., and C. L. Penner. *Counseling for Sexual Disorders*. Waco, Tex.: Word, 1990.

Smedes, L. B. *Sex for Christians*. Grand Rapids: Eerdmans, 1976.

Stafford, T. *A Love Story: Questions and Answers on Sex*. Grand Rapids: Zondervan, 1977.

Notes

1. G. R. Collins, *Christian Counseling: A Comprehensive Guide* (Waco, Tex.: Word, 1980).

2. W. H. Masters, V. E. Johnson, and R. C. Kolodny, *Masters and Johnson on Sex and Human Loving* (Boston: Little, Brown, 1986), 283.

3. R. Crooks and K. Baur, *Our Sexuality*, 4th ed. (New York: Benjamin-Cummings, 1990).

4. G. Wood and E. Ruddock, *Vitalogy* (Chicago: Vitalogy Association, 1918).

5. Two passages that are most often used to condemn masturbation are Genesis 38:8–10 and 1 Corinthians 6:9. However, most scholars examining these passages do not see them addressing the issue of masturbation.

6. R. E. Butman, "Masturbation," in *Baker Encyclopedia of Psychology* (Grand Rapids: Baker, 1985).

7. R. J. Foster, *Money, Sex and Power* (San Francisco: Harper & Row, 1985).

8. Consider the variety of positions taken by Christians on this issue: Stephen Grunlan, in his book *Marriage and the Family: A Christian Perspective* (Zondervan, 1984) gives three reasons why Christians should avoid masturbation: First, there is no biological necessity for masturbation; second, masturbation is a solo act, and God created us as sexual beings to bring men and women together; third, the fantasies and thought life that accompany the act are sinful. By contrast, James Dobson, in his popular "Focus on the Family" film series, accepts masturbation as a normal part of growing up unless it becomes excessive. Charlie Shedd, in *The Stork Is Dead* (Word, 1976), speaks of masturbation as a "gift from God." David Seamands (in J. A. Petersen's *For Families Only*, Tyndale, 1977) says, "It's high time we stop making such a big deal of masturbation and give it the well-deserved unimportance it merits."

9. J. D. Atwood and J. Gagnon, "Masturbatory Behavior in College Youth," *Journal of Sex Education and Therapy* 13, no. 2 (1987): 35–42.

10. Ibid.

11. R. Clifford, "Development of Masturbation in College Women," *Archives of Sexual Behavior* 7 (1978): 559–73.

12. E. Hamilton, *Sex with Love* (Boston: Beacon Press, 1978), 33.

13. G. K. Olson, *Counseling Teenagers* (Loveland, Colo.: Group Books, 1984).

14. W. R. Johnson, *Masturbation* (New York: Sex Information and Education Council of the U.S., n.d.).

15. M. A. Mayo, *A Christian Guide to Sexual Counseling* (Grand Rapids: Zondervan, 1987), 193.

16. L. Smedes, *Sex for Christians* (Grand Rapids: Eerdmans, 1976).

17. D. A. Seamands, "Sex, Inside and Outside of Marriage," in *The Secrets of our Sexuality*, ed. G. R. Collins (Waco, Tex.: Word, 1976), 156.

18. Butman, "Masturbation," 688.

19. R. Sorenson, *Adolescent Sexuality in Contemporary America* (New York: World, 1973).

20. S. A. Grunlan, *Marriage and the Family: A Christian Perspective* (Grand Rapids: Zondervan, 1984), 122.

21. D. Marshall, "A Deadly Shame," *Parents of Teenagers* (August–September 1990).

OBSESSIONS
and COMPULSIONS

☑ **WHAT THE STRUGGLE LOOKS LIKE**

It is not unusual for preschoolers to insist on certain kinds of routines. They may need a drink of water before going to bed, or they may want a particular doll with them in bed every night—and no other doll will do. They may insist that their shirt be put on before their pants. They may require that the same glass be used for their milk at every meal. The attention to regular patterns among young children is an attempt to control their environment and their own behavior. The more predictable they can make their lives, the more secure they feel.

In the same way that fears turn into phobias, these kinds of routines may turn into maladaptive rituals and preoccupations. Routines may become an *obsessive-compulsive personality style* characterized by a pervasive tendency to be preoccupied with concerns of neatness, orderliness, punctuality, control, efficiency, hard work, rigid adherence to rules, and perfection in every way.[1] Mild compulsivity or perfectionism, if handled well, may be an asset. Often, however, these traits lead to problems.

Obsessions are intrusive and recurring thoughts, ideas, fears, or doubts that certain people cannot prevent from bombarding their conscious awareness. Though they want to avoid them, they cannot keep from ruminating and worrying about them. These ruminations rarely serve any constructive purpose and often paralyze any capacity to take action.

Compulsions are repetitive, nonproductive impulses that people feel required to carry out over and over again, even against their better judgement. The compulsion may be as absurd as counting every tile on a bathroom floor or washing one's hands every fifteen minutes. I treated one young man who routinely measured his nose. Failure to carry out certain self-prescribed rituals gives compulsive people a terrible sense of impending catastrophe. Compulsions often occur with obsessions and vice versa, but not always.

Obsessive-compulsive behavior is fairly common. Most of us know people who are regarded as perfectionistic worriers, who are indecisive, meticulous, or inflexible. Obsessive-compulsive symptoms are considered pathological only when at least five of the following events occur:[2]

1. Perfectionism that interferes with task completion. For example, the inability to complete a project because self-imposed strict standards are not being met.
2. Preoccupation with details, rules, lists, order, organization, or schedules to the extent that the major point of the activity is lost.
3. Unreasonable insistence that others submit to exact ways of doing things, or unreasonable reluctance to allow others to do something because of the conviction that it will not be done correctly.
4. Excessive devotion to productivity to the exclusion of leisure activities and friendships.
5. Indecisiveness due to total avoidance, postponement, or protraction of decision making. For example those who cannot get assignments done on time because of concentration on priorities. They fear making mistakes.
6. Overconscientiousness, scrupulosity, and inflexibility about matters of morality, ethics, or values (not accounted for by cultural or religious identification).
7. Restricted expression of affection.
8. Lack of generosity in giving time, money, or gifts when no personal gain is likely to result.
9. Inability to discard worn-out or worthless objects even when they have no sentimental value.

Although obsessive-compulsive disorder is more prevalent among adults than among young people, it often has a youthful onset. Obsessive-compulsive adolescents show an average age of onset of about ten years and more than half of all cases of the problem begin before age twenty. It occurs about equally between males and females.[3]

☑ WHY THE STRUGGLE HAPPENS

In spite of much effort devoted to development of a theory of the origins of obsessive-compulsive disorder, its causes are largely unknown. Nevertheless, there are several suggested reasons for its occurrence.

Biology

To date, biological approaches to the understanding of this disorder have yielded only traces of definitive information. Genetics appears to have a weak influence that may predispose some people to develop problems with obsessions and compulsions. But no biochemical or structural deficits can explain its emergence.[4]

Case Description

Rick, fifteen, is the only child of middle-class, emotionally stable parents. He enjoyed a happy childhood free from any significant problems, but during the fourth grade his parents sought professional help because they thought he might have a learning disability. Rick was very nervous about tests, and he spent hours on homework that should have taken only minutes. An evaluation by a learning specialist revealed no significant pathology. He and his parents were counseled briefly, and the next few years passed without any major difficulties. In fact, Rick was considered a model child by his parents' friends. He was always well behaved, orderly, and "mature" for his age. His bedroom was a showroom of neatness.

About the time Rick entered high school, however, things began to worsen. Rick started doing very poorly in school. His parents realized it wasn't due to a lack of "smarts," however. Rick read his assignments over and over looking for errors. It was not unusual for him to recopy a written assignment four or five times. Regardless of how good his work was, it never seemed to be good enough for him. He developed perfectionistic rituals like keeping the inside of his locker extremely clean and organized. Three times after he locked it he would check his locker to be sure it was secure. Rick's waking life became governed by rituals, and he was terrorized by thoughts that if he failed to carry them out "something terrible" would happen.

Fear Reduction

Obsessions and compulsions are attempts to master the environment and feel safe. Perfectionistic behavior enables people to avoid the anxiety and fear that accompany less than perfect performance. By doing the "right" thing people troubled in this area are certain of their behavior and thus reduce their fear of making a mistake or otherwise not being acceptable. Fear is also reduced by engaging in behavior that postpones undesirable events. By counting objects, for example, teens may delay imagined catastrophes.

Self-Doubt

Unfortunately, self-doubts dominate many adolescents' feelings about themselves. This may contribute to occurrences of obsessions and compulsions in susceptible teens. Young people who repeat behavior doubt that they performed the behavior correctly. They become anxious and are compelled to repeat the act again. Orderliness and organization may also be vain attempts to help them dismantle their self-doubt. Having everything "in its place" provides psychological balance and lets them know they are okay because their things are okay.

Guilt

Compulsivity may be a counteraction to the desire to be sloppy, messy, and disorganized. The guilt of having "forbidden" wishes fuels perfectionistic behavior. Instead of being the slobs they want to be, they become models of orderliness. Instead of stealing and cheating, they become models of virtue and are horrified by the misbehavior of others. They become overly scrupulous and feel guilt over minor misdeeds. They even feel guilty for not being constructive during their leisure time.

Parental Expectations

Many children learn from their parents that things must be done in a specific and exact manner to be acceptable. Overly strict parents with high expectations, who are themselves rigid and perfectionistic, do not tolerate children's deficiencies and inconsistencies. Their home emphasizes etiquette and cleanliness. They both model and reinforce compulsive behavior. If the children do not rebel against their perfectionistic behavior along the way, they will probably react by becoming overly conscientious and perfectionistic.

☑ HOW TO HELP

Obsessive-compulsive disorder is not easy to treat. It requires months of work and relapses are not uncommon. The following techniques should be, as always, undergirded by personal acceptance and reflective listening.

Pinpoint the Severity

At the beginning of treatment assess the intensity of the adolescents' obsessions and compulsions. The Compulsiveness Inventory is an eleven-item scale designed to measure compulsive behavior that is common in the normal population. This scale focuses specifically on overconcern that decisions and tasks be completed perfectly according to rigid well-established norms. The Obsessive-Compulsive Scale is a twenty-item instrument that measures tendencies to obsessive thoughts and compulsive behaviors. Both are found in *Helping the Struggling Adolescent: A Counseling Guide*.

Facilitate a Slow Pace

Obsessive-compulsive individuals are very tense. They are almost continually hurried to the point where they can't relax or slow down. It is up to counselors to set a slow pace. Be aware of your tone and attitude. The last thing they need are driving and pressured counselors. You may eventually approach this hurriedness directly by asking them how they rest and relax. Sometimes all they need is "permission" to lighten up.

Explain the Problem

Simply labeling struggles and discussing their nature relieves anxiety and a great deal of stress in distraught adolescents. Labeling helps teens know that they are not alone in their struggles. I remember a spiritually sensitive teenager, fighting a compulsion, who was relieved to find that she was not possessed by a demon! Explain the dynamics of the struggle. Make a distinction between obsessive thoughts and compulsive behavior. Tell them it is normally understood to be a means of coping with anxiety and stress and that they can learn new ways of coping with anxiety that are more constructive. Counselors, however, must use labels cautiously. If a teen grapples with mild symptoms of the disorder, it may be best to avoid anything that feels like a clinical diagnosis. A label may be self-fulfilling.

Encourage Feelings

Open expression of feelings prevents compulsive rituals and obsessive thoughts from becoming more intense. The difficulty for those who battle this problem is that they often are not aware of their feelings. For this reason they can benefit from keeping a "feeling log." It is a place for them to record what they feel, not what they *should* feel. Suggest that troubled adolescents keep track of their feelings by recording them throughout the day. Have them note what happens, what they say to themselves, and what they feel as a result. Of course, this assignment may become a compulsion. They may become more concerned about carrying out the assignment correctly than actually becoming more aware of their emotions. Tell them there is no right or wrong way to do this exercise and that it needn't be done consistently. Use the log in your sessions to process their feelings. Facilitate their expression.

Steer Clear of Superstition

Superstition promotes compulsive behavior. To ward off bad luck young people battling this problem may, for example, always sharpen their pencils at predetermined times, or they may wear certain colors on specific days. If they grew up in a home where parents knocked on wood for luck, never walked under ladders, and so on, help them see that they can make free choices and do not have to imitate these habits. Another means of staying clear of solidifying these rituals is to have them purposely vary their behavior. For example, ask them to dress in a different order or walk home from school along a different route, or sit in a different area of the cafeteria. This gives them permission to be flexible and creative. Of course, for hard-core obsessive compulsives, any variation in routines will be difficult and should not be forced.

Use Reconditioning

Perfectionism is associated with avoidance of anxiety. It is necessary to recondition young people so that compulsive behavior is no longer necessary to avoid anxiety.[5] They may behave without rituals or perfectionism and still feel good. Teach them to relax on cue. Urge them to breathe deeply, for example, just before a task in order to prevent the usual rise of anxiety. The section on anxiety outlines several relaxation strategies that may be used for this purpose.

Another avenue is to teach relaxation and then desensitize clients by showing that their not performing compulsive rituals does not result in disaster. While they are relaxed, ask the teens to imagine themselves not following their usual perfectionistic and compulsive behavior. Each time they imagine that scene, they will become less anxious about giving up their compulsions.

For example, if adolescents are obsessed with and compulsive about having trash in the trash can, help them relax. Once they are in a state of relaxation ask them to see themselves in their mind's eye sitting at a desk in their bedroom. Ask them to imagine that they just threw a piece of paper into their trash can under the desk. Lead them to imagine that they do not immediately empty the trash can into the garbage can in the garage. Let them image that they simply keep studying while the paper lies in the bottom of the trash can. They will probably experience at least mild anxiety at this image. Urge them to relax more deeply. Then, have them image themselves tossing another piece of paper into the trash can, and so on. Each time they visualize the scene their anxiety lessens, and the exercise brings them closer to letting go of their compulsion.

Teach Constructive Behavior

Perfectionistic behavior is unnecessary and inefficient. Show the young person how he or she may use good intentions more constructively. For example, challenge a young woman to substitute different behavior or at least repetition, if she takes two hours in the bathroom washing in a particular way several times, arranging her toothbrush and paste, hanging the towels perfectly, and so on. Rather than washing four times, urge her to wash only twice. Rather than washing each finger individually, suggest that she wash all fingers of one hand together. Rather than hanging the towels several times until they are perfect, tell her that she may have two tries and then she must quit. This will help cut her time in half and help her see that her rituals are unnecessary.

The idea is for the teens to recognize the positive value in their behavior and eliminate unnecessary repetition. Take the pressure off by telling them that failures are okay, and challenge them to keep trying until they succeed.

Reinforce Noncompulsiveness

Counselors should praise any sign of better self-control and reduction of perfectionism. Congratulate them on their progress. If they have been struggling with the need at school to hand in assignments that are not perfect, applaud them for turning in papers regardless of their quality and extent of completion. Focus on their new ability to control their rituals, not on the result of the control. You may also suggest that they reward themselves when they break compulsive habits by doing something they enjoy.

Practice Thought-Stopping

Obsessive thoughts have been successfully treated using the thought-stopping technique developed by Joseph Wolpe.[6] It involves telling clients to focus on their obsessive thoughts for a moment and shouting "stop!" This will distract them, and they will momentarily interrupt the obsessive thoughts. The procedure is repeated several times until clients can silently give the command to themselves and thereby stop the obsession. Another variation of this strategy is to have clients wear a rubber band around the wrist and snap it whenever they sense a buildup of an obsession. It is also helpful to have a thought to substitute for the obsession once it is stopped.[7] For example, the person who is obsessed with an image of a gory accident can stop the thought and substitute a picture of an ocean scene.

Consider Medical Consultation

Some of the most successful treatments for severe obsessive compulsive disorder have included medication. Antidepressant medications such as clomipramine and imipramine (both inhibitors of serotonin) have helped many people suffering with this problem. Unfortunately, these medications have a number of significant side effects that must be outweighed by their benefits.[8]

Model Spontaneity

It is no secret that some counselors have mild characteristics of obsessive-compulsive disorder. We are often organized, neat, punctual, hard working, efficient, controlled, driven, and even perfectionistic. After all, these character-istics may have been what got some of us through graduate school. As we work with young people who struggle with obsessions and compulsions, however, we must be aware of our own tendencies in this direction and "loosen up." Model humor, spontaneity and fun. I have often found it helpful to allow clients to laugh at their "strange" habits.

I referred earlier to the compulsive patient who was obsessed with his nose. About every ten minutes he would measure it with a little wire he kept in his pocket. After a half hour of watching him, I smiled and said, "I have never met anyone so serious about his nose." He burst into laughter and the tension was broken. "Doc," he said, "it's crazy but for some reason I have to measure my nose." Unless it creates extreme anxiety in your clients, be genuinely spontaneous in your sessions. Say things like "Normally I . . . but today I feel like . . . ." Try sitting in different places in your office. The point is to model spontaneous behavior that does not cause you anxiety.

☑ WHEN TO REFER

Refer adolescents struggling with obsessions and compulsions to psycho-logically astute physicians or psychiatrists if the symptoms are severe enough to warrant consideration of medication. Refer clients to other competent coun-selors or psychologists when, after three months of regular therapy, they show no decrease in their ritualistic behavior or if they are becoming increasingly depressed. In this case a more severe underlying disorder may be operating, and a second opinion might help therapists make this determination. Obsessional thoughts and rituals sometimes operate as a defense against a more serious mental disorder such as schizophrenia.

Where To Go for Additional Help

Adams, P. L. *Obsessive Children*. New York: Brunner-Mazel, 1973.

Rachman, S. J., and R. J. Hodgson. *Obsessions and Compulsions*. Englewood Cliffs, N.J.: Prentice-Hall, 1980.

Rapoport, J. L. *The Boy Who Couldn't Stop Washing: The Experience and Treatment of Obsessive-Compulsive Disorder*. New York: Plume, 1990.

Salzman, L. *Psychotherapy of the Obsessive Personality*. New York: Aronson, 1980.

Notes

1. C. M. Berry, "Obsessive-Compulsive Disorder," in *Baker Encyclopedia of Psychology*, ed. D. G. Benner (Grand Rapids: Baker, 1985).

2. American Psychiatric Association, *Diagnostic and Statistical Manual of Mental Disorders*, 3d ed. rev. (Washington, D.C.: American Psychiatric Association, 1987).

3. C. E. Hollingsworth et al., "Long-Term Outcome of Obsessive-Compulsive Disorder in Childhood," *Journal of the American Academy of Child Psychiatry* 19 (1980): 134–44.

4. E. T. Sturgis, "Obsessional and Compulsive Disorder," in *Comprehensive Handbook of Psychopathology*, ed. H. E. Adams and P. B. Sutker (New York: Plenum, 1984).

5. L. Salzman and F. H. Thaler, "Obsessive-Compulsive Disorders: A Review of the Literature," *American Journal of Psychiatry* 138 (1981): 286–96.

6. J. Wolpe, *Psychotherapy by Reciprocal Inhibition* (Stanford, Calif.: Stanford Univ. Press, 1958).

7. D. C. Rimm, "Thought Stopping and Covert Assertion in the Treatment of Phobias," *Journal of Consulting and Clinical Psychology* 41 (1973): 466–67.

8. E. T. Sturgis and V. Meyer, "Obsessive-Compulsive Disorder," in *Handbook of Clinical Behavior Therapy*, ed. S. M. Turnger, K. C. Calhoun, and H. E. Adams (New York: Wiley, 1980).

PANIC ATTACKS

☑ WHAT THE STRUGGLE LOOKS LIKE

Fear is when you look up and see a half-ton weight about to fall on your head. In a panic attack you feel the same fright but don't know why.

It is estimated that up to six percent of the people in the United States have at some time in their lives been diagnosed as having problems with panic attacks. However, since anxiety reactions rarely require hospitalization, statistics on the incidence of the disorder are difficult to compile. Until recently panic attacks were believed to be confined to adults. Research is showing that this is not true.[1] About sixty-five percent of all cases begin between the ages of ten and twenty-nine.[2] In a survey of 338 high school students, thirty-two percent reported experiencing at least one panic attack that meets clinical diagnostic criteria in the *Diagnostic and Statistical Manual* (3d ed. rev. [DSM-III-R]). In addition, five percent of the students reported experiencing panic severely and frequently enough to fulfill the diagnostic criteria of panic disorder. Surprisingly, this researcher found that fewer than half the students surveyed with panic disorder reported any contact with mental health services.[3] In spite of this, many professionals report an increase in the incidence of panic symptoms in adolescents.[4]

A panic disorder is characterized by sudden, brief attacks of acute anxiety and extreme autonomic arousal. The individual experiences intense apprehension and terror and a sense that something dreadful is about to happen. Attacks are usually unexpected and sudden, lasting anywhere from a few seconds to an hour or more. Most commonly they last about three or four minutes. The anxiety mounts to high intensity and then subsides, all in the absence of any obvious cause.

A person's first panic attack, according to Stewart Agras at Stanford University, usually occurs in a public place. The victim of the attack suddenly feels ill, notices a fast and erratic heartbeat, experiences a tight feeling in the chest, breathes rapidly, and may feel faint. The rapid breathing leads to chemical changes that cause tingling in the hands and feet, and numbness around the mouth.[5]

Adolescents struggling with panic feel that they are losing control. Physiological symptoms, together with the sense of impending death or catastrophe, make panic attacks truly terrifying. They are real experiences and must not be downplayed by therapists. To underestimate, dismiss, or laugh at the irrationality of the attacks will only make it worse.

The symptoms of panic are so markedly physical that in the eighteenth century the disorder was termed "hysterical vertigo" in an attempt to describe the sensations of dizziness often reported by patients.[6] To be clinically diagnosed today with panic disorder the person must have at least four of the following symptoms during at least one of the attacks:

1. Shortness of breath or smothering sensations
2. Dizziness, unsteady feelings, or faintness
3. Palpitations or accelerated heart rate
4. Trembling or shaking
5. Sweating
6. Choking
7. Nausea or abdominal distress
8. Depersonalization or derealization
9. Numbness or tingling sensations
10. Flushes or chills
11. Chest pain or discomfort
12. Fear of dying
13. Fear of going crazy or of doing something uncontrolled[7]

Symptoms vary from one person to another, but they usually include varying combinations of the above signs. If the attack lasts more than a few minutes, the victim may frantically implore someone to summon a doctor or to be taken to a hospital emergency room. After medical treatment has been administered, usually in the form of verbal reassurance and a minor tranquilizer, one generally feels better. In fact, the patient may feel ridiculous after arriving at the hospital when the physician or nurse attempts to ascertain the presenting problem.

Attacks vary in frequency, but generally occur from several times a day to once a month or even less often. They may occur during the day, or the person may be sound asleep when awakened with a strong sense of apprehension that quickly develops into a full-blown attack. Between attacks the person may be mildly anxious or tense, but one can also be relatively unperturbed.

Clinicians often misdiagnose panic disorder as agoraphobia—the fear of open places. Since people who struggle with panic attacks do not know when an attack will strike, they may anticipate its disastrous occurrence and become reluctant to venture far from home. The real fear here is not going out of the house. It is a fear that the panic symptoms will occur while they are walking on the streets, while driving, or out with friends. Once they learn how to control the attacks, they typically resume their normal lifestyle.

Case Description

Tina was a vivacious cheerleader and a senior in high school. She first came in for therapy at the request of her physician. She believed she had a physical disorder because of her attacks. Her medical examinations, however, revealed no physical problems that could account for the dramatic experience of the panic attacks. Because of the discrepancy between the intensity of her experience and the failure of her physician to find any significant disorder, she was convinced that the doctor had made a mistake and that she was suffering from a very serious but hidden physical disorder. She described her attacks as "horrendous." "I can't predict when the next one will come, but when it does I know my legs will cave in and I'll feel as if I can't breathe. It feels as though my throat is closing up, and my heart wants to jump right out of my chest!"

Tina was terrified. Since she could not predict when her "illness" was going to occur, she was constantly on the alert for symptoms to appear. She was especially fearful that one would strike while she was doing a routine on the cheer squad during a game. One time, to get out of a game when she thought she might have an attack, she even reported to her captain that she was sick. She kept a thermos of ice water and some cold face cloths handy to place on her neck whenever she started feeling weak. This seemed to make her feel better, but she was desperate to alleviate her terror permanently. At the time she came in for counseling, she had already been to several physicians, most of whom had suggested psychological treatment. She was relieved finally to learn that she was struggling with a common form of anxiety—panic disorder.

☑ WHY THE STRUGGLE HAPPENS

Panic disorder may have distinct diagnostic criteria, but its causes are clouded. Certainly, its etiology has much in common with general anxiety. You may wish to refer to the section on anxiety. Here are some of the possible reasons for the occurrence of panic attacks.

Genetics

Studies have shown that panic disorder runs in the family. Children of anxiety-disorder parents are more than seven times as likely than others to be victims of the same problem.[8] Another researcher found that if an identical twin suffers from panic disorder or agoraphobia with panic attacks, the other twin will likely also suffer from panic attacks.[9]

Physical Disorders

Anxiety symptoms may be caused by physical disorders that mimic anxiety reactions. Here are some examples: Hyperthyroidism, cocaine abuse, alcohol withdrawal, diabetes, hypoglycemia, psychomotor epilepsy. There are numerous others. For this reason, a complete medical examination by a physician is necessary when treating an anxiety disorder.

Family Environment

Disabling anxiety often originates in dysfunctional families. This condition in adolescents or young adults should prompt counselors to investigate the families' role. While external stress may be beyond the patients' control, it may be affected for better or worse by their families. Moreover, families may cause anxiety directly through mistreatment, substance abuse, or marital problems that disrupt family relationships.[10]

Fear of Independence

To complete the individuation process begun in adolescence, young adults need to gain psychological and geographical independence from both home and parents. It is during this growing apart that they are most vulnerable to anxiety. Anticipation of leaving home has been especially difficult for many adolescents in the current generation. Today's adolescents are not prepared to separate from their parents and become independent. The disappearance of the extended family support system, the loss of the economic importance of children as members of a family work force, and overly indulgent parents are some of the reasons for this phenomenon. In any case, fear of independence is a causal factor of panic cited by some.[11]

☑ HOW TO HELP

The following techniques should be undergirded by personal acceptance and reflective listening. They are designed to create alternatives for adolescents to replace dysfunctional behaviors and attitudes.

Pinpoint the Severity

While specific symptoms of panic disorder are difficult to assess through a rapid assessment instrument, therapists may quickly gain a clinical picture of the symptoms through interview. Assess the occurrence of specific characteristics of the attacks and their frequency. Although it is designed to measure the amount, degree, or severity of generalized anxiety, the Clinical Anxiety Scale may be used in conjunction with assessing panic. It is found in *Helping the Struggling Adolescent: A Counseling Guide*.

Require a Medical Examination

A careful physical examination with particular attention to panic attack symptoms cannot be overemphasized. Prior to embarking on a psychological treatment approach, organic disorders must be adequately ruled out. Certain antipanic drugs like alprazolam (Xanax), imipramine (Tofranil), and phenelzine (Nardil) may be helpful for those who suffer from extreme attacks of panic. The question, of course, is how the side effects of the medication will affect patients. Psychologically astute physicians or psychiatrists will generally prescribe the lowest dosage needed for the shortest period of time if medication is seen as necessary.[12]

Generally, once an effective drug regime has been found, patients are kept on the medication for six months with dosages tapering off gradually over the next three months. Of course, if medication is prescribed, adolescents continue under medical supervision throughout treatment. Patients' misunderstandings about medications and their alarm concerning side effects are often the main cause of their noncompliance and their dropping out of treatment. Therefore, encourage clients to contact their physicians whenever they have questions or concerns related to their medical treatment.

Discuss the Nature of the Struggle

Once medical examinations are over and diagnoses of panic disorder are completed, therapists should fully discuss the nature of the disorder and its treatment with the young victims. They need to hear that their problem has a name and that much is known about it. In addition to providing information and answering questions during office sessions, clinicians may refer adolescents to one of several books written about panic disorder for the lay reader. Three excellent books for this purpose are listed under "Where To Go for Additional Help" at the end of this section: *Panic: Facing Fears, Phobias, and Anxiety*; *Overcoming Anxiety*; and *The Anxiety Disease*.

Prescribe a Diary

It is helpful to have adolescents keep diaries or logs of symptoms. Ask them to record the time and setting of each attack, to rate its intensity on a zero-to-ten scale, its duration, any medication taken and side effects experienced, and an account of their experience together with any questions. These records will prove helpful in assessing their response to treatment.

Insure a Proper Diet

Just as there is a definite connection between diet and physical illness, so there is between diet and anxiety. The key is to improve adolescents' vitality by avoiding foods with added sugar, caffeine, salt, and artificial additives. Instead, urge them to eat more fresh fruit and vegetables, whole-grain breads, and lean meat and fish. This diet will help adolescents feel more energized and less susceptible to panic.

Encourage Avoidance of Caffeine

Caffeine triggers the release of adrenaline and has been linked to panic attacks. Research at the Yale University School of Medicine has shown that when people with anxiety disorders are given caffeine, they register significant increases in anxiety, nervousness, fear, nausea, palpitations, restlessness, and tremors. People struggling with panic attacks show marked signs of anxiety when using products containing caffeine. While most teens do not drink coffee, they may be drinking soft drinks that contain significant amounts of caffeine.

Teach Breathing Exercises

When undergoing attacks, victims breathe shallow rapid breaths from the chest. By changing their breathing patterns during attacks, they may reverse the body's panic-provoking symptoms. Urge them to breathe from the diaphragm and use the lower part of their lungs with each breath so that the stomach expands instead of the chest. While they may learn a breathing exercise in a matter of minutes and experience some immediate benefits, the profound effects of the exercise may not be fully appreciated until months of persistent practice have passed.

Here are some suggested steps for helping adolescents master deep breathing:

1. Have the clients lie down, bend their knees, and move their feet about eight inches apart. Make sure the spine is straight.
2. Ask them to become aware of their tension and their natural breathing.
3. Ask them to place one hand on the abdomen and one hand on the chest.
4. Instruct them to inhale slowly and deeply through the nose into the abdomen to push up the hand as much as comfort allows. The chest should move only a little and only with the abdomen.
5. Instruct them to inhale through the nose and exhale through the mouth, making a quiet, relaxing whooshing sound like the wind as they blow gently out. Allow them to take long, slow, deep breaths that raise and lower the abdomen. Remind them to focus on the sound and feeling of breathing as they become more and more relaxed.
6. After about five or ten minutes of this, ask them to become aware of their tension again. Allow them to compare the tension they felt moments before doing the exercise.
7. Assign them to continue deep breathing once or twice a day for about five minutes at a time.
8. Encourage them to practice the breathing exercise whenever they feel tense. They may do it while sitting or standing. The value is in allowing them to gain control over their moments of anxiety.[13]

Practice Autogenics

Autogenic Training is a systematic program that teaches adolescents to respond quickly and effectively to their own verbal commands to relax and return to a balanced, normal state. It is one of the most effective and comprehensive reducers of stress and has been used successfully with panic disorder. The goal is to reverse the "fight-or-flight" alarm state and to get physical, mental, and emotional processes normalized when they begin to get out of balance. Essentially, the method is to relax in a comfortable position and concentrate passively on verbal formulas suggesting warmth and heaviness in one's arms and legs.[14]

In doing this exercise, it is essential that clients maintain an attitude of passive concentration. That is, they are to go through the exercise without any expectations and to let whatever happens happen. Passive concentration does not mean "spacing out" or going to sleep. They should be alert to the experience but attempt to refrain from analyzing it.

It is important to keep external stimuli to a minimum. The room should be quiet, moderately warm, and the light low. They may either sit in a comfortable arm chair (a recliner works best) or lie on their backs with their heads supported. Follow these suggestions:

> Say to the counselee, "Make yourself comfortable. Allow your body to be relaxed and your eyes closed. Scan your body for tension and relax. I am going to speak some sentences, and I want you to repeat them silently to yourself. Repeat the following about four times: 'My right arm is heavy.' [Allow about thirty seconds of silence after each phrase and then move to the next one.] Repeat these sentences four times: 'My left arm is heavy'; 'Both of my arms are heavy'; 'My right leg is heavy'; 'My left leg is heavy'; 'Both of my legs are heavy.' When you open your eyes you will feel refreshed and alert."[15]

If this exercise works well for your counselees, you may wish to extend it with additional suggestions. For example, "My right arm is heavy and warm," and so on. Panic victims may also benefit from repeating the phrase, "My heartbeat is calm and regular." Have adolescents practice this exercise on their own. They will eventually achieve this relaxed state upon their own verbal command when they feel anxiety coming on.

Practice Guided Imaginal Coping

Our thoughts, images, and other mental activities may be harmful when they upset us. Guided imagery provides an avenue for adolescents to replace troubling thoughts with pleasant ones. The goal is to reduce and control mental anxiety. Research has shown that treatment incorporating guided imagery reduces panic attack frequency and duration.[16] By using pleasant visual images, adolescents control upsetting thoughts and enjoy a deep state of physical relaxation.

When beginning the exercise, it is important to let clients know that they should not get upset as unwanted thoughts come to mind. This happens even to the most practiced of individuals in guided imagery. Knowing that unwanted thoughts may come will help them react to them calmly and not get upset. Tell them to let the thoughts pass gently.

The basic technique involves asking counselees to select a clear image of a pleasant setting. For example, a tropical island just as the morning rains are ending, a sandy white beach with gentle palm trees, or a meadow in a green valley with clouds drifting overhead. With any scene that seems to work best for the adolescent, improvise from a script like the following:

> Picture yourself on a mountaintop, above a tropical rain forest on a small island. The morning rains have finished, and the wind is carrying the clouds away. The sky is clear and blue, with the warm tropical sun shining down. You can see below you the bright green trees in the rain forest. The raindrops on the leaves are reflecting the bright morning sun. Artistically scattered within the dense greenery are bright, colorful flowers: reds, yellows, and blues. In the distance you see a line of coconut palms all along the sugar-white, sand beach. Beyond that, as far as you can see, is crystal-clear and brilliantly blue water. The sky is clear except for one small fluffy cloud that floats overhead on the gentle breeze. . . . Now, count from one to three. As you take a deep breath, silently say each number. When you reach three, open your eyes. You will be relaxed and alert. The world around you will seem slower and more calm; you will be more relaxed and peaceful.[17]

For more scripts and further elaboration of this technique, you may find *Stress Management* by Edward Charlesworth and Ronald Nathan helpful.

Encourage Laughter Therapy

"Laughter can provide immediate relief from life's daily pressures," says Joel Goodman, editor of *Laughing Matters* magazine. "But it also builds up immunity to stress for the long haul." Other experts agree. "Laughter is not only as good a method of stress relief as a massage, a hot bath or exercise; it's essential to stress relief," says Steve Allen, Jr., M.D., son of comedian Steve Allen. Laughing, like aerobic exercise, also diffuses physical tension directly. It triggers a sequence of actions in which muscle tension first increases, then decreases. That is why much hilarity can make us "weak with laughter." It also decreases production of adrenaline and cortisone. Adolescents are not too young to be caught up in a spinning vortex of conflicts and confusion. They need to be reminded to "lighten up." Prescribe three belly laughs daily!

Explore Adolescents' Preferences in Music

When young David played his harp for troubled King Saul, he became one of history's first-known music therapists. Today's music therapists talk about two kinds of music. The first is stimulating music that sets people to clapping their hands, tapping their toes, or dancing. The second is calming music, which has a much slower, easier rhythm (about sixty beats per minute). Calming music has been used to reduce distress and pain among people in dentists' offices, coronary-care units and migraine-headache clinics.

The right music can take a person in a matter of minutes from a highly tense state of panic to a relaxed yet alert state. A young woman I once treated for panic disorder almost always had an attack while at a nightclub where loud rock music was played. Relaxing music triggers the release of endorphins in the brain that make us feel less anxious. Most adolescents, of course, prefer very stimulating music. Young people struggling with panic attacks, however, can usually be convinced to replace Aerosmith or the Red Hot Chili Peppers with something more calming, if it will help them avoid future attacks. While I have had little success in motivating teenagers to play *Harpsichord Concerto in F Minor* in their Walkmans, I have seen several enjoy the benefits of listening to a selection of environmental sounds or soft jazz.

Implement a Desensitization Strategy

If counselees are particularly fearful of situations where they have had panic attacks, it is important to practice *in vivo* desensitization. Have adolescents gradually reenter the feared situation, accompanied by a trusted companion. Beneficial results are optimal if this can be done with their therapists. This exercise may be helpful in reducing anticipatory anxiety and phobic avoidance once the panic has been controlled. It allows them to resume their normal activities and regain confidence.

☑ WHEN TO REFER

Refer depressed adolescents to psychologically astute physicians or psychiatrists when physical symptoms are present or when the depression is severe enough to warrant medication for temporary relief.

Refer them also to other competent counselors or psychologists when, over time, they feel more out of control and increasingly depressed, hopeless, or suicidal. And refer them if you recognize that you are encouraging dependence in already-depressed and dependent adolescents (so that you yourself will feel needed and powerful).

Where To Go for Additional Help

Agras, S. *Panic: Facing Fears, Phobias, and Anxiety.* New York: W. H. Freeman, 1985.
Benson, H. *The Relaxation Response.* New York: Morrow, 1975.
Charlesworth, E. A., and R. G. Nathan. *Stress Management: A Comprehensive Guide to Wellness.* New York: Ballantine, 1984.
Colten, M. E., and S. Gore. *Adolescent Stress: Causes and Consequences.* Hawthorne, N.Y.: Aldine de Gruyter, 1991.
Davis, M., M. McKay, and E. R. Eshelman. *The Relaxation and Stress Reduction Workbook.* Richmond: Calif.: New Harbinger, 1980.
Hart, A. D. *Adrenalin and Stress.* Waco, Tex.: Word, 1986.
————. *Overcoming Anxiety.* Waco, Tex.: Word, 1989.
Marks, I. M. *Living with Fear.* New York: McGraw-Hill, 1978.
Osborn, C. *Release From Fear and Anxiety.* Waco, Tex.: Word, 1978.
Sheehan, D. V. *The Anxiety Disease.* New York: Scribner, 1984.
Walker, E. *Learn to Relax.* Englewood Cliffs, N. J.: Prentice-Hall, 1975.

Notes

1. C. Hayword, J. D. Killen, and C. B. Taylor, "Panic Attacks in Young Adolescents," *American Journal of Psychiatry* 8 (1989): 1061–62.

2. M. R. Von Korff, W. W. Eaton, and P. M. Keyl, "The Epidemiology of Panic Attacks and Panic Disorder: Results of Three Community Surveys," *American Journal of Epidemiology* 122 (1985): 970–81. Also see M. Giesecke, "Panic Disorder in University Students: A Review," *Journal of American College Health* 36 (1987): 149–57.

3. G. D. Zgourides and R. Warren, "Prevalence of Panic in Adolescents: A Brief Report," *Psychological Reports* 3 (1988): 935–37.

4. W. K. Silverman, J. A. Cerny, W. B. Nelles, and A. E. Burke, "Behavior Problems in Children of Parents with Anxiety Disorders," *Journal of the American Academy of Child and Adolescent Psychiatry* 6 (1988): 779–84.

5. S. Argas, *Panic: Facing Fears, Phobias, and Anxiety* (New York: W. H. Freeman, 1985).

6. Ibid.

7. *Diagnostic and Statistical Manual III–R* (Washington, D.C.: American Psychiatric Association, 1987), 238.

8. Silverman et al., "Behavior Problems in Children of Parents with Anxiety Disorders."

9. S. Torgersen, "Genetics of Panic Disorder," *Psychiatria-Fennica: 1989 Supplement* (1988): 29–34.

10. Silverman et al., "Behavior Problems in Children of Parents with Anxiety Disorders."

11. D. E. Gredanus et al., "Anxiety in Young Adults," *Medical Aspects of Human Sexuality* 12 (1986): 76–83.

12. For an excellent review of the importance of a medical evaluation for panic-attack victims, see A. Raj and D. V. Shehan, "Medical Evaluation of Panic Attacks," *Journal of Clinical Psychiatry* 48 (1987): 309–13.

13. M. Davis, M. McKay, and E. R. Eshelman, *The Relaxation and Stress Reduction Workbook* (Oakland, Calif.: New Harbinger, 1980). The exercise was adapted from this workbook. You will find several other breathing exercises in this excellent resource.

14. For a thorough understanding of this technique you may wish to consult W. Luthe, *Autogenic Therapy* (New York: Grune and Stratton, 1969).

15. Adapted from Davis et al., *Relaxation and Stress Reduction Workbook*, 81–89.

16. P. L. Watkins and E. T. Sturgis, "Guided Imaginal Coping: An Integrative Treatment for Panic Disorder," *Journal of Behavioral Therapy and Experimental Psychiatry* 19 (1988): 147–55.

17. E. A. Charlesworth and R. G. Nathan, *Stress Management: A Comprehensive Guide to Wellness* (New York: Ballantine, 1984), 141–46.

PARENTS

☑ WHAT THE STRUGGLE LOOKS LIKE

Mark Twain said, "When I was seven my father knew everything. When I was fourteen my father knew nothing. But when I was twenty-one I was amazed how much the old man had learned in just seven years."

While teenagers usually do grow out of their struggles with mom and dad, that doesn't offer much solace to adolescents or to their parents. The problem is almost inevitable. Accounts of stress and strain between adolescents and their elders date back virtually as far as recorded history. Despite considerable love between most teens and their parents, they can't help sparring. Increasing autonomy in adolescence almost necessitates difficult periods for adolescents and parents. Parents need to be needed. Adolescents need not to need them. Haim Ginott, in *Between Parent and Teenager*, wrote, "Teenagers are like a person needing a loan but wishing they were financially independent."[1]

Although adolescence is not a tumultuous ordeal for most families, research reveals that more than twenty percent of adolescents experience excessive argumentativeness directed at either parent (more often with their mothers than with their fathers).[2] Conflict between adolescents and their parents is different from conflict between peers. With parents the conflict is over both content, as in how late to stay out, and the process by which decisions are to be made. In other words, both the rules and the way the rules are made may become subjects of controversy. The process usually relates to a perceived lack of freedom by adolescents.

The content of parent-adolescent struggles frequently focuses on one of the following areas.[3]

- *Social life and customs.* This probably creates more discord than any other area. It includes conflict over everything from teenagers' choice of friends to the choice of clothes and hair styles. One of the most common complaints of parents is that their teens are never home and spend no time with the family.[4] Curfew hours, dating, and certain activities are also examples of social-life conflicts.
- *Responsibility issues.* Parents want teenagers to care for their personal

208

belongings and to be responsible in money matters and use of the telephone and the car.

- *School performance.* Grades, study habits, attendance, and general attitudes toward learning receive a great deal of attention from parents. Sometimes pressure on adolescents to succeed also contributes to the problem.
- *Family relationships.* Quarreling with siblings, relationships with relatives, and the amount of autonomy from the family is grist for the conflict mill.
- *Values and morals.* Parents are concerned especially with their children's sexual behavior, drinking, smoking, use of drugs, basic honesty, staying out of trouble, and church attendance.

The ages of young people play a role in the focus of parent-adolescent conflicts. Girls are increasingly in conflict with their parents about boyfriends from age twelve on, with the peak years being fourteen and fifteen. The same conflict for boys about girlfriends peaks at age sixteen. The sex of adolescents is another factor influencing conflict. Girls report a greater number of family problems than do boys.[5]

Socioeconomic status is another well-documented determinant of conflict. Low-income families are more often concerned about obedience and respect, whereas middle-income families are more concerned with grades and achievement. Some researchers have also found that the larger the family the greater degree of parent-youth conflict.[6]

☑ WHY THE STRUGGLE HAPPENS

No list of reasons for parent-adolescent conflict is exhaustive. The following are some of the most frequently cited sources for chronic adolescent struggles with their parents.

Marital Instability

One of the most important influences upon young people is the emotional climate of their parents' relationship. Numerous research studies emphasize the positive relationship of stable marital adjustment and family cooperation.[7] When parents are not getting along with each other, teenagers feel threatened, afraid, and angry. Unstable homes are a significant cause of adolescent rebellion against parents.

Generational Differences

Personality differences between parents and adolescents are a major source of conflict. While not all adults or youths fit the stereotypes, experts have noted that parents see teenagers as too inexperienced, naïve, and reckless. While adults are careful and sometimes skeptical, adolescents tend to be adventurous and idealistic. Adults value the past and are generally contented; adolescents

Case Description

The Johnson family was in a stalemate. They had waged a heated battle for several months before the parents called a truce and retreated to a counselor for help. The atmosphere in the counselor's office during the initial session was very tense and emotionally charged. The clash was over the selection of a particular group of friends by Glen, their fourteen-year-old son. He wanted to hang out with guys his parents didn't approve of. His mother called them "ruffians" and explained that they were a terrible influence on her son. They were kids Glen had met at school, and his parents wanted him to run with the group of teens at church. Glen said his school friends were "cool," while he was quick to label his parents' choice as "a group of nerds."

About a month ago, Glen's dad laid down the law and demanded that he not see his friends on the weekend. When his father saw Glen at the mall with them on a Friday evening the battle escalated to a fierce war. In the first session, neither Glen nor his parents could finish a sentence before one of them would jump in to defend a position. Their communication strategy was predictable: "frontal attack," resulting in rage, defensiveness, or passive withdrawal. Both sides were obsessed with being right and having their way. The issue, of course, spilled into every part of their relationship, to the point that even the smallest of annoyances would evolve into a major debate.

view the past as irrelevant and want reform. Adults want to stay youthful; adolescents want to be grown-up.[8] Perennial generational differences account for a sizable portion of parent-adolescent struggles.

Poor Communication

Parents teach communication skills to their children. If they do not model and practice effective styles of communication, they may be planting seeds for discord in the teen years. Poor parent-child communications during the earlier years backfire in adolescence with hostility and rebellion. Instead of openly discussing issues and arriving at mutually agreed upon solutions, or spending time with their adolescents in leisure activities, these parents resort to snooping, interrogating, and blaming. They do this in a futile attempt to maintain control—not to have a relationship.

Lack of Trust

Some conflict occurs because adolescents use discord as a means of testing the relational waters with their parents. Teens will put out a piece of information designed to upset or irritate their parents. They do this, consciously or not, to see whether their parents can be trusted with what is really on their teenagers' minds. If the parents overreact, they lose.[9] Deciphering these kinds of hidden messages requires sensitive and empathic parents. The more self-control and calmness parents display, the more open and sharing teenagers become.

Parental Expectations

Some parents almost see adolescence as a disease, a period of transitory sickness. Bruce Narramore's helpful book, *Adolescence Is Not an Illness*, is an attempt to dispel that myth.[10] The point is that many a parent-adolescent struggle happens because conflicts are expected. Parents, hearing of other parents' "war stories," have stereotyped images of teenagers. Parents often create attitudes, perceptions, and responses to teenagers that are built upon myths. For example, they may have heard, and consequently believe, that adolescents are "explosive" and "totally out of control." These expectations and fears may exacerbate normal human friction.[11]

Changing Roles and Rules

Much of what was acceptable for adolescents to do when they were children is no longer acceptable now that they are teenagers. As children make the transition into adolescence, both they and their parents are redefining roles and rules. For example, they are negotiating curfew and the kinds of clothes, music, and friends they will have. Deciding what is now acceptable and unacceptable behavior may cause strain in parent-child relationships.

☑ HOW TO HELP

The following techniques should be undergirded by personal acceptance and reflective listening. They are designed to create alternatives for adolescents to replace dysfunctional behaviors and attitudes.

Pinpoint the Severity

At the beginning of counseling, it is helpful to assess intensity of parent-adolescent struggle. The Child's Attitude Toward Father (CAF) and Mother (CAM) Scales are designed to measure problems children have with their parents. Each of these is a twenty-five-item scale designed to measure the extent, degree, or severity of problems children have with their fathers or mothers. The CAF and CAM are located in *Helping the Struggling Adolescent: A Counseling Guide*.

Provide Comfort

Adolescents love and resent their parents at the same time. They themselves find this ambivalence difficult to accept. They understandably think that something is inherently wrong for them to feel two ways about the people who provide for them. Sensitive counselors can spare young people a great deal of unhealthful guilt by showing them how "normal" their mixed-up feelings are, that the conflict is a natural part of growing up. It may be beneficial for counselors to voice adolescents' ambivalent feelings. For example, "You seem to feel two ways about your dad. You admire him, but he also makes you angry." A calm, uncritical statement like this helps youth see that their "crazy" feelings are understandable. You obviously shouldn't say, "Make up your mind! Which way do you feel?"

Understand Family Origins

While most parents try do their best in rearing their children, sometimes teenagers' conflicts with parents stem from sincere but dysfunctional parenting. Effective counselors must be aware of these styles, not to label or blame parents, but to empower them to break out of their unhealthful ways. Keith Olson, in his valuable book *Counseling Teenagers*, notes several patterns of damaging parenting styles that influence parent-adolescent struggles.

Perfectionistic parents don't see good as good enough. Their teenagers can never do anything right and consequently suffer from feelings of inadequacy.

Rejecting parents are perhaps the most damaging because they direct their rejection squarely at their children instead of at their performance. The most extreme form comes in physical abuse.

Overprotective parents have a difficult time letting go, and they continue to do things for the children long after such help is necessary. This creates an aching feeling of helplessness and inadequacy within adolescents.

Overindulgent parents give too many things to their children. The result is usually selfish, demanding adolescents who believe everyone else owes them.

Overpermissive parents provide a free environment with few rules and few expectations. Adolescents who are brought up in this way usually make disastrous interpersonal adjustments because they are not accustomed to adapting to others.

Severe parents are harsh and excessive in their punishment. While adolescents reared in these homes carry a huge pack of guilt, they will eventually rebel against this form of treatment (often as a way of hurting the severe parents).

Inconsistent parents shift from one pattern to another without any logical rationale. This confusion leaves adolescents with no solid moral basis to live by. They often become skilled manipulators and make others angry.

Double-binding parents trap their adolescents in no-win situations. No matter what the adolescents do, they can't feel good. Parents use double binds as a means of subtle and insidious control.

A knowledge of these parenting styles may help counselors identify potential sources of conflict and work to modify them. For more about these patterns you will find Olson's *Christian Counseling* useful.

Encourage Parents and Consider Training

Being parents of adolescents can be overwhelming. At times almost all parents feel discouraged or confused. If you sense that adolescents' struggles would be alleviated with the help of parental support and training, incorporate this into your counseling. Tension between parents and teens may sometimes be reduced by giving parents a boost of encouragement and objective guidance. Often the mistakes they have made are what stand out to parents, to the neglect of all the positive things they've done and said. Ease their consciences by letting them know that there has never been a perfect parent. Alert them to the fundamental dangers of overprotection, overpermissiveness, overrestrictiveness and overmaticulousness. Consider principles of effective parent-child communication and behavior management. A number of helpful books for parents of adolescents are on the market. Some are noted at the end of this section.

Explore Communication Skills

Communication is at the heart of harmony between parents and children. With developing autonomy in the teen years, adolescents deserve more egalitarian communication patterns than parents developed when their teens were children. How well the family negotiates this shift may be the critical factor in how smoothly they get along. Research has revealed a number of patterns of communication in families. Unspoken rules about who can talk to whom and about what are not unusual. But in some families these rules may cause so much dysfunction that teenagers who want their dads to know something tell mom, and mom tells dad. Communication styles like this obviously create parent-teen problems.

Effective counselors may help families implement open, honest, democratic communication and problem-solving skills that are essential if families are to overcome conflicts. Both parents and adolescents must learn a number of communication guidelines in order to maintain open and nondefensive positions and thereby avoid blaming and interrogating.

Sven Wahlroos, in *Family Communication*, lists a number of rules to help adolescents and parents speak to one another so that genuine understanding is achieved.[12]

- Remember that actions speak louder than words.
- Define what is important and ignore what isn't.
- Be as realistic as possible.
- Be clear and specific.
- Be as positive as possible.
- Check out your assumptions.
- Recognize that it is all right for two people to view the same thing differently.
- Recognize that your family members know you well.
- Keep discussions from turning into arguments.
- Become aware of and express your true feelings.

- Accept all feelings and try to understand them.
- Be considerate and respectful.
- Do not preach or lecture; ask questions instead.
- Do not use excuses.
- Do not nag, yell, or whine.
- Know when to use humor and when to be serious.
- Above all, listen.

A list like this is much easier to talk about than it is to follow. You may wish to highlight and practice two or three of these rules for parents and teens in specific situations. Providing them with the entire list at once may be overwhelming.

In a survey of adolescents, one researcher collected teenagers' advice to their parents on communication. Here it is: (1) Listen and understand; (2) be upfront and honest; (3) don't cop out when tough subjects come up; (4) trust us and let us learn from our own mistakes; (5) don't live in the past; (6) discipline, don't dominate; (7) compromise; (8) show that you love, care, and will be there.[13]

While effective communication may not be a panacea, and it may seem too simple to some, research has made it abundantly clear that to teach parents and teenagers skills such as clarifying content and reflecting feeling is well worth counselors' efforts.[14]

Teach Fair Fighting

Adolescents and parents who are in conflict often engage in "dirty fighting." For example, they resort to switching the subject, bringing up more than one accusation at a time, interrupting, attributing guilt, sarcasm, or silence. When chronic arguing of this nature is the problem, it is generally best to see both the adolescent and the parents at the same time, at least for a few sessions. Together, they can learn how to fight fairly.

The technique outlined below was developed by George Bach. It is a means to reaching a resolution, most typically after a complaint or frustration doesn't seem to simmer down after an emotional blowup. The fair fight allows parents and adolescents to express their frustrations in a more rational mode. Bach states that "the only kinds of specific issues that are not negotiable under the fair fight format are disputes over behaviors that are beyond willful control and therefore not open to change by an act of will."[15] These include alcohol, smoking, and problems of mood swings or social withdrawal. The nine steps of fair fighting emphasize how a conflict is resolved rather than the content of the dispute. The following is a brief summary of the strategy as applied to the parent-adolescent struggle. A more detailed description can be found in *Creative Aggression*.

Step 1.   An adolescent with a complaint asks the parent to engage in a fair fight. If the parent agrees, a time and place for the fight is set.

Step 2.   Neutral people (family members) should be present at the agreed-upon time. Before beginning the fair fight, the adolescent and the parent should have a strategy session with a neutral observer to help define the complaint. The strategy session should be open so that all who are involved can listen.

Step 3. The initiator of the fight, in this case the adolescent, states the complaint.

Step 4. The parent must repeat the complaint, not word for word, but accurately reflecting its essence and the feelings of the adolescent. From this point on in the fight, each participant must repeat every statement made by the other during the fight.

Step 5. The adolescent states a "demand for change." This must be a change in behavior, not attitude.

Step 6. The parent responds to the complaint and the demand for the change.

Step 7. The fair fight alternates back and forth with direct, simple statements.

Step 8. The fight is ended when parent and adolescent agree on change, one of the two rejects a resolution, or when the two sides establish specific conditions for partial change.

Step 9. At a future meeting the success or failure of the agreement is discussed by the parent and adolescent.

Explore Runaway Potential

A frightening number of adolescents see running away as their only alternative to conflict with their parents. These teens survive on the streets and are often referred to as "children of the night." They turn to drugs, crime, and prostitution as the means of coping with their pain. Both runaway girls and boys are often offered a roof over their heads and the promise of protection if they sell their bodies. In a strange way, a dangerous pimp becomes their substitute parent. Some runaways eventually return home; others make it on their own or die young. Most homeless street kids are from white, middle-class, mainstream homes. However, a crisis such as divorce or physical or sexual abuse by a parent usually precipitates such drastic behavior.[16]

Counselors working with adolescents who struggle with severe conflicts with their parents must consider the possibility that young people may run away. Adolescents who are thinking about running away are typically depressed, insecure, impulsive, and wrestling with seemingly unmanageable problems.[17] Arguments with parents are the number-one reason young people give for leaving.[18] The National Runaway Youth Program promotes assistance to youths who are apt to run away and vulnerable to dangerous encounters. Aid is offered nationwide through this toll-free number: 800/999-9999. Your community social service agencies may be of assistance with this problem as well.

☑ WHEN TO REFER

Refer adolescents who struggle with chronic conflict with their parents to other competent counselors or psychologists when, over time, counselees feel more out of control and increasingly frustrated. Refer them if you recognize that you are getting caught in a triangle between adolescents and their parents. In other words, if you feel a strong and consistent pull to side with adolescents for unhealthful reasons (so they will like you, for example), you should consider referral.

Where To Go for Additional Help

Bach, G. B., and H. Goldberg. *Creative Aggression: The Art of Assertive Living.* New York: Avon, 1974.

Bell, R., and L. Wildflower. *Talking with Your Teenager: A Book for Parents.* New York: Random House, 1983.

Campbell, D. *How To Really Love Your Teenager.* Wheaton, Ill.: Victor, 1981.

Davitz, L., and J. Davitz. *How to Live (Almost) Happily with a Teenager.* Minneapolis: Winston, 1982.

Ginott, H. G. *Between Parent and Teenager.* New York: Avon, 1969.

Gnagey, T. D. *How To Put Up with Parents: A Guide for Teenagers.* Ottawa, Ill.: Facilitation House, 1975.

McIntire, R. *Losing Control of Your Teenager: Ten Rules for Raising an Adult While Keeping a Friend.* Amherst, Mass.: Human Resources Development Press, 1985.

Meier, P. D. *Christian Child-Rearing and Personality Development.* Grand Rapids: Baker, 1977.

Narramore, S. B. *Help! I'm a Parent.* Grand Rapids: Zondervan, 1972.

————. *Parenting with Love and Limits.* Grand Rapids: Zondervan, 1979.

————. *You Can Be a Better Parent.* Grand Rapids: Zondervan, 1979.

————. *Adolescence Is Not an Illness.* Old Tappan, N.J.: Revell, 1980.

Patterson, G., and M. Forgatch. *Parents and Adolescents Living Together.* Eugene, Oreg.: Castalia Publishing, 1987.

Ridenour, F. *What Teenagers Wish Their Parents Knew About Kids.* Waco, Tex.: Word, 1982.

Ross, L. *A Kid's Goal-Setting Guide (for Parents).* Wheaton, Ill.: Tyndale, 1985.

Scott, B. *Relief for Hurting Parents.* Nashville: Oliver-Nelson, 1989.

Weinhause, E., and K. Friedman. *Stop Struggling with Your Teen.* New York: Penguin, 1984.

Youniss, J., and J. Smollar. *Adolescent Relations with Mothers, Fathers, and Friends.* Chicago: Univ. of Chicago Press, 1985.

Notes

1. H. G. Ginott, *Between Parent and Teenager* (New York: Avon, 1969).

2. J. D. Balswick and C. Macrides, "Parental Stimulus for Adolescent Rebellion," *Adolescence* 10 (1975): 253–66.

3. J. A. Hall, "Parent-Adolescent Conflict: An Empirical Review," *Adolescence* 22 (1987): 767–89.

4. M. Felson and M. Gottfredson, "Social Indicators of Adolescent Activities Near Peers and Parents," *Journal of Marriage and the Family* 46 (1984): 709–14.

5. D. R. Papini et al., "Early Adolescent Age and Gender Differences in Patterns of Emotional Self-Disclosure to Parents and Friends," *Adolescence* 25 (1990): 959–76.

6. Avery Bell, "Family Structure and Parent-Adolescent Relationships: Does Family Structure Really Make a Difference?" *Journal of Marriage and Family Therapy* 47 (1985): 503–8.

7. B. Burman, R. S. John, and G. Margolin, "Effects of Marital and Parent-Child Relations on Children's Adjustment," *Journal of Family Psychology* 1 (1987): 91–108.

8. F. P. Rice, *The Adolescent: Development, Relationships and Culture* (Boston: Allyn and Bacon, 1990).

9. L. Ross, *A Kid's Goal-Setting Guide (for Parents)* (Wheaton, Ill.: Tyndale, 1985).

10. S. B. Narramore, *Adolescence Is Not an Illness* (Old Tappan, N.J.: Revell, 1980).

11. G. K. Olson, *Counseling Teenagers: The Complete Christian Guide to Understanding and Helping Adolescents* (Loveland, Colo.: Group Books, 1984).

12. S. Wahroos, *Family Communication* (New York: Macmillan, 1974).

13. J. Normon and M. W. Harris, *The Private Life of the American Teenager* (New York: Rawson, Wade, 1981).

14. J. Alexander and B. V. Parsons, *Functional Family Therapy* (Monterey, Calif.: Brooks-Cole, 1982).

15. G. B. Bach and H. Goldberg, *Creative Aggression: The Art of Assertive Living* (New York: Avon, 1974).

16. J. J. Christensen, "Survival on the Streets: Homeless Teens and What You Can Do To Help," *Youth!* (March 1991): 26–31.

17. B. Benalcazar, "Study of Fifteen Runaway Patients," *Adolescence* 17 (1987): 553–66.

18. E. Spillane-Grieco, "Characteristics of a Helpful Relationship: A Study of Empathetic Understanding and Positive Appeal Between Runaways and Their Parents," *Adolescence* 19 (1984): 63–75.

PEER PRESSURE

☑ WHAT THE STRUGGLE LOOKS LIKE

In a cartoon, a boy with spiked hair is talking with his dad. The caption says, "But, Dad, I gotta be different. How else can I be like the other kids?"

All of us want to please others. We want to be liked, respected, and accepted. The people around us have a substantial influence on what we do, think, and say. And it's a good thing! Our desire to accommodate ourselves to the group norm is one of the most civilizing forces in society. But it also has the potential to create a great deal of personal conflict and loss of self-esteem. This harm is perhaps greater for adolescents than for any other group.

Young people change their speech, clothing, behavior, thinking, and even values to fit in with their cohorts. Peer pressure doesn't have to be bad, however. Joining a scout troop, playing tennis, even attending church and reading the Bible can be the result of peer pressure. Traveling between the child world they left and the adult world they have not yet reached, teens turn to each other for support; that support may lead in positive directions.

But negative consequences also result from peer pressure. Dropping out of school, experimenting with drugs, racism, and shoplifting are just a few examples. Premarital sex is another behavior that is often the result of peer pressure. In fact, love is one of the least-named reasons teens give for having sex. Peer pressure is number one.[1] Negative peer pressure occurs when young people feel forced to do something they really don't want to do—something they would not have done on their own—in order to be part of the gang.

Peer pressure is not a phenomenon that suddenly occurs in adolescence. The need to be accepted by our peers is seen in our earliest friendships. But it is during adolescence that we become more acutely aware of peer pressure because the stakes and risks are higher. The natural and healthful individuation process may explode into a tumultuous eruption of rebellion against parental values because of peer influences.

Before examining the causes and interventions for peer pressure it may be helpful to take a quick look at the kinds of peer groups influencing today's teens. Sociologists have discovered a variety of specific high school groups:

Case Description

Connie, a fifteen-year-old, came to counseling at the insistence of her mom and dad. She was doing about average in school and attended her youth group at church frequently. But Connie's recent behavior caused her parents a great deal of concern. First of all, she was part of a neighborhood party that got out of hand and had to be broken up by the police. She was brought home by the father of one of her friends, and he reported to Connie's parents that she had been drinking.

This was a surprise to her parents. They didn't suspect that Connie was involved in this kind of activity. At church and at home she seemed like a different person. She dressed differently and acted differently. Her parents later learned that Connie would take a different set of clothes to school in her gym bag and change in the restroom before classes began. At school she didn't hang out with her church friends, but was trying to break into a group of students that had very different values. Her parents were especially concerned about the older boys she was dating. After three or four counseling sessions, Connie admitted that she would do just about anything to be accepted by "the popular" students. She felt phony and hollow.

Jocks are usually males that are consumed by athletics. They tend to make average to above-average grades; they are clean-cut, friendly, and self-confident.

Motorheads are also usually male, and they are consumed by cars. They make below-average grades, are rude to teachers, and wear clothes dirtied by working on their cars.

Freaks consist of both males and females that are into drugs. They are unconcerned about school and frequently skip classes.[2]

Rah-rahs are the socially elite, the female equivalent of jocks.

Politicos are the governing elite who run student government. They intercede with the school administration and are generally well liked.

Intellectuals are the academic elite, known for their ability to breeze through classes with ease.

Greasers are throwbacks to the fifties and tend toward the delinquent side. They smoke marijuana, drink, and are ambivalent about school.

Grinds are a very small group of math wizards that spend most of their time in math lab. With the exception of the politicos, all of these groups occupy specific territory on school campuses—places where they congregate when not in class.

Students who do not fit into one of these sociological categories make up the silent majority. They attend school regularly, are involved in various interest groups off and on campus, and have friends like themselves.[3]

☑ WHY THE STRUGGLE HAPPENS

Many factors influence struggles with negative peer pressure. The following are just a few of the most commonly cited "causes."

Insecurity

The more insecure young people are about their own worth, the more they tend to look to others for direction in making their decisions. In their need to belong, adolescents are susceptible to the influences of their peers. It helps them keep from "looking stupid" in their friends' eyes if they are doing just what their friends would do. Teenagers achieve a false sense of security that quickly disappears when they encounter even a small dose of rejection.

Parental Relationships

One of the strongest and most consistent findings concerning peer pressure is its relationship to family interactions. Research links high peer conformity to poor parent-child relationships. Antagonism, rejection, poor communication, extreme authoritarianism, and permissiveness at home are strongly linked with adolescents' susceptibility to peer influence.[4]

Lack of Assertiveness

Learning to "just say no" isn't always that easy. Some adolescents give in to negative peer pressure because they do not have the interpersonal skills that are needed to stay their ground, express their genuine feelings, and choose their own behavior. They are like a feather in the wind, blown about by any prevailing opinion and unable to influence their environment.

Faulty Thinking

Sometimes young people act on beliefs that are irrational—beliefs that have little or no basis in reality. With little evidence they conclude, "I have to do whatever anyone else wants to do in order to be his or her friend," or "I have to dress a certain way and talk about certain things in order to be popular." They base all of their decisions on faulty thinking.

☑ HOW TO HELP

The following techniques are designed to give struggling adolescents inner strength to resist negative peer pressure. They should be thought of as working with and undergirded by personal acceptance and reflective listening.

Pinpoint the Severity

At the beginning of treatment it is helpful to assess the intensity of adolescents' struggle with peer pressure. I know of no clinical assessment of negative peer influence. But Bill Sanders, in his book *Tough Turf: A Teen Survival Manual*, has developed a helpful questionnaire that can serve as a springboard for self-examination and discussion. It can also be found in *Helping the Struggling Adolescent: A Counseling Guide.*

Ease Parents' Concerns

Parents generally worry about the impact of peer pressure on their children, but most of their worries are unfounded. Most adolescents continue to live by their parents' values regarding religion, education, politics, and careers. Although adolescents spend less time with their parents and more time with their friends than they did as children, they still turn to their parents for advice and guidance on the important issues in their lives. Moreover, when asked who is most influential and most important in their lives, most adolescents name their parents, not their friends.[5]

Effective counselors will empathize with parents' concerns, but will also help them see the big picture of adolescent transition. During teen years, conflict between parents and children is at its height. Typical adolescents are overly concerned about establishing their independence, while at the same time, most parents are overly concerned with maintaining control to counteract the presumed peer pressure. Parents often worry that the first year or so of adolescence is only the tip of the iceberg, that their conflicts are going to get worse rather than better. In reality, however, the reverse usually occurs after that first year or two.

Explore Helpful Pressures

Adolescents may be empowered by examining in what ways their peers are influencing them. One of the least threatening means to heighten this awareness is to help adolescents explore how their friends influence them in positive ways. For example, friends may help them try out for a team, get better grades, get in shape, run for class office, save money, and so on. This discussion may lead to an exploration of how they are being influenced in negative ways.

Take an Inventory of Their Experiences

Help adolescents achieve perspective by examining past decisions based on negative peer pressure. Ask them to list how they have responded to situations in the past few months, how things turned out, and what they have learned in the process. Ask whether they would do the same again. This helps them see who is "bad news" and to make conscious decisions about who will be their friends. The inventory can also help young people localize areas where they are especially prone to giving in to negative peer pressure.

Boost Self-Confidence

Many of the principles discussed in the section on inferiority (for example, developing positive self-statements, modifying unrealistic standards, confronting destructive tendencies, and exploring theology) can be used to help boost the confidence of adolescents who battle peer pressure.

Question Self-Talk

Adolescents who give in to peer pressure often have automatic thoughts that keep them from standing their own ground. They are irrational thoughts that perpetuate a fear of rejection. A student, for example, may think, "I look silly," whenever someone looks at him or her. The thought just pops into mind automatically. Help adolescents question the validity of these thoughts by first discovering what their self-talk is. These thoughts are usually lightening fast and difficult to catch.

To identify them have counselees recall the thoughts they had just prior to the start of a feeling. For example, what judgments of their experience did they make just before feeling insecure. It may be helpful to reconstruct a situation that led to giving in to something they didn't want to do. Lift out the self-talk statements and explore how changing their thinking (that is, substituting rational thoughts for faulty logic) may help them resist giving in. Have them imagine potential situations that may be difficult, and help them prepare self-talk statements that will give them inner strength and self-respect. For example, "I can stand up for what I believe," "I am a person of integrity," or "I believe in me."[6]

Help Them Challenge the System

Teenagers often believe they must go along with the crowd to be popular. Explore with them what might happen if they were to buck the system. What if they were to walk out of a movie that offends them? Would their friends think they were wimps? How do they know? If their friends were to look down on them for standing up for their beliefs, explore the value of relationships with those people. Empower young people to question the behaviors of others and decide for themselves how they want to direct their lives. Challenge teenagers to break out of the expected mold and to influence their environment. Use the illustration of a thermostat. Most young people act like thermometers. They have no control over their environment and adjust to everything around them. Thermostats, on the other hand, influence their environment. It is an old cliché, but new to most adolescents.

Teach Assertiveness

Perhaps the most effective strategy for helping adolescents withstand negative peer influence is assertiveness training. It has been found to help youths resist drug use, negative sexual behavior, and other actions.[7] Teenagers can learn to use nonverbal skills to bolster their ability to be assertive—to express feelings, ask for what they want, or say no to something they don't want. They can be taught to look directly at others when addressing them, maintain an open rather than a closed posture, and literally "stand their ground" by not physically backing away from others. Adolescents can also learn to be assertive by expressing their feelings and desires. Struggling adolescents often evaluate their feelings for appropriateness. They are asking, "What *should* I be feeling?" rather than "What *am* I feeling?" Once they have learned to identify their feelings, encourage young people to express them in peer groups.

Learning to be assertive requires practice. Have adolescents write out descriptions of two or three situations where they become especially passive (for example, drinking at a party in order to be accepted by others). Next, have them write how they would like to act in such circumstances. Help them practice assertive responses in those situations. Have them use "I" statements, simple requests, nonverbal behaviors, and so on.

For more information on assertiveness training you may find *Your Perfect Right* (Alberti and Emmons) and *Asserting Yourself* (Bower) helpful. For assertiveness training within a Christian context, *Beyond Assertiveness* (Faul and Augsburger) and *The Assertive Christian* (Emmons and Richardson) are useful.

☑ WHEN TO REFER

Refer adolescents who struggle with negative peer pressure to other competent counselors or psychologists when, over time, they feel more out of control and increasingly give in to peer influence. Refer them also if you recognize that you are encouraging adolescents to depend upon you to make decisions for them.

Where To Go for Additional Help

Adler, R. B. *Confidence in Communication: A Guide to Assertive and Social Skills.* New York: Holt, Rinehart, 1974.

Alberti, R. E., and M. L. Emmons. *Your Perfect Right: A Guide to Assertive Behavior.* San Luis Obispo, Calif.: Impact Publishers, 1978.

Bower, G., and S. Bower. *Asserting Yourself: A Practical Guide for Positive Change.* Reading, Mass.: Addison-Wesley, 1976.

Emmons, M., and D. Richardson. *The Assertive Christian.* Minneapolis: Winston, 1981.

Faul, J., and D. W. Augsburger. *Beyond Assertiveness.* Waco, Tex.: Word, 1983.

Hartley, F. *Dare To Be Different.* Old Tappan, N.J.: Revell, 1980.

Sanders, B. *Tough Turf: A Teen Survival Manual.* Old Tappan, N.J.: Revell, 1986.

Scott, S. *How To Say No and Keep Your Friends.* Amherst, Mass.: Human Resource Development Press, 1986.

_____. *Peer Pressure Reversal: An Adult Guide To Developing a Responsible Child.* Amherst, Mass.: Human Resource Development Press, 1985.

Notes

1. *Psychology Today* (May 1989): 10.

2. M. H. Leona, "An Examination of Adolescent Clique Language in a Suburban Secondary School," *Adolescence* 13 (1978): 496–502.

3. R. W. Larkin, *Suburban Youth in Cultural Crisis* (New York: Oxford Univ. Press, 1979).

4. J. E. Marcia, "Identity in Adolescence," in *Handbook of Adolescent Psychology*, ed. J. Adelson (New York: Wiley, 1980).

5. J. Williamson and L. Campbell, "Parents and Their Children Comment on Adolescence," *Adolescence* 20 (1985): 745–48.

6. A. T. Beck, *Cognitive Therapy and Emotional Disorders* (New York: New American Library, 1979).

7. J. M. Williams and D. W. Hall, "Conformity to Peer Influence: The Impact of Assertion Training on College Students," *Journal of College Student Development* 29 (1988): 466–71.

PHOBIAS

☑ WHAT THE STRUGGLE LOOKS LIKE

Fear is both common and natural. Some people are afraid to walk through certain sections of town late at night. Others fear vicious dogs or tornadoes. Those are reasonable, appropriate fears that help us survive.

A phobia, however, is irrational and inappropriate. A phobia is experienced in situations that present no real threat. It is not adaptive or natural. A phobia is an intense, irrational fear that greatly interferes with a person's life. The fear revolves around some object, event, activity, or situation. As a result, phobic individuals begin to structure most, if not all, of their daily activities around that which they fear. And they will do almost anything to avoid confronting that fear.

Most people define their behavior based on prior knowledge. People with phobias tend to think the worst of a situation. For example, people who are claustrophobic in a small dark room might think the ceiling will collapse on them or that they will suffocate because they will get trapped with no air.

It can be difficult to distinguish a phobic person from one who is experiencing a panic disorder, but there are distinctions. A panic attack seems to appear suddenly, with no obvious precipitating factor. A phobia, by contrast, appears to be much more directed and specific. Phobic people are overcome with anxiety only in the presence of what they fear (e.g., an elevator or a dog). The section on panic attacks may be helpful for further comparisons.

Approximately seventy-seven out of a thousand people in the general population suffer from some type of phobic disorder. The most common phobia treated by therapists is agoraphobia—fear of venturing out into open or public spaces like stores, restaurants, theaters, or public transportation. Phobias are common at all levels of society, at all ages, and in both sexes.

Phobic reactions usually have three components. The first is *cognitive*. The phobic individual may report negative thoughts like "I know I am going to make a fool of myself" or "I'm going to die." The second is *behavioral*. The phobic person will generally avoid the feared situation. And last, the person may experience a whole range of *physiological* responses in the presence of phobic stimuli.[1]

Literally hundreds of phobias have been identified. In fact, the number is indefinite because phobic reactions may occur with almost any situation or object. *Blakiston's Gould Medical Dictionary* lists 368 different phobias.[2] Some common phobias along with their uncommon names are cats (ailourophobia), thunder (asterophobia), dirt (mysophobia), snakes (ophidiophobia), and stage fright (topophobia). The most widely accepted classification system, the *Diagnostic and Statistical Manual* (3d ed. rev. [DSM-III-R]), subdivides phobias into three groups: simple phobias, social phobias and agoraphobia.[3] Counselors working with teens should be familiar with each of these phobias.

Simple Phobia. These involve maladaptive fear and avoidance of discrete objects or situations. They are sometimes called specific phobias because the range of phobic stimuli is narrower than in other phobic disorders—everything from acrophobia (fear of high places) to zoophobia (fear of animals). Some of the most common simple phobias are fear of animals and insects such as birds, cats, dogs, bees, spiders, snakes, or moths. Others include fear of disease or illness like cancer or a heart attack.[4] These phobias rarely cause a serious problem for the phobic person, unless the feared stimulus happens to be something that is commonly or out of necessity encountered (such as a person who fears elevators but lives in a high-rise apartment). Simple phobias are experienced more by women. One researcher found that ninety-five percent of animal phobics are women. This figure is accepted for postpubescent individuals, but before puberty, fears of animals are found commonly in boys as well as girls.[5]

Social Phobia. This is characterized by excessive anxiety in social situations such as parties, meetings, interviews, making complaints, writing in public, interacting with the opposite sex or with teachers. These people are especially fearful of potential public scrutiny and evaluation. For fear of looking ridiculous, social phobics may refuse to sit facing another person at the lunch table. They may avoid going swimming since swimming involves exposing their bodies to the view of others. This is obviously quite maladaptive since it interferes with important areas of normal social functioning and development for adolescents. Social phobia is rarely reported before puberty and most frequently begins in the late teens.[6]

Counselors must make the important distinction between adolescents struggling with social phobia and adolescents struggling with social inadequacy. Young people may experience anxiety in social situations simply because of poor social skills. This is not the same as social phobia. This has significant implications for treatment. If young people are experiencing anxiety caused by skill deficiency, anxiety reduction procedures will not be effective. They need assertiveness and social-skills training. See the section on inferiority for a discussion of this treatment approach.

Case Description

Laura came to counseling at the insistence of her parents. Her mom and dad were prominent and wealthy members of their community. Laura was their first child and they had high expectations for her. They brought her to counseling because, according to her father, she had "low self-esteem." As it turned out, Laura was struggling with a social phobia. She would suffer intense anxiety in a social situation that she saw as potentially awkward or embarrassing. The straw that broke the camel's back for her parents was when she retreated to her room at a recent family reunion where she was expected to be with her relatives from around the country. It was apparent that Laura was not lacking social skills; she simply feared being evaluated by others. She dreaded the thought of doing something embarrassing and having others talk about it.

Agoraphobia. This term dates back to ancient Greece and literally means "fear of the marketplace." The most common clinical feature is a fear of leaving a familiar setting. The agoraphobic becomes anxious at the thought of leaving home or being outside, particularly when alone. Many phobic persons rarely, if ever, go out in public, but they can often function fairly well within the home. Many agoraphobics also suffer from panic attacks. Fear of having a panic attack outside the home is often cited as the reason for staying home. As with panic disorders, onset of agoraphobia is generally in adolescence, and it usually follows a course of repeated episodes of anxiety interspersed with mild, diffuse anxiety. Agoraphobia is three times more likely to occur in women than in men. More than any other phobia, agoraphobia is frequently accompanied by a variety of other problems such as depression or the abuse of alcohol.

☑ WHY THE STRUGGLE HAPPENS

Phobias rarely materialize out of nowhere. While it is difficult to pinpoint a single causal factor, most agree that phobias are generated out of a combination of the following reasons.

Biology

Recently, biological theories have put forth the notion of "preparedness" to explain some phobic behavior. They have noticed that symptoms do not appear at random. They argue that our biological constitutions cause us to be more "prepared" to avoid certain situations or objects. In other words, certain phobias may be indicative of some sort of biological predispositions to avoid certain dangers.[7]

Conditioning

Under some circumstances phobias may be learned from frightening experiences. For example, being bitten by a dog may lead to a persistent, unreasonable fear of something that bears little relationship to the likelihood of being bitten again. Once acquired, the phobic person may extend any such excessive fear to other stimuli, such as all four-legged animals. A classic psychological experiment by John Watson demonstrated that unreasonable fears may be learned from unpleasant experiences, not only directly but indirectly through association with a fear-provoking event. Working with "Albert" (an eleven-month-old boy), Watson made a loud banging noise every time the boy reached out toward a white rat. Over a seven-day period Albert gradually came to show fear in the presence of the white rat, without any noise being made, and his fear subsequently "generalized" to include all furry objects.[8] While ample research confirms that phobias can result from conditioning, it is usually agreed that origins of phobias are more complex.

Modeling

Many fears in childhood are acquired by observing and imitating parents who are frightened by dentists, storms, darkness, and so on. Children have even been observed in new situations to look at their parents to see how they are reacting before they will show their own reactions. Verbal as well as behavioral messages may generate fear in children. Youngsters may become terrorized by the dire warnings that "spiders can kill you" or that "strangers will kidnap you and kill you." Young people may become phobic of what they were taught to fear.[9]

Displacement

Displacement is the process by which feelings and attitudes are transferred from their real source to a previously neutral object or situation. Freud was the first to describe the origin of phobias in displacement. He wrote about his conversations with the father of "Little Hans," a five-year-old boy who was afraid of horses. Freud's analysis of the information he obtained suggested that Hans was really afraid that his father was angry at him, and he had displaced his fear onto horses to minimize his anxiety (he could more easily avoid horses than his father).[10]

G. Keith Olson illustrates this causal factor in describing an adolescent who became phobic of sharp knifes. Olson explains, "A few months ago, during an angry fight with her mother while they were in the kitchen, [the adolescent] saw a sharp knife and thought of stabbing her mother with it. The thought horrified her. She felt guilty and afraid, and she repressed it as quickly and as thoroughly as she could."[11] From that experience forward, she was desperately afraid of knives.

☑ HOW TO HELP

The following techniques should be thought of as working with and, as always, undergirded by personal acceptance and reflective listening. They are designed to create alternatives for adolescents to replace dysfunctional behaviors and attitudes.

Pinpoint the Severity

At the beginning of treatment it is helpful to assess the intensity of adolescents' phobias. A number of assessments that work nicely with phobic struggles are available. The Fear Questionnaire is a twenty-four-item instrument developed to assess the outcome of work with phobic patients. The Fear Survey Schedule-II is a fifty-one-item instrument designed to measure fear responses. It lists potential fear-evoking situations and stimuli. Adolescents rate their level of discomfort or distress. The Mobility Inventory for Agoraphobia measures the severity of agoraphobic avoidance behavior. It is a twenty-seven-item instrument. Each of these measures is found in *Helping the Struggling Adolescent: A Counseling Guide*.

Examine Secondary Gains

Some phobias enable people to feel "privileged." They may receive a great deal of attention and love for remaining fearful of birds, for example. These fringe benefits of their phobia are called *secondary gains*. Do phobic young people fear a loss of attention if they do not maintain their dysfunctional behavior? How badly do they *really* want to overcome their phobic struggles? Ask them what good things they will have to give up if they do not have their fears. Using a scale of one to ten, ask them to estimate how badly they want to overcome their fears.

Inspire Optimism

As adolescents see themselves to be more effective in confronting challenging situations, their levels of anxiety diminish and so do their phobias. Albert Bandura of Stanford University calls this self-efficacy and has shown the importance of clients' belief in their ability to overcome their struggles. While actually behaving in successful ways is one of the best ways to instill this kind of optimism, verbal persuasion from respected therapists has also been shown to have a positive influence.[12] Knowing that others believe they can succeed helps struggling adolescents also believe they can.

Practice Relaxation Techniques

Phobic adolescents must acquire the basic tools of relaxation. This process should begin in the first few sessions. Several relaxation techniques are discussed in the sections on anxiety and panic attack. They include deep muscle relaxation, breathing exercises, autogenics, and biofeedback. It may take adolescents a while to learn to use these exercises, but with practice they will soon be able to relax and thereby experience a sense of control over their physiological responses to their phobias.

Teach Coping Skills

Once young people have begun to master relaxation techniques, they are ready to learn coping skills. The first step is to have them make a list of all current life situations that trigger their fear and anxiety. They should be as specific as possible and try to come up with at least twenty items (they may range from very mild discomfort to the most dreaded experiences). Have them arrange lists into a hierarchy by ranking the stressful experiences in order from the least to the most anxiety-producing. Each item should represent an increase in stress over the last item, and the increases should be in approximately equal increments.

The rating system is based on *Subjective Units of Distress* (suds). Total relaxation is zero suds, while the most stressful situation in the hierarchy is rated at one hundred suds. All others fall somewhere in between and are assigned suds scores based on their subjective impression of where each situation falls relative to their most relaxed or most anxious states. For example, if the most stressful item in the hierarchy, "making conversation with attractive members of the opposite sex," is ranked at one hundred suds, then "thinking about calling a member of the opposite sex" might be ranked sixty-five suds, and "seeing an attractive member of the opposite sex from across the room" might rank down around thirty-five suds. Allow clients to be the experts on how they react to each situation and decide where each stressful event fits. On a list of twenty items, they may be separated by increments of five suds.

Once the hierarchy is in place, use it to desensitize adolescents to their strongest fears. Start with the first scene (lowest suds) and build a clear picture of the situation for them to see in their imagination. Ask them to hold the stressful image for about a half minute. Ask them to notice the beginning of any tension in their bodies. Ask them to use the tension as a signal for deep muscle relaxation or deep breathing. They will relax away the tension as they imagine the stressful situation.

After they have imagined a particular scene without anxiety or tension, go on to the next item in the hierarchy. Move through the entire hierarchy of stressful situations using this same procedure. Make sure the scenes are vivid and real to them. With each step they will use early signs of tension as their signal to relax. Repeat the exercise and assign them to do it on their own. Once they have mastered those items with the highest suds, they will have a much stronger degree of confidence to battle their fears in actual situations.

Work on Inner Dialogue

Teach adolescents that their thoughts do not need to intensify fear. Instead, how they think can act as a tranquilizer for their tension and push away their panic.[13] They can tell themselves to relax in the middle of a phobic reaction by beginning to repeat to themselves a series of fear-conquering statements such as "There is nothing to worry about"; "This won't last long"; "Nothing can hurt me here"; "I can relax." In the midst of fearful situations, the more attention they give to their coping monologue, the quicker they will experience physiological relief. Let them make their own lists of inner dialogue statements that will help them inoculate themselves against phobia. Then ask them to practice these in actual situations.

Practice *In Vivo* Coping and Systematic Desensitization

For phobia treatment to be effective, adolescents must have opportunities to transfer their coping skills from the counselor's office to "real life." They must confront the feared stimuli through direct exposure (*in vivo*). A substantial body of evidence has accumulated that attests to the superiority of this technique.[14] In this strategy adolescents are actually exposed to crowded shopping malls, birds, airplanes, snakes, or whatever.

One of the most thoroughly researched *in vivo* treatments for phobic disorders is participant modeling developed by Albert Bandura and his colleagues.[15] Therapists accompany adolescents and assist them in any way that helps them conquer their irrational fears. Therapists may simply be there for encouragement and support or, even better, to model nonphobic behavior. A preliminary step in conducting this kind of modeling may include a graded hierarchy of fear-provoking situations that will allow patients systematically to desensitize themselves to the feared object.[16]

In the case of snake phobics, for example, an initial hierarchy item might include looking at or touching a picture of a snake.[17] Intermediate items might include putting hands on the glass of the cage housing a real snake. The next step is to put their faces up to the glass. Once the hierarchy has been constructed, therapists then model for clients each of the graded tasks on the hierarchy. After the modeling of all the graded tasks of the hierarchy, therapists again model one of the first hierarchy items and instruct the adolescents to repeat the behavior. This step is repeated with each item.[18] Of course, using the skills in the face of the feared object will be more difficult than in an imagined scene. Setbacks are inevitable. This performance-based strategy is sometimes impossible, for example, in the case of fear of death or fear of injury. In these cases, imaginal exposure becomes the treatment of choice.

Create "Win" Situations

It is crucial for adolescents to accomplish something on their own. This allows them to break patterns of possible dependency. To accomplish this counselors may provide homework assignments. These should be very small at first to insure success. For example, if you are working with social phobia, you may give the assignment of buying a newspaper from a machine in a public place. Eventually assign clients to go into a store to buy a newspaper from a clerk. Next, into a library to check out a book, and so on. This strengthens their belief in their abilities and gives them efficacy for future situations.

Explore Other "Frightening" Emotions

Adolescents struggling with phobic disorders may be dealing with any number of unexpressed feelings. After they have faced what initially appeared to be overwhelming situational fears, they may then be ready to face other fearful emotions. With a solid platform of trust where therapists have helped clients take behavioral risks with their environment, the next step is often to take risks with feelings that seem dreadful. It may be anger, guilt, resentment, or a number of other "unsafe" feelings. In any case, therapists may help young people deal with safe dosages of feelings, working toward the goal of enabling them to manage the fears that surround them.

☑ WHEN TO REFER

Refer adolescents to psychiatrists for evaluation whenever drugs are involved. If during any point in treatment the phobic behavior is exacerbated or seems to be becoming entrenched, consultation or referral is necessary. Phobias can also play a part in other mental disorders, such as schizophrenia. In these cases, they serve to stabilize a fragile ego and prevent further overwhelming anxiety and decompensation. The phobia thus serves a different purpose for these individuals than it does for the "true" phobic. If you are not trained in the treatment of this serious illness where phobia is simply a component, referral is paramount.

Where To Go for Additional Help

Agras, S. *Panic: Facing Fears, Phobias, and Anxiety.* New York: W. H. Freeman, 1985.

Bourne, E. J. *The Anxiety and Phobia Workbook.* Oakland, Calif.: New Harbinger, 1989.

Davis, M., M. McKay, and E. R. Eshclman. *The Relaxation and Stress Reduction Workbook.* Richmond: Calif.: New Harbinger, 1980.

Meichenbaum, D. H. *Cognitive-Behavior Modification.* New York: Plenum, 1974.

Wanderer, Z. *Acquiring Courage,* 1990. This in an audio cassette program for the "rapid treatment of phobias." It applies the techniques of implosion therapy in a self-help style. I recommend that this be used in conjunction with a competent psychotherapist.

The Phobia Society of America lists more than one thousand phobia specialists in North America. To receive general information on phobias or the latest information in effective treatment of phobias, write to the Phobia Society of America, Department R, 133 Rollins Avenue, Suite 4B, Rockville, MD 20852-4004.

Notes

1. P. J. Lang, "Fear Reduction and Fear Behavior: Problems in Treating a Construct," in *Research in Psychotherapy,* vol. 3, ed. J. M. Shlien (Washington, D.C.: American Psychological Association, 1968).

2. A. Osol, *Blakiston's Gould Medical Dictionary,* 3d ed. (New York: McGraw-Hill, 1972).

3. *Diagnostic and Statistical Manual III–R* (Washington, D.C.: American Psychiatric Association, 1987).

4. I. M. Marks, *Fears and Phobias* (New York: Academic Press, 1969).

5. J. W. McFarlan, L. Allen, and M. P. Hanzik, *A Developmental Study of the Behavior Problems of Normal Children Between 21 Months and 14 Years* (Los Angeles: Univ. of California Press, 1954).

6. S. Shafer, "Aspects of Phobic Illness: A Study of 90 Personal Cases," *British Journal of Medical Psychology* 49 (1976): 221–36.

7. M. E. P. Seligman, "Phobias and Preparedness," *Behavior Therapy* 2 (1971): 307–20.

8. J. B. Watson and R. Rayner, "Conditioned Emotional Reactions," *Journal of Experimental Psychology* 3 (1920): 1–14.

9. J. L. Deverensky, "Children's Fears: A Developmental Comparison of Normal and Exceptional Children," *Journal of Genetic Psychology* 135 (1979): 11–21.

10. S. Freud, "Analysis of a Phobia in a Five-Year-Old Boy," standard ed., vol. 10. (1909; reprint, London: Hogarth, 1955).

11. G. K. Olson, *Counseling Teenagers: The Complete Christian Guide to Understanding and Helping Adolescents* (Loveland, Colo.: Group Publishing, 1984), 303.

12. A. Bandura, "Self-Efficacy Mechanism in Human Agency," *American Psychologist* 37 (1982): 122–47.

13. D. H. Meichenbaum, *Cognitive-Behavior Modification* (New York: Plenum, 1974).

14. A. Bandura, "Self-Efficacy: Toward a Unifying Theory of Behavioral Change," *Psychological Review* 84 (1977): 191–215.

15. A. Bandura, R. W. Jeffery, and C. Wright, "Efficacy of Participant Modeling As a Function of Response Induction Aids," *Journal of Abnormal Psychology* 83 (1974): 56–64.

16. The theory underlying this technique was designed by Joseph Wolpe, who believed that phobias are not explained by unconscious conflicts but through undergoing traumatic experiences. See J. Wolpe, "Experimental Neuroses As Learned Behavior," *British Journal of Psychology* 43 (1952): 243–52.

17. You can find photos of many feared objects for this purpose in a standard encyclopedia.

18. Bandura, "Self-Efficacy Mechanism in Human Agency."

PORNOGRAPHY

☑ WHAT THE STRUGGLE LOOKS LIKE

The reading of sexually explicit materials or looking at pictures of sexual acts has been around for a long time. Cave drawings depict sexual activity. Erotic art of ancient Greece, India, Africa, and Japan indicates the cultural universality of such interest.

Today, it is practically impossible to find a high school student in America who has not come across some form of sexually explicit material. Although "adult" bookstores and movie theaters cater to people twenty-one or older, inquisitive teenagers have ample opportunities to experience erotica and pornography. Magazines, best selling novels, advertisements, comic books, and general-release movies guarantee that anyone remotely interested in viewing such materials has the opportunity. Chances for doing so are not limited to sneaking a look at a friend's collection of *Playboy* centerfolds. Adolescents may experience pornography on the telephone through so-called "Dial-a-Porn" services, through VCRs and the neighborhood video store, and on late-night cable television. Josh McDowell and Dick Day in *Why Wait?* report that experts estimate that as much as seventy percent of all pornography ends up in the possession of teenagers.[1]

Counselors of adolescents may expect to find more and more young people in their offices who struggle with pornography. With its widespread dissemination and efforts to achieve glossy respectability, pornography was estimated in 1982 to be a five-billion-dollar business in the United States. Instead of being a fringe influence on society, its moral values pour into the mainstream.[2]

Defining pornography is not a simple matter in part because different kinds of pornography have been identified. In the view of many, *violent pornography* champions the notion that sexual violence, usually directed against women, is normal. *Degrading pornography* debases and dehumanizes women even if the material does not depict explicit violent behavior. In contrast to degrading and violent pornography, *erotica* advocates the view that nonviolent and nondegrading sexual expressions are normal and serve a useful purpose.[3] Of course, the lines of demarcation become fuzzy when using an ambiguous

Case Description

Before I had even said hello, Ron was confessing his problem. "I can't stop thinking about sex. I have never told anyone, but I can't stand it any more." Ron was fighting back his tears. "I am getting scared. Last week I stole money from my mom to buy more pornography, and I think she knows what I am doing." As a senior in high school, Ron's existence seemed to be consumed by sex. He saw his first piece of pornography, a *Playboy* magazine, in a neighbor's trash can when he was nine. When he came to my office he was hooked on "the hard stuff"—mostly magazines but he also used dial-a-porn services from time to time.

Ron has a pattern of binging on pornography. He buys or steals about four magazines every couple of weeks and hides them inside his record album jackets in his bedroom. He uses them for several days as he masturbates, and then goes through great pains to destroy them. It is his ritual by which he promises himself and God that he will never do it again.

term like *degrading*. Some prefer the general definition of Langly Longford: "Pornography is that which exploits and dehumanizes sex, so that human beings are treated as things, and women in particular as sex objects."[4]

There are arguments over almost all definitions of pornography, but, as Richard Foster says, "That should not obscure its existence. There is a world of difference between the nude figures in the Sistine Chapel and those in a 'skin' magazine, and any reasonable person knows the difference."[5]

While almost every adolescent has been exposed to pornography, male adolescents are about three times more likely than females to report being sexually aroused by it.[6] While not all males become obsessed with it, adolescents who tell their counselors that they battle it probably feel like hostages to their preoccupation with it. They may indeed be addicted.

Dale Ryan, known to some as "the missionary to the addicted," identifies five aspects of addiction. The first is *tolerance*; the addict needs to see more to achieve the same degree of mood alteration. The second is *withdrawal*; the addict would be very uncomfortable not to continue. The third is *self-deception*; the addict denies that the behavior is really affecting oneself. The fourth part is *the loss of will power*. Finally, the behavior process causes *real problems* in the person's life.[7]

Sexual addiction has been described by Patrick Carnes as "the athlete's foot of the mind."[8] It never goes away. It continually asks to be scratched, promising relief. To scratch, however, is to cause pain and to intensify the itch. This section is to aid counselors to help teens who need spiritual and therapeutic healing for the intensity of addiction to pornography.

☑ WHY THE STRUGGLE HAPPENS

Numerous reasons explain why some teenagers grapple with pornography. The following are only a few of the most commonly cited factors.

Curiosity

According to John Court, "Pornography is a significant factor in shaping the sexual mores and attitudes of teenagers."[9] While it may hinder healthful development, a young person will seek out pornography as a source of knowledge and comparative information about sexual behavior. Court also points out that while certain well-chosen sexually explicit materials may educate young people, studies have shown that pornography has the same beneficial effects.[10]

Physiological Desires

Teenagers are physically ready for sex far sooner than they are for social intimacy and the responsibilities of marriage. Masturbation is a natural "safety valve" while nature is synchronizing growth in young people's lives. The problem for some teenagers is that the safety valve may become an all-consuming obsession. Frederick Buechner, acclaimed author and Presbyterian minister, has written, "Lust is the ape that gibbers in our loins. Tame him as we will by day, he rages all the wilder in our dreams by night. Just when we think we're safe from him, he raises up his ugly head and smirks, and there's no river in the world flows cold and strong enough to strike him down. Almighty God, why dost thou deck men out with such a loathsome toy?"[11] Agonizing adolescents are not too young too understand this plaintive query.

Availability

Magazines like *Playboy, Penthouse, Hustler,* and dozens of others are available at neighborhood stores. R-rated, NC–17-rated, and X-rated movies are everywhere. Porno shops abound. Erotic art has been legitimized. The advent of videotape and cable television has added new dimensions to availability of pornography. A University of Utah psychologist studied junior high customers of a New York dial-a-porn service. He found that without exception the adolescents became addicted to listening to explicit adult sex by phone. In several cases the children made more than three hundred telephone calls before parents received enormous phone bills and ended the practice.[12] Adolescents seeking access to pornography will manage to obtain it.

Faulty Thinking

Generally, adolescents who become addicted to pornography do not perceive themselves as worthwhile. They use pornography as a way of making their isolation bearable. Out of this thinking come denial and distortions that keep them from confronting their temptations.

The Addictive Cycle

Addiction to pornography follows a four-step cycle, which, according to Patrick Carnes, intensifies with each repetition:

1. *Preoccupation*—the trance or mood when the addict is completely

engrossed with thoughts of sex. This mental state creates an obsessive search for sexual stimulation.

2. *Ritualization*—the addict's special routine leading up to masturbation or other sexual behavior. The ritual intensifies the preoccupation, adding arousal and excitement.

3. *Compulsive sexual behavior*—the actual sex act, which is the goal of the preoccupation and ritualization. The true addict is unable to control or stop this behavior.

4. *Despair*—the feeling of utter hopelessness about one's behavior and powerlessness in the face of it.[13]

☑ HOW TO HELP

The following strategies should be undergirded with empathy, personal acceptance, and reflective listening. With this sensitive struggle, it is imperative that counselors be slow to condemn and quick to listen and understand.

Pinpoint the Severity

In treating the combat with pornography it is crucial to assess the degree to which adolescents are "addicted." The Sexual Addiction Screening Test is designed to evaluate the likelihood of sexual addiction. The test is a fourteen-page questionnaire that assesses all aspects of sexually addictive behavior. The Sexual Addiction Screening Test is available from

Patrick J. Carnes
Institute for Behavioral Medicine
4101 Golden Valley Road
Golden Valley, MN 55422
612/588-2771

If adolescents show signs of addiction, the following is a place to begin preparing for work with this problem.

Instill Hope

Affirm the courage the youth have demonstrated in their asking for help with such a difficult matter. Confession of the attraction that pornography holds for them is like a healing ointment that brings immediate relief, if not the much-needed long-term cure. Knowing that they may talk about their problem in a nonjudgmental setting is a boon to the ease they seek. But adolescents also need to know that there is a permanent way out of this problem. Hope will energize optimism and fuel the steps toward complete recovery.

Understand Its Pull

Since teenagers are immoderately curious about the opposite sex, pornography reaches out and pulls them in like a magnet. Pornography draws on their need to know about the unknown. If young people may talk openly with counselors about the attractiveness of pornography, they will be taking the first step toward gaining control over the power of this pernicious vice. Much of adolescent energy that would be used in devouring pornography will then be immediately directed into positive action. According to Keith Olson, "Simply talking about the desires and conflicts in a non-judgmental setting will reduce the chances of sexual acting-out."[14]

Understand Its Serious Damage

In the early 1970s it was widely publicized that pornography is benign or beneficial. Following a massive increase in its availability and the appearance of violent and child pornography, further research has shown the earlier optimism by secularists to be misplaced. Several lines of evidence show that in many sex crimes pornography has been among the triggering influences—especially in cases of rape.[15]

Pornography promotes the myth that women want to be raped. Victims are often depicted as secretly desiring sexual assault and deriving pleasure from violent sex. Evidence suggests that the depiction of a woman becoming aroused while being raped is strongly associated with potential violence against women. In one study forty-one percent of the participants reported that after seeing such a scene they might rape if they were certain of not being caught.[16] Regardless of whether the act is actually carried out, exposure to violent pornography does reduce sensitivity to rape victims.[17] Callousness toward women is seen in such statements as "a woman doesn't mean no until she slaps you." As one researcher put it, "Pornography promotes a climate in which acts of sexual hostility directed against women are not only tolerated ideologically, but encouraged."[18]

Understand Its Relational Damage

Pornography contributes to unrealistic expectations about sexuality. Even so-called soft porn like *Playboy* magazine presents a world of sexual fantasy that distorts meaningful relationships. The staged photo sessions and dye-transfer printing cover a multitude of flaws. The glossy photos that appear on the pages of these magazines have been air brushed beyond reality.

Researchers have found that after repeated exposure to pornography, men and women become less satisfied with the physical appeal of "real" partners.[19] Pornography also perpetuates the myth that a "real man" is always ready for sex and that sex may be experienced without regard for the other person. Pornography by its nature debases sexuality and creates relational damage. In pornography goodness and purity are ridiculed in favor of lust and immorality. Researchers have found that the consequences of viewing nonaggressive pornography may include increased aggressive sexual fantasies, aggressive behavior against women, and acceptance of antifemale attitudes and beliefs about sexual behavior that are not conducive to respect for the opposite sex.[20]

Understand Its Power

Pornography represents a powerful mechanism for learning because pornographic images are paired with the powerful reinforcer of sexual arousal and aggressive arousal, which by context leads to mislabeling of the experience as sexual.[21] The "forbidden fruit" hypothesis argued that liberalization of laws related to pornography would result in reduced interest and a withering of the market. Evidence for this view has obviously been found faulty. In recent years the porn market has escalated to an unprecedented degree. The violent and degrading nature of much of these materials is certainly market driven. Sales are not just to the one-time curiosity seeker. The billion-dollar business is based on repeat customers.

Focus on the Beliefs

In counseling, focus should not be simply on a "sexual problem." The addiction may be interpreted as symptomatic or symbolic of other needs that are not being met. These unmet needs may be seen in four core beliefs that are central to adolescents who are wrapped up in this painful conflict.

1. "I am basically a bad, unworthy person." Young people see themselves in a secret world in which only they know the whole truth. Each effort to quit adds to the sense of worthlessness. Adolescents recovering from an obsession with pornography may say "I am a worthwhile person."
2. "No one would love me as I am." Adolescents who see themselves as unworthy add the parallel belief that no one else would love them either. Rejection and abandonment are constantly feared. Adolescents recovering from an obsession with pornography may say "I am loved and accepted by people who know me as I am."
3. "My needs are never going to be met if I have to depend on others." Believing they are unworthy and unlovable, adolescents will conclude that they cannot depend on others. After all, who would listen or sympathize with those who are unlovable? They are convinced they are never going to have what other healthy people have. Adolescents recovering from an obsession with pornography can say "My needs may be met by others if I let them know what I need."
4. "Sex is my most important need." Adolescents who have fallen into this line of thinking eventually substitute sexual obsession for people. Using pornography becomes their primary source of comfort. Adolescents recovering from an obsession with pornography may say, "Sex is but one expression of who I am."[22]

Interrupt the Addictive System

In his book *Out of the Shadows*, Patrick Carnes adapts the twelve steps of Alcoholics Anonymous to use with those struggling with addiction to sex. Leading young people through these steps has been shown to result in a fundamental altering of the addictive system. As with Alcoholics Anonymous, this Twelve-Step approach has been found to work best for sexual addicts in a group setting. Seeing and hearing other sexual addicts facing reality and coming to grips with their lives is one of its strong points. A professional organization that provides information on these groups is

National Council on Sexual Addiction Problems
22937 Arlington Avenue, Suite 201
Torrance, CA 90501
213/534-1792

The greatest potential for long-lasting change is in the process of individual counseling coupled with a Twelve-Step group. The goal is to integrate the young people's addictive needs into a healthy self so that the needs are met, rather than acted out. Here are the Twelve Steps for Sexual Addicts:

1. We admitted we were powerless over our sexual addiction—that our lives had become unmanageable.
2. We came to believe that a Power greater than ourselves could restore us to sanity.
3. We made a decision to turn our will and our lives over to the care of God as we understood Him.
4. We made a searching and fearless moral inventory of ourselves.
5. We admitted to God, to ourselves, and to another human being the exact nature of our wrongs.
6. We were entirely ready to have God remove all these defects of character.
7. We humbly asked Him to remove our shortcomings.
8. We made a list of all persons we had harmed, and became willing to make amends to them all.
9. We made direct amends to such people wherever possible, except when to do so would injure them or others.
10. We continued to take personal inventory, and when we were wrong promptly admitted it.
11. We sought through prayer and meditation to improve our conscious contact with God as we understood Him, praying only for knowledge of His will for us and the power to carry that out.
12. Having had a spiritual awakening as the result of these steps, we tried to carry this message to others and to practice these principles in all our matters.[23]

☑ WHEN TO REFER

Refer adolescents struggling with the lure of pornography to other counselors or psychologists if you are embarrassed, ill-at-ease, overly curious, or uncertain how to proceed. Counselors referring adolescents with this problem should go to great lengths to let the young people know that it is not a personal rejection of them. Let them know how sincerely you want them to receive the best help available.

Refer adolescents to other competent counselors or psychologists when, over time, the young people are feeling more out of control and increasingly obsessed with pornographic material.

Where To Go for Additional Help

Bowen, N. H. "Pornography: Research Review and Implications for Counseling." *Journal of Counseling and Development* 65 (1987): 345–50.

Carnes, P. *Out of the Shadows*. Minneapolis: CompCare, 1983.

Court, J. H. *Pornography: A Christian Critique*. Downers Grove, Ill.: InterVarsity Press, 1980.

Mayo, M. A. *A Christian Guide to Sexual Counseling*. Grand Rapids: Zondervan, 1987.

Penner, J. J., and C. L. Penner. *Counseling for Sexual Disorders*. Waco, Tex.: Word, 1990.

Smedes, L. B. *Sex for Christians*. Grand Rapids: Eerdmans, 1976.

Stafford, T. *A Love Story: Questions and Answers on Sex*. Grand Rapids: Zondervan, 1977.

Zillmann, D., and J. Bryant. *Pornography: Research Advances and Policy Considerations*. Hillsdale, N.J.: Lawrence Erlbaum Associates, 1989.

Notes

1. J. McDowell and D. Day, *Why Wait? What You Need to Know About the Teen Sexuality Crisis* (San Bernardino, Calif.: Here's Life, 1987).

2. J. H. Court, "Pornography," *Baker Encyclopedia of Psychology*, ed. D. G. Benner (Grand Rapids: Baker, 1985).

3. W. A. Fisher and A. Barak, "Sex Education As a Corrective: Immunizing Against Possible Effect of Pornography," in *Pornography: Research Advances and Policy Considerations*, ed. D. Zillman and J. Bryant (Hillsdale, N.J.: Lawrence Erlbaum Associates, 1989), 289–320.

4. L. Longford, *Pornography: The Longford Report* (London: Coronet, 1972).

5. R. J. Foster, *Money, Sex and Power* (San Francisco: Harper & Row, 1985).

6. P. Y. Miller and W. Simon, "The Development of Sexuality in Adolescence," in *Handbook of Adolescent Psychology*, ed. J. Adelson (New York: Wiley, 1980).

7. M. G. Maudlin, "Addicts in the Pew," *Christianity Today* (22 July 1991): 19–20.

8. P. Carnes, *Out of the Shadows: Understanding Sexual Addiction* (Minneapolis: CompCare, 1983), vii.

9. J. H. Court, "Pornography," *Dictionary of Pastoral Care and Counseling*, ed. R. J. Hunter (Nashville: Abingdon, 1990).

10. Court, "Pornography," *Baker Encyclopedia*.

11. F. Buechner, *Godric* (New York: Harper & Row, 1980), 153.

12. T. Minnery, "Pornography: The Human Tragedy," *Christianity Today* (7 March 1986).

13. P. Carnes, *Out of the Shadows*, 9.

14. G. K. Olson, *Counseling Teenagers: The Complete Christian Guide to Understanding and Helping Adolescents* (Loveland, Colo.: Group Books, 1984).

15. Court, "Pornography," *Dictionary of Pastoral Care*.

16. S. Feshbach and N. Malamuth, "Sex and Aggression: Proving the Link," *Psychology Today* (1978): 110.

17. D. Linz, "Exposure to Sexually Explicit Materials and Attitudes Toward Rape: A Comparison of Study Results," *Journal of Sex Research* 26 (1985): 50–84.

18. S. Brownmiller, *Against Our Will: Men, Women and Rape* (New York: Simon & Schuster, 1975), 395.

19. D. Zillmann and J. Bryant, "Pornography's Impact on Sexual Satisfaction," *Journal of Applied Social Psychology* 18 (1988): 438–53.

20. D. Byrne and K. Kelley, "Introduction: Pornography and Sex Research," in *Pornography and Sexual Aggression*, ed. N. M. Malamut and E. Donnersten (Orlando, Fla.: Academic Press, 1984), 1–9.

21. R. A. Baron and D. Byrne, *Social Psychology* (Boston: Allyn & Bacon, 1977).

22. For a more thorough discussion of these beliefs and how to facilitate their change, see Carnes, *Out of the Shadows*.

23. Carnes, *Out of the Shadows*, 137. For a Christian evaluation of the Twelve-Step method see T. Stafford, "The Hidden Gospel of the 12 Steps," *Christianity Today* (22 July 1991).

PROMISCUITY and PREMARITAL SEX

☑ WHAT THE STRUGGLE LOOKS LIKE

Every adolescent walks along the moral precipice of premarital sex. In spite of efforts to install safety rails, more and more young people are falling off the cliff. Statistics are startling. By age twenty, eighty-one percent of today's unmarried males and sixty-seven percent of today's unmarried females have had sexual intercourse. Most research shows that the average age for first having sex is fifteen for girls and fourteen for boys.[1]

☑ WHY THE STRUGGLE HAPPENS

Adolescents who are sexually active engage in intercourse for different reasons. Though their motives may appear similar on the surface, they often have diverse origins.

Curiosity

Going through puberty is like exchanging a Volkswagon bug for a red Corvette and being told you can't drive over thirty miles per hour until you are married. When it comes to sex, most adolescents' curiosity is in high gear. When young people reach puberty, changes occur that make them physically capable of sex and they want to experiment, not wait. They are curious about the unknown, especially when it is prohibited. They want to see for themselves if sex is as great as "everyone" says it is.

Environmental Stimulation

It has been said that the typical adolescent "faces more sexual temptation on his way to school each morning than his grandfather did on Saturday night when he was out looking for it!"[2] Only a hermit in today's society stands a chance of escaping the bombardment of provocative images used by Madison Avenue. Sex sells and no one can avoid the hundreds of titillating images that flash before us daily. Sex is used to sell everything from deodorants to soda pop. Sexy images are described in top forty songs. They are blatantly depicted

Case Description

Julie, seventeen, came into counseling depressed and plagued with guilt. After a few sessions of talking around these ambiguous emotions the real issue emerged. Through a stream of tears (with ten minutes left in the session), Julie began to tell how she was sleeping with her boyfriend. She was madly in love, but terribly burdened by her sexual activity. Three weeks ago she missed her period and was scared to death that she was pregnant. It turned out to be a false alarm, but Julie (along with her boyfriend) vowed to quit. In spite of sincere intentions, she found it to be impossible. She came to counseling, without her parents' knowing and with resistance from her boyfriend, to get help. She wanted desperately to stop but didn't know how.

on MTV, network television, movies, books, magazines, and newspapers. Today's adolescent cannot avoid sexual stimulation from the everyday environment.

The Media's Message

Thirty years ago a teenager's behavior was influenced by peers, parents, teachers, relatives, and religious leaders. Today television, radio, and movies have replaced most of those influences. While adolescents are still shaped by peers and parents, the media rank third in influencing values. And the media value sex. It has been estimated that ten years of viewing television provides 92,000 scenes of sexual activity.[3] What is doubly disturbing is how sex is portrayed in the media. Sex on TV rarely depicts the unsettling but real consequences. Every day 33,000 Americans become infected with a sexually transmitted disease. But when was the last time you saw an actor or actress portray a character with VD, AIDS, or an unwanted pregnancy? The message from the media is that "everybody's doing it" with no guilt and no worry, just fun.

Peer Pressure

A young person reared by good parents with solid morals and wholesome values will still be pushed to become sexually active. The ideals of goodness and purity in many cases are offset by the greater pressure of the "you'd do it if you loved me" argument. While girls may often be coerced by their dates, both sexes are pressured by their peers, young men to be macho, and young women to be liberated. In the locker room or at a slumber party, one's sexual "track record" is a sign of "mature" behavior, a passage to adulthood. On some high school and secular college campuses, the term *virgin* is used in a derogatory way, like "nerd" or "jerk."

Society also does its share to pressure teens. It portrays sex as natural and "hip." A smash single on the pop charts has the chorus "Sex is natural, sex is good, not everybody does it but everybody should." If you are a celibate teenager, you may be tempted to wonder if you're a freak. If not a freak, perhaps a nerd.

Emotional Longings

Why do so many adolescents succumb to temptation and engage in premarital sex? One reason is that they mistake sex for intimacy. Many sexual encounters, especially for girls, occur out of a desperate need to be loved. A *Seventeen* magazine survey reports that most girls opt for affection over sex. In fact, only 1.1 percent of the girls surveyed say sex is more important than affection.[4] Adolescents are not so much seeking a sexual experience as they are longing for a loving relationship. The phrases "making love" and "being intimate" are often used as synonyms for sexual intercourse. Adolescents searching for security and a sense of identity make up for the shortage of love they receive from their parents by sleeping around. They mistakenly come to believe that real emotional sharing, openness, and love come through sexual intercourse.

☑ HOW TO HELP

Rarely will adolescents enter counseling for help with the moral issues involved in premarital sex. Many who engage in sexual intercourse do not see it as a struggle, and those who do are too embarrassed to talk about it. Problems with premarital sex are usually uncovered after a considerable amount of work in other areas (e.g., depression, guilt, problems with parents, etc.). When adolescents are courageous enough to bring their agony into the open, it is like a merit badge in empathic listening for counselors. It is a rare but encouraging sign that the teens are trusting their counselors and looking to them for help.

Assess the Facts

In assessing the intensity of adolescents' sexual activity, the goal is to have an accurate understanding of how it affects their lives and how they have been coping with the matter up to this point. While some instruments are available to help in assessing the depth of this problem, their use is too threatening for most adolescents. The severity of the strain can be assessed easily enough through direct yet sensitive questioning:

- "How often do you have intercourse?"
- "When was the first time?"
- "When was the last time you had intercourse?"
- "How many different partners have you been with?"
- "Have you taken precautions against pregnancy and sexually transmitted diseases?"
- "Is the intercourse usually planned ahead of time, or is more spontaneous?"
- "Does it normally take place in the same location (your home or car)?"

- "Is it something you enjoy, or are you pressured into it?"
- "Do you talk about it with anyone else?"
- "What do you see as your primary reason for engaging in it?"
- "On a scale of one to ten, how badly do you want to quit doing it and wait for marriage?"
- "In what ways (if any), have you attempted to quit having sex?"

Examine Your Attitudes

It is easy for the counselor to be drawn into subjective responses to adolescents who report sexual activity. In examining "why sex talks with adolescents go wrong," Gordon Jensen and Myra Robbins report that counselors may (1) fail to listen; (2) take a condemning, moralizing attitude; (3) transmit inaccurate information; (4) show shock or excessive curiosity; (5) fail to keep confidentiality; or (6) too readily give "easy answers."[5]

To avoid these pitfalls effective counselors must be aware of their own attitudes toward teenage sexuality. Are you embarrassed, shocked, angered, overly curious, etc.? If you are unable to respond with an understanding and compassionate attitude, which may still acknowledge the reality of sin, then you are not in a position to help teenagers who face this problem.

Demonstrate Forgiveness

A study at the University of Wisconsin–Madison shows that the people who come to psychologists with issues of premarital sex see their primary problem as the sense of guilt that results from it.[6] This is especially true for adolescents in the church. If they are already involved in sexual activity, they are probably plagued with guilt. They need to hear that God forgives and helps people to begin again. They need to hear that no matter what they have done, no matter how many times they have broken their own standard, Jesus Christ is ready to heal and to purify.

Young people with guilt from sexual behavior may be on the brink of losing hope of ever again living a holy lifestyle. Because of one bad experience some young people will say, "Why should I even try again to do right after what I have already done?" They assume that their past has already mortgaged their future and that they are left morally bankrupt. While sex outside of marriage is sinful (see 1 Cor. 6:12–20), young people need to know that it is never too late for forgiveness. And counselors have a beautiful opportunity to demonstrate that very fact.

Reframe the Concept of Waiting

When adolescents are in love, the frustration of waiting is hard to take. However, by discussing the ways in which waiting can help their relationship, young people may begin to change their attitude and see waiting as a challenge rather than a duty. When two people are sleeping together but not living together, sex tends to become larger than life. It becomes a consuming passion that excludes other ways of experiencing love.

When sex is put on hold, however, it frees a couple to channel their love into getting to know each other better. Also, the way two young people respond to sexual pressures tends to set the course for their responses to other pressures later in life. Do they give in or help each other stand strong? Each time a problem or pressure arises and the couple is able to solve it together, their love will grow. Framing the wait in positive terms may do much to empower a young couple concerned about their sexual future.

Be Prepared for Rationalizations

Sooner or later adolescents who experience stress in this area will ask, "Why does it matter? We are going to get married and have sex anyway. What difference does the date of a wedding ceremony make?" The question begs for a counterpoint.

Colleen Kelly Mast, creator of *Sex Respect,* points out that premarital sex may fool a young person into marrying the wrong person: "Because sex is so powerful, it creates very strong emotional bonds between partners. These bonds can make us believe a relationship is deeper than it really is, that we know our partners much better than we actually do. Or, because we've had sex, we may be tempted to hang on to the relationship, not out of love, but just to 'save face.' "[7]

Another common rationalization for premarital sex is "I owe it to him." If a girl thinks she owes a boy sex, it is normally because he wants her to think so. A girl with this concern needs to be shown her dignity as a person. She needs objective feedback to show that respect is actually expressed through concern, not manipulation. All rationalizations, however, must be listened to at the emotional level from which they rise. Once counselors have listened fully to adolescents, the possibilities of helping relationships are greatly increased.

Explore How Sex Affects Future Relationships

One study of adolescent sexuality concluded that premarital sex creates "emotional deprivation," a restricted range of feelings.[8] In other words this behavior has long-term emotional results that are generally characterized by guilt, jealousy, fear, anxiety, insecurity, anger, and depression. Few adolescents realize that premarital sex may be a great source of distrust in a later marriage. The suspicion is well founded. People who cannot control themselves before marriage may have a difficult time controlling themselves after marriage. Premarital sex does not necessarily lead to extramarital sex; it simply increases the odds that it will. This understanding will do much to motivate the adolescent who values a secure marital relationship later on.

Explore How Sex Affects Spirituality

If the adolescents you work with value their relationship with God, it is important to discuss ways that premarital sex will impact them spiritually. In fact, for religiously committed adolescents, this will probably be of great concern. Discuss ways that the joy of relating to God fades when they begin to do the opposite of what is best for them. Prayer and worship become meaningless, and if they continue to engage in premarital sex, they will be shot through with heavy doses of guilt. Few activities do more to nag at the conscience of committed Christian young people than premarital sex.[9]

One note of caution: In exploring this issue guard against conveying the idea that sex is bad. God created human bodies capable of sexual intimacy and orgasm. As with other parts of his creation God called sexual human beings "good." Adolescents with overly active consciences can distort God's gift of sex and set themselves up for years of sexual anxiety as married adults.

Provide Helpful Literature

Generally it is not helpful to recommend a book to struggling adolescents. They simply don't read books about depression, anger, sibling rivalry, and so on. However, young people are usually eager to read anything on sexuality. In fact, a teacher has half jokingly said that many young people's first examination of the encyclopedia results from a rumor that there is detailed sexual information in it.

Reading material will help teenagers secure accurate information about questions they may be hesitant to ask. Tim Stafford's book *A Love Story* is a classic written in question-and-answer format. It covers a number of topics, including premarital sex, masturbation, dating, and several others. A more recent work by Stafford, *Worth the Wait*, also speaks to teens about the frustration of premarital sex. It addresses such things as why sex is so attractive, how to build healthful relationships, twenty questions for choosing the right person at the right time, finding forgiveness, and how to say no and stick with it. Both books are straightforward, filled with insight and sensitivity, and eagerly read by most teenagers. Another book that addresses issues of premarital sex and is often helpful to young people is James Dobson's *Preparing for Adolescence: Straight Talk to Teens and Parents*.

Set Up Safeguards

The time to look for a fire escape is before the building is ablaze. Young people often find themselves in situations from which they cannot escape. Once they've let their hormones loose, they will have trouble harnessing them again. The solution is to stop the tragedy before it begins. By helping young people decide ahead of time what they may and may not do, you are helping them draw lines that they do not want to cross over. One example might be to guard against being alone as a couple in an empty house. More than half of today's teenagers first had intercourse in their own or their partner's house (usually between 3:00 and 5:00 P.M.).[10] Other suggestions might include avoidance of a certain style of provocative dress, parking in a car, and certain parties. A couple should also always have an activity planned ahead of time when going out on a date. By setting up safeguards, adolescents define specific areas they will not enter and thereby avoid potentially dangerous situations.

Respect the Value of Romance

Setting up safeguards does not mean avoiding romance. According to Erik Erikson, if by late adolescence young people have not been involved in romantic love relationships, they may settle for a series of impersonal relationships; and they may suffer from a permanent sense of depersonalization.[11] However, youth may enjoy the glory of romance and get relational needs met without having sexual intercourse. As a counselor, you may help embattled adolescents become aware of their relational longings and be assertive in getting them met through nonsexual means.

Encourage Community

Adolescents often feel terribly alone in their difficult battle for sexual purity, even within the church. A sensitive and caring community offers great refuge in the midst of battle. Remind Christian teens that God is with them every moment (see Deut. 31:8), and that they have power to resist even the strongest urges (see Phil. 4:13). Of course, these messages are heard best from respected peers. Knowing there are others fighting yet drawing on God's strength does much for adolescents who feel isolated in this war.[12] Relationships build convictions.

Focus on Relational Needs

The problem facing adolescents who scuffle temptation to engage in sex outside of marriage is not just a sexual one. It is a relational one as well. Teens need to learn to get their relational needs met without having to resort to sex. Intercourse is not the price they have to pay for warmth, intimacy, or romance. Helping adolescents to become aware of the particular needs that underlie sex and helping them become assertive in getting those needs met in other ways will quiet the battle. For example, some teens become sexually active to develop autonomy and assert separate identity from parental authority. The privacy of sex helps prove to adolescents that they are no longer dependent children. Once they understand the strength of their drive for autonomy they may choose to channel it in ways that will serve them better.

Understand Sexually Transmitted Diseases

No discussion of premarital sex would be complete without emphasizing the importance of counselors' knowledge of Sexually Transmitted Diseases (STD). It is estimated that 2.5 million teens are infected with STD each year. That means that every thirteen seconds a teen in the U.S. contracts a sexually transmitted disease. Sexually active adolescents should be questioned directly but sensitively about STD. They may be too embarrassed to ask about their symptoms and may need encouragement to talk about it. The risk of infection with STD increases enormously in relation to the number of different people with whom they have had sexual contact. The fewer the number of contacts, the lower the risk.[13] The most common STDs and their symptoms are these:

Gonorrhea. A woman may have no signs or symptoms or she may have burning urination, vaginal discharge, fever, or stomach pain. A man will see whitish discharge from his penis and feel itching or burning when urinating. Symptoms usually appear two to eight days after contact.

Chlamydia. This disease is twice as common as gonorrhea. Its symptoms resemble mild gonorrhea and they often appear at the same time. Chlamydia appears from one to five weeks after contact.

Syphilis. The person infected with syphilis gets a sore, sometimes painful, on the sex organs or mouth. The sore will slowly disappear even without treatment, but the disease has not gone away. Several weeks later other signs will appear, including low fever, sore throat, sores, or rashes.

Herpes. Officially, this is herpes simplex virus type 2 (HSV-2). It may be extremely painful or very mild. A man will see a small sore or cluster of blisters on his penis. A woman may have blisters in or around her vagina. She may have fever and headaches. Without treatment, symptoms disappear in a week or two, but the herpes virus doesn't leave the body.

An adolescent who is found to have STD should be referred to a physician immediately. Serious danger results from failure to treat. The disease may cause irreparable damage to female reproductive organs, sterility in men and women, arthritis, heart disease, or even eye infection serious enough to end in blindness. Some of these effects show up years after the disease is first contracted. Medical treatment is essential. Refer adolescents to physicians even if they think they only wonder whether they may have been exposed to a sexually transmitted disease. And of course if tests are positive, they must tell anyone with whom they have had sex to go at once for a test.

Understand AIDS

More than eighteen thousand people in their twenties have been diagnosed with AIDS (acquired immunodeficiency syndrome) and most of them were probably infected with the virus while they were teenagers.[14] It is a disease in which the body's immune system breaks down. It is caused by the human immunodeficiency virus (HIV). People infected with HIV may appear completely healthy, but they may also develop many health problems that signal the onset of AIDS, including extreme weight loss, severe pneumonia, a form of cancer, and damage to the nervous system. A person becomes infected when HIV is introduced into the bloodstream, most commonly through homosexual or heterosexual intercourse or by sharing drug needles or syringes with infected people.[15]

Several excellent books on understanding and counseling people with AIDS are available. Michael J. Christensen's *The Samaritan's Imperative: Compassionate Ministry to People Living with AIDS* (Abingdon, 1991) stresses a back-to-basics approach to dealing with AIDS patients that includes fresh insight on love, acceptance, and forgiveness. For a resource that is specifically written for professional practitioners in a Christian context, Gregg R. Albers's *Counseling and AIDS* (Word, 1990) will be of interest. It includes advice on everything from counseling those who need AIDS testing to counseling the families of AIDS patients.

☑ WHEN TO REFER

Refer adolescents if your attitude threatens them (evaluative, vindictive, and so on) or if you are too shocked or embarrassed to continue counseling. Nonunderstanding may drive worried adolescents back into further immorality. Referral is necessary if you feel a strong and persistent sexual attraction to the counselee. As always, referrals must be made with sensitivity so as not to be misinterpreted by clients as rejection. They need to know that referrals are common and are designed for their benefit.

Where To Go for Additional Help

Dobson, J. *Preparing for Adolescence: Straight Talk to Teens and Parents*. Ventura, Calif.: Vision House, 1984.

Howard, M. *How To Help Your Teenager Postpone Sexual Involvement*. New York: Crossroad-Continuum, 1991.

McDowell, J., and D. Day. *Why Wait? What You Need To Know About the Teen Sexuality Crisis*. San Bernardino, Calif.: Here's Life, 1987.

Mayo, M. A. *A Christian Guide to Sexual Counseling: Recovering the Mystery and Reality of "One Flesh."* Grand Rapids: Zondervan, 1987.

Smedes, L. B. *Sex for Christians*. Grand Rapids: Eerdmans, 1976.

Stafford, T. *Worth the Wait: Love, Sex, and Keeping the Dream Alive*. Grand Rapids: Zondervan, 1990.

_____. *A Love Story: Questions and Answers on Sex*. Grand Rapids: Zondervan, 1977.

Notes

1. J. McDowell and D. Day, *Why Wait? What You Need To Know About the Teen Sexuality Crisis* (San Bernardino, Calif.: Here's Life, 1987).

2. C. K. Mast, *Sex Respect: An Option of True Sexual Freedom*, A Public Health Workbook for Students (Bradley, Ill.: Respect, 1986).

3. McDowell and Day, *Why Wait?* 40.

4. J. Gaylin, "What Girls Really Look for in Boys," *Seventeen* (March 1978), 107–13.

5. G. Jensen and M. Robbins, "Ten Reasons Why Sex Talks with Adolescents Go Wrong," *Medical Aspects of Human Sexuality* (July 1975): 7.

6. McDowell and Day, *Why Wait?* 261.

7. Mast, *Sex Respect*.

8. G. R. Collins, *Christian Counseling; A Comprehensive Guide* (Waco, Tex.: Word, 1980).

9. L. Jensen, R. J. Newell, and T. Holman, "Sexual Behavior, Church Attendance, and Permissive Beliefs Among Unmarried Young Men and Women," *Journal for the Scientific Study of Religion* 29, no. 1 (1990): 113–17.

10. R. Coles and G. Stokes, *Sex and the American Teenager* (New York: Harper & Row, 1985).

11. E. H. Erikson, *Identity: Youth and Crisis* (New York: Norton, 1968).

12. J. P. Roche, "Premarital Sex: Attitudes and Behavior by Dating Stage," *Adolescence* 21 (1986): 107–21.

13. F. Wattleton, "American Teens: Sexually Active, Sexually Illiterate," *Curriculum Review* 27 (1988): 16–23.

14. Ibid.

15. L. L. Lockhart and J. S. Wodarski, "Facing the Unknown: Children and Adolescents with AIDS," *Journal of the National Association of Social Workers* 34 (1989): 215–22.

SCHIZOPHRENIA

☑ WHAT THE STRUGGLE LOOKS LIKE

A patient of mine once told me a joke with this punch line: The difference between schizophrenics and neurotics is that neurotics say that $1 + 1 = 2$ and they can't stand it. Schizophrenics say that $1 + 1 = 11$, and they love it!

Plenty of humor has been derived from this problem, but schizophrenia is not a joke. It is a painful group of diseases characterized by a loss of contact with reality. At some point in the illness several features may become prominent: hallucinations, delusions, decreased self-care and social inappropriateness, or markedly disturbed thinking. The schizophrenic's personality becomes severely disorganized, and one often requires acute management and treatment in a hospital during the more active phases of the illness.

Schizophrenia is considered by many to be the leading mental health problem in the United States. At least one out of every one hundred people is likely to suffer an episode of schizophrenia during his or her life. One hundred thousand new cases are added each year. Schizophrenia requires more hospital beds than any other medical or psychiatric condition and more hospital beds than cancer, heart disease, arthritis, and diabetes combined.[1] The treatment and rehabilitation of people suffering from schizophrenia today is estimated to cost over twenty billion dollars each year. Schizophrenia may prevent young people from completing late-adolescence and ruin a promising future. It is a disheartening societal and personal problem that cries out for solution.

Schizophrenia in teenagers has been a concern since the early 1900s. It used to be called adolescent insanity. In 1911, the famous Swiss psychiatrist who coined the term *schizophrenia*, Eugene Bleuler, wrote, "The adolescent age period seems to offer a particular predisposition to this disease."[2] Subsequent research and clinical observations confirm that most forms of schizophrenic disturbance tend to appear first during or soon after adolescence.[3] In fact, it is the most common diagnosis among adolescents in mental hospitals.

The *Diagnostic and Statistical Manual of Mental Disorders* (3d ed. rev. [DSM-III-R]) recognizes five types of schizophrenia:

1. *Disorganized.* This usually begins in early adolescence and is marked by

The DSM-III-R Criteria for Schizophrenia[4]

A. At least two of the following symptoms:
1. Bizarre thinking and delusions: thoughts that are blatantly untrue, such as that the person's brain is being controlled by a television station or that others are broadcasting one's thoughts
2. Grandiose, religious, nihilistic, or persecutory delusions
3. Prominent hallucinations such as voices conversing with each other or one voice keeping a running commentary on the patient's thoughts and behaviors
4. Prominent hallucinations on several occasions, with the content of words having no apparent relationship to depression or elation
5. Incoherent thinking, marked loosening of associations, illogical thinking, or marked poverty of content of speech if associated with at least one of the following:
   a. Blunted, flat, or inappropriate affect
   b. Delusions or hallucinations
   c. Catatonic or other grossly disorganized behavior
B. Deterioration from previous level of functioning in areas such as school, work, social relations, self-care, or failure to achieve expected level of development
C. Duration: Continual signs of the disorder for at least six months at some time during the person's life, with some signs at present
D. During the early and the residual phases, at least two of the following present but not owing to a mood disturbance or drug abuse: social withdrawal, digressive vague speech, illogical thinking and loosening of associations; peculiar, odd behavior; grossly disorganized behavior or blunted, flat, or inappropriate affect

incoherence, loose associations in thought and speech, and flat, inappropriate, or silly affect. No elaborate delusional system is present. The clinician is more likely to see fragmented delusions or disorganized hallucinations. Without treatment this type will suffer chronic and extreme social impairment.

2. *Catatonic.* This type most often begins between the ages of fifteen and twenty-five following some type of emotional trauma. It is characterized by a major psychomotor disturbance that may include rigidity, excitement, or a stupor. Mutism is common. The prognosis for recovery after a single catatonic episode is more favorable than for recovery from other types.

3. *Paranoid.* This type tends to occur after adolescence around the age of thirty. Symptoms include delusions and/or hallucinations of persecution or grandiosity.

4. *Undifferentiated.* Psychotic symptoms (delusions, hallucination, incoherence, or severely disorganized behavior) are present, but the patient's clinical picture either does not meet the criteria for any of the

three forms mentioned above or it meets the criteria of more than one of them.

5. *Residual.* This diagnosis is used when a history of schizophrenia exists, but the current evaluation of the patient no longer indicates significant psychotic symptoms.

Clinical studies of adolescents suffering from schizophrenia indicate that only about thirty-five percent initially show clear signs of a schizophrenic breakdown. The rest tend to present a masked or mixed picture in which features of schizophrenia are secondary to or even obscured by other kinds of problems or complaints. Two kinds of mixed-symptom pictures are likely to be seen—one is depressive, the other antisocial. In one picture the young person shows some signs of schizophrenia but complains primarily of depression, with a loss of interest in people or activities, feelings of hopelessness, and even suicidal thoughts. In the other picture indications of schizophrenia are present but overshadowed by an apparent antisocial personality disorder and a turbulent history of family conflict and truancy. Schizophrenia may be difficult to detect in adolescents who show signs primarily of depression or antisocial features. Still, these symptoms may alert the clinician to its presence.[5]

Three guidelines should provide the basis of diagnosis of schizophrenia in adolescents:

1. *Persistence of the Schizophrenic Features.* The longer the schizophrenic features in a mixed clinical picture persist, the more likely a diagnosis of schizophrenia becomes. Emerging schizophrenia is especially clear when these features remain after other kinds of presenting complaints have become less noticeable. For example, they may no longer complain of depression but they are still not thinking coherently.

2. *Extent of Usual Adolescent Concerns.* Disturbed adolescents who are becoming schizophrenic show a marked inability or reluctance to grapple with usual adolescent concerns. If teens are not involved in such age-appropriate concerns as adapting to bodily changes, increasing their interest in self-care, attaining independence from parents, and gaining social skills in relating to the opposite sex, a diagnosis of schizophrenia becomes more likely. It is as though these troubled young people are skirting around adolescence through pseudomaturity or avoiding it by being overly immature.[6] Neither pattern in and of itself, of course, is conclusive evidence of schizophrenia.

3. *Prominence of Formal Manifestations of Disturbance.* Here we are concerned with how young people are saying or doing something peculiar rather than what they are actually saying or doing. Among disturbed adolescents, the likelihood of an emerging schizophrenic disorder increases in direct relation to the prominence of formal manifestations. In other words, it is not so much peculiar thought content but peculiar ways in which this content is arrived at and expressed that point to schizophrenia in teen years.

It is helpful to establish a distinctive profile of impairment in adolescent schizophrenia. A team of researchers studying hundreds of thirteen- to eighteen-year-olds diagnosed with schizophrenia found several symptomatic factors. Here are five of the highest rated characteristics.

1. *Bizarre Cognition*. These adolescents may substitute, confuse, or misuse pronouns in conversation. For example, one may use one's name rather than "I" when referring to oneself in conversation. Speech is disconnected or incoherent and one may report hearing voices or other hallucinations.

2. *Bizarre Action*. Schizophrenic adolescents may display odd postures, movements, or facial expressions. They may shut out sounds by putting their fingers in their ears, and they may rock back and forth while sitting or standing.

3. *Social Withdrawal*. These adolescents may seem to be in their own little world. They may have a blank stare or faraway look in their eyes. They may walk around oblivious to others around them or they may simply look puzzled.

4. *Emotional Detachment*. They tend to keep their emotional distance and may even seem apathetic. These adolescents seem to lack appropriate feelings, and they may be unaware of how others are feeling around them. They have a "blunted affect."

5. *Poor Emotional Control*. These young people may become explosively upset if things do not go their way. They may become easily outraged with their peers and express their anger in an unbridled fashion.[7]

Before we discuss etiology and treatment of schizophrenia it is important to understand a common distinction. The more severely disabled a schizophrenic disturbance is and the longer it persists, the more likely it is to be classified as *chronic*. This is also labeled as *process* or *typical* schizophrenia. Three features are associated with chronicity. The first is *an insidious onset*, which means that the person's functioning slowly deteriorates over a period of months or even years in the absence of any clearly precipitating stressors. The second is *symptom tolerance*, which occurs when the person displays little concern about the schizophrenic features. And the third is *prior maladjustment*, which means that the person was experiencing interpersonal and school difficulties even before the insidious onset began.[8]

Acute schizophrenia, sometimes known as *reactive* or *atypical* schizophrenia, on the other hand, begins rapidly in response to clear stressful experiences. Acutely schizophrenic individuals tend to recognize and worry about the unusual nature of their symptoms. One may say, "I feel as if I am going crazy. I just can't seem to think straight." Typically, their families and friends are surprised at their suddenly becoming disturbed. Acute schizophrenia responds more quickly and successfully to treatment than chronic cases.[9] After five years, eighty to ninety percent of acute schizophrenics are rated recovered or improved as compared to fifty to sixty percent for chronic schizophrenics.[10]

Case Description

Rick is a sixteen-year-old. About six months ago he was considered a creative, yet quiet, adolescent with a bright future. He had many friends, was well liked, and had never been involved in any serious disciplinary difficulty. Shortly before beginning his sophomore year he was in a minor automobile accident. He suffered no head injury or any other physical distress for that matter, but since that time he began to sleep poorly and have nightmares. More surprisingly, he would frequently lose his temper as never before. For seemingly no reason, he would slam his bedroom door or yell obscenities at his parents. For the first time he began to do poorly in school. He was even apprehended by the police for illegally attempting to enter the school building at night. At that point his parents sought the help of the school counselor.

In the counselor's office Rick displayed very little emotion and mostly stared at the wall. He expressed no concern about his failing grades. The counselor knew Rick's problem was beyond his training, and he referred Rick to a clinical psychologist. A psychological examination clearly identified features of a schizophrenic disturbance. For example, Rick had poor reality testing and an impaired capacity for social judgments. He showed signs of impulsive reactions to fairly clearly defined situations. Rick was diagnosed with acute undifferentiated schizophrenia and was hospitalized for further evaluation, pharmacological treatment, and psychotherapy.

☑ WHY THE STRUGGLE HAPPENS

The search for the causes of schizophrenia has baffled investigators for more than a hundred years. It is most commonly thought, as it is with almost all other disorders, that schizophrenia is the result of a complex interaction of several factors.

Biochemistry

In the past few decades, researchers have concentrated a great amount of effort on understanding the brain's function in schizophrenia. Many conclude that the neurotransmitter, dopamine, is the cause of some forms of schizophrenia. The basis for a biochemical theory of schizophrenia lies in the following observations: (1) Schizophrenic-like reactions may be created by hallucinogenic drugs such as LSD; (2) hallucinogenic drugs affect the chemical balance of the brain's regulatory centers and are similar to chemical compounds, such as dopamine, normally found in the brain; (3) dopamine is known to be involved in the normal functioning of the brain; (4) antipsychotic medications reduce the level of dopamine in the brain; and (5) certain drugs (like amphetamines) that increase the level of dopamine may intensify symptoms in schizophrenics and produce schizophrenic-like symptoms in nonschizophrenics. While the biochemical theory is sufficiently promising to warrant further investigation, it is certainly not seen as conclusive.

Genetics

The tendency of schizophrenia to run in families is offered as evidence to support the idea of a genetic transmission of biochemical abnormalities in the brain. While the rate at which schizophrenia occurs in the general population is about one percent, children of one schizophrenic parent have a ten percent chance of developing schizophrenia. Children of two schizophrenic parents have about a forty percent chance.[11] In spite of strong evidence for a genetic link to schizophrenia, this theory has its critics. Its strength, however, is that the biochemical predisposition or vulnerability to schizophrenia is inherited rather than schizophrenia itself. The question is not whether there is an influence, but rather how much influence genetic factors have.

Family Factors

A family environment characterized by excessive distortions in communication, a hostile, confused, or ambivalent emotional climate, and destructive marital interactions has been linked to the genesis of schizophrenia.[12] Interpersonal communication in the context of family life is worth highlighting as a key element in the socialization process. According to theorists in this area, communication in schizophrenogenic homes is characterized by a vague, fragmented, ambivalent, contradictory quality. The situation creates a double-bind situation where the child cannot win.

The double messages usually involve an "impossible" appeal to come closer yet stay away. Such messages occur over and over again. For example, a mother may invite a child to kiss her while assuming a cold, rejecting posture. A father may encourage self-reliance while subtly maintaining control. These parents may "push" the child away and then accuse the child of not loving them. I once observed a father picking up his teenage daughter who was recovering from a reactive schizophrenia attack at the hospital. He seemed very glad to see her, gave her a hug, then said, "Is that how you are wearing your hair these days? Wait 'til your mother sees you!" This kind of paradoxical communication during the important early years of development obviously creates fear and confusion. While some children learn to cope with this environment, many others imitate the vague amorphous style of sending double meanings.[13] Obviously, family factors cannot fully explain and predict schizophrenia.

Peer Relations

Friendship patterns of adolescents may be significant in determining whether young people are at risk of schizophrenia. Those who have very few friends, who see their "friends" only infrequently and have little in common with them, and who are involved in exploitive rather than mutual relationships with them are more predisposed to schizophrenia than young people who, even if they have a relatively inactive social life, carry on at least a few really close and mutual friendships.[14]

☑ HOW TO HELP

Robert Carson, author of a chapter on schizophrenia in the voluminous *Comprehensive Handbook of Psychopathology*, wrote: "The author who undertakes to write a handbook chapter on the phenomena conventionally included under the rubric schizophrenia—questions of his own sanity and proper intellectual humility aside—faces an enormously intimidating task."[15] I couldn't agree more. Thousands of books and scholarly articles have been written on the treatment of schizophrenia. This brief section provides only a cursory overview, and is perhaps most helpful for the counselor who is not going to treat schizophrenic adolescents clinically, but wants to be knowledgeable about current treatment strategies and how to find competent help for young people.

Treatment of schizophrenia has changed significantly in the past forty years. Up until the development of antipsychotic drugs in the early 1950s, schizophrenic patients were confined for years in large state-run institutions, sometimes for the remainder of their lives. Antipsychotic medication revolutionized this treatment and paved the way for community mental health centers and deinstitutionalization in the 1960s and 1970s. With these medications, the length of hospital stays was reduced from years to weeks. The contemporary treatment of schizophrenia involves a combination of the following strategies:

Know Your Limits

Schizophrenia is a serious illness that requires treatment by trained professionals. This generally means clinical psychologists or psychiatrists. If you are not trained and experienced in the treatment of schizophrenia, the greatest service you can perform is as a bridge to programs or people who are experts in meeting the needs of schizophrenics and their families. Your local telephone directory or directory assistance is one of the most immediate means of accessing such a service. To find agencies in your area, look up the following listings in your directory: adolescent clinics, county department of health, mental health clinics, general hospitals, and psychiatric hospitals.

When psychiatric treatment within an explicitly Christian context is desired, three programs are worth investigating: The Minirth-Meier hospitals, the Rapha hospitals, and New Life Treatment Centers. All offer professional treatment in hospitals staffed by people committed to Christ-centered psychiatric treatment. All programs have several locations across the United States where treatment is immediately available. For additional information about Rapha, call 800/227-2657 (in Texas call 800/445-2657); regarding Minirth-Meier services, call 800/877-4673; for New Life, call 800/227-LIFE.

Pinpoint the Severity

As with almost all psychological struggles, it is helpful to assess the severity of the problem. Psychological assessments for schizophrenia are complex and require specific training. Most psychologists who assess schizophrenia rely on a battery of instruments that include the Minnesota Multiphasic Personality Inventory, the Millon Clinical Multiaxial Inventory, the Wechsler Adult Intelligence Scale, the Thematic Apperception Test, the Rorschach Ink Blot test, and many others. In addition to these measures, an extensive clinical interview would occur that notes interview behavior (speech patterns, appearance, style of relating, and so on), and details client history.

Work at a Positive Therapeutic Alliance

The treatment of schizophrenia depends on the stage of the disorder, the depth of regression, the grasp on reality that remains, and patients' desire for therapy. In any case, however, it is necessary from the outset to work at establishing a positive working relationship. This may try the patience of even the most sensitive of therapists. Schizophrenic adolescents may view therapists' attempts to establish supportive relationships as exploitive acts. Gentle inquiries into their personal histories may be seen as hostile efforts to interrogate them. Helping them clarify the reality of a situation may lead patients to spew out vulgar accusations. Persons working with schizophrenic adolescents should be prepared for a slow and difficult road to the establishment of positive therapeutic alliances.

Avoid Exotic Spiritualizing

A young woman came to see me after four unsuccessful exorcisms had been conducted on her at her church. A sincere minister and two "lay counselors" had been working with her for months. The damage was horrendous. They didn't know her bizarre symptoms were signs of schizophrenia. They labeled her "demon possessed." It can be very harmful to assume exotic or supernatural causes like demon possession. There is no need to give Satan free publicity. And the hopelessness such a label engenders in the victim can often do more harm than the original disease. Misdiagnosing those who suffer from schizophrenia as demon possession places blame on the patients for what they have little or no control over. Archibald Hart has pointed to several dangers of falsely attributing psychological problems to demons: "It removes the victim from responsibility for recognizing and confessing human sinfulness. It enhances Satan's power inappropriately. But most importantly, it delays the introduction of effective therapy. And a delay in the treatment of schizophrenia can decrease the likelihood of the sufferer's return to normality."[16] Rodger Bufford's book *Counseling and the Demonic* is an excellent resource in discerning the spiritual and the physical.

Identify Thoughts and Feelings

Schizophrenics often hide inner experiences. Therapists need to remember that the emotional responses of schizophrenics are appropriate to their perceptions of reality. Therapists must continually seek to empathize with and understand schizophrenic patients. Symptoms may express patients' feelings. Schizophrenic clients, for example, may choose to remain silent throughout treatment time. When they finally feel safe and trusting enough to communicate with the therapist, a revelation of all that was absorbed during the silence—a prevention of rejection—may come forward. Making an accurate interpretation or clarification of what patients are thinking and feeling may make them feel secure enough to relinquish some psychotic manifestations.

Understand the Major Phases of Treatment

Treatment for schizophrenia today involves a mixture of hospitalization, antipsychotic medication, psychosocial therapy, and family intervention. The treatment is often divided into two major phases, the acute and the aftercare. The goal of the first stage is to reduce disruptive symptoms, reestablish contact with reality, prevent harm to self, and improve psychosocial functioning. This usually takes place in a hospital setting over the course of about a month in public psychiatric hospitals. In a private psychiatric hospital, the stay may continue for six months or more, depending on need and the patient's insurance coverage. Disruptive symptoms are reduced primarily through a combination of antipsychotic drugs and psychosocial therapy.

The goal of the aftercare phase is to assist in the continuing recovery in the community. It also assists adolescents in reentry into the mainstream of school and the developmental tasks of adolescence. This is where patients' families become especially important. With proper training and counseling, families may do much to relieve the pressure of coping and aid in the recovery process. The goal of family intervention is to establish a clear, practical set of guidelines for living with patients; it is not necessarily to resolve past family conflicts, and it is certainly not to fix the blame on anyone for an adolescent's condition. Some of the resources noted at the end of this chapter may be particularly helpful in guiding family members through this difficult experience. The emotional climate of the home may have decided effects on recovery and relapse rates.[17]

Hospitalize When Necessary

Hospitalization certainly has its downside. It is a major life disruption that removes young people from their normal surroundings of home and school, threatens their self-esteem, and often produces a stigma evidenced by reactions from their friends, teachers, and others. But insufficient treatment of a serious disorder like schizophrenia is much too high a price to pay for trying to avoid these problems. At least three circumstances necessitate hospitalization of a troubled adolescent:

1. When a more thorough evaluation is required than can be accomplished on an outpatient basis
2. When the adolescent is already out of control and potentially dangerous to himself or herself or to others
3. When environmental stress has become intolerable[18]

Understand the Importance of Medication

Psychotropic medications decrease adolescents' confusion, stabilize emotions, and diminish social withdrawal. Medication allows the work of psychosocial therapy to take place. One researcher cites three principal uses of these medications: (1) to bring clients out of acute schizophrenic crises; (2) to facilitate management and control of clients; and (3) to prevent recurrence of schizophrenic symptoms.[19]

The most widely used group of antipsychotic drugs is classified chemically as phenothiazines, and of these the best known is marketed under the trade name Thorazine. Another commonly prescribed drug for schizophrenia is haloperidol (Haldol). While these medications may bring relief to schizophrenic symptoms, they unfortunately have unpleasant side effects that often lead patients to discontinue using them. For this reason they are sometimes called neuroleptics because, in addition to their beneficial effects, they have side effects similar to behavioral manifestations of neurological diseases.

Consider Group Therapy

Group treatment is commonly used in the hospital setting. It is also widely used in the treatment of schizophrenia following discharge from hospitals. It can be a powerful strategy because it "forces" patients into a certain amount of social interaction and helps prevent the social isolation that is so common among schizophrenics. One study, for example, found that after two years, forty percent of individual therapy patients had to be rehospitalized, but only twenty-four percent of group patients had to return to the hospital.[20] Many clinicians agree that in an outpatient setting, group therapy, in conjunction with individual therapy and medication, is fairly effective in preventing further rehospitalization. However, research has also given us guidelines for knowing when it is most effective. For example, group therapy is less effective and may even be detrimental for acutely psychotic individuals.[21]

Consider a Social-Learning Approach

Rather than trying to change the whole schizophrenic syndrome, social-learning techniques usually focus on target behavior patterns that are interfering with adolescents' functioning. Such programs are often termed token economies. This strategy has been successful in increasing appropriate behavior (such as social interaction) and in eliminating or decreasing inappropriate behavior (such as noncompliance, hallucinations, and delusional speech). Most often these treatment programs are established in institutional settings where they are more easily implemented.[22] But they also may be used in some form in the home during aftercare to provide continuity and structure for the recovering adolescent.

☑ WHEN TO REFER

Appropriate referral of schizophrenic adolescents is imperative. Obviously, if you do not have clinical training and experience with this disorder, referral is a necessity. Remember, the sooner effective treatment is begun, the better the prognosis.

If you are treating schizophrenic adolescents and they are showing increased signs of psychotic defenses such as hallucinations or delusions or anxiety, despite your efforts to help contain them, you should refer. If medication is needed or their current medication is ineffective, refer schizophrenic adolescents to a psychiatrist. They need psychiatric evaluation in order to determine whether increasing the dosage of the present medication or changing the medication is advisable.

If, despite every effort to help, adolescents are unable to maintain adequate contact with reality or to control destructive impulses, you have a psychiatric emergency on your hands. Their judgment is impaired and their delusional system adds to the feeling of being out of control. You must take action to insure the safety of patients and others. Most state hospitals and general hospitals have psychiatric emergency units in which adolescents' need for hospitalization can be evaluated.

If the family environment seems to exacerbate symptoms, referral to a day care center may be appropriate. If after time patients are able to return to stable functioning, a socialization group may be an appropriate referral. This allows them to maintain active engagement in a social environment. Many mental health centers and hospital outpatient departments provide groups for previously hospitalized clients where they may form friendships and practice social skills.

Referral to other therapists is necessary if clients see the therapist as the personification of something or someone they despise (a "bad" parent, for example). This can be discussed with patients and, if appropriate, their families, and the therapist can explain that continuation of treatment under this circumstance would be unproductive and perhaps dangerous.

Where To Go for Additional Help

Arieti, A. *Interpretation of Schizophrenia.* 2d ed. New York: Basic Books, 1974.
_____. *Understanding and Helping the Schizophrenic.* New York: Basic Books, 1979.
Bufford, R. K. *Counseling and the Demonic.* Waco, Tex.: Word Books, 1988.
Hatfield, A. *Coping with Mental Illness in the Family: The Family Guide.* Washington, D.C.: National Alliance for the Mentally Ill, 1982.
Torrey, E. F. *Surviving Schizophrenia: A Family Manual.* New York: Harper & Row, 1983.
Walsh, M. E. *Schizophrenia: Straight Talk for Families.* New York: Warner Books, 1985.

Waso, M. *Coping with Schizophrenia: A Survival Manual for Parents, Relatives and Friends.* Palo Alto, Calif.: Science and Behavior Books, 1982.
The National Alliance for the Mentally Ill. This is a nationwide advocacy organization with more than 25,000 members in 300 state and local chapters. It assists families with schizophrenic members by exchanging information on treatment and financial resources, hospital procedures, and common experiences. The address of the national office is National Alliance for the Mentally Ill, 1200 15th Street N.W., Suite 400, Washington, DC 20005. The telephone number is 202/833-3530.

Notes

1. D. C. Kimmel and I. B. Weiner, *Adolescence: A Developmental Transition* (Hillsdale, N.J.: Lawrence Erlbaum Associates, 1985).

2. E. Bleuler, *Dementia Praecox or the Group of Schizophrenias,* tr. J. Zinkin (1911; reprint, New York: International Universities Press, 1950).

3. A. Arieti, *Interpretation of Schizophrenia,* 2d ed. (New York: Basic Books, 1974).

4. Adapted from American Psychiatric Association, "The Diagnostic and Statistical Manual of Mental Disorders," 3d ed., rev. (Washington, D.C.: American Psychiatric Association, 1987).

5. S. C. Feinstein and D. Miller, "Psychoses of Adolescence," in *Basic Handbook of Child Psychiatry,* vol 2., ed. J. D. Noshpitz (New York: Basic Books, 1979).

6. I. B. Weiner, "Adjustment to Adolescence," in *International Encyclopedia of Neurology, Psychiatry, Psychoanalysis, and Psychology,* ed. B. B. Wolman (Princeton, N.J.: Van Nostrand Reinhold, 1977).

7. G. Spivack, P. E. Haimes, and J. Spotts, "Adolescent Symptomatology and Its Measurement," *American Journal of Mental Deficiency* 72 (1967): 74–95.

8. Weiner, "Adjustment to Adolescence."

9. J. H. Stephens, "Long-term Prognosis and Follow-up in Schizophrenia," *Schizophrenia Bulletin* 4 (1978): 25–47.

10. R. W. White and N. F. Watt, *The Abnormal Personality,* 5th ed. (New York: Wiley, 1981).

11. J. R. Asarnow and M. J. Goldstein, "Schizophrenia During Adolescence and a Developmental Perspective on Risk Research," *Clinical Psychology Review* 9 (1986): 211–35.

12. L. C. Waynne, M. L. Toohey, and J. Doane, "Family Studies," in *Disorders of the Schizophrenic Syndrome,* ed. L. Bellak (New York: Basic Books, 1979).

13. G. Batson et al., "Toward a Theory of Schizophrenia," *Behavioral Sciences* 1 (1956): 251–64.

14. D. Kreisman, "Social Interaction and Intimacy in Preschizophrenic Adolescence," in *The Psychopathology of Adolescence,* ed. J. Zubin and A. M. Freedman (New York: Grune and Straton, 1970).

15. R. C. Carson, "The Schizophrenias," in *Comprehensive Handbook of Psychopathology,* ed. H. E. Adams and P. B. Sutker (New York: Plenum, 1983), 411.

16. A. Hart, "Regeneration, Deliverance, or Therapy?" *Leadership* 12 (Summer 1991): 74.

17. C. W. McGill and E. Lee, "Family Psychoeducational Intervention in the Treatment of Schizophrenia," *Bulletin of the Menninger Clinic* 50 (1986): 269–86.

18. B. G. Winsberg et al., "Home vs. Hospital Care of Children With Behavioral Disorders," *Archives of General Psychiatry* 37 (1980): 413–18.

19. H. E. Lehmann, "The Somatic and Pharmacologic Treatments of Schizophrenia," *Schizophrenia Bulletin* 13 (1974): 27–45.

20. C. P. O'Brien, K. B. Hamm, and B. A. Ray, "Group vs. Individual Psychotherapy With Schizophrenics: A Controlled Outcome Study," *Archives of General Psychiatry* 27 (1972): 474–85.

21. Ibid.

22. R. P. Liberman et al., "Interventions With Psychotic Behaviors," in *Innovative Treatment Methods in Psychopathology,* ed. K. S. Calhoun, H. E. Adams, and K. M. Mitchell (New York: Wiley, 1974).

SCHOOLWORK

☑ WHAT THE STRUGGLE LOOKS LIKE

Sharon handed her report card to her dad. While her father stood silent and in a state of shock, Sharon asked, "Dad, do you think those grades are the result of heredity or environment?" Ron came home with a report card displaying four F's and a C. When his parents asked about the problem, he said, "I guess I've been concentrating too hard on one subject."

Both Sharon and Ron used humor to deflect the pain of their problems with schoolwork, but for parents of underachieving students, failing school is no laughing matter. The problem is grim and gargantuan. Millions of adolescents perform poorly in math and reading. It is now estimated that thirty percent of our nation's youth are failing to acquire the basic education and skills needed to obtain secure jobs.[1]

Adolescents who struggle with schoolwork do not always look the same. Some sit in the back of crowded classrooms, chewing gum or a strand of hair, hoping teachers will not call on them. Some train teachers to leave them alone by maintaining a hostile silence whenever they're called upon. Some become the class clowns, blurting out irrelevant remarks whenever the class becomes quiet. Some steal homework from classmates or turn in blank test papers (on multiple-choice tests they circle all the A's). Some suffer crippling anxiety over their school performance, fainting or throwing up during major exams. Some come to class late, skip classes or even whole days of school. Some get suspended or expelled. Some drop out.

In spite of their different coping styles, each of these adolescents is battling with the same problem—underachievement in school. They are what some education specialists call "sleepers." They are capable young people who are not doing well in school.

While some of these students may have slipped through the screening system with learning disabilities (they are generally identified and placed in special classes),[2] many have average IQ's but fight against two common problems: (1) lack of motivation, and (2) lack of study skills.

Motivation is the engine that drives behavior. Almost all activity is initiated

Case Description

Allen, a fourteen-year-old, had done relatively well in his elementary school years. But after only four months of high school it became apparent that he was laboring to keep his head above water. Allen felt tense and inadequate, he would lose his concentration quickly, and he rarely completed all of his homework. He reported that he would read a chapter in one of his textbooks and later have no recall of its contents. In his own words, he was "dragged" into the counselor's office by his parents, who began the session by reciting a list of Allen's academic failures. The pressure Allen was feeling from his parents was horrendous. They expected him to perform at the top of his class, yet he had few of the skills needed simply to survive.

and continued because of motivation. When motivation is high, students are said to be high achievers. Students with high-achievement motivation set goals and are persistent in trying to meet them. Students who lack motivation are often labeled "underachievers." They are not motivated to meet academic goals and therefore do not work up to their potential. Their feelings of frustration at school do not lead to problem solving, but to a lack of motivation and an avoidance of the real problems. Estimates of underachievement range from fifteen to forty percent of all adolescents.[3]

Poor study skills also contribute to adolescents' difficulties with schoolwork. A sure sign of this problem emerges when homework becomes a major source of conflict in the family. Surveys reveal that sixty percent of seventeen-year-olds in the United States do less than five hours of homework per week. Six percent say they have no homework, and seven percent acknowledge that they are assigned homework but they simply do not complete it. Only six percent do more than ten hours of homework per week.[4] Study skills are a major factor in whether students do homework at all. Knowledge of how to study efficiently and motivation to learn are the greatest needs of adolescents who have trouble with schoolwork.

☑ WHY THE STRUGGLE HAPPENS

Many factors contribute to failure at school. Adolescents who have difficulty with schoolwork bring together a unique combination of "causes." The behavioral and attitudinal patterns that result from these influences may persist throughout young people's lives and govern their opportunities for future work if intervention is not sought.

Lack of Information

Many students simply do not know how to study. Their poor academic performance is a result of the poor study habits they developed or picked up from a variety of sources. They were never taught effective study skills. For example, they never learned how to use the library, take notes in class, organize a scheme to study for exams, or separate the important from the trivial. To criticize these students for not studying better is like complaining that an automobile is faulty when the only difficulty is an empty gas tank.

Psychological Problems

Fear of failure, dependency, inferiority, and critical attitudes may lead to teenagers not wanting to try to study or to ineffective study. Perfectionism can lead to procrastination or failure to complete assignments. Students with more severe psychological problems almost always experience difficulties with studying. For example, traumatic family conflicts may cause children to have difficulty concentrating. And battles with depression or anxiety are obviously detrimental to academic achievement. Medication or drug use may cause a lethargy that interferes with study. Psychological problems have a powerful impact on schoolwork.

Parental Influence

When parents hold unreasonably high expectations, their children often develop a fear of failure and low motivation. Adolescents may "get even" with their overly controlling parents by giving up in school.[5] Since they cannot consistently be good enough to please their parents, they stop trying. The reverse may also be true and just as detrimental. That is, if parents give little encouragement, underestimate their children, and communicate very low aspirations, their children may respond accordingly.

Some parents become so absorbed in their own affairs that they express no interest in their children's schoolwork. Some parents who are overly permissive expect no compliance, and their children do not learn discipline. Therefore, they have little motivation. Children who are overly protected also have difficulty at school. They do not learn to set goals, be self-motivated, or to work under even minimal stress. Parents have a great influence on whether children succeed or fail at school.

Low Self-Esteem

Feeling worthless is a major factor in low motivation. Students who suffer from feeling inferior often see themselves as helpless. They almost appear to want to fail. Failure becomes a way to confirm their low self-regard. The result of a poor self-concept is an "I can't" attitude that leads to almost no motivation for success in the classroom. These adolescents underestimate their abilities and have low aspirations. You may find the section on inferiority helpful when dealing with these students.

Poor Environment

Just as students' home life influences their level of enthusiasm for learning, so does school environment. The learning atmosphere in a school system or in a particular class relates directly to levels of motivation. A school should have the feel of excitement and a spirit of optimism about learning. Young people develop an interest in learning when their instructors are actively interested in the success of their learning. Some adolescents fail at school simply because instructors who "go through the motions" have turned them off to the excitement of learning.

External Locus of Control

According to some researchers, the concept of locus of control encapsulates the single most important personality dynamic associated with underachievement.[6] Locus of control refers to a person's belief about who controls the future. Adolescents high in internal locus of control believe themselves responsible for their own success. If they do badly on a test, for example, such persons are likely to blame themselves for not studying enough, for not paying attention in class, or for staying up too late. Adolescents high in external locus of control believe the factors that control success are outside themselves. For example, they may blame a teacher for their failure on an exam, or bad luck, or unfair questions. Struggling students are most often very high externals. They assume little responsibility for their failure and are therefore prone to give up. They develop what Martin Seligman calls "learned helplessness."[7] The student says, "I can't do it, so why try?"

☑ HOW TO HELP

Literally dozens and dozens of effective interventions are available to help adolescents having problems with schoolwork. The following techniques are a place to begin. They should, as always, be undergirded with personal acceptance and reflective listening. The ultimate goal is to help young people internalize effective study skills and heighten motivation so that they can face academic challenges with only limited assistance.

Consider the Family Context

When adolescents come to counseling for academic struggles, one of the first questions to ask is, "What role does this crisis play within the young person's family?" If tension exists between the parents, if there has been a recent divorce, or even a new sibling, academic problems may serve as a diversion from the real issue. Adolescent anxiety, anger, or depression about home life drains young people emotionally and makes concentration at school next to impossible. On the other hand, youth who compete with successful siblings may opt for failure as a means to gain attention at home. In any case, the family context is an important consideration and worthy of exploration in counseling.

Focus on Encouragement

The foundation of any work with adolescents who have trouble at school must be to encourage an "I can" attitude. Adolescents must be able to sense acceptance of themselves by their parents and counselors, and parents and counselors must avoid sarcasm and teasing at all costs. Criticism of any kind will most likely squelch any opportunity for effective intervention. Effective counselors and parents work diligently to distinguish students' self-worth from their academic performance.

Examine Study Conditions

High school students should have adequate conditions to study on their own. The best setting for most should be as quiet and uncluttered as possible. A desk in a bedroom is ideal. A bright light should come from the direction opposite the writing side (to avoid shadows). Interruptions and distractions should be minimized. Students should not accept telephone calls during study time. Dictionaries and other reference books should be available and easily accessible as well as pens, pencils, and paper. Students should also create a system that fits their style to organize their various courses in a notebook. These conditions can be discussed with adolescents and their parents. The goal is to create the best study conditions, not to force them into a setup that they will resist. Some young people, for example, may find a desk in their room too isolating. They may prefer working at a kitchen table. The key is to have a regular place and time to study.

Build Self-Esteem by Assuring Successful Achievement

The old adage that "nothing succeeds like success" is not just a cliché. It is the truth. Adolescents who are failing school need hope. They need to see signs of possibilities, signs that help them believe they can succeed. This can be done by placing them in classes that are challenging but not over their heads. Students who have failed a great deal in the past should be able to succeed about ninety percent of the time in order to like what they are doing. Discuss this principle with teachers to get their suggestions of what can be done to facilitate success. With a sense of achievement they begin to feel like winners, and are eager to master new material and skills. Self-esteem is not a prerequisite for academic achievement; it is the consequence of success.

Explore How To Study

Some students have never been taught how to study. Explore with them how they prepare for exams, write papers, and do homework. If they are at all motivated to do better, you can help them by showing them more effective ways to study. One of the most straightforward, effective, and researched methods of how to study effectively is called SQ4R—survey, question, read, recite, write, review.[8]

Survey. The goal of surveying is to determine what important questions are answered in a textbook chapter. The students go first to the beginning and end of the chapter to look for any stated objectives, a list of questions, or a chapter summary. They read these first to discover the questions they should be able to answer after completing the chapter. Next is the survey. This is the process of quickly skimming the chapter to determine what important questions it answers. They are to read titles and subtitles, and examine any illustrations, pictures, or charts. This gives them a basic understanding of what the chapter is about.

Question. A part of surveying is turning titles and subtitles into questions. For example, students who keep in mind the title of this book and the subject of this section of the book would combine them and turn them into "What are the ways to help adolescents who struggle with schoolwork?" By generating questions as they survey, students keep alert to important points in the chapter. After completing their survey, they should have a list of questions. If a chapter does not have subtitles, the lead sentences of paragraphs can be used. Before reading, students may wish to attempt to answer the questions they have formulated. They can then test their answers against the book.

Read. Next, students read to find full answers to their questions. They do not need to pore over every word and minute detail. Their goal is to answer their questions. They are to read as quickly as they can, and to read selectively to find answers to questions. If they come to an answer to a question they did not anticipate, they slow down, formulate the question, and make sure they know the answer.

Recite and Write. After students have read the answers to the questions from their survey, and developed new questions and answers that they hadn't anticipated, they are to recite the answers. Just because they have read the chapter doesn't mean that they really know what it is about. Having them talk out loud about the concepts they've found helps them to get a better grasp of the content of the chapter. They are also to write a summary "self-discussion."

Review. The final step in the SQ4R method is to review the chapter. This may be done at any time. For example, in preparing for an exam, students may quiz themselves on questions they generated until they know they could give accurate answers if those questions should appear on their exam. When they know they can answer correctly and make accurate summaries, students will be more confident and perform better on examinations.

With the SQ4R method students spend less time memorizing facts they will soon forget. Instead, they focus on key concepts rather than details, and they don't waste time reading and looking for things they already know. They are also equipped for a thorough review for test preparation. High school students who have learned the SQ4R method of studying have been shown to improve their school performance significantly.[9]

Explore Class Attendance and Note Taking

Attending class is such an obviously useful thing to do that it is almost embarrassing to have to bring it up. Unfortunately, some adolescents need encouragement in simply being there when class opens. They need to understand the important relationship between attending class and the grades they receive. Eighty-five percent of students with a B average or higher almost always attend class.[10]

Students troubled by schoolwork also need guidance in how to take notes in class. A helpful note-taking strategy is to record notes on the right-hand side of the page, leaving the left-hand side for study questions. Students should be encouraged to write down the major ideas and statements in the lecture and not every word. After the lecture, they should take a few minutes to turn their notes into questions. The main theme and subtopics may be turned into questions and recorded next to the lecture notes. The point is to go to class looking for questions and answers.

Consider Rewards

Most parents have already used positive reinforcers, such as the privilege of watching television after studying. Rewards can sometimes be useful in motivating the unmotivated. A struggling student with a new driver's license, for example, may be highly motivated by the availability of the family car, once certain conditions have been met. Threatening kids with punishment for bad grades, however, is another popular method that does not work very well. Positive rewards work better. The best motivator of all is success. Focus on increasing the positive rather than diminishing the negative.

Explore Getting a Tutor

One of the most direct ways of improving the performance of students who are troubled by schoolwork is through professional tutors. This may be an especially helpful alternative for students who resist placement in schools for special education. Students may stay in public school and parents may use the money they would have spent on tuition to hire tutors to work with their children at home. Some tutors are experts in particular academic subjects; others can be hired to teach general study skills.

Research in education reinforces the gains that may be achieved from one-on-one instruction. An area college or university education department is an excellent resource for tutors. Some high schools have tutoring programs. And an increasing number of corporations sell tutorial services. One of them, Sylvan Learning Centers, increased from 200 franchise holders to 450 in two years. Adolescents often develop relationships with their tutors that resemble the bond between clients and therapists. And that student/tutor bond has similar therapeutic effects. Some embattled students may find it easier to form relationships with adults they identify as tutors than with adults they call parents, or shrinks or therapists. For students with emotional problems as well as academic struggles, however, the combination of tutoring and psychotherapy produces outstanding, even dramatic results.

Consider Private Schools

Some parents are frustrated by their experiences with public schools and may find a high-performance prep school or a Christian school a positive alternative. Generally, these schools are orderly, safe, wholesome, and traditional in instruction. Sometimes the challenge of a rigorous program is precisely what an unruly or unmotivated student needs. To locate a Christian school in a specific area these organizations can be helpful:

Association of Christian Schools, International
P.O. Box 4097
Whittier, CA 80607

Christian Schools International
3350 E. Paris Avenue S.E.
Grand Rapids, MI 49512

National Association of Private Schools
2021 K St., N.W.
Washington, DC 20006
(For locating preparatory schools)

☑ WHEN TO REFER

Refer struggling students to education specialists for evaluation if you suspect a learning disability. Most learning disabled, mentally retarded, and emotionally disturbed students have been identified and placed in special classes or assigned to resource teachers for special help. But occasionally they are missed. Refer students to other competent counselors or psychologists when, over time, they are not making progress in their school performance.

Where To Go for Additional Help

Felton, G. S., and B. E. Biggs. *Up from Under-Achievement*. Springfield, Ill.: Charles C. Thomas, 1977.
Lillie, D. L., and P. A. Place. *Partners: A Guide To Working with Schools for Parents of Children with Special Instructional Needs*. Glenview, Ill.: Scott, Foresman, 1982.
Nemko, M., and B. Nemko. *How To Get a "Private School" Education in a Public School*. Washington, D.C: Acropolis Books, 1986.
Rich, D. *Mega Skills: How Families Can Help Children Succeed in School and Beyond*. Boston: Houghton-Mifflin, 1988.
Robinson, F. *Effective Study*. New York: Harper & Row, 1970.
Wrenn, C. G., and S. Schwaryrock. *Grades: What's So Important About Them, Anyway?* Circle Pines, Minn.: American Guidance Service, 1970.
Zifferblatt, S. M. *Improving Study and Homework Behaviors*. Champaign, Ill.: Research Press, 1970.

Notes

1. Education Commission of the States, "Securing Our Future: The Report of the National Forum for Youth At Risk" (Denver: Education Commission of the States, 1988).

2. "Learning disabilities" is a generic phrase describing problems that an estimated six to ten percent of otherwise normal students encounter in taking in, processing, and retrieving information. The most familiar is dyslexia, a neurological disorder that causes students to reverse letters and misread words.

3. C. A. Asbury, "Selected Factors Influencing Over- and Underachievement in Young School-age Children." *Review of Educational Research* 44 (1974): 409–28.

4. National Assessment of Educational Progress, *Newsletter* 11 (1978): 1–3.

5. K. Metcalf and E. Gaier, "Patterns of Middle-Class Parenting and Adolescent Underachievement," *Adolescence* 22 (1987): 919–28.

6. L. Nielsen, *How To Motivate Adolescents* (Englewood Cliffs, N.J.: Prentice-Hall, 1982).

7. M. Seligman, *Learned Optimism* (New York: Knopf, 1991).

8. F. P. Robinson, *Effective Study* (New York: Harper & Row, 1970).

9. J. M. Greiner and P. Karoly, "Effects of Self-Control Training on Study Activity and Academic Performance: An Analysis of Self-Monitoring, Self-Reward, and Systematic Planning Components," *Journal of Counseling Psychology* 23 (1976): 495–502.

10. H. C. Lindgren, *The Psychology of College Success* (New York: Wiley, 1969).

SHYNESS

☑ WHAT THE STRUGGLE LOOKS LIKE

Some adolescents are socially invisible. They are not noticed or selected as leaders. They do not participate much in class or other social activities. They do not stand up for their own rights, and they are too timid to express their opinions on matters that concern them. They are afraid to ask others out on dates. They feel awkward and tense in social situations. They seek quiet corners at parties. Because they want to be liked, they are easily influenced by others and lack self-confidence. These are the adolescents who struggle with shyness.

Shyness is fear to meet people and discomfort in their presence. At its core is anxiety about being evaluated by others and consequently rejected. In its extreme form, shyness becomes a social phobia (see the section on phobia). While many adolescents recognize shyness in themselves, it would probably come as a surprise to them to learn that only seven percent of Americans claim they have never experienced attacks of shyness.[1]

Anyone who writes about shyness owes an enormous debt to Philip G. Zimbardo of Stanford University, who has studied shyness for more than two decades. Much of what I have written here was inspired by his work. His research reveals that more than eighty percent of high school and college students perceive themselves as shy at times, and forty percent report current shyness and embarrassment around peers. Symptoms include blushing, inability to make eye contact, an avoidance of social gatherings, a tendency to speak in a voice almost too low to be heard, clammy hands, dry mouth, excessive perspiration, trembling hands and legs, pounding heart, queasy stomach, a sinking feeling, or even a sudden need to go to the bathroom.[2]

Shy adolescents suffer numerous disadvantages. Compared with others, shy people are more likely to be anxious, depressed, lonely, have lower self-esteem, and regard their social networks as less supportive and less satisfying. Unlike introverts, shy people are not happy to be by themselves or to participate minimally in social encounters.[3] Zimbardo likens shyness to a prison that is every bit as real and in some ways more restricting than iron bars.[4]

Case Description

Martha, age fifteen, came to counseling at the encouragement of her mother who described her as "a wallflower." In the first session Martha barely said a word. She seemed cold and emotionally aloof. She was, however, visibly upset at having to be in counseling. It was almost as though she were using her silence as a weapon to preserve her sense of dignity. To talk freely with the counselor would mean that she had lost the power struggle with her mom. There was more to her silence, however, than not losing that battle.

Therapy progressed slowly at first, but after three or four sessions, Martha confessed her dread of being with people whom she did not already know. She wanted to meet other people but was terribly fearful of doing or saying something that would embarrass her. To avoid having to sit uncomfortably next to another student, she walked alone to and from school and always arrived at her classes just as they were beginning. She confessed that she had even retreated to the isolation of a bathroom stall for safety. Martha arranged much of her life so as to avoid situations where she might be put on the spot.

☑ WHY THE STRUGGLE HAPPENS

For many years researchers have attempted to make sense out of the complexities of shyness. The following is not an exhaustive list of causes.

Learned Helplessness

One of the ways adolescents learn their social style is by trying behaviors out and receiving various rewards and punishments. Over time they develop expectations concerning the likely results of their behaviors. If their behaviors achieve desired goals, they develop positive expectations. They also learn what doesn't work. They learn to expect a negative response to their behavior, and they make choices to avoid that behavior again. Helplessness is learned when expectations, either positive or negative, are not present. For example if young people are in new social situations where they do not know what to expect, they will probably become anxious and clam up. It is almost as if they are visiting a foreign country where they do not understand the language. They feel helpless and give up trying to communicate. This may also happen if their behaviors produce inconsistent rewards (whether real or simply perceived). If they do not know what to expect they become helpless. They become shy.[5]

Formality

Formal situations can elicit shyness. Religious ceremonies, graduations, weddings, funerals, and important meetings all have a greater number of rules than other situations. People want to do the right thing. A mistake in a formal setting can be embarrassing. And the likelihood of making a mistake becomes greater where there are more spoken and unspoken rules. Formality makes teens feel exposed and vulnerable. Of course, formality often results in situational shyness, but for some teens, every interaction is "formal."

Social Attention

Adolescents do not want to be ignored. But being conspicuous or being stared at also tends to cause social anxiety. Shyness is likely to be the reaction of a girl in a group of boys. Physical handicaps frequently result in shyness. These adolescents may avoid others so as not to be stared at or talked about. Even subtle handicaps like learning disabilities or expressive language problems may lead to social withdrawal. An example is adolescents who arrive late at gatherings and find everyone stopping to look at them as they enter. While a few adolescents love the attention, many shrink away and look for a place to hide to avoid all eyes upon them. It's the middle ground of social attention that produces psychological comfort for most young people.

Novelty

Teens often deplore new social environments. For many, a new social setting is about as comfortable as a new pair of tight shoes. Adolescents are having a hard enough time dealing with their changing bodies without the discomfort of a strange social context. The threatening social situation is likely to make young people inhibited and careful in their behavior. Generally, this guardedness is relaxed after they grow more accustomed to the setting. However, some teens never seem to jump over the hurdle of novelty. They maintain their role as the "new kid" and incorporate shyness into their basic social style.

Heredity

Some researchers blame genetics for shyness. They say shyness runs in families. The evidence is not conclusive, but a study conducted by psychologists at Yale and Harvard revealed that ten to fifteen percent of us are born with a propensity to become shy. This shyness is seen in infants and toddlers who turn away from strangers and hide behind parents when spoken to, even by adults they know. Jerome Kagan of Harvard reports that shy infants and toddlers develop a rapid heart rate and become wary, withdrawn, reserved, and silent when faced with unfamiliar people or new situations. Their hypersensitivity makes them uncomfortable, self-conscious, even panicky in social settings. Of course, circumstances play a role in determining whether an inherited tendency to become shy is expressed. The Yale-Harvard study revealed that two-thirds of shy children had older siblings who perhaps bullied or belittled them, shaking their self-confidence.

Parental Modeling

Shy parents often produce shy children, but this does not mean shyness is in the genes. Adolescents are prone to fall into the same social styles of their adult models. If they hear their parents discuss others in fearful or mistrustful terms and they see their parents avoid social settings, they may acquire a habit of being quiet and shy. A strict behaviorist would say that shyness is a learned phobic reaction.

Parental Overprotection

Adolescents who have been overly protected by their parents are frequently dependent, passive, and shy. They have been limited in their opportunities to be adventurous, and thus have not learned to trust themselves in dealing with their social environment.

Self-Labeling

A self-perpetuating pattern is set when adolescents perceive and accept themselves as shy. They view the world through timid glasses and don't recognize that they have a choice in eye wear. It is as if they are out to prove that they are shy. Experiences that present contrary findings are warded off. Their belief prevents them from taking actions that could lead them to get what they want and counteract their feelings of inferiority. They have labeled themselves as shy "and that settles it."

☑ HOW TO HELP

Shyness does not have to be a permanent part of people's personalities. The following techniques are designed to help shy adolescents overcome the anxiety that fuels their social style and acquire a sense of security in social situations. As always, these techniques should be undergirded by personal acceptance and reflective listening.

Pinpoint the Severity

It is helpful to assess the severity of adolescents' shyness. One of the best known measures of shyness, the Stanford Shyness Survey, was developed by Zimbardo. It is found in *Helping the Struggling Adolescent: A Counseling Guide.*

Emphasize Warmth and Acceptance

Although "unconditional positive regard" is taken for granted in most of the sections of this book, shyness demands a reemphasis. The more warmth and acceptance given to shy adolescents the better. If they experience love and acceptance from you, they may then generalize the experience and realize that others can accept them too. Provide them with safe places to let down their social guard, places where they will not be embarrassed or ashamed, where they do not even have to think of being rejected. In doing this you are also modeling effective social interaction. You may find it helpful to review "Characteristics of Effective Helping" and "The Heart of Helping" in Part One.

Help Them Understand Their Shyness

Adolescents, like all of us, have a need to explain their experiences. Understanding shyness is no exception. Experiments have demonstrated the value of people understanding why they are shy. Three therapy groups of shy people received the same treatment with the exception of an explanation of shyness. Those in one group were helped to understand their shyness by an explanation of the role of their developmental history and childhood experiences. Another group was shown how shyness usually results from their thinking styles and self-perceptions. The third group received counseling that did not focus on finding explanations for shyness. In general, the first two approaches, which helped the shy people understand their shyness, were more effective than the third approach, which did not. When shy adolescents are helped to understand their shyness, they become more amenable to change.[6]

Implement Social Skills Training

Research has shown that social skills are best learned in group settings designed to provide the following experiences: (1) a description and rationale for new behaviors that are to be learned; (2) a demonstration of new behaviors through modeling; (3) practice of new behaviors with feedback about how one is doing; and (4) transfer of new behaviors to the natural environment. These training groups generally proceed gradually to allow clients to progress at their own pace.[7]

If a group setting is not possible, it is still necessary to implement social skill training strategies. Here are some techniques that are particularly useful in counseling shy adolescents.

1. Help them rehearse what they want to say in specific situations. Ask them to write out complaints, compliments, questions, or whatever. Then have them read aloud from their papers and role play specific situations. If possible, have them use the telephone to express themselves while in your office. Then ask them to do it face-to-face with you.

2. Help them practice smiling and making eye contact. Ask them to look in the mirror as practice. Give them assignments to smile and make eye contact with five strangers each day.

3. Work to improve their speaking voice and volume. Teach them to experiment with volume levels. Sometimes a tape recorder is helpful in giving them objective feedback.

4. Ask them to observe and take notes on behavior patterns of people they respect. Help them to see how others laugh at themselves when things go wrong. Help them to practice modeling behavior. Ask them to practice giving compliments, asking questions, and sharing experiences they've recently had.

5. Guide them in an exploration of their true selves. Shy adolescents often believe they have to be someone they aren't. Help them accept and

appreciate their peculiarities as special traits that make them distinctive and interesting (rather than unattractive).

6. Explore their use of humor. I often find that quiet adolescents have a wonderful sense of humor. Sometimes they need only to be encouraged to try it out. If appropriate, have them call a store to ask about a product and have them see if they can make the person on the telephone laugh.

7. Review their appearance. This idea may sound ridiculous, but research speaks loudly about the importance of physical appearance and social interactions.[8] Physical appearance has a profound impact on first impressions. Dressing appropriately makes young people more appealing to others and helps them feel better about themselves.

Use Relaxation Techniques

Reducing anxiety in social settings involves two basic steps. The first is to develop self-relaxation skills. The second is to use these skills during social interaction. Self-relaxation involves awareness of muscle tension and strategies of deep muscle relaxation. This technique along with others is described in detail in the section on anxiety. Once relaxation techniques have been mastered they may be applied to shyness by having adolescents imagine real-life social situations that cause anxiety. Ask them to place themselves there as fully as possible. Then let them practice their self-relaxation techniques until they can see themselves in those situations without anxiety.

The use of imagery to promote self-relaxation is based on the procedure of systematic desensitization developed by Joseph Wolpe.[9] The next step is to let them practice these relaxation techniques in actual situations. This will help them reduce their social anxiety and give them control over their seemingly uncontrollable social anxiety.

Teach Positive Self-Talk

Shy behavior is what people do, not what they are. And much of what we do comes from what we think. A very destructive aspect of shyness is young people's acceptance of the idea that they are shy by nature and little can be done to improve things. This belief is supported by numerous irrational assumptions and expectations that have caused them to talk themselves into "being shy." These assumptions include "Everyone must like me," "It is awful to make a mistake in front of others," "I need to be perfect," and "I can't control what I do in a social setting." Consider the thoughts going through the minds of shy adolescents who want to ask someone for a date.

Anxiety is understandable, but clients will multiply the natural apprehension with thoughts like "What if she says no? That would mean I am terrible! I would feel like a jerk and never ask anyone else out again. I can't take that risk. I don't think I will call her."

The challenge facing a therapist is to help a shy young man say something more along the lines of "If she says no, that would be unfortunate, but it certainly wouldn't be the end of the world. What would I have to lose? In fact, I can only gain. If she says yes, great! If not, I still have the satisfaction of knowing I tried and I won't be any worse off." Shyness generally results from viewing social interactions as times when people are evaluating adolescents crippled by shyness. This attitude is bound to make young people feel anxious and appear anxious. With this pattern of thinking, it is not surprising that shy adolescents expect the worst and don't enjoy socializing.

Adolescents who overcome shyness do so with positive self-talk. They see social interactions as opportunities to make new friends and have fun. One previously shy adolescent I worked with did a major shift in his thinking and had a sentence he repeated to himself whenever he started to feel shy: "The party is where I am." This helped him remember that he did not have to depend on another person's evaluation to have self-worth.

Donald Meichenbaum has developed a therapeutic approach built on use of self-statements as coping skills. He presents three major steps to overcome social anxiety.[10] If a young person wants to meet a stranger, for example, the first step is to prepare for the challenge. This is done through self-statements like "I know how to relax when I get nervous; besides, I am allowed to make mistakes." Next is learning to keep cool during the interaction. The young person may say, "I can handle this. My nervousness is natural and I am doing fine. I am going to focus on the other person, not myself." Finally comes self-reinforcement. Here the adolescent may say, "I survived it and that is success. It is getting easier each time."

Implement Assertiveness Training

Assertiveness is an attitude and a way of acting in any situation where people need to express feelings, ask for what they want, or say no to something they don't want. Several studies have demonstrated the usefulness of this technique with shy adolescents. After a month-long assertiveness-training program, thirteen-year-olds earned higher self-concept scores, became more confident, and more willing to speak up in their classes.[11] Even with as little as twelve hours of assertiveness training, high school students had improved their self-esteem and their relationships with teachers. Moreover, students with the lowest self-esteem scores at the outset made the greatest improvements.[12]

Learning to be assertive involves developing nonverbal skills. These include looking directly at other people when addressing them, maintaining an open rather than a closed posture, and literally "standing their ground" by not physically backing away from other people.

Learning to be assertive also involves an expression of feelings and desires. Feelings are neither "right" nor "wrong," but they give people energy. Feelings simply exist. Shy adolescents often evaluate their feelings for appropriateness. They ask, "What should I be feeling?" rather than "What am I feeling?" Once they have learned to identify their feelings, encourage expression of them, first with counselors and then in their environment. Shy adolescents keep their feelings to themselves also because they assume others already know what they want. They need to see that people around them are not mind readers.

Learning to be assertive requires practice. Ask adolescents to write out descriptions of two or three situations where they become especially passive and shy (for example, getting shortchanged in the cafeteria at lunch). Next, ask them to write how they would like to react in those situations. Practice with them assertive responses. Help them use "I" statements, simple requests (not demands), nonverbal behaviors, and so on.

Space does not permit an adequate description of these important techniques. For more information on assertiveness training you may find *Your Perfect Right* by Alberti and Emmons, and *Asserting Yourself* by Bower to be helpful. For assertiveness training in a Christian context, *Beyond Assertiveness* by Faul and Augsburger, and *The Assertive Christian* by Emmons and Richardson are useful.

Encourage Volunteering

Sharing not only feelings, but talents and knowledge as well, according to Zimbardo, helps alleviate shyness.[13] Adolescents do not need to join the Peace Corps, however, to share their abilities. For example, if a shy fourteen-year-old girl has knowledge of photography and enjoys it, urge her to use it to help others. A youth minister, for example, may ask her to chronicle a choir trip on film. This not only increases her self-esteem, but her interest can become an entry into less frightening conversations with others. Encourage shy young people to volunteer for activities. A small job at a party may be a great aid in overcoming social awkwardness. They may be given something to do, such as helping serve or cleaning up. It's their reason for being there. While shy adolescents do not want the spotlight, social assignments or special roles give them reasons to initiate conversation and interaction. These may go a long way in helping them feel good about themselves and secure enough to take more social risks.

☑ WHEN TO REFER

Refer shy adolescents if you cannot genuinely accept them or if you find yourself becoming impatient with their seeming inability to master social skills. Refer them to other competent counselors or psychologists when, over time, they are not progressing in the struggle to overcome shyness. If you recognize that you are encouraging dependence in an already shy and dependent adolescent, you should consider referral.

Where To Go for Additional Help

Adler, R. B. *Confidence in Communication: A Guide to Assertive and Social Skills.* New York: Holt, Rinehart, 1974.

Alberti, R. E., and M. L. Emmons. *Your Perfect Right: A Guide to Assertive Behavior.* San Luis Obispo, Calif.: Impact Publishers, 1978.

Bower, G., and S. Bower. *Asserting Yourself: A Practical Guide for Positive Change.* Reading, Mass.: Addison-Wesley, 1976.

Daly, J. A., and J. C. McCroskey. *Avoiding Communication: Shyness, Reticence, and Communication Apprehension.* Beverly Hills: Sage Publications, 1984.

Emmons, M., and D. Richardson. *The Assertive Christian.* Minneapolis: Winston Press, 1981.

Faul, J., and D. Augsburger. *Beyond Assertiveness.* Waco, Tex.: Word, 1983.

Gilmartin, B. G. *Shyness and Love: Causes, Consequences and Treatment.* New York: University Press of America, 1987.

Jones, W. H., J. M. Cheek, and S. R. Briggs, eds. *Shyness: Perspective on Research and Treatment.* New York: Plenum, 1986.

Zimbardo, P. G. *Shyness: What It Is, What To Do About It.* Reading, Mass.: Addison-Wesley, 1977.

_____. *Shyness Clinic.* New York: Biomonitoring Applications, 1978.

_____. *The Shy Child.* New York: McGraw-Hill, 1981.

Notes

1. P. G. Zimbardo, "Shyness," in *Dictionary of Pastoral Care and Counseling*, ed. R. J. Hunter (Nashville: Abingdon, 1990).

2. P. G. Zimbardo, *Shyness: What It Is, What To Do About It* (Reading, Mass.: Addison-Wesley, 1977).

3. B. M. DePaulo et al., "Are Shy People Reluctant To Ask for Help?" *Journal of Personality and Social Psychology* 56 (1989): 834–44.

4. Zimbardo, *Shyness: What It Is.*

5. M. E. Seligman, *Helplessness: On Depression, Development and Death* (San Francisco: W. H. Freeman, 1975).

6. M. A. Hoffman and H. Teglasi, "The Role of Causal Attributions in Counseling Shy Subjects," *Journal of Counseling Psychology* 29 (1982): 132–39.

7. R. M. Eisler and L. W. Frederksen, *Perfecting Social Skills: A Guide to Interpersonal Behavior* (New York: Plenum, 1980).

8. R. E. Glasgow and H. Arkowitz, "The Behavioral Assessment of Male and Female Social Competence in Dyadic Heterosexual Interactions," *Behavior Therapy* 6 (1975): 488–98.

9. J. Wolpe, *The Practice of Behavior Therapy* (New York: Pergamon, 1974).

10. D. Meichenbaum, *Cognitive-Behavior Modification* (New York: Plenum, 1977).

11. S. Wehr and M. Kaufman, "The Effects of Assertive Training on Performance in Highly Anxious Adolescents," *Adolescence* 22 (1987): 195–205.

12. J. Stake, C. Deville, and C. Pennell, "The Effects of Assertive Training on the Performance and Self-Esteem of Adolescent Girls," *Journal of Youth and Adolescence* 12 (1983): 435–43.

13. Zimbardo, *Shyness: What It Is.*

SIBLINGS

☑ WHAT THE STRUGGLE LOOKS LIKE

Rivalry between brothers and sisters has been written about from the earliest recorded history. From the biblical account of Cain and Abel to the make-believe world of Cinderella and her step-sisters, sibling conflicts have formed the basis for untold numbers of stories. Our interest in the sibling bond, however, is not limited to literature. Ever since the prominent psychoanalyst of the early 1900s, Alfred Adler, wrote about the first-born child in a family being "dethroned" by the competition, jealousy, and hostility of a younger brother or sister, sibling rivalry has been the topic of study for numerous researchers.

Growing up in a family context that includes brothers and sisters is an experience that eighty percent of American children share.[1] Children with siblings often spend more time with one another than they do with either parent. Siblings have a tremendous influence on child development. The presence of a second sibling acts as an incentive for change. The first child is pushed to differentiate from the other, usually toward the values of the parents, in order to retain his or her "favored" position. The first child's growth is typically accelerated while the younger child is likely to maintain a more adaptive position, which requires more attention from parents.

According to one study, the most frequent type of aggression occurring in American society is between youthful siblings. These reports indicate that forty percent of brothers and sisters hit one another with harmful objects at least once during a given year, and more than eighty percent engage in some form of violence against a sibling.[2] Other researchers have found statistics to be less dramatic.[3] Some researchers have found sibling conflict to be the most intense among sibs of the same sex.[4] Others have found close-age spacing to intensify sibling conflict while others have found it to promote stronger ties.[5] Although experts quibble about the exact figures and disagree about research methodology, most agree that sibling rivalry is indeed common, if not normal.

Three forms of sibling rivalry have been identified: *Heir/Heiress*, where siblings perceive that one child is the parents' favorite. *Competitor*, where

281

Case Description

Corey, a fourteen-year-old, was engaged in extreme sibling rivalry with his brother Doug, age sixteen. Almost every look and gesture provoked verbal or physical battle. They were in constant competition for attention from others. They argued over who sat where in the family car, what TV shows to watch, who was better at basketball, and on and on. More than once valuable objects were broken as a result of one of their tussles. Doug remembers Corey once cutting the telephone cord with a pair of scissors while he was talking on the phone. Corey recalls Doug threatening him with a hot iron for spilling milk on his homework. During the first session they reeled off their stories of sibling conflict. They were brought into counseling by their mother, a single parent, who simply felt that she had lost control of both of them.

siblings perceive that the parent-favored child changes depending on current behavior. And *Peers*, where siblings perceive that each is recognized as special to parents and therefore conflicts are minimal.[6]

Failure to resolve rivalry may lead to residual and persistent envy, manipulation, scheming, plotting, grudges, alienation, revenge, sabotage, or even vendettas.[7] Happily, these situations are the exceptions, but effective therapeutic intervention helps to ensure that siblings overcome their inevitable conflicts.

Before exploring the causes and treatment of sibling rivalry it is important to note briefly three unique characteristics of human beings. These traits get to the root of all human conflict. First, each person sees and experiences the world through his or her own perceptual framework. Second, humans are intentional, willful beings with goals to be fulfilled. Third, humans are social beings who live out their identity within the context of family and other persons. In short, to be human means to have conflict.[8] Siblings do not have an option whether to have conflict, only how to deal with it.

☑ WHY THE STRUGGLE HAPPENS

Many factors lie behind sibling rivalry. The following are just a few of the most commonly cited.

Favoritism

Children depend so much on their parents for love, attention, and fulfillment of their needs that they simply do not like to share their parents with anyone. This is especially true if they perceive, even irrationally, that their parents are playing favorites. Parental favoritism toward one child may spark tremendous resentment in siblings. Joseph and his coat of many colors is a biblical example of jealousy over perceived parental favoritism.

Displaced Anger

Sometimes hostile feelings that originate in other relationships, for example with parents, are taken out on younger siblings. Children may pick fights with siblings as a way to release frustration about matters that are totally unrelated. Brothers or sisters may be convenient marks for a needed physically and emotionally cathartic experience.

Feelings of Inferiority

If children have to live in the shadow of talented siblings' achievements, they tend to feel robbed of their individuality. The competition doesn't seem fair. Adolescents troubled with this problem feel that all of their actions and accomplishments are compared with those of their siblings. One continually hears people say, "You're John's brother? Wow, you have some big shoes to fill." To balance the scales, younger siblings may try, unsuccessfully, to take their rivals down a few notches by showing hostility toward them.[9]

Developmental Changes

Identity issues and self-consciousness add a great deal to the causation of sibling rivalry during adolescence. Teenagers, more than any other age group, may be angered by even a minor assault on their dignity and self-worth. This may include teasing, bossiness, sarcasm, criticism, or unfair treatment. During these years of continual change, the body's chemistry may interact with emotional processing and contribute to short fuses and emotional blowups with siblings. Hormone levels in adolescents, for example, have been shown to be related to anger.[10]

Environment

The structure of some households may promote conflict between siblings. They may compete for property, space, and other tangible goods that they share by virtue of their environment. For example, siblings may become involved in disputes over the use of the bathroom or telephone. Interestingly, when people are placed in situations that create conflict, they are more likely to attribute the origins of conflict to each other than to the situation of which they both are victims.

☑ HOW TO HELP

The following strategies have been found useful in reducing arguments and fights among or between siblings. Typically, a combination of these techniques works best. As always, they should be undergirded with personal acceptance and reflective listening.

Pinpoint the Severity

At the beginning of treatment it is helpful to assess the intensity of adolescents' struggles with sibling conflict. While I know of no direct measure of sibling rivalry, a measure of anger can help pinpoint the severity. The State-Trait Anger Scale is a fifteen-item instrument that assesses anger both as an emotional state that varies in intensity and as a relatively stable personality trait (how frequently an adolescent feels state-anger over time). The Novaco Anger Scale is another instrument that may be helpful in pinpointing the severity of one's anger. Both are found in *Helping the Struggling Adolescent: A Counseling Guide*. To assess further the intensity of conflicts, an interview should include questions related to the breaking of objects and physical injury.

Explore the Issue with Parents

When young people experience serious conflict with siblings, it is helpful to assess the situation with the parents. Are they treating all of their children fairly and still allowing for their uniqueness? Help them avoid comparing one child with another (as in the question, "Why don't you work hard in school like your sister?"). Hold up a figurative mirror to the parents to help them recognize the subtle signs of favoritism. Do they baby one sibling? Do they call one child by an endearing term? Do they spend more time or money on one child? Do they constantly belittle one child's interests, abilities, or performance? Do they recognize and affirm the uniqueness of each child? Encourage them to spend time alone with each child. Every child should have a meaningful experience, for example, a trip alone with a parent—with no other siblings to compete with. Help parents plan times for one of their children to be their "only" child. Middle children, in particular, tend to suffer from parental neglect, and a focused experience will do much to boost their self-worth.

Include Both Siblings

Sometimes parents will bring in one child for counseling, seeing that child as the primary instigator of the sibling conflicts. Insist on seeing both of the siblings together. You may elect to see them in individual sessions eventually, but it is important to observe their interactions firsthand. Remember to show respect for each adolescent, understand both perceptions without openly taking sides, and summarize the situation and positions frequently. If they will not agree to be in the same room together, it is best to back down and start where they are willing to begin.

Assign an Anger Log

This assignment is designed to heighten teens' awareness of where, when, why, and how often they get angry. It is a diary-like means of analyzing provocative sibling incidents. In the event of any conflict, ask them to record (1) the time, (2) where they were, (3) what happened, (4) who was present, (5) what they did or said, (6) the result, (7) how they felt afterward, and

(8) what they would do differently. Ask that they bring the log to each session. Review the log and role-play situations from it to teach improvement techniques.

Uncover the True Source of Conflict

At times sibling conflict is nothing more than the blatant irritation that comes from living with a brother or sister. At other times conflict may be a symptom of an emotion that is buried deep below the surface. Angry adolescents, for example, may be mad at their fathers for embarrassing them in front of their friends, or at teachers for unfair grades. Since adults are more difficult to confront, young people may take out their frustrations on siblings. Examine any potential sources of frustration with clients. The rivalry may be only a guise for the real problem.

Examine Assumptions

People inevitably make assumptions about their siblings' behavior that have no basis in reality, and, in turn, they act on these assumptions without ever checking their validity. For example, one may assume that a brother who forgets to report a phone message does so on purpose, or one may assume that a sister "lost" a favorite cassette tape in retaliation for a real or imagined offense. Adolescents may never reveal these assumptions to others. However, as they keep them from the light of examination they lead only to further destructive conflict. Help them explore whether or not the assumptions they are acting upon are true.

Teach the "Anger Control Chain"

Extensive research has revealed the power that comes from learning anger management. Raymond Novaco has designed a program that centers around "the five links in the anger control chain"—triggers, cues, reminders, reducers, and self-evaluation. This intervention strategy is described in the section on anger.

Teach Conflict Management

When two siblings are in conflict, they have four major choices about the direction they will take. Help adolescents recognize that *they* make the choice. According to Joyce Hocker Frost and William W. Wilmot, adolescents may choose to (1) avoid the conflict, (2) maintain it at its present level, (3) escalate it, or (4) reduce it.[11] Explore the tactics of each response. Avoiding the true conflict may be accomplished by postponing or refusing to recognize the conflict. To maintain the conflict they may strike a bargain that temporarily maintains the status quo but does not resolve the conflict. They may escalate the conflict by calling each other names, by pulling in other issues that are tangentially related to the real conflict, or by threatening each other. Finally, they may choose to reduce the conflict in the following ways.

- Resist tendencies to attack, criticize, or use emotionally loaded words.
- Break the conflict into smaller issues and deal with them one at a time.
- Ask for more information about the other person's point of view and attempt to empathize with the other's experience.
- Talk about what each is genuinely feeling without accusing one another.
- State the positions of each side clearly and concisely until both can articulate the other's point of view.
- Compromise by agreeing on an alternative that resolves the conflict; each loses something and each wins something.

Another basic guideline for creative conflict management is effective communication. It consists of attentive and reflective listening and sending messages. In sending messages, it is important for young people to remember that all communication is a matter of perceptions and perspectives, not many facts. On the receiving end the key is to avoid distortions. Two things should be practiced for effective receiving of communication. First, listen to both the verbal and nonverbal messages. Second, check with the sender to see whether messages are being understood correctly. Take time in the session to practice these skills with clients.

Consider Contracting

When a repetitive and predictable sibling dispute over an issue becomes apparent, a contract may be useful. For instance, if two sisters routinely argue over the use of the stereo, a contract over the shared use of it may ease tension. First, define the goals of the contract. Allow each to voice her concerns. Next discuss an agreed-upon plan to achieve the goals. The two should write the contract together, clearly stating requests, definable behaviors, times, and so on. The contract should be put into writing and signed and dated by each sib. This signifies their commitment. Post the contract as a visual reminder.[12]

Detect Abuse

It is becoming more apparent that some siblings suffer from the nightmare of a still largely undetected form of abuse from their siblings. It may be physical, emotional, or sexual. If you suspect serious abuse, do not rationalize it away by saying, "Kids will be kids," or, "It's only normal sibling rivalry." Calling sibling abuse nothing more than sibling rivalry is like labeling physical abuse nothing more than a little discipline. For further help in working with these terrible cases you will find the book *Perilous Rivalry* useful.

Teach Forgiveness

Angry adolescents who are full of hatred toward siblings ultimately need the healing of forgiveness. They need to forgive brother or sister as well as themselves. Forgiveness holds more promise for aiding effective resolution of chronic sibling rivalry than any therapeutic intervention. The memory of hurtful events will continue to cause anger, bitterness, and resentment throughout adult life. The solution, in these cases, lies not in forgetting or even in conflict-management techniques, but in breaking the power of memories to re-create feelings of hurt at some later date. The solution is found in forgiveness.[13] For techniques and strategies that facilitate this process, see the section on forgiveness.

☑ WHEN TO REFER

Refer adolescents who struggle with sibling conflict to other competent counselors or psychologists when, over time, they become more out of control and increasingly combative. Refer them if you recognize that you have not dealt with issues regarding your own siblings that may be interfering with treatment.

Where To Go for Additional Help

Faber, A., and E. Maslish. *Siblings Without Rivalry: How To Help Your Children Live Together So You Can Live Too.* New York: Norton, 1987.

Lush, J. *Mothers and Sons: Raising Boys To Be Men.* New York: Revell, 1988.

Ostrovsky, E. *Sibling Rivalry: A Guide for Parents Who Want To Understand and Control Conflict Between Their Children.* New York: Cornerstone Library, 1970.

Sloan, H. R. *Stop That Fighting: A Short, Step-By-Step Guide for Turning Sibling Rivalry into Peaceful Coexistence.* Fountain Valley, Calif.: Telesis, 1976.

Sutton-Smith, B., and B. G. Rosenberg. *The Sibling.* New York: Holt, Rinehart, 1970.

Wiehe, V. R. *Perilous Rivalry: When Siblings Become Abusive.* Lexington, Mass.: Lexington Books, 1991.

Notes

1. P. H. Mussen, J. J. Conger, and J. Kagan, *Child Development and Personality* (New York: Harper & Row, 1974).

2. R. Felson, "Aggression and Violence Between Siblings," *Social Psychology Quarterly* 46 (1983): 271–85.

3. B. Sutton-Smith and B. G. Rosenberg, *The Sibling* (New York: Holt, Rinehart, 1970).

4. V. G. Cicirelli, "A Comparison of College Women's Feelings Toward Their Siblings and Parents," *Journal of Marriage and the Family* 42 (1980): 111–18.

5. S. Bank and M. D. Kahn, "Sisterhood–Brotherhood Is Powerful: Sibling Sub-systems and Family Therapy," *Family Process* 14 (1975): 311–37.

6. C. E. Calladine, "Sibling Rivalry: A Parent Education Perspective," *Child Welfare* 5 (1983): 421–27.

7. E. A. Loomis, "Sibling Rivalry," in *Baker Encyclopedia of Psychology*, ed. D. G. Benner (Grand Rapids: Baker, 1985).

8. D. Lewis, "Conflict and Conflict Management," in *Dictionary of Pastoral Care and Counseling*, ed. R. J. Hunter (Nashville: Abingdon, 1990).

9. J. H. Pfauts, "The Sibling Relationship: A Forgotten Dimension," *Social Work* 21 (1976): 200–204.

10. E. J. Susman et al., "Hormones, Emotional Dispositions, and Aggressive Attributes in Young Adolescents," *Child Development* 58 (1987): 1114-34.

11. J. Hocker Frost and W. W. Wilmot, *Interpersonal Conflict* (Dubuque, Ia.: William C. Brown, 1978).

12. Calladine, "Sibling Rivalry," 421–27.

13. A. Hart, *Unlocking the Mystery of Your Emotions* (Dallas: Word, 1989).

SLEEP DISTURBANCE

☑ WHAT THE STRUGGLE LOOKS LIKE

Humans spend about one-third of their time asleep. That's about twenty-five years over an average lifetime. Sleep is more than the absence of wakefulness. It is a positive phenomenon that brings rest, restoration, and rejuvenation. Many people, however, are painfully aware that sleep is not always sweet slumber. Disturbed sleep strongly influences waking behaviors and plays a significant role in feelings of well-being. Sleep problems are not trivial and they can no longer be viewed as obscure, even among adolescents.

Toward the end of the 1970s, researchers at Stanford University found evidence to dispute the assumption that sleep disturbance occurs predominantly among adults. They found that approximately thirteen percent of adolescents suffer from chronic sleep disturbances. In addition, thirty-eight percent complain of occasional poor sleep. Other research has reported that close to fifty percent of the adolescent population will suffer from mild to severe sleep disturbance. Furthermore, an unknown number of adolescent insomniacs remain undiagnosed and rely on alcohol or habit-forming medication to help them sleep.[1] Without proper intervention, this malady may continue into adulthood and diminish the quality of life and learning.

Sleep disorders include any disruption of the onset or termination of sleep, or any of a number of difficulties occurring during sleep that disrupt normal sleep cycles.[2] A chronic sleep disturbance is defined by three parameters: when a period of forty-five minutes or longer is required to fall asleep on three or more nights a week, when one or more awakenings followed by at least thirty minutes of wakefulness occur on three or more nights a week, and when three or more awakenings occur on three or more nights a week.

Some 120 disorders of sleep and arousal have been identified.[3] Most do not merely disrupt sleep; they affect a person twenty-four hours a day. Sleep disorders, according to the *Diagnostic and Statistical Manual* (3d ed. rev. [DSM-III-R]), are divided into two major subgroups: the *Dyssomnias* and the *Parasomnias*. In the Dyssomnias the predominant disturbance is in the amount, quality, or timing of sleep. They include Insomnia (difficulty initiating or

288

Case Description

Keith is a fifteen-year-old who awakens almost every morning about 2:00 to ruminate on his anxieties. He then has tremendous difficulty resuming his sleep. Keith dreads crawling into bed each night. He is tired of counting sheep, only to find his mind wandering back to the anxieties of the day. He lies there for at least an hour trying to fall asleep. He looks at the clock repeatedly, which, of course, only makes him more anxious. He goes through most days feeling haggard and cranky. Sometimes after school he tries to catch up on his sleep by taking naps. Keith has experienced this pattern for several months. He is not depressed, just tired.

maintaining sleep), Hypersomnia (excessive daytime sleepiness), and Sleep-Wake Schedule Disorder (a mismatch between the normal sleep-wake schedule that is demanded by environment and circadian rhythm [twenty-four-hour cycles]).

In the Parasomnias, the predominant disturbance is an abnormal event occurring during sleep. They include Dream Anxiety Disorder (repeated awakenings from sleep with detailed recall of frightening dreams), Sleep Terror Disorder (repeated episodes of abrupt awakening from sleep, usually beginning with panicky screams), and Sleepwalking Disorder (repeated episodes of a sequence of complex behaviors that progress to leaving the bed and walking about, with the person unaware of the episode or not later remembering it).

Other disorders affecting sleep include Sleep Apnea, which is a cessation of breathing that arouses the patient from sleep. Obstructed nasal passages or weak tissue in the throat may restrict the flow of air over the soft palate and trigger an oxygen deprivation. When this occurs, the person then wakes enough only to change positions, often gasping for air, but not enough to remember the disturbance. Sleep apnea may be fatal and should be treated by qualified physicians. Through reconstructive surgery of the nasal passages or soft palate, patients may be completely cured.

Narcolepsy is another sleep disturbance. It is characterized by recurrent sleep attacks appearing abruptly and inappropriately even during the day. For no apparent reason, the person suddenly falls asleep. I strongly recommend referral to a competent neurologist for this problem.

Of all the sleep disorders, insomnia is by far the most common. About fifteen percent of the general population consider insomnia a serious problem for which professional help is occasionally sought. It is the sleep disorder that counselors working with adolescents are most likely to see. It is also a common symptom of other problems, such as depression or drug or alcohol abuse.

Sleep complaints among adolescents are usually associated with daytime fatigue, irritability, or depression. They may describe themselves in negative terms such as anxious, tense, or moody. They often experience problems with school attendance and academic performance.[4]

Before exploring causes and treatment strategies for these disorders, it may be useful to quickly review the stages of sleep. The development of the electroencephalogram (EEG) has allowed researchers to measure central nervous system activity during sleep. Sleep can be classified into two major periods or stages: rapid eye movement sleep (REM) and non-rapid eye movement sleep (NREM). REM sleep is characterized by frequent bursts of rapid, jerky eye movements associated with slow, low-voltage brain waves. These eye movements occur infrequently in NREM sleep, which is associated with slow brain waves. NREM stages appear to be important in recovery from muscular fatigue while REM sleep appears to be more important in learning and psychological adjustment. Dreaming usually occurs during REM sleep.

Normal sleep has four or five ninety-minute cycles of NREM sleep alternating with REM sleep in periods lasting an average of fifteen minutes. REM periods get longer later at night, so most of the total REM time is in the last third of sleep. For more on these stages, see the book *Better Sleep*.

☑ WHY THE STRUGGLE HAPPENS

It is impossible to list all the factors contributing to sleep disturbances. The problem is unique for each individual. Nevertheless, many researchers group the causes under the following three major headings.

Physical Influences

Allergies, asthma, or side effects of alcohol, prescribed medications, and illegal drugs may influence sleep patterns. These physical causes are primarily a medical concern and are usually revealed in a careful medical evaluation.

Psychological Influences

A number of psychological influences may affect sleep. Anxiety and depression are two of the most common. Depression is highly correlated with early waking and with inability to return to sleep. Anxiety is associated with difficulty falling asleep upon going to bed. Anxiety, tension, and worry also account for a great deal of poor sleep. Some describe these tendencies as a "fear of letting go." Insomniacs, for example, often have trouble letting go not only of physical tension but also of thoughts (unsolved problems and so on).

Behavioral Influences

Some people have lifestyles, habits, and behavioral patterns that are not conducive to sound sleep. Some of these habits include irregular bedtimes and rising hours, long daytime naps, and the excessive consumption of foods and drinks containing caffeine (such as chocolate, coffee, tea, and soft drinks).

☑ HOW TO HELP

Most sleep experts believe that if poor sleepers are to achieve meaningful and consistent change in sleep habits, they must acquire sleep skills and be able to utilize them successfully when necessary. These skills include (1) the ability to measure objectively one's own sleep, (2) mastery of basic relaxation techniques, (3) recognition and control of thoughts and perceptions that may interfere with sound sleep, and (4) analysis of one's sleep environment. The following techniques are designed to help counselors teach these skills to adolescents struggling with sleep disorders. As always they should be thought of as undergirded by personal acceptance and reflective listening.

Consult a Sleep Expert

Worldwide, only about five or six hundred specialists identify themselves as somnologists (specialists in the study and treatment of sleep disorders). They bring their expertise from the fields of neurology, psychiatry, clinical and experimental psychology, internal medicine, pediatrics, pharmacology, and many other disciplines. While these experts may not be readily available to you for consultation, many practitioners with a wealth of experience work with sleep disorders. Medical institutions are generally the most helpful in guiding you to a sleep disorder expert (also consult the Association of Sleep Disorder Centers noted at the end of this section). Before moving into a treatment plan, counselors should advise adolescents with this problem to have careful physical and neurological examinations, even if clients are obviously experiencing stress. Once physiological problems have been ruled out, psychological counseling may be effective.

Measure Sleeping Patterns

Objective measures of sleep are best achieved in a laboratory. Many major medical schools and hospitals have sleep labs designed for this purpose.[5] However, where this option is impossible or impractical, clients may enlist the assistance of friends or parents to help monitor their sleep. Encourage adolescents to keep accurate sleep diaries, recording approximate bedtime, number of sleep interruptions, and time of arousal. Many may find that they get more sleep than they thought. Monitoring one's sleep provides a useful assessment of the variety of factors related to sleep interference. Continued use of sleep diaries may also help clients monitor their improvement.

Here is an example of a sleep diary page to be completed each day. It is important to let young people know that they should not be concerned with answering the questions perfectly. It is generally best for them to fill in their diaries for at least two to three weeks before a helpful review can be made.

Understand Sleep Medications

Because many sleep disorders have been viewed historically as medical problems, the most common treatment has been a variety of prescription and nonprescription drugs. In fact, sleep medications are among the most widely prescribed medications in the United States. It has been reported that forty percent of insomniacs use sleep medication almost nightly. Another twenty-six percent use them occasionally. However, studies have shown that most drugs

---

Daily Sleep Diary

- Date: _____

- Approximate total time sleeping: _____

- Approximate time required to fall asleep: _____

- Time I went to bed: _____

- Time I fell asleep: _____

- Number of times I woke up during the night: _____

- Length of time I stayed awake during each uptime: _____

- Time I woke up for the day: _____

- Time and effect of last meal or snack before going to bed: ____

  _____

- How rested did I feel this morning, on a scale of 1 to 5? _____

- How free of physical tension was I when I went to bed
  (1 to 5)? _____

- How free of mental activity was I when I went to bed
  (1 to 5)? _____

- If I exercised today, did it have a positive or negative effect? ___

  _____

- What special circumstances or experiences affected my sleep?

  _____

---

designed to alleviate sleep problems actually make sleep more difficult rather than better because our bodies eventually develop tolerance to the medication.[6] At that point, a cycle evolves in which sleeplessness leads to drug taking, which leads to dependence and more drug taking. This dependency may become a greater problem than the initial insomnia. Medications (1) may alter sleep stages, (2) cause rebound insomnia, (3) increase daytime anxiety levels, and (4) ultimately require increased dosages of medication. Only in the most extreme cases should treatment with sleeping pills be considered. The techniques in this section are designed to prevent adolescents from using and becoming dependent on prescription and nonprescription drugs.

Teach New Sleeping Habits

Adolescents' sleeping environment is critical. The bedroom and normal bedtime may be signals for troubled youth to start worrying. Clients have learned negative association through repeated practice, but it can be unlearned with habit-reformation techniques. This strategy involves repeatedly substituting one behavior for another until the new behavior becomes a habit. That is, going to bed at the same time and getting out of bed at the same time consistently. It may mean using the bed and bedroom for nothing but sleep. Ask teens to choose other places to do homework, listen to music, worry, talk on the phone, eat, or do anything else that is not sleep-related. This allows them slowly to learn to associate the bedroom with sleep only.

Successful intervention with adolescents who have poor sleeping habits are common. For example, one researcher reports a typical case of an adolescent insomniac who had the habit of awakening regularly at 2:00 A.M. to ruminate on his worries. He seldom resumed sleep. To break this habit, his counselor simply advised him, upon awakening, to write a list of his worries on a notepad by the bed. By learning to do something constructive with his worries rather than staying awake to ponder them, he was able to alleviate the problem. Within five weeks, his early-morning waking habit was broken and he slept until his alarm went off at 7:00.[7]

Incorporate Relaxation Techniques

Relaxation techniques may be used to eliminate stress and tension from the skeletal and visceral muscles. Learning to use these techniques has been shown to be an important step in acquiring sound sleep. Invariably, teens who suffer from sleep problems at night are subject to nervousness, anxiety, and worry during the day. At bedtime they often show high levels of physical tension and mental arousal. In these cases, relaxation strategies may be practiced upon retiring to help prepare both minds and bodies for sleep. A high degree of success in treating poor sleepers has been reported by those using progressive relaxation methods.[8] In one published case, a thirteen-year-old male was taught to perform relaxation exercises prior to going to sleep and upon premature waking. His sleep was significantly improved by the eighth week.[9]

Progressive relaxation involves systematically tensing and relaxing the muscle groups in the body. Each time a muscle is tensed and relaxed, the level of tension in the body becomes lower and lower, ultimately eliminating tension. This strategy, along with several others, is described in the section on anxiety. Encourage adolescents who have sleep problems to practice progressive relaxation two or three times a day to increase the possibility of spontaneous relaxation at bedtime.

Use Cognitive Focusing

This cognitive strategy is best used to help adolescents return to sleep upon waking in the night. It is not uncommon for insomniacs to begin worrying that they will not get back to sleep or to begin thinking other negative thoughts once they have awakened prematurely. Cognitive focusing involves thinking positive, calming, reassuring thoughts. Cognitive focusing is often coupled with deep breathing. It is important for young people to develop positive thoughts to replace negative ones. Just trying to stop thinking negatively does not work. Many find it useful to focus their thoughts upon their breathing. For example, upon inhaling they may say to themselves, "I am," and upon exhaling they say, "relaxed." The repetition of these thoughts coupled with breathing calmly helps keep them from negative thinking and allows them to fall back to sleep.

Explore Exercise and Nutrition

Effects of exercise on sleep have been studied extensively. Studies have shown that even a simple regular exercise routine helps people sleep better compared to those who are completely sedentary. While exercise may enhance sleep for some, it does not always create a greater need for sleep nor does it produce more sound sleep. The time of exercise seems to be the most important element in determining whether it will adversely affect sleep. Studies indicate that exercise about two hours before bedtime increases metabolic responses that interfere with the onset of sleep. Exercise must be consistent, balanced, and scheduled for several hours before bedtime.[10]

Nutritional requirements must also be consistent for optimal effects. An overabundance of one particular food group may increase sleep disturbances, as will excessive weight change. Coffee, tea, and cola beverages containing caffeine drunk late in the day may also complicate sleep patterns. As a stimulant, caffeine has a peak effect two to four hours after it is consumed, and it may continue to affect a person for as long as seven hours.

Explore Napping

As a general rule, insomniacs should avoid napping. Naps, especially for adolescents, reinforce poor nighttime sleep routine. Studies have shown that napping cannot substitute for a solid night of good sleep. Encourage adolescents who nap to stay up during the day so that they will be more likely to sleep during the night. Sometimes this simple intervention is all it takes to bring relief to insomniacs.

Explore Environmental Factors

Often, a simple consideration of environmental influences will bring some relief to the person struggling with poor sleep. Noise is an obvious problem. If clients are particularly sensitive to noise, take stock of the noise situation with them. While soundproofing a bedroom is usually not an option, an alternative is to experiment with various types of "white noise" such as fans, air conditioners, or audio tapes of ocean waves or rain. Ear plugs may be helpful with some people, but they should be used only with a physician's approval because of possible ear infection. If clients are disturbed or awakened by too much light, consider different light-blocking curtains or eye shades.

Ask about the quality of their mattresses as well as their bedroom temperature. When room temperature rises above seventy-five degrees, people become more restless and wake up more often. The optimum bedroom range is between sixty-five and seventy degrees Fahrenheit. Remove watches that beep or clocks that chime on the hour. They cause insomniacs to count each hour that passes and subtly keep them awake as they anticipate the next chime. In short, use a commonsense approach and explore every environmental factor that might influence sleep.

☑ WHEN TO REFER

Refer adolescents who struggle with sleep disorders to psychologically astute physicians or psychiatrists for complete physical examination at the beginning of treatment. This should occur even if physical symptoms are not present. If over time they suffer increasingly from sleep disturbance, refer them to other competent counselors or psychologists.

Where To Go for Additional Help

American Medical Association. *Guide to Better Sleep*. New York: Random House, 1984.
Catalano, E. M. *Getting To Sleep*. Oakland, Calif.: New Harbinger, 1990.
Coates, T. J., and C. E. Thoresen. *How To Sleep Better*. Englewood Cliffs, N.J.: Prentice-Hall, 1977.
Cryer, B., and E. S. Kaplan. *Inside Insomnia: How To Sleep Better Tonight*. New York: Villard Books, 1986.
Lacks, P. *Behavioral Treatment for Persistent Insomnia*. New York: Pergamon Press, 1987.
Association of Sleep Disorder Centers (P.O. Box 2604, Del Mar, CA 92014) maintains a list of accredited sleep disorder centers.

Notes

1. J. R. Morrison and B. Storey, "Adolescent Insomnia," *Clearing House* 60 (1986): 110–14.

2. J. H. Jennison, "Sleep and Sleep Disorders," in *Dictionary of Pastoral Care and Counseling*, ed. R. J. Hunter (Nashville: Abingdon, 1990).

3. American Medical Association, *Guide to Better Sleep* (New York: Random House, 1984).

4. T. J. Coates and C. E. Thoresen, *How To Sleep Better* (Englewood Cliffs, N.J.: Prentice-Hall, 1977).

5. In 1975 only five medical institutions in the United States had centers devoted to the diagnosis and treatment of sleep problems. Today more than a hundred sleep disorder centers operate under common accrediting requirements.

6. D. R. Anderson, "Treatment of Insomnia in a 13-Year-Old Boy by Relaxation Training and Reduction of Parental Attention," *Journal of Behavioral Therapy* 10 (1979): 263–65.

7. J. R. Morrison, E. Kujawa, and B. A. Storey, "Causes and Treatment of Insomnia Among Adolescents," *Journal of School Health* 55 (1985): 148–50.

8. Coates and Thorsesen, *How To Sleep Better*.

9. Anderson, "Treatment of Insomnia."

10. R. D. Bootzin, "Effects on Self-Control Procedures for Insomnia," in *Behavioral Self-Management: Strategies, Techniques, and Outcomes*, ed. R. B. Stuart (New York: Brunner-Mazel, 1977).

SPIRITUAL DOUBT

☑ **WHAT THE STRUGGLE LOOKS LIKE**

Adolescents' quest for identity cannot avoid faith issues. Like trying on different styles of clothing, teenagers question religion and search for a faith that feels right. As a result, they may accuse the church of being a collection of hypocrites and totally reject the family's religious values. By contrast, they may become increasingly committed and involved in their faith. In either case, teenagers are trying to find their own expression of faith, and it often involves a struggle with spiritual doubt.

Spiritual doubt is characterized by an absence of either assent or dissent to a religious proposition. It is not the same as unbelief, which is a conviction that something is false. Psychologically, doubt is often accompanied by anxiety or depression. For some it may become obsessional and especially troubling.[1]

Religious beliefs change as children enter and pass through adolescence. Teens, for example, are less likely than children to believe in literal translations of the Bible. Children report that they believe in God because their parents told them God exists. Adolescents, in contrast, rely more on rational thinking in their faith than on parental precepts. They believe in God, for example, because the universe is orderly.[2]

Among the more extensive studies of how faith changes as people age is the work of James Fowler. From his research, Fowler delineated six stages of faith development.[3] Three of his six stages shed light on the development of adolescent faith and the issues of spiritual doubt.

- *Stage 2: Mythical–literal faith.* This is the level where adolescents begin their journey of faith. Operating at the pre-teen concrete level, they respond to religion according to their cognitive capacity. Persons at this stage view religious stories and music in literal, concrete ways. They perceive God in human form somewhere in the sky. They simply accept their religious heritage and ask no questions.
- *Stage 3: Synthetic–conventional faith.* In early adolescence, with their increased capacity to think abstractly (i.e., formal operations), adolescents' principle task is to relate their own religious views with

296

Case Description

Russ, seventeen, a thoughtful and articulate high school student, grew up in the church. His parents were strong lay people and active in the life of their local church. Russ can't remember the last time he missed a church service. He enjoyed his youth group and was respected as a young leader. Secretly, however, Russ battled spiritual doubt. He questioned everything from the Bible to the existence of God. His prayers had dwindled down to a single word, *why?* Russ was especially concerned that he was a Christian only because he grew up in a Christian home. He was afraid his faith was built on selfish motivations.

incompatible views of others. They may conceive of God as a personal advisor and guide, but in a less personalized fashion than previously.

- *Stage 4: Individual–reflective faith.* Not all adolescents reach this stage in their faith development. However, those who do will engage in critical self-reflection and examination of their beliefs and values. Their questioning leads to individual and personal religious beliefs. They view God in more abstract ways, not as a personal advisor, but as a spirit embodying moral truths and personal presence.

The seeds of doubt are usually planted in Stage 3 of Fowler's model, but it is toward the start of Stage 4 that the struggle with doubt shows visible signs of growth and maturity. Spiritual maturity is broached when people have internalized their values and beliefs into an integrated faith by which to live.

☑ WHY THE STRUGGLE HAPPENS

The causes of spiritual doubt are not easily identified. However, some of the following may be contributing factors.

The Nature of Growth

Spiritual development does not progress at a steady direction toward a pinnacle of maturity. Feelings of emptiness are a part of human existence, even on the spiritual journey. Young people may experience an emotional rush during the days, weeks or even months following a new spiritual commitment, but eventually this energy dissipates and questions arise that may cause doubt. This process is natural. It is endemic to spiritual growth. Some theologians see doubting as a dynamic ancillary to belief and not necessarily in opposition to it. A strong faith is not the result of avoiding questions, but of working with doubt. If there are no mountains without valleys, can there be faith without doubt or answers without questions?

Unsettling New Insights

Swiss psychologist Jean Piaget theorized that in two different ways people come to understand new information: *assimilation* and *accommodation*. Assimilation is the process by which people make an effort to take new information and join it to their existing thinking. The new experience may fit easily, or may require minor adjustment. Accommodation, on the other hand, is necessary when new experiences stretch people beyond their comfortable limits, when they do not fit within their current beliefs, and when they go beyond their structure of thought. A completely new insight regarding God is an example. Radical new ways of thinking about spiritual matters may launch adolescents into debilitating doubt.

Lack of Models

Teenagers need models of vibrant spirituality in whom they have respect and confidence. They need to see faith lived out in peers as well as adults. Unhealthful models in places of spiritual authority only compound the struggle. If young people lack a formative community of friends who share a common faith, they may have difficulty developing religious commitment and therefore struggle with spiritual doubt.[4] Most sociologists believe that faith is kept alive by a human as well as a divine support system. It is hard to keep on believing in a flat earth unless you are surrounded and supported by others who believe in a flat earth.

Idealistic Thinking

Because adolescents are so strongly idealistic, they may easily suffer disillusionment and disappointment with the church. No church can adequately fulfill every ideal of every person. Young people are bound to be disappointed and even critical of their religiously committed parents and church. Difficulty in coping with their own temptations further contributes to their disillusionment. They may begin to think the Christian life is an impossible ideal. This state of mind leads, obviously, to a struggle with doubt.

Unpleasant Church Experiences

Adolescents are more emotional than cognitive. They remember feelings more readily than facts. Concerning their church, they know exactly how they feel about last Sunday's service even when they cannot remember what was said or taught. An unpleasant feeling at church is more important than the sermon content in determining whether young people are drawn to a religious context. If adolescents do not have positive feelings about their churches they may experience spiritual doubt.[5]

☑ HOW TO HELP

The following techniques, used in combination with personal acceptance and reflective listening, may be useful in helping young people face their doubts. These techniques are designed to create alternatives for replacing dysfunctional behaviors and attitudes.

Pinpoint the Severity

At the beginning of "doubt-work," it is helpful to assess the intensity of clients' struggle with spiritual doubt. The Inventory of Religious Belief, a fifteen-item scale designed to measure the degree of acceptance or rejection of Christian doctrine, may be used to help pinpoint the intensity of the struggle. It is found in *Helping the Struggling Adolescent: A Counseling Guide*.

Examine Your Own Spiritual Growth

It is crucial for those who work with adolescents struggling with doubt to know where they themselves stand in their spiritual well-being. Is your personal faith alive and fresh? Are you struggling in Fowler's Synthetic-Conventional stage of faith like adolescents with whom you are working? Are you dealing with unresolved spiritual conflicts that will negatively influence your relationships with adolescents? Modeling how you deal with spiritual struggles may be very useful in helping adolescents, but when your spiritual deficiencies are overwhelming and difficult to articulate, you will probably help doubters most by referring them to other spiritually sensitive counselors.

Affirm the Honest Quest

Some people feel uneasy with, or even resent, adolescents with doubts. They lose sight of the fact that faith matures because of, not in spite of, doubt. They forget that serious questions not asked will not produce the richness and depth of an adequate answer. The most destructive thing counselors or parents can do to teenagers passing through periods of honest uncertainty is to attempt to silence their doubts and encourage their repression. "Repressed doubts have a high rate of resurrection," according to John Powell, "and doubts that are plowed under will only grow new roots."[6]

Although the Bible strongly warns against unbelief, not a single passage forbids the asking of critical questions. Doubt and belief are compatible. As odd as this may sound, doubt is not a hazard to faith; it may be the necessary catalyst that will bring a developing faith to maturity. Frederick Buechner put it nicely: "Doubt is the ants in the pants of the seat of faith."[7] Affirm honest adolescents who admit doubt. Your acceptance of their doubts as worthy of serious discussion will lay the foundation for them to construct a stronger faith.

Avoid Pat Answers

Doubting adolescents often ask dozens of questions. It seems that if they only had answers to their questions their doubts would dissipate. Don't be deceived. Doubters who ask for answers do not necessarily expect them or want them. Don't answer doubters' questions prematurely or supply them with heavy books to do the answering for you. Adolescents who struggle with doubt are usually more concerned to have a relationship with God than they are to have answers about God.

Focus on Relationships

Adolescent identity formation takes place in relationships. So does faith development. Creating a place to belong is one of the secrets of the success of youth organizations like Young Life, Youth for Christ, and Fellowship of Christian Athletes. Role models who are living out faithful lifestyles increase the opportunity for young people to integrate a more secure faith into their identity. To help adolescents fighting spiritual doubt, make sure they are part of a vital youth group that embraces healthful faith principles.

If young people are part of religious communities that do not meet their needs for peer relationships and adult role models, they should look elsewhere. An emphasis on relationships is crucial in helping them define their relationship to God. Adolescents who struggle with spiritual doubt are not searching for an explanation. They are longing for a relationship. To locate an area Young Life group, call 719/473-4262. For more information on Youth for Christ, call 913/262-1700, and for Fellowship of Christian Athletes, call 816/921-0909.

Consider the Church Context

Adolescents' religious community must be considered and understood. Research has identified several elements essential to healthful adolescent faith development.[8] To help insure a spiritual commitment, the church must address and satisfy these needs.

1. *Security in freedom.* The church must afford young people opportunities to test values in an atmosphere of respect. It must avoid merely demanding obedience to authority.
2. *Significance and status.* The church must afford adolescents opportunities to earn respect through responsible activity within it.
3. *Idealism and altruism.* The church must embrace the idealism of youth and help them develop altruistic attitudes and behaviors through service.
4. *Love.* The church must discuss all aspects of love, including sexual love, in an open and supportive manner.
5. *Meaning for life.* The church must assist adolescents in discussions about their quest for meaning, including the questions they have about faith.

If it is apparent that adolescents are struggling in their faith because some of these elements are absent in their church, explore alternatives.

Confront Irrational Thinking

Most adolescents who struggle with spiritual doubt are also burdened with guilt. Be sensitive to these feelings and help them dispute irrational "oughts" and "shoulds." What are their unrealistic expectations about their spiritual development? Perhaps they believe they should never question the Bible or even their pastor. Maybe they think they should never allow their thoughts to be distracted while they are praying. These kinds of distortions and unrealistic expectations are generally unspoken. Counselors must listen carefully to detect them. For additional suggestions on alleviating this component see the section on guilt.

Help Ease the Pressure

For parents who have adolescents in rebellion against the family faith, it is important, in helping them, to avoid the battle of forced attendance. This is especially true for older adolescents. Allowing teenagers to choose noninvolvement doesn't need to imply passivity or lack of spiritual concern on the part of parents. It may involve meaningful discussions to help both sides clarify their views and find solutions. For example, if young people find Sunday worship boring or irrelevant, they may choose to attend a weekly youth group meeting instead. Or they might like to try another church. This process is not easy for parents. It takes courage and some risk. But parents may believe that God will continue to operate in the lives of their sons and daughters even though they are making unsettling choices.

Explore Inaccurate Theology

Listen carefully to the comments of young people. Notice what they reveal about their beliefs concerning God. Keith Olson points out that adolescents troubled over issues of faith often hold blatantly incorrect concepts of God.[9] Effective counselors must discover and help correct these beliefs. Some of the most common inaccurate beliefs include: "God will never allow a real tragedy to strike a faithful believer"; "God punishes us by causing accidents"; "God will accept nothing but absolute perfection"; "God is going to destroy the world." Help adolescents avoid faulty theology that will result in their putting God into a box.[10] Christian counselors and parents must correct misinformation in an understanding yet gentle and compassionate manner.

☑ WHEN TO REFER

Refer adolescents who struggle with spiritual doubt to other competent counselors or psychologists when, over time, they feel more frustrated, depressed, or hopeless. You should also refer teenagers if you recognize that you are uncomfortable with their doubts and even subtly condemn them for their sincere search.

Where To Go for Additional Help

Benner, D. G. *Psychotherapy and the Spiritual Quest*. Grand Rapids: Baker, 1988.
Fowler, J. *Stages of Faith*. New York: Harper & Row, 1981.
Gillespie, V. B. *The Dynamics of Religious Conversion: Identity and Transformation* (Birmingham, Ala.: Religious Education Press, 1991).
Guinness, O. *In Two Minds: The Dilemma of Doubt and How To Resolve It*. Downers Grove, Ill.: InterVarsity Press, 1976.

Parks, S. *The Critical Years: The Young Adult Search for a Faith To Live By*. San Francisco: Harper & Row, 1986.

Shelton, C. *Adolescent Spirituality*. New York: Cross Road, 1989.

Steele, L. *On the Way: A Practical Theology of Christian Formation*. Grand Rapids: Baker, 1990.

Notes

1. J. R. Beck, "Doubt," in *Baker Encyclopedia of Psychology*, ed. D. G. Benner (Grand Rapids: Baker, 1985).

2. P. Benson, M. Donahue, and J. Erickson, "Adolescence and Religion: Review of the Literature from 1970–1986," *Research in the Social Scientific Study of Religion* 1 (1989): 153–81.

3. J. Fowler, *Stages of Faith* (New York: Harper & Row, 1981).

4. W. Rice, *Junior High Ministry*, rev. ed. (Grand Rapids: Zondervan, 1987).

5. R. Campbell, *How To Really Love Your Teenager* (Wheaton, Ill.: Victor, 1985).

6. J. Powell, *A Reason To Live, a Reason To Die* (Allen, Tex.: Argus Communications, 1972).

7. F. Buechner, *Wishful Thinking* (San Francisco: Harper & Row, 1973).

8. R. Goldman, *Readiness for Religion* (London: Routledge Kegan Paul, 1965).

9. G. K. Olson, *Counseling Teenagers: The Complete Christian Guide to Understanding and Helping Adolescents* (Loveland, Colo.: Group Books, 1984).

10. J. B. Phillips, *Your God Is Too Small* (New York: Macmillan, 1969).

STUTTERING

☑ WHAT THE STRUGGLE LOOKS LIKE

Stuttering is painful and frustrating at any age, but particularly for the teenager who is on a quest for a stable identity. Stuttering is the condition in which the flow of speech is broken by abnormal stoppages, repetitions, or prolongations of sounds and syllables. In addition, stutterers may show unusual facial and body movements associated with their efforts to speak. Some are fluent with friends or when alone, but stutter severely with others, especially with authority figures. While some young people stutter with everyone, many stutter only under certain circumstances. In general stutterers are average or above average in intelligence.[1]

Some stuttering is typical and temporary in young children and is called *developmental* stuttering. The onset is usually between two and four years of age and lasts only a few months. *Persistent* stuttering starts between three and eight years of age and persists unless some effective intervention is employed. Stuttering that appears after age five is considered more serious than stuttering at a younger age.[2]

Several million preschoolers stutter. About seventy-five percent of ten-year-olds who stutter remain stutterers throughout life, and about one percent (two million) of all adolescents struggle with stuttering. At all ages, from four to eight times as many males stutter than females.[3]

☑ WHY THE STRUGGLE HAPPENS

The causes of stuttering are not clear. No single theory of its origin is widely accepted. Here are some of the more commonly noted contributing factors.[4]

Physiological Influences

The likelihood of becoming a stutterer is, in large part, influenced by heredity. The direct physical cause is believed to be an auditory perceptual defect. Stutterers receive delayed feedback from their own speech. Another

Case Description

Ryan is a thirteen-year-old who first began to stutter when he was about six. Within the last few years he has stuttered more and more frequently, and his parents became increasingly concerned about his entering adolescence with this problem. His parents used to try to help him by having him repeat words properly. Rather than helping him, however, Ryan became more anxious and his stuttering increased. He is now seeing a speech and language pathologist. He was brought in for psychological counseling by his parents because he was showing signs of depression and low self-esteem. At the root of his struggle, however, was his problem with stuttering.

theory holds that one side of the brain has not achieved the level of influence necessary for smooth speech.

Stressors

Stressful situations like fatigue, school pressures, separation from significant others, and changes at critical stages of development, may lead to stuttering. Tension causes susceptible individuals to lose control of their delicate speech muscles, and nonfluent speech becomes their way of indicating fear or reluctance. If the pattern continues, persistent stuttering may result. It is generally understood that proneness to stuttering is increased by stressful situations.

Parental Expectations

Unrealistic parental expectations generate anxiety in children. Stuttering may result from tension caused by parents who try to force young children to speak at levels beyond their normal developmental stage. Perfectionistic parents may also generate this tension by making their children feel compelled to live up to standards that are either impossible or unusually difficult. If parents overreact to normal speech difficulties ("Be more careful when you talk" or "Start again and speak more slowly"), a child may become more self-conscious about speaking. Parents' forceful attempts to reduce children's nonfluency in public may lead to more hesitation and therefore compound the problem.

Expression of Conflict

Unexpressed feelings of anger are thought, by some, to be a cause of stuttering. This idea is analogous to the automobile driver who has one foot pressing the gas pedal while their other foot holds down the brake. Stutterers are seen as wanting to express themselves but at the same time wanting to hold back. While some recognize this internal conflict as a cause, relatively little research is available to support this belief.

☑ HOW TO HELP

Stuttering is a specialized area of intervention. The following techniques are not exhaustive and they should be thought of as working with recommendations or interventions of a qualified speech-language pathologist.

Provide an Accepting and Calm Atmosphere

It is essential to provide a peaceful and emotionally supportive atmosphere when working with adolescents who stutter. Speak in a soft voice, slowing down your own verbal pace. This helps set the tempo and create a climate that allows stutterers to relax and release tensions that often underlie stuttering. Listen patiently and carefully to what they say, and do not focus on how it is said.

Consult a Specialist

Adolescents who stutter are more likely to come to counseling because of other problems, such as anxiety, fear, depression, frustration, feelings of inferiority, or guilt. However, these problems are often a result of stuttering. If young people struggle with these kinds of problems and also stutter, consult a specialist. Serious intervention for stuttering requires the specialized treatment of a speech-language pathologist.

Heighten Awareness

Adolescent stutterers are certainly aware of their problem. But it can be helpful to enhance their motivation by reviewing in detail the patterns of speech that result from their stuttering. It is also helpful to discuss the types of words, behaviors, and situations that elicit the most stuttering. Identifying trouble areas can help you target helpful treatment strategies (e.g., the relaxation techniques noted below).[5]

Explore the Use of Paced Speech

After consulting a speech-language pathologist, and with his or her recommendation, you may want to employ the oldest means of improving fluency—speech pacing. Through this method adolescents learn to speak in a rhythmically paced manner. Using metronomes to practice with, adolescents speak in time with a slow beat, then at normal speed, and eventually without its use. This technique should be used only in consultation with an expert.[6]

Negate Anticipation Anxiety

Anticipation is the worst enemy of stutterers. Give young stutterers "permission" to take chances and be spontaneous. Release the burden of guilt, self doubt, and inhibition. Stutterers need space and emotional freedom. Try to instill courage in them. Significant others in their environment should be encouraged to help in this way also. This will allow them to "let 'er rip," as a stuttering scholar from the University of Wisconsin says. [7]

Implement Relaxation Techniques

Adolescents with this problem may benefit from a number of relaxation techniques. Once mastered, they provide clients with a sense of control in the midst of a struggle that seems beyond their control. Deep muscle relaxation, biofeedback, deep breathing, guided imagery, and autogenics may all be used. These techniques, along with others, are described in the sections on anxiety and panic attacks.

Consider Group Treatment

Many experts agree that group therapy offers positive experiences to stutterers that cannot be found in individual sessions. For example, in these groups, adolescents share experiences and feelings with others who suffer from the same problem. Young people also find that they are not the only ones having a battle with stuttering, and, more importantly, they may benefit from the therapeutic experiences of other stutterers.[8]

☑ WHEN TO REFER

Adolescents with fluency problems may respond relatively quickly to some of these techniques. However, if they continue to stutter after intervention strategies to help reduce anxiety, consult specialists. Most young people who struggle with stuttering into the teen years do require specialized professional help. The probability of spontaneous remission is practically nonexistent.[9] While general counselors can help adolescents with anxiety issues and self-esteem problems, experts in speech therapy should be consulted. Qualified speech and language pathologists may be obtained through a referral from the American Speech and Hearing Association in Washington, D.C. Speech therapists will evaluate the problem, make recommendations, or treat clients as necessary. Qualified speech-language pathologists are trained at the master's or doctoral degree level, and many hold the Certificate of Clinical Competence (CCC) from the American Speech-Language-Hearing Association (ASHA) and/or a license from your state.

Where To Go for Additional Help

Ainsworth, S. *Stuttering: What It Is and What To Do About It.* Lincoln, Neb.: Cliffs Notes, 1975.

Bryngelson, B., M. E. Chapman, and O. K. Hansen. *Know Yourself: Guide for Those Who Stutter.* Minneapolis: Burgess, 1966.

Couture, E. G. *Stuttering.* Englewood Cliffs, N.J.: Prentice-Hall, 1982.

Schwartz, M. F. *Stuttering Solved.* Philadelphia: Lippincott, 1976.

Starkweather, C. W., S. R. Gottwald, and M. M. Halfond. *Stuttering Prevention: A Clinical Method.* Englewood Cliffs, N.J.: Prentice-Hall, 1990.

Van Riper, C. *The Treatment of Stuttering.* Englewood Cliffs, N.J.: Prentice-Hall, 1973.

Notes

1. E. G. Couture, *Stuttering* (Englewood Cliffs, N.J.: Prentice-Hall, 1982).

2. C. E. Schaefer and H. L. Millmann, *How To Help Children with Common Problems (New York: Van Nostrand Reinhold, 1981)*.

3. Ibid.

4. Ibid.

5. B. P. Ryan and Van Kirk B. Ryan, "Programmed Stuttering Therapy for Children: Comparison of Four Establishment Programs," *Journal of Fluency Disorders* 8 (1983): 291–321.

6. J. Pill, "A Comparison Between Two Treatment Programs for Stuttering: A Personal Account," *Journal of Fluency Disorders* 13 (1988): 385–98.

7. G. F. Johnson, "Ten Commandments for Long-Term Maintenance of Acceptable Self-Help Skills for Persons Who Are Hard-Core Stutterers," *Journal of Fluency Disorders* 12 (1987): 9–18.

8. Couture, *Stuttering.*

9. R. Ladouceur and L. Saint-Laurent, "Stuttering: A Multidimensional Treatment and Evaluation Package," *Journal of Fluency Disorders* 11 (1986): 93–103.

SUICIDE

☑ WHAT THE STRUGGLE LOOKS LIKE

Suicide is a raging epidemic in America. Each year the national statistics on suicide climb—especially for adolescents. Suicide is the second-leading cause of death for thirteen- to nineteen-year-olds. Because many suicides, however, are disguised as accidents, it may be the number-one cause of teenage death. Since the 1950s the number of suicides among youth has tripled.[1]

The problem of adolescent suicides assumes even greater proportions when we consider unsuccessful suicide attempts. Some believe that for every adolescent who commits suicide, at least a hundred teenagers attempt it.[2] That adds up to a potential of two million teen-suicide attempts each year.

Sooner or later, people working with adolescents will face the problem of suicide, and this forces them to know what the struggle looks like. The symptoms of suicide are only signals and may not mean that an adolescent is on the verge of committing suicide. However, each sign should be taken seriously. If a young person's symptoms go unnoticed, he or she may resort to drastic measures as a cry for help. Some ninety percent of teenage suicides take place at home between 3:00 P.M. and midnight—the time and place a suicide attempt is most easily discovered.[3] Here are warning signs:

- *A history of problems:* Suicide is a process and rarely an impulsive act.
- *Decline in performance:* Grades drop; the young person no longer wants to compete.
- *A recent traumatic event:* Physical illness, failure in school, breakup of a romance, or divorce of parents may intensify already-present suicidal thoughts.
- *Communication problems:* Suicide may become an inarticulate cry for help by adolescents who have difficulty expressing their feelings.
- *Irrational outbursts:* Suicidal youth may suddenly become quick-tempered, cry easily, or become easily upset by trivial things.
- *Depression:* An enormous sense of sadness is almost always a warning sign.

- *A recent holiday:* Although suicides are fewer than many expect during the Christmas season, the days that follow a holiday show a release of the suppressing effect and contain a significantly higher number of suicides.[4]
- *Change in eating or sleeping habits:* Adolescents begin to sleep or eat much more or much less than they usually do.
- *Talk about suicide:* Experts estimate that about eighty percent of persons who take their lives have talked about it with others.
- *Drugs and alcohol:* When abuse occurs, the possibility of suicide must at least be considered.
- *Withdrawal:* Rather than taking initiative for new experiences, the suicidal teen may spend long hours alone in silence or listening to music.
- *Lack of hope:* "Life just isn't worth living" is the attitude, and the youths see their future as something they cannot control.
- *Tunnel vision:* The suicidal life is often viewed in rigid situations; life is black or white.

☑ WHY THE STRUGGLE HAPPENS

Every suicide is an attempt to say "I need help." A combination of faulty reasoning and a deep sense of hopelessness is nearly always present in young people struggling with suicide. Below are some of the specific motivators that often drive adolescents to take their lives.[5] Keep in mind, however, that usually a combination of several factors makes suicide a serious option.

To Escape

This is perhaps the most common reason we attribute to suicide and it is often a valid assessment. People who consider suicide see no hope for resolution of their life situations. This hopelessness is fueled by irrational thinking that pulls them into deeper despair. The hope that may be obvious to counselors and others may be difficult for suicidal adolescents to see. They view death as the only way to avoid pain. Young people who use sleep to avoid problems are especially at risk, symbolically equating death with prolonged sleep.

To Be Punished

With an overly sensitized conscience, some adolescents devalue themselves. Because of their sins and shortcomings, they believe death is what they deserve. They feel that they have committed the unpardonable sin, and for this they will burn in hell. Whether it be fornication, masturbation, abortion, or simply "evil thoughts," youth who attempt suicide as a means of punishment see no other option for absolving their unbearable guilt.

To Punish Others

Suicide is sometimes directed toward one or more survivors. The eighteen-year-old who overdoses on pills and stabs himself in the abdomen after

Case Description

Tim, sixteen, is a "C" student. He has long hair, and most days wears faded jeans and a flannel shirt. His jacket has "Pink Floyd" scrawled on the back in ball-point pen. Tim lives at home with his mother. His dad left when he was in the third grade. Tim came in for counseling at his mother's insistence. She described him as "a loner, always listening to his music and never interested in getting a job." Two months earlier Tim had slit his wrists and run into where his mother was sleeping to wave the spurting blood over her bed. Tim's suicide attempt was more of an angry cry for help than anything else. He used this ugly gesture to "get back" at his mom for pressuring him "to be the perfect son." Feeling he had no other means of communication, he resorted to this frightening option.

rejection by his girlfriend really wants, in a distorted way, to make her suffer. In his desire to punish her he says, "She'll know she loves me when I'm dead." It is not always clear, however, whom suicidal adolescents are wanting to punish. The hostility is usually directed toward the person who the adolescent believes will find the body.

To Manipulate Others

When manipulating others is the primary motive for suicide or attempted suicide, adolescents are seeking specific objects or actions. They may feel that attempted suicide will bring about a specific result, like getting mom and dad back together after a stormy separation. While teenagers use threats of suicide to control parents, friends, counselors, or others, threats should be taken seriously. Taking their suicide seriously does not necessarily mean giving in to manipulative demands, but it does mean doing more than simply acknowledging the threat. Manipulators sometimes succeed in taking their own lives.

To Gain Attention

Few behaviors command more attention than suicide. The shocking news of a young life abruptly ended startles us to the core. Even a mere acquaintance suddenly becomes meaningfully important when word of the death is received—"I saw him only yesterday. How can he be dead?" People lavish attention on the previously ignored youth who have attempted suicide. Seeing how much concern suicide generates causes other young people to consider the option. It is not uncommon for schools to experience cluster suicides, where one tragedy triggers three or four more. The attention received through death is even reflected in the literature students are often required to read. Nearly every early adolescent identifies with Tom Sawyer's ploy to allow his Aunt Polly to think he has drowned. He delights in the expressions of love he observes as he surreptitiously attends his own funeral.

To Be Reunited with a Deceased Loved One

Suicide is sometimes an attempt to join someone who has died. It is an ancient motive with roots in multiple cultures. In Western culture this idea of joining a deceased loved one persists most commonly among older persons. However, it is by no means limited to the graying population. For this reason, pay careful attention to adolescents' views on death lest suicide attempts follow deaths of loved ones. Suicide for some Christian adolescents with a distorted theology may be an attempt to join Jesus in heaven.

To Express Love

Suicide may also be a tragic way of saying "I love you." Adolescents in love can be extremely loyal and intense. In a distorted and confused way, they may believe that death alone will communicate the great strength of their love. The thought of living without each other is so strong that both partners, like Romeo and Juliet, commit suicide, or a girl may vow to take her life if her boyfriend dies.

To Avoid Being a "Burden"

Some adolescents take their lives to avoid being problems to those around them. If they were out of the way, they believe that things would be better for everyone. They may see themselves as the root cause of mom and dad's fighting. Or they may believe they were unwanted biological "accidents." More than seventy percent of young people who attempt suicide are from broken homes. Even in homes with stable relationships, adolescents may feel they are an embarrassment or burden to their families. Tragically, this motivation for suicide robs survivors of any opportunity to prove otherwise.

☑ HOW TO HELP

Adolescents who are considering suicide often make last-ditch efforts to get help with what they perceive as intolerable problems. Usually they have been struggling with problems and no resolution is in sight. The way their cry for help is met or ignored will influence the likelihood of future attempts at self-destruction.

Pinpoint the Severity

When counseling adolescents who battle suicidal thoughts, it is helpful to determine the likelihood that they will act on them. The Self-Rating Depression Scale, the Generalized Contentment Scale, and the Dysfunctional Attitude Scale described in the section on depression may be used with the suicidal teen. Additionally, the Reasons for Living Inventory specifically measures the seriousness of a person who talks about committing suicide. Each of these measures can be found in my book *Helping the Struggling Adolescent: A Counseling Guide*.

Focus on Feelings

Getting suicidal adolescents to share their feelings is vital to recovery. The driving force behind suicidal thought is often buried beneath feelings that the adolescents have never revealed to anyone. Suicidal youth are usually overwhelmed with guilt, helplessness, and rejection. Arguing about the validity of these feelings only adds to the load. Troubled adolescents need understanding, not debate.

Don't Dismiss the Trivial

Teenagers' concerns or problems should never be ignored or played down. The underlying message of effective suicide intervention must be "I care about you and I take you seriously." Failing to make the soccer team may seem relatively insignificant to an adult, but teenagers have committed suicide over less than that. Adolescents' concerns are intensely real and must be respected. They are never inconsequential.

Be Specific

If adolescents are depressed but have never expressed suicidal thoughts, do not hesitate to ask whether they have ever considered this option. Talking about suicide directly will not plant the idea. Instead, talking will help young people express any frightening thoughts that may be present and will often diminish any compulsion to act on them. Ask how often they have thought about suicide. Do they know how and where they would attempt it? Most suicidal teens feel no one cares, and asking specific questions lets them know that somebody does.

Explore Personal History

To assess the level of suicide risk, it is helpful to know whether clients have attempted suicide in the past. Four of five young people who kill themselves have attempted suicide more than once.[6] Talking about a previous attempt—how long ago it happened, why it occurred, and its lethality—may help counselors understand the seriousness of the attempt and any possible secondary gains such as attention or new expressions of love. Exploring clients' interpretations of the suicides of friends or family members are also helpful in discerning their perspectives on life and death. When "significant others" deal with stress by attempting suicide, it becomes a viable option to troubled teens.

Discover the Plan

If adolescents express suicidal thoughts, find out the method they might use. Simply ask, "Do you have a plan?" Determine whether their plan includes location and time of day. The risk of actual suicide is probably not so serious without a well-thought-out means. Teenagers who have thought in specific terms about how and when they will commit suicide (with a gun, in the bedroom, on Monday) are much closer to attempting suicide than those who have not. The more specific the plan, the greater the risk. In discussing the plan, it is best to use the past tense. "How were you thinking of going about this?" is better than "How are you thinking. . . ." This indicates you and the adolescent are moving beyond suicide to positive alternatives.

Assess the Lethality of the Plan

If an adolescent does disclose a plan, it is important to ask yourself how deadly the method is likely to be. Using a gun, lying down in front of a moving train, or hanging oneself is a greater danger than slashing one's wrists or taking pills. While these latter methods may be lethal, they often involve less risk. It is also important to understand the adolescent's perception of the deadliness of the chosen method. Swallowing a bottle of aspirin will not normally kill a person. However, if an adolescent thinks a bottle of aspirin is lethal, then one is serious about suicide. Also, the method sometimes symbolizes something privately important to the adolescent. A certain gun, a specific knife, a particular medication may carry a message the youth wants to communicate. It is important to discuss these specifics.

Make a Written Contract

Written contracts with adolescents may be a useful preventive measure, although contracts come with no guarantee. Even if suicidal adolescents seem to have improved, it is important to make the topic easy to talk about. Many counselors have talked with persons threatening suicide who left the session saying, "This really helped; I feel better now," only to learn that they were found dead with a revolver in their hand later that evening. By having adolescents formally sign an agreement to contact you if they get suicidal, you are communicating the importance to you of their lives.

The contract should emphasize that they *will* contact you, not that they will just *try* to. When you are not going to be available, you must have a backup counselor or a suicide hot line, with instructions written into the contracts. These contracts are not a mere formality. They meaningfully express the value you place upon adolescents' lives. And remember, most teenagers who plan suicide attempts desperately want to be stopped.

Take Note of Increased Energy

The greatest danger of suicide is in the first three months following a period of deep depression. When adolescents seem to be doing better, the danger of suicide may be greater. Severely depressed teens don't have the ability to do everyday tasks, let alone kill themselves. However, as the depression lifts, the ability to act on earlier suicide plans increases.

"Sterilize" the Home of Lethal Means

Although determined suicidal persons can always find a way to kill themselves, there are advantages in clearing the home of easily available lethal materials. Counselors should tell parents and their adolescents how suicidal feelings come and go and that the availability of a means for suicide may trigger the attempt. To decrease the likelihood of impulsive suicidal behavior it is best to make the home as safe as possible. Remove poisons, firearms, lethal medications, and razor blades. Restrict driving privileges of suicidal adolescents. Although they may protest these measures, they represent tangible proofs that their parents and their counselors want them to live. This reassurance of parental and counselor concern may play a larger role in prevention than cleansing the house of lethal means.

Hospitalize If Necessary

Adolescents who have specific plans for carrying out suicide should not be left alone. The revelation of specific plans indicates that clients have already decided to commit suicide.[7] Your decision to use an inpatient-treatment setting until you are sure continued risk of suicide is minimal sends a clear message to adolescents that you have heard their cries for help and are taking them seriously. A word of caution: clients may view hospitalization as rejection or abandonment. Be careful. Important factors in deciding on hospitalization include the pervasiveness of current stresses, the degree of impulse control, availability of an adequate support system among family and friends, and the willingness and ability of counselors to become involved in crisis management beyond the regular counseling hour.

Take Care of Yourself

Few situations drain counselors of more energy than working with people on the brink of suicide. Paradoxically, ability to help suicidal adolescents is dependent on counselors' ability to maintain personal power, perspective, and vitality for living. You must take care of yourself. These measures include consulting with colleagues, exercising, enjoying diversion, and taking time to pray. When you work with suicidal teens, you do not work alone. God is with you.

Don't Beat Yourself

Sadly, no matter how hard we try and how skilled we become, we will face times when we are unable to prevent struggling adolescents from taking their lives. The tendency of most counselors is to take on a disproportionate amount of responsibility and punish themselves with guilt for not doing enough. Some may even be tempted to quit counseling altogether because of this "failure." Obviously, if you find yourself stuck in a depressed state, unable to move beyond grief, you need to seek professional help.

☑ WHEN TO REFER

Refer suicidal adolescents to other competent counselors or psychologists when, over time, the teens continue to feel more out of control and increasingly suicidal. Refer counselees when you recognize that you are unable genuinely to invest the energy it takes to help suicidal adolescents discover constructive alternatives. As mentioned above, also consider hospitalization when you assess the likelihood of suicide to be critically dangerous and other alternatives are not available.

Where To Go for Additional Help

"Adolescent Suicide: Mental Health Challenge." Public Affairs Pamphlets No. 569. Public Affairs Committee, Inc., 389 Park Ave. S., New York, NY 10016 (fifty cents each).

American Association of Suicidology, 2429 South Ash, Denver, CO 80222. This organization distributes booklets and pamphlets, publishes a journal and newsletter, and conducts educational seminars on suicide prevention.

Blackburn, B. *What You Should Know About Suicide*. Waco, Tex.: Word, 1982.

International Association for Suicide Prevention, 1811 Trousdale Drive, Burlingame, CA 94010. This worldwide organization, with headquarters in Vienna, Austria, trains people and provides information about suicide prevention.

National Committee on Youth Suicide Prevention, 666 Fifth Avenue, 23d Floor, New York, NY 10103. The aim of this organization is to increase public awareness of youth suicide by providing information and developing youth suicide prevention programs in local communities.

Suicide Information Center, 6377 Apopka Place, San Diego, CA 92119. This organization maintains an updated list of materials on suicide and prevention. Free book lists, cassette tapes, and articles are available.

Notes

1. H. C. Fishman, *Treating Troubled Adolescents: A Family Therapy Approach* (New York: Basic Books, 1988).

2. I. B. Weiner, "Psychopathology in Adolescence," in *Handbook of Adolescent Psychology*, ed. J. Adelson (New York: Wiley, 1980).

3. M. D. Stein and J. K. Davis, *Therapies for Adolescents* (San Francisco: Jossey-Bass, 1982).

4. T. Sparhawk, "Traditional Holidays and Suicide," *Psychological Reports* 60 (1987): 245–46.

5. For more detailed descriptions of many of these motivations see B. Blackburn, *What You Should Know About Suicide* (Waco, Tex.: Word, 1982), and G. K. Olson, *Counseling Teenagers* (Loveland, Colo.: Group Books, 1984).

6. D. Eble, "Too Young To Die," *Christianity Today* (20 March 1987): 19–24.

7. W. Reid, *The Treatment of Psychiatric Disorders: Revised for the DSM-III-R* (New York: Brunner-Mazel, 1989).

INDEX

Abbott and Costello, 33
Abuse, 12, 47–53, 57, 68, 93–94, 97–100;
   detection of, 286
"Academy Award Recovery," 138
Acceptance, 17, 25, 48, 58, 80–81, 89, 95,
   121, 123, 127, 133, 136, 146, 150, 155–56,
   162–63, 165–66, 173–74, 176, 184–85,
   187, 193, 201, 211, 220, 227, 236–37, 249,
   266–67, 275, 277, 283, 291, 298–99
Acquired Immunodeficiency Syndrome, 249
Acting out, 22–23, 88
Active listening, 29–31, 33–39
Adam and Eve, 146, 149
Addiction, 158, 235, 238
Adler, Alfred, 281
Aerosmith, 206
Agras, Stewart, 113, 198
AIDS, 243, 249
Albers, Gregg R., 249
Alberti, R. E., 223, 279
Alcohol, 47, 68, 93–103, 134, 143, 200, 214,
   226, 288–90, 309
Alcoholics Anonymous, 101, 103–4, 238
Allen, Steve, Jr., 205
Alliance for Invitational Education, 171
American Anorexia Nervosa Aid Society, 116
American Anorexia Nervosa Association, 105,
   117
American Speech and Hearing Association, 306
Anger, 12, 22–23, 32, 35, 41, 50–52, 55–64,
   115, 119–22, 132–36, 139, 148, 160, 231,
   246–47, 254, 266, 283–86; chronic, 55,
   57, 62–63; control, 12, 59–60
"Anger Control Chain," 59–60, 285
"Anger log," 284
Anorexia nervosa, 105–6, 111–14, 116–17
Anxiety, 22, 42, 50, 65–75, 88, 102, 113,
   115–16, 127–29, 131, 143, 154, 159, 162,
   176, 178, 183, 185, 187, 192–96, 198,
   200–204, 206, 224–29, 231, 246–47, 261,
   263, 265–66, 272, 274–75, 277–78, 290,
   292–93, 296; chronic, 65–67, 71
Appearance, physical, 163–67, 237, 258, 277
Are You Dying To Be Thin Scale, 111
Arguments, 214, 286, 288, 300
Aristotle, 31
Arterburn, Stephen, 93
Assertiveness, 150, 220, 225; training, 51,
   222–23, 278–79
Association of Christian Schools, International,
   270
Association of Sleep Disorder Centers, 291,
   295
"Athlete's foot of the mind," 234
Augsburger, David W., 223, 279
Autogenics, 203, 228, 306
Autonomy, 115–16, 169, 175, 208–9, 213, 248
Avoidance, 155, 184, 187, 191, 194

Bach, George, 214
Bagby, Daniel G., 58
Bandura, Albert, 228, 230
Beatles, the, 173
Beck Depression Inventory, 136
Bible characters, 31, 38, 55, 119, 145, 180,
   186, 205, 282
Biblical principles, 123, 172, 186
Biochemical factors, 105, 191, 255
Biofeedback, 72–73, 228, 306
Biology, 78, 109, 191, 226
Blackburn, B., 305
Blame, 44, 50, 58, 212, 258–59, 266, 274
Bleuler, Eugene, 251
Body: changes, 253; functions, 186; image,
   76–86; shape, 107, 165
Boredom, 38, 82, 107, 176, 184
Bower, G. and S., 223, 279
Bowlby, John, 133
Bryant, William Cullen, 133
Buechner, Frederick, 235, 299
Bufford, Rodger, 258
Bulimia Test, 111
Burns, Jim, 93
Cain and Abel, 281
Campolo, Tony, 173–74
Campus Crusade, 126
Carlson, David, 166
Carlson, Dwight, 130
Carnes, Patrick, 234–36, 238, 241
Carpenter, Karen, 106
Carson, Robert, 257
Center for Self-Esteem, 171
Center for the Study of Anorexia and Bulimia,
   117
Century HealthCare Corporation, 100
Charlesworth, Edward, 25
Cherry, Frank, 138
Child's Attitude Toward Father/Mother Scale,
   211
Children of Alcoholics Foundation, 98
Christensen, Michael J., 249
Christian Association for Psychological Studies
   (CAPS), 43
Christian Schools International, 270
Church, 140, 144–45, 152, 173–74, 182, 186,
   209–10, 218–19, 245, 248, 258, 296–98,
   300
Clarification, 31, 33–34, 66, 90, 100
Clinical Anxiety Scale, 69
Cognitive factors, 102, 114–16, 162, 181, 293
Collins, Gary, 27, 74, 135, 146, 166
"Common cold of psychopathology," 87
Communication: problems, 308; skills, 210, 213
Community, sense of, 90, 174, 179, 248, 298
Compassion Book Service, 141
Compassionate Friends, 141
Competition, 148, 163, 281–83

Compulsions, 187, 190–96, 236
Compulsive Eating Scale, 80
Compulsiveness Inventory, 193
Confidentiality, 48, 99, 245
Contract, 83, 286, 313
Coping ability, 22, 24, 36, 49, 58, 65, 71, 204, 215, 229–30, 244, 259, 263, 278, 298
Cosgrove, Mark, 55, 63
Courage, 69, 148, 177, 179, 185
Court, John, 235
Cousins, Norman, 36
Curiosity, 185, 235–36, 238–39, 242, 245
Danzinger, Paula, 79
Date rape, 52–53
Dating, 110, 120, 153, 158, 175
Day, Dick, 233
DeBakey, Michael, et al.,84
Decisions, 112, 125–31, 133, 193; making, 126, 128–29, 191; moral, 128; simple, 126, 128
Delayed intervention, 49, 52
Demon possession, 258
Depersonalization, 133, 199, 248
Depression, 12, 23, 35, 41, 47, 49, 76, 87–91, 94, 106–8, 110, 113, 131, 133, 143, 154, 162, 164, 176–77, 206, 215, 226, 243–44, 246–47, 252–53, 265–66, 272, 289–90, 296, 304–5, 308, 311, 313
Desensitization, 206, 230, 277
Developmental changes, 57, 109, 283, 304
Diagnostic and Statistical Manual. See DSM–III–R
Diary, 59, 81–82, 202, 284, 291–92
Diet, 41, 68, 79–80, 84, 88, 105, 202
Discipline, 214, 265, 286
Disorders, 105, 109–11, 113, 115, 117, 135, 143, 162, 200–3, 205, 224, 252–53, 258–59, 261, 270, 289, 295
Displacement, 22, 227
Disputation, 179, 181
Dobson, James, 247
Double-binding parents, 212, 256
Doubt, 12, 20–22, 42, 49, 51, 93, 299
Drinking, 17, 23, 42, 95–97, 203, 209, 219, 223. *See also* Alcohol
Drugs, 17, 42, 93–103, 134, 143, 201, 209, 215, 218–19, 231, 255, 290–92, 309. *See also* Medications
DSM–III–R, 65, 94–95, 111, 132, 198, 225, 251–52, 288
Dysfunctional Attitude Scale, 90
Eating disorders, 12, 41, 44, 47, 76–77, 105–17, 143
Eating style, 78, 81–82, 83
Eckman, Paul, 55
Einstein, 12
Ellis, Albert, 67
Embarrassment, 226, 239, 244–45, 248, 250, 268, 273, 275, 285
Emmons, M. L., 223, 279
Environment, 206, 265, 278; family, 201, 212, 256, 261, 283; influence on, 220, 222;

influence of, 184, 242–43, 263, 265, 275, 276, 289, 291–92, 294
Erikson, Erik, 15, 18–19, 247, 133
Exercise: physical, 41, 59, 71–73, 83–84, 91, 103, 105–8, 113, 294; breathing, 203, 207, 228
Exodus International, 160
Expectations, 20–21, 57, 68, 83, 85, 89, 98, 109–10, 134, 163–65, 175, 193, 204, 211–12, 273, 277; parental, 304; unrealistic, 126, 144–45, 147–48, 165, 237, 300
Eye contact, 272, 276
Facial Action Coding System, 55
Failure, 106, 114, 126, 137, 149, 162–63, 170, 176, 187, 190, 200, 308
Faith: Fowler's stages of, 296, 299; issues, 180, 296
Family, 207–16; conflicts, 259, 265; environment, 201, 256, 259, 261, 266, 281; factors, 16, 20, 79, 83, 97, 106, 110–11, 113, 115–17, 138–39, 148, 154, 156, 184, 189, 200, 256; origins, 156, 212. *See also* Parents
Fantasies, 139, 156, 183, 187, 189
Faul, J., 223, 279
Favoritism, 282, 284
Fear(s), 20, 22, 35, 41, 49, 56, 59–60, 65–66, 70, 108, 139, 145, 157, 178, 185, 190, 201–2, 215, 222, 224–31, 246, 256, 265, 272, 279, 289–90; of dying, 199; reduction, 192; repressed, 159
Fear Questionnaire, 228
Fear Survey Schedule–II, 228
"Feeling log," 194
Fellowship of Christian Athletes, 300
Femininity, 156, 158
Focus on the Family, 43
Foster, Richard, 234
Fowler, James, 296
Frankl, Viktor, 68
Friends, 23, 41, 56, 59, 69, 76, 95, 107, 111, 116, 119, 138, 140, 150, 160, 167–69, 174, 177, 180, 199, 208, 210–11, 219–22, 256, 278, 285, 291, 298, 303, 310, 312
Friesen, Gary, 127
Frost, Joyce Hocker, 285
Frustration, 23, 56, 58, 60–62
Future, facing the, 23, 66, 89, 114, 126, 128–29, 135, 139–40, 156, 164, 167, 176–77, 245–46, 264, 266
Gallup Poll, 20, 76
Generalized Contentment Scale, 90
Genetics, 78, 191, 200, 256, 274
Genuineness, 27–29
Ginott, Haim, 208
Glasser, William, 23
Goldfarb Fear of Fat Scale, 111
Goodman, Joel, 205
Graham, Sylvester, 182
Group: norm, 218; therapy, 52, 260; treatment, 115–16, 306
Grunlan, Stephen, 187, 189
Guerin, Philip J., Jr., 115

Guided imagery, 204, 306
Guilt, 18, 115, 132, 134–36, 139, 142–51, 171, 183, 186–87, 192–93, 211–12, 214, 231, 243–47, 300–01, 305, 309, 312, 314; false, 147–48; irrational, 144–45
Guilt Scale, 147
Hallucinations, 251–52, 254, 260–61
Halvorson, Patricia, 112, 114
Hamilton, Eleanor, 184
Handicaps, 165, 274
Hare Self-Esteem Scale, 166
Hart, Archibald, 73, 75, 87, 119, 258
"Hassle log," 59–60
Helplessness, 47, 87, 89, 134, 163, 212, 266, 273
Heredity, 98, 263, 274, 303
History, personal, 113–14, 135, 156, 308, 312
Holy Spirit, 12, 25, 123–24, 129–30, 146
Home life, 265–66. See also Family factors
Homework, 168, 192, 230, 263–64, 267, 282, 293; for clients, 166
Homosexuals Anonymous, 160
Hope(fulness), 12, 16–17, 25, 52, 55, 71, 77, 90, 236, 245, 267
Hopelessness, 236, 253, 258, 309
Hormones, 15, 19, 247, 283
Horney, Karen, 148
Hospitalization, 103, 112–13, 117, 135, 198, 251, 257, 259–61, 291, 314–15
Hostility, 22–23, 159
Houston, Whitney, 175
Humiliation, 57, 67, 76, 166, 186
Humility, 122, 164, 166, 171
Humor, 214, 251, 263, 277
"I can" attitude, 266
Identity, 15, 19, 244, 248, 282–83, 296, 300
Imagery exercises, 61
Impulsive behavior, 215, 255
Inadequacy, 116, 149, 162
Individuation, 55, 70
Inferiority, 115, 143, 149, 161–71, 180, 221, 225, 265, 275, 283
Inner dialogue, 229–30
Internal Versus External Control of Weight Scale, 80
Intimacy, 235, 244, 247–48
Inventory of Religious Belief, 299
Isolation, 175–76, 178
"I" statements, 223, 279
James, John, 138
Jargon, adolescent, 33, 219
"Jellyfish in armor," 174
Jensen, Gordon, 245
Jesus, 27, 31, 119–20, 122–23, 140, 146–47, 180, 187, 311
Jiminy Cricket, 145
Johnston, Jerry, 97
Jung, Carl, 39
Kagan, Jerome, 274
Kinsey Report, 153
Kohlberg, Lawrence, 21
Kushner, Harold, 37
La Rochefoucauld, Duc François de, 137

Labeling, 17, 60, 194
Language, 12, 16, 33, 47, 61–62, 99–100, 219
Legalism, 68, 120, 145
Lewis, Huey, 150
Lifegate services, 100
"Little Hans," 227
Locus of control, 163, 266
Loneliness, 12, 90, 107, 110, 143, 172–81, 184, 272; five "Cs" of, 174
Longford, Langly, 234
Love, 110, 116, 120, 125, 140, 143, 146, 150, 160, 163–64, 166–67, 178, 208, 211, 214, 218, 228, 238, 243–49, 251, 274–75, 282, 300; expressing, 311
MTV, 243
Mace, David, 55
Mallory, James, 158
Maltz, Maxwell, 162
Manipulation, 56, 116, 246, 282
Manning, Doug, 132
Masculinity, 155–56, 158–59
Mast, Colleen Kelly, 246
Masturbation, 143, 154, 156, 181–89, 235–36, 247, 309
Mayo, Mary Ann, 186
McDowell, Josh, 233
Media, 97, 176, 243
Medications, 196, 201, 255, 257, 259–60, 291–92
Meeks, John E., 95
Meichenbaum, Donald, 278
Memories, 22, 62, 123–24, 133, 138–40, 159, 182
Merton, Thomas, 178
Mindbody, Inc., 73
Minirth-Meier Hospitals, 43, 100, 257
Minnesota Multiphasic Personality Inventory, 258
Minuchin, Salvadore, 110–11, 115
Misdiagnosis, 258
Misinformation, 31, 158
Mobility Inventory for Agoraphobia, 228
Modeling/models, 121, 165, 196, 227, 230, 274–76, 299–300
Mood swings, 20, 94, 100, 214
Motivation, 263–66, 315; lack of, 269–70
Narramore, Bruce, 143, 151, 165, 211
Nathan, Ronald, 205
National Alliance for the Mentally Ill, 262
National Committee on Youth Suicide Prevention, 315
National Council on Sexual Addiction Problems, 239
National Institute of Drug Abuse, 104
National Institute of Mental Health, 95
National Institutes of Health, 77
National Runaway Youth Program, 215
Neuman, Patricia, 112, 114
New Life Treatment Centers, 43, 100, 113
Newton, Miller, 100
Nicolosi, Joseph, 159
"Night Stalker," 148
No-win situations, 212

Noncompliance, 202, 260
Nonverbal skills, 222, 278
Nouwen, Henri, 125
Novaco, Raymond, 59, 60
Novaco Anger Scale, 58, 284
O'Neill, Cherry Boone, 106
Oaks Treatment Center, 84
Oates, Wayne, 133
Obsessions, 108, 120, 126, 190–96, 235, 238
"Offender bashing," 51
Ogilvie, Lloyd, 125
Olson, Keith, 160, 212, 227, 237, 301
Opposite-sex relationships, 156, 159
Optimism, 179, 228, 236–37, 266
"Oughts," 144, 300
Overcomers Outreach, 102
Overpermissiveness, 212–13
Overprotectiveness, 79, 111, 164, 212–13
Panic attacks, 12, 42, 44, 58, 66–67, 102,
    159, 198–207, 224
Parents: 116, 122, 136, 146, 156, 165, 175,
    192–93, 207–16, 221, 243–44, 248, 265,
    274, 281, 284, 301, 304, 308, 310, 313–14.
    See also Family
Parents Anonymous, 52
Parents United, 52
Pat answers, 70, 299
Pattison, Mansell, 153
Peace Corps, 279
Peers, 12, 97, 111, 115–16, 167, 218–23, 243,
    256
Perception exercise, 33
Perfectionism, 47, 68, 108–9, 114, 116, 144,
    147, 150, 164, 190–96, 212, 265, 304
Performance, 209, 212, 230, 263–64, 267–70,
    284, 289, 308
Permission, 50, 138, 150, 193–94
Permissiveness, 68, 220
Personality, 56, 98; assessment, 130–31
Peter Pan, 87
Petersen, J. A., 189
Phobias, 12, 65, 202, 224–32
Physical: abuse, 47, 52; activity, 59, 84, 159;
    changes, 19; disorders, 68, 200; examina-
    tion, 69, 80, 85; influences, 165, 290
Physiological factors, 199, 235, 303
Piaget, Jean, 23–24, 146
Pinocchio, 145
Polson, Beth, 100
Powell, John, 299
Prayer, 20, 61, 74–75, 101, 123, 127–28, 130,
    140, 178, 186–87, 239, 246, 314
Premarital sex, 17, 128, 143, 218, 242–48
Preoccupations, 190, 234–36
Problem solving, 168–69, 213
Promiscuity, 22, 94, 242–50
Psychic armor, 163
Psychological services, 12, 23, 42–44, 53, 62,
    74, 91
Psychosis, 23, 87, 252–53, 259
Rape, 52–53, 183, 237
Rapha Hospitals, 43, 100, 113, 158, 257
Rational Emotive Therapy, 67

Rationalization, 246, 286
Real Self minus Ideal Self, 162
Reasons for Living Inventory, 311
Reassurance, 51–52, 66, 149, 185, 199
Rebellion, 16–17
Red Hot Chili Peppers, 206
Reflective listening, 121, 127, 136–37, 146,
    166, 184, 193, 201, 211, 220, 227, 236,
    266, 275, 283, 286, 291, 298
Regression, 23, 134
Reik, Theodore, 31
Reisman, David, 177
Rejection, 57, 67, 89, 109, 152, 173–74, 176,
    184, 188, 212, 220, 222, 238, 240, 250,
    259, 299, 310, 312, 314
Relational: damage, 237, needs, 248; style, 258
Relationships, 108, 111, 115–16, 119–21,
    133–36, 146, 149–50, 153–56, 158–60,
    165–68, 175–80, 184, 187, 246
Relaxation, 159, 194–95, 205; techniques, 159,
    228–29, 277, 291, 293, 305–6
Religion, 20, 175, 221, 273, 296
Remuda Ranch, 113
Repression, 22, 50
Resentment, 119–20, 124, 132, 231, 282, 286
Revenge, 119–20
Revictimization, 50
Richardson, David, 223, 279
Ridley, Charles, 164
Robbins, Myra, 245
Rogers, Carl, 25
Roosevelt, Franklin, 70
Rorschach Ink Blot Test, 258
Rules, 208, 211–14, 273
Runaway potential, 215
Ryan, Dale, 234
Same-sex relationships, 156, 159–60
Sanders, Bill, 220
Sarcasm, 57, 214, 267, 283
Satan, 146, 186
Saving face, 246
Sawyer, Tom, 310
"Scarfing," 188
Schizophrenia, 12, 196, 231, 251–60
School, 22, 41, 139, 148, 162, 167, 209, 263–
    70, 304; Christian, 269–70
Seamands, David, 123–24, 187, 189
Secondary gains, 149, 228
Self: harm to, 259; ideal, 162; views of, 16
Self-: -acceptance, 123, 162–63, 165;
    -affirmation, 167; -awareness, 115, 167;
    -care, 251–53; -centeredness, 37, 183;
    -concept, 163, 170, 278; -condemnation,
    166, 170–71; -confidence, 115, 159, 163,
    221, 274; -consciousness, 57, 66, 162, 283;
    -control, 211; -criticism, 106, 144; -decep-
    tion, 234; -denial, 129, 167; -depreciation,
    162; -doubt, 67, 305; -efficacy, 163, 166,
    169; -esteem, 47, 57, 76–77, 81, 98, 115–
    16, 149, 162–67, 169–72, 187, 218, 226,
    259, 265, 267, 272, 278–79; -exploration,
    184; -ideal, 163; -imposed guilt, 147;
    -inventory, 25–26, 29; -labeling, 194, 275;

-loathing, 18; -love, 163–64, 166–67; -mutilation, 41; -negation, 164; -perceptions, 276; -pity, 132, 178; -punishment, 79, 143, 149; -recovery, 52; -reflection, 297; -statements, 278; -talk, 61, 67, 71, 102, 169, 179, 222; -worth, 16, 27, 57, 267, 278, 283–84
Self-Rating Depression Inventory, 311
Seligman, Martin, 266
Sexual abuse, 47–48, 52–53, 158, 215
Sexuality, 20, 22, 153–54, 157–58, 182, 184, 234–37, 239, 242, 244, 247–49
Sexually transmitted diseases (STDs), 243–44, 248–49
Shame, 20, 31, 38, 275
Shedd, Charlie, 189
"Shoulds," 144, 148, 300
Shyness, 158, 180, 272–80
Siblings, 116, 141, 156, 209, 266, 274, 281–87; rivalry, 12, 247, 281–84, 286
Significance, 176, 300
Silver, Larry, 95
Sin, unpardonable, 309
Sleep, 12, 66, 288–96, 309
Smedes, Lewis, 186
Smith, Blaine, 127–30
Smoking, 17, 96, 209, 214
Snooping, 210
Social: adjustment, 162; assignments, 279; changes, 20; comparison, 176; environment, 110, 136, 274; inappropriateness, 251; interaction, 260, 275, 277; isolation, 176; learning, 57, 260; phobia, 225–26, 230, 272; pressure, 145; rewards, 89–90; risks, 179–80; skills, 158–59, 167, 180, 226, 253, 261, 276, 279; support, 136, 139, 160; withdrawal, 87, 94, 214, 252, 254, 260, 274
Socioeconomic status, 209
Solitude, 177–79
Speech, 303–6; patterns, 258
Spiegel, Y., 133
Spiritual: authority, 298; counsel, 131; doubt, 12, 296–301
Spirituality, 52, 246, 258, 297–99
SQ4R, 267–68
Stafford, Tim, 247
Standards: strict, 191; unrealistic, 170
Stanford Shyness Survey, 275
State-Trait Anger Scale, 284
Stealing, 128, 193
Stereotypes, 153, 209
Street children, 215
Streisand, Barbra, 178
Stress, 19, 28, 65, 67, 69, 73, 88, 102, 109, 304
Studying, 209, 264, 266–67, 269
Subjective Units of Distress (suds), 229
Success, 109, 113, 158, 162–63, 167, 170

Suicide, 12, 49–50, 91, 253, 308–15; prevention, 315; risk, 50, 312
Support group, 44
Survivors, 48, 51–52
Switzer, David, 133, 136
Sylvan Learning Centers, 269
Symptom tolerance, 254
Tabooed pleasures, 17
Teasing, 57
Temper tantrums, 23
Temperature dots, 73
Tension, 22, 59, 62, 66, 68, 71–72, 107, 304
Theology, 153, 311; faulty, 121, 165, 171, 301; personal, 186
Therapeutic alliance, 113, 160
Thermostat, illustration of, 222
Thinking, 71, 276, 298; faulty, 114, 127, 165, 220, 235; irrational, 60, 90, 300, 309
Thought control, 159, 291
Thought-stopping, 195
Tillich, Paul, 69
Timidity, 165, 182, 272, 275
Tournier, Paul, 25, 175
Tranquilizers, 68, 93, 96, 98, 199, 229
Treatment, 12, 41, 44, 84, 100, 112, 115–16, 306; phases of, 259
Trust, 26, 36, 47, 50, 70, 113–14, 116, 119, 128, 133, 151, 164; lack of, 210
Twain, Mark, 28
Twelve-step approach, 238–39
"Tyranny of the Shoulds," 148
Underachievement, 263–64, 266
Van Pelt, Rich, 95
Venereal disease, 42. See also STDs
Violators, 119, 122
Violence, 52, 56; against women, 237
Voltaire, 30
Wagner, Maurice, 170
Wahlroos, Sven, 213
"Wanna be's," 17
Warmbrod, Mary Elizabeth Taylor, 138
Warmth, 25, 27–29, 90, 98, 204, 248, 275
Warshaw, Robin, 53
Watson, John, 227
Weatherhead, Leslie, 124
Wechsler Adult Intelligence Scale, 258
Weight: fluctuation, 108; graph, 81, 84; loss, 80, 84–85, 105–6, 113–14, 249
White, John, 152
White, Joseph, 102
Wilmot, William W., 285
Wilson, Earl, 147, 156, 158
"Win" situations, 230
Wolpe, Joseph, 195, 232, 277
Women's roles, 19
Wright, H. Norman, 61
Young Life, 300
Youth for Christ, 300
Zimbardo, Philip G., 272, 275, 279